Over the past couple of decades there have been episodes of particularly rapid growth in output per head in a number of countries throughout the world, in particular in the UK since the early 1980s. To understand this phenomenon requires a detailed analysis of these productivity changes using data for individual firms. These changes in average performance for the economy as a whole can be related to changes in the spread between the productivity leaders and laggards. Drawing on research carried out under the leadership of the National Institute of Economic and Social Research in London, and with the help of the Fulbright Commission, the contributors to this volume provide a comparative analysis of data for a number of different countries. Chapters cover the UK, the USA, Canada, Japan, Australia, Belgium, Norway and Sweden, and comparisons also include Germany and the Netherlands. Using a variety of the most up-to-date methods of analysis, the contributors estimate the importance of a variety of different factors. Changes in competitive conditions, skills, innovation and the growth of small firms each have their part to play, as does the closure of the least productive establishments. The research in the UK was financed by the ESRC.

Sources of productivity growth

THE NATIONAL INSTITUTE OF ECONOMIC AND SOCIAL RESEARCH

The National Institute of Economic and Social Research is an independent, non-profit-making body, founded in 1938. It has as its aim the promotion of realistic research, particularly in the field of economics. It conducts research by its own research staff and in cooperation with universities and other academic bodies.

Sources of productivity growth

Edited by

DAVID G. MAYES
The Reserve Bank of New Zealand

CAMBRIDGE
UNIVERSITY PRESS

338.06
S724

Published by the Press Syndicate of the University of Cambridge
The Pitt Building, Trumpington Street, Cambridge CB2 1RP
40 West 20th Street, New York, NY 10011-4211, USA
10 Stamford Road, Oakleigh, Melbourne 3166, Australia

First published 1996

Printed in Great Britain at the University Press, Cambridge

A catalogue record for this book is available from the British Library

Library of Congress cataloguing in publication data applied for

ISBN 0 521 55437 3 hardback

Acknowledgements

Melanie Lansbury and David Mayes gratefully acknowledge financial support from the Economic and Social Research Council, grant no. R000231195 for the research behind chapters 2, 3 and 4 and towards the costs of the colloquium. The participants also thank the Fulbright Commission and the British Academy whose grants made the meeting and the book possible. Richard Caves and Peter Hart have provided continuing advice and encouragement. The National Institute of Economic and Social Research hosted the colloquium.

Contents

Tables

Figures

xx   List of figures

Contributors

Martin Neil Baily, *University of Maryland and National Bureau of Economic Research, USA.*
John R. Baldwin, *Micro-Economics Analysis Division, Statistics Canada, and Economic Growth Group, Canadian Institute for Economic Research.*
Eric J. Bartelsman, *Board of Governors of the Federal Reserve System, USA.*
Gavin Cameron, *Nuffield College, Oxford.*
Keith Cowling, *University of Warwick.*
Finn R. Førsund, *Department of Economics, University of Oslo, Centre for Applied Research in Business and Economics, Oslo.*
John Haltiwanger, *University of Maryland and National Bureau of Economic Research, USA.*
Chris Harris, *Bureau of Industry Economics, Department of Industry, Science and Technology, Canberra, Australia.*
Lennart Hjalmarsson, *Göteborg University, Sweden.*
Melanie Lansbury, *National Institute of Economic and Social Research, London.*
Amador Malnero, *Université Catholique de Louvain, Belgium.*
David G. Mayes, *Reserve Bank of New Zealand.*
Geoff Mason, *National Institute of Economic and Social Research, London.*
John Muellbauer, *Nuffield College, Oxford.*
Mary O'Mahony, *National Instituteof Economic and Social Research, London.*
Akio Torii, *Department of Business Administration, Yokohama National University, Japan.*
Henry Tulkens, *Université Catholique de Louvain and Facultés Universitaires Saint-Louis, Brussels, Belgium.*
Bart van Ark, *University of Groningen, The Netherlands.*
Guy Vernon, *University of Warwick.*
Karin Wagner, *Wissenschaftszentrum für Sozialforschung, Berlin, Germany.*
Bo Walfridson, *Göteborg University, Sweden.*

1   Introduction

DAVID G. MAYES

It seems only a few years ago that the focus of concern over the subject of productivity lay on the slowdown which affected much of OECD after the first oil shock in 1973. Worries were expressed that the slowdown might be enduring and there was extensive debate over the cause (see, for example, Wenban-Smith, 1981). The 1980s have seen a turnround in this performance with productivity accelerating again. In the case of the UK the extent of the acceleration has been so great that it has been called the Thatcher miracle (Muellbauer, 1986; Oulton, 1987), reflecting the major policy change which took place during the period. To some extent this acceleration is merely a catching up of the progress foregone during the 1970s and represents a return to the longer-run rates of productivity growth observed in the 1950s and 1960s. However, hypotheses abound to explain behaviour in the 1980s. In this book we focus on one group of such analyses, those which draw on detailed data on individual businesses across the whole of industry.

The book is the culmination of nearly two decades of research into productivity using data drawn from the Annual Censuses of Production in the UK and other major OECD countries. The research has involved international collaboration throughout and the current book, although it emphasises the experience of the UK, contains work on the United States, Canada, Japan, Australia, Belgium, Norway, Sweden and Mexico. The genesis of the work has varied across the participating countries.In the case of the UK it began with work at the National Economic Development Office in 1976, undertaken as part of the Industrial Strategy being developed by the government of the day. NEDO was concerned to identify industries where there was potential for productivity improvement, which could be addressed by its working groups. In particular it wanted to look for

1

industries where there was a long 'tail' of less productive firms. In those cases it was suggested that it would be possible to assist firms in attaining the best practice for that industry, by a combination of information and analysis of the ways in which such transformations could be achieved.

The UK analysis typified that in the other countries in that it required access to the confidential data obtained from the Annual Censuses of Production. This was obtained with the assistance of what was then the Business Statistics Office (now the Central Statistical Office) in Newport. Information relating to individual businesses cannot be released because of the terms of the Statistics of Trade Act which guarantee confidentiality so the results were presented as parameters of the distribution of productivity in each of over 150 industries within manufacturing. From the early days, the work benefited from collaboration with Professor Richard Caves at Harvard, who was instrumental in bringing together many of the foreign collaborators.

The current joint work has been made possible by research funding in the UK by the Economic and Social Research Council who provided a grant to Mayes and Lansbury, by a grant from the Fulbright Commission to set up a symposium to discuss the results at the National Institute of Economic and Social Research in London in February, 1994, and by support from the British Academy for the travel costs of the Australian and Japanese participants. This book is derived from the papers discussed at that symposium.

What is productivity?

This book is largely about labour productivity – output per unit of labour input. Just looking at labour productivity presents an easy opportunity for distortion as output will vary according to the amount of capital available. A firm with more up to date equipment will be able to produce more output per person. In the same way a firm that works two or three shifts will be able to produce more per unit of capital than one which works a single shift. However, it is labour productivity which is the main policy variable which governments concentrate on as it is this which determines incomes per head. Nevertheless the work of O'Mahony in Chapter 8 and Oulton (1994) considers total factor productivity as well, exploring the extent to which the results for labour alone can be rather misleading.

For many comparative purposes it is therefore necessary to try to eliminate the various factors which might cause labour productivity to vary other than the activities of labour itself in the production process. Since output involves the transformation of inputs using labour and capital, the simplest element required for a helpful comparison is to ensure that inputs, whether of materials or capital in the form of buildings, equipment and machinery are fully compatible. This similarity also needs to extend to the product and to the techniques used to produce it.

This is a very tall order as with outside commodities a large part of the ability to compete comes from differentiating the product. It is thus difficult to make highly detailed comparisons across firms. Indeed one might feel that the only way to make such comparisons was to pick different establishments from within the same organisation as in the comparisons of the production of photographic paper and water heaters in Chapter 9 by Chris Harris and of bank branches by Henry Tulkens and Amador Malnero in Chapter 10. Here, however, the problem is different – if we look at comparisons within a single firm many of the sources of variation which are most important are omitted. Management styles and structures will tend to be the same. Training programmes will tend to be common to all plants within the group. It is just these differences which are most important in between-company studies as these variables are subject to choice by the firm.

It is for this reason that Mason and van Ark in Chapter 6, while considering just a small number of firms in detail, pick for their comparison, not plants that are closely matched (along the lines explored in Mayes, 1983, for example) but firms that are each typical of the industry in the country from which they come. Thus in the case of the comparison of biscuit-making which is considered in detail in the chapter, the type of biscuit commonly produced in the UK is different from that commonly produced in Germany or the Netherlands. In the UK the typical biscuit is a relatively straightforward product, at most involving a chocolate coating. In the continental case a much more complex product is involved, often entailing multi-stage baking. It is thus not surprising that the latter should be more labour intensive.

Mason and van Ark therefore approach the comparison differently by looking at common and identifiable activities in the production process, such as maintenance, reprogramming machinery, supervision and so on. Clearly it may still be difficult to get exact comparisons as more complex machines are often more difficult to maintain or operate, particularly in the engineering firms they compare. (This is by no means a universal finding as newer machines attempt to have more user friendly programming structures. They also incorporate more self-checking and adjustment, requiring less operator intervention. As a result the craft skills involved in production may actually be reduced, despite the ability to produce more sophisticated products. Indeed the greatest skills may come from the successful operation of traditional wood fired ovens in baking.)

There is a further and more pertinent reason for focusing on labour productivity which stems from the accumulated result of the programme of research undertaken at the National Institute of Economic and Social Research in London (clearly summarised in Prais *et al.*, 1970). Although in some instances it is possible to explain the UK's lower productivity levels compared with its competitors in Europe and North America in terms of material inputs, the age of machinery and the nature of the products and lengths of production runs employed, there is still a pervasive shortfall in productivity. Although it is difficult to pin down the exact causes of this shortfall (for this reason this type of discrepancy has been labelled as X-inefficiency by Leibenstein, 1976) most of the factors which have been identified are alterable and hence this is of great policy significance for those who wish to see productivity and competitiveness improved, with its consequent benefits for increasing real incomes and reducing unemployment.

These factors include the skills of the labour force and the nature of its training, production organisation, human resource development programmes and the whole range of management operations. Mason and van Ark show that not only is the stock of skills in the UK low compared with the Netherlands and Germany, particularly at the intermediate level, but that this lack of skills has a clear impact on efficiency and the ability to undertake various tasks. In particular it reduces the flexibility of the labour force. This results in interruptions to the smooth flow of work, the need to employ larger numbers of staff in order to get the necessary specialisms (while more qualified employees could do all of the tasks themselves) and a lower ability to innovate and bring through new ideas and processes into production. In the past the lack of flexibility in the labour force was in part due to deliberate rigidities agreed with trade unions. (While such agreements may originally have been a means of ensuring the quality of those to be employed, many had become outdated.)

Determinants of productivity

The level of productivity which prevails is largely the result of a combination of choices made by firms and the efforts of those that work in them. The primary determinant of productivity lies in product and process innovation including the skills of the labour force as well as the technology embodied in machinery. In many instances it is possible to map out what is achievable with a given range of inputs using a particular technology.

While not so rigorous a concept as we observe in the operation of specific processes, such as electricity generation, it is nevertheless possible to map out what is feasible. With the important role played by human intervention in the production process, particularly in service industries the scope for departure from the feasible standard is very considerable.

The chapters by Melanie Lansbury and David Mayes and by Henry Tulkens and Amador Malnero illustrate two approaches to this and Chris Harris describes some others. The Tulkens and Malnero case takes a large number of bank branches and maps out the relationship between their inputs and outputs. Since bank branches have both multiple inputs and multiple outputs it is necessary to express both inputs and outputs as indices after weighting the components. This then enables us to graph actual performance and identify those establishments with the highest productivity (figure 1.1). It is thus possible to see what can be achieved on the basis of the best which has been achieved. Lansbury and Mayes employ a rather different technique by suggesting that it is possible to estimate a production function for each industry they consider. This suggests that a specific and identifiable relationship exists linking inputs to outputs, which is common across firms in the industry that use the same technology.

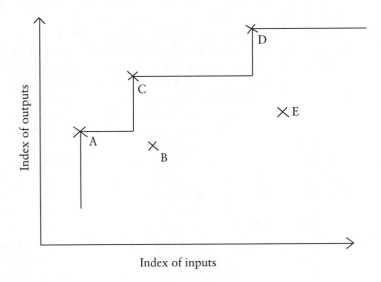

Index of inputs

Figure 1.1   *Frontier of actual performance*

The continuous line shows the frontier of performance actually achieved. Points A, C and D lie on the frontier. C produces more output with less input than B and clearly out-performs it, similarly for D over E. No attempt is made to link A and C or C and D and suggest that intermediate points on that line should theoretically be attainable; only actual recorded performance is admitted.

Both these approaches have drawbacks. The Tulkens and Malnero method requires quite a large data set of establishments with similar sizes if the 'frontier' of best attainable productivity is not to be too ragged. The Lansbury and Mayes 'frontier production function' on the other hand imposes strong assumptions on the behaviour of the industry. So while it may produce a productivity frontier for a wide range of inputs, that frontier may be a very inexact representation of the data.

Technical, allocative and X-inefficiency

Actual productivity will depart from that theoretically achievable for a number of reasons but Farrell (1957) has distinguished neatly between suboptimality because the firm has chosen an inappropriate combination of labour and capital and inefficient use of the combination which has been chosen. Thus in the second case, even given the shortfall in productivity due to a poor combination of inputs it would be possible to have higher productivity if they had been used more efficiently. He labels the two sources of inefficiency 'allocative' and 'technical' inefficiency respectively. Lansbury and Mayes concern themselves primarily with the second area but Walfridson and Hjalmarsson distinguish both sources. Indeed they take the analysis further in two respects, first by allowing for the fact that the scale of operation will also have an effect on productivity and second by placing the whole analysis in a dynamic framework. Tybout and Westbrook (1994) also provides a three-way split, separating out scale effects from changes in share and a residual which itself comprises both the shift in the frontier and movements with respect to it.

Farrell's decomposition is not the only way of looking at departures from optimality. Leibenstein (1976) attempted a different definition of the extent of waste stemming from inefficient production by coining the term 'X-inefficiency' – that element in the system which is left when all the factors relating to the nature of outputs, inputs and the production technology have been taken into account. In Chapter 15 Torii explores a means of relating allocative, technical and X-inefficiency. These attempts to disentangle the different sources of discrepancies in productivity and more importantly their contribution to changes in measured productivity lie at the heart of the analysis in this book. As explained in the next section, although it may be possible to separate out these factors in theory, it is much more difficult in practice and we normally either have to isolate only some factors or make quite strong assumptions in order to perform the decomposition.

Economies of scale

The consequences of scale are straightforward and well known, enabling a spreading of fixed costs over a larger amount of output. While typically this is applied to capital, it applies just as well to labour. In larger establishments the workforce can specialise and they can run larger batches without having to reset equipment. Such gains also occur across time as the workforce can learn how to operate new production techniques with increasing skill and hence can increase their productivity through learning. Such learning curves tend to become flatter the more experience develops but refinements in the process or the next innovation can make them important on a continuing basis.

This ability to spread costs across outputs also applies to spreading costs across related activities. We have already noted that multi-skilling enables employees to do a number of jobs and hence avoid idle time. Most firms also produce a range of products. In these circumstances production of one product benefits from production of the other. This may involve joint use of equipment or joint use of staff. Lessons learnt in one production process can be applied in another. A business operating without these interlinkages will tend to have lower productivity although it may be possible to obtain them externally, say by marketing agreements or by buying in components required in small numbers from others who by supplying a large range of firms can themselves reap the economies of scale. All these external economies will lead to variation in productivity among firms if they are not equally available to all of them.

Dynamic adjustment

While productivity, even with a fully efficient workforce, will vary with the nature of their inputs, their combination and their scale, these outcomes do not occur within a static framework. The firm is striving to achieve an optimum position not just in a changing world but in a world where its past actions govern the scope for actions in the present and future. Thus it can be a slow process to change fixed capital, to implement new techniques or even products. Although there may be fairly substantial scope for altering the size of the labour force it too has restrictions on the rate it can change, both through training and through learning by experience.

Walfridson and Hjalmarsson do not incorporate a fully dynamic framework but they go a long towards doing so.

Perhaps the simplest example of this adjustment problem is revealed by the behaviour of productivity over the economic cycle. When the economy is growing at its fastest, productivity also tends to grow rapidly as firms strive to meet that demand. Firms are also likely to be expanding capacity rapidly during the upturn, providing newer machinery that will help raise productivity even further. However, as growth slows those that have most recently expanded capacity find that they cannot utilise it fully. Because of the costs of hiring and firing, firms will only adjust their labour force downwards relatively slowly in the hope that the fluctuation will be short-lived. As a consequence their productivity will fall. When the costs rise too far, labour has to be cut back markedly, restoring productivity levels.

The behaviour of productivity over the cycle is one of the preoccupations of this book. During the 1980s in the UK productivity rose rapidly both in the sharp downturn at the beginning of the period and during the stronger growth of the second half of the decade. It was only with the recession at the end of the period that productivity growth began to slip back. It is this consistency in prolonged productivity growth which contributes to the Thatcher miracle. Part of the argument is that the severity of the 1979–82 recession was so great that harsh decisions were made to restructure companies, in many cases making up for failures to act over an extended period. What Lansbury and Mayes show in Chapter 2 is that there are important differences in the structure of the components of productivity growth between the periods of output decline and growth. In the recession important contributions to productivity growth in the economy as a whole came from the closure of the worst performing plants rather than from an increase in the share of growing plants with above average productivity, which characterised the recovery. There is also a considerable switch in the industries within manufacturing which were making the most important contributions to growth.

Decomposing productivity growth by category of business

The most common disaggregation of businesses is clearly by industry as this is the form in which the statistics are available. Similarly decompositions are often possible by size. Beyond that it is usually very difficult to explain the contribution of particular types of firm. Chapters 11 and 12 are an exception to this. The importance of different groups of establishments to the overall change in productivity is explored in more detail by Martin Neil Baily, Eric Bartelsman and James Haltiwanger for the USA and John Baldwin for Canada. In those two instances, because they have full databases in which they can trace the performance of individual plants across time, they can see how plants of different types contribute to productivity growth. In the case of Canada, for example, Baldwin notes that it is the increasing importance of small firms that has helped reduce aggregate productivity growth as small firms tend to have below average productivity. The authors are also able to distinguish performance by ownership – both according to whether the business is foreign or domestic owned or whether it is independent or part of a larger group. (Takeovers and mergers themselves can alter productivity performance.)

Measuring productivity

As we have noted, it is one thing to be able to say that we can in theoretical terms decompose productivity into a series of component determinants. It is quite another to suggest that we can distinguish these influences in practice. To summarise, we need to be able to measure inputs: labour, capital and materials (in the widest sense of the word); outputs, whether of goods or services; and the technologies employed in a way that we can make comparisons across firms, industries, countries and over time – a short list but a formidable problem in almost all its aspects.

Starting with inputs, labour presents a straightforward series of problems. A measure of the amount of labour available would probably be best measured in person-hours rather than just number of people employed as the latter poses several difficulties:

- employees may work different numbers of hours in the day. A one hour reduction in the working week might appear to be a fall in productivity
- some employees will be full-time and others part-time. Even if treating them as single group can be avoided it will usually only be possible to multiply the part-time employees by a standard factor to compute their full-time equivalent. If there were no variations among the firms to be studied in how they use part-time employees then there would be no problem, but this is highly unlikely.

However, hours themselves are not without problems. It has been observed that the productivity of standard and overtime hours differs (Leslie and Wise, 1980). It appears that because overtime hours are better paid than standard hours there is a drop off in productivity in the last few standard hours to ensure that overtime is activated. There is thus no clear homogeneity in either hours or people. We are all aware that our productivity drops as we become tired from working long hours.

People themselves are not homogeneous, nor is their role in the production process. We might therefore wish to distinguish between tasks and skills as does Harris in Chapter 9 and Mason and van Ark in Chapter 6. In general, however, it has to be said the data available to us relating to the whole range of plants across industry do not permit the use of refined labour input variables.

Capital itself is a heterogeneous item and we would normally wish to distinguish between buildings, works, land, equipment and vehicles and would probably wish to separate out computer and IT equipment from the rest, as is the case in the national balance sheets. The problem in this case, however, lies with valuation. Capital depreciates. We may know what it cost to buy – historic cost – and in some cases we will know its value written down for depreciation purposes or even then revalued to replacement cost. However, this will tend to come from detailed studies and only be available for a limited number of enterprises. Aggregate official figures for industries in the UK draw on the figures for capital *investment* available each year and build up the capital *stock* figures from then, making assumptions about life lengths of assets and the distribution of scrapping round the average life (this is described in detail in Mayes and Young, 1994). The accuracy of the results is sensitive to the assumptions and it has been widely argued that the published UK capital stock figures may be erroneous by as much as a third (see the summary in *Ibid.*). However, more recent work at the National Institute in a project for the Central Statistical Office suggests that the extent of overestimation may be relatively small.

When it comes to individual businesses no such data exist on a coherent basis. Although the same investment figures have been recorded each year, the data are not held in the form of a business database where individual businesses can be identified in successive years. (The National Institute is now undertaking a joint project with the Central Statistical Office, with the assistance of the Economic and Social Research Council, which will establish just such a database. When this is complete it will then be possible to undertake longitudinal studies at the level of the individual establishment for the UK of the same sort that are undertaken in Chapters 11 to 14 for Canada, the USA, Sweden and Norway.) Unfortunately it is also difficult to make use of company accounts in generating the appropriate variables as a single company may include several different businesses or establishments spread over a variety of industries. Following Mayes and Young (1994) the Central Statistical Office is investigating whether more appropriate information can be obtained by direct estimation but even if implemented it will be several years before it becomes available.

There are also problems of comparison for material inputs when these are not of a direct commodity nature but since the chapters in this book deal largely with valued added or net output rather than gross output we shall not explore them here. More important is the issue of the measurement of output. In most industries the nature of output varies quite considerably, hence the use of values or a single price deflator may be substantially misleading – take the example of biscuits that we have already mentioned (see Chapter 6), the much more complex continental biscuits are not directly comparable with the mass produced UK variety. Compared with many other areas of manufacturing biscuit-making might appear one of the more homogeneous activities. The problem becomes much greater when making comparisons over time as it becomes very difficult to take account of quality changes (as Keith Cowling points out in his comments on Chapter 5). Failing to take account of quality change can result in substantial undervaluation of the improvement that has taken place as a price index not adjusted for quality will effectively underestimate output.

However, industries making products have a major advantage over those producing services as here it becomes difficult to measure output at all. Indeed, in some cases the labour input is used as a means of quantifying the output – a self-defeating approach from our point of view although understandable in the circumstances. In these cases it becomes necessary to find a series of measures which indicate the extent of output. This may reflect the extent of the service: ton-miles shipped for transport, to take one of the examples considered by Chris Harris in Chapter 9, or numbers of counter transactions in the case of Henry Tulkens in Chapter 10. All of these are somewhat unsatisfactory but they enable us to put together a data envelope which sets out a whole range of measures which between them cover the various aspects of the production of the particular service.

Part of the problems of comparability occur simply because of the classifications we use for industries. These definitions put together for statistical purposes may be very broad and hence comprise many very different activities. Manufacturing is inherently heterogeneous, a single plant covering not just the manufacturing process but the ordering, the R&D, the sales, security, the maintenance of the building and so on. Since some firms contract out various of these items and others do not we have a clear problem of comparability.

This heterogeneity presents particular problems if we wish to estimate production functions or take account of technological change. For a production function to make proper sense it should apply to a single technology, otherwise it becomes a hybrid. In practice this will mean that most estimated production functions covered in this book, certainly all those in

Chapter 4 by Lansbury and Mayes, will be only approximate. This gives a further problem when trying to look at the question of efficiency, as the estimated frontier of performance may in fact refer to a plant in a different segment of the industry and hence be unattainable by the firm in question. In these circumstances efficiency measures may be rather more indicators of heterogeneity in an industry than of strict technical inefficiency. For this reason Chapter 4 explores the extent to which the measures of inefficiency which are computed are related to other indicators of heterogeneity. While there is a clear link, the bulk of the variation is due to other factors, most of which remain unexplained.

Unless it is possible to get information directly from plants it is very difficult to get any measures of the nature of the technologies employed in production or the nature of the changes that are taking place. Cameron and Muellbauer in Chapter 7 discuss the extent to which measures of R&D capital or of R&D activity can indicate the pace of change within industries but these will be imperfect indicators of the degree of variety of products and processes being employed.

Productivity at the level of the firm, the industry and the economy

Our basic concern in this book is to use detailed data to explain the dramatic improvements in productivity in UK industry during the 1980s. Aggregate studies have been able to isolate various facets of the problem but they have not been able to isolate the extent to which the improvement in productivity is due to existing firms improving their efficiency relative to the feasible frontier, the extent that that frontier has itself shifted and thereby increased the scope for productivity gains, or whether the gain is a purely arithmetic one as the least productive firms have gone out of business and the structure of the economy has moved towards the higher productivity and higher productivity growth sectors. By concentrating on information collected at the level of the individual business (giving between 15,000 and 20,000 data points in most years) as part of the Annual Census of Production, an approach to these questions can be explored.

Production functions can be estimated for each year, and measures of inefficiency relative to those frontiers can be calculated. Comparisons across years will indicate the extent of technical change. However, these results will be at the industry level. Even if detailed results could be obtained the requirements of confidentiality would preclude researchers from being able to relate them to individual observations. In the case of the research into the USA (Baily, Bartelsmann and Haltiwanger), Canada

(Baldwin) and Japan (Torii) no such constraint applies as the authors are able to access the data directly. This is not because confidentiality is not respected but because the statistical agencies responsible for collecting and distributing the results of investigations are able to impose strict conditions on the potential users making them behave in a manner consistent with the role played by wages.

On the basis of these results it is possible to observe that, indeed, much of the improvement in productivity in these economies has come from firm entry and exit ('churning'). Furthermore there have been sectoral shifts moving activity towards the higher productivity industries. Only limited improvements in productive efficiency have been observed. Industries as a whole seemed to have moved their productivity upwards in line with the industrywide improvements that have become available. Evidence for some sort of clear miracle in the improvement of existing firms remains elusive.

Productivity and growth

Productivity growth and output growth tend to be positively linked although this is rather more an example of the operation of the statistical association spelt out in Verdoorn's Law than it is of a clear and generally accepted economic framework. Nevertheless it is clear from the work in Chapter 2 and Chapters 11 and 12 that there is a correlation between output growth and productivity growth at the industry level as well as for the whole economy. However, once we consider the individual businesses that make up that productivity, growth is rather less obvious as it is not just a matter of the fastest growing businesses having the most rapid rises in productivity. The observed correlation stems from a combination of the higher productivity firms increasing their market share, the businesses which cease trading having below average productivity and new entrants having higher productivity than the firms they replace. Only part of the explanation comes from the growth productivity in existing firms. Even so Finn Førsund (Chapter 14) finds that Verdoorn's Law applies at the micro level.

Sources of productivity growth

There are two sorts of answer that can be put forward to the question 'what are the sources of productivity growth?' The first relates to the broad determinants through technological innovation – the sorts of issues addressed by Cameron and Muellbauer in Chapter 7. Here following the sorts of approach suggested *inter alia* by endogenous growth theory (Romer,1990a) it is the stock of highly trained human capital which makes the major contribution to growth, through innovation. That innovation covers products as well as production processes. This contribution is thoroughly dynamic in concept. Thus if skilled personnel can acquire the necessary training or qualifications the market should be fairly buoyant throughout.

The second approach is to explore the extent to which businesses have benefited from this increase in skill level in terms of making innovations.

However, there is a narrower approach to answering the question of the sources of productivity growth, which is to unpick the components of any increase in productivity and see how this can be assigned among the competing hypotheses at the level of the individual business. It is this approach we follow in this book, identifying the importance of changes in physical capital, human capital, the composition of outputs, technological development and changes in the scale of operations. We look at the performance of groups of individual firms within industries. In particular we balance out the potential gains from different types of firms – small, large, diversified, growing, contracting, and so on. (Both Lennart Hjalmarsson and Finn Førsund find that for their respective countries of Sweden and Norway detailed data can be exploited.) Wilfridson and Hjalmarsson decompose the data using a Tornqvist index to allow the assessment of the contribution due to capacity utilisation, lagged adjustment in the process of price response, variation in inputs, technological change embodied in new equipment and a ubiquitous residual. Interestingly enough, during the downturn of the 1970s the fall in capacity utilisation appeared a strong determinant of the productivity slowdown. In the upturn of the 1980s on the other hand it was capital formation which was the driving force.

Førsund's decomposition comes to somewhat different conclusions, and shows that where productivity has been increasing more rapidly this has been due to the outward movement of technological possibilities in shifting the production frontier, rather than any net movement towards the frontier. Førsund uses a Malmquist index to combine inputs in order to make comparisons over time using a piecewise linear frontier rather than the continuous frontier production functions of Lansbury and Mayes in Chapter 4 or the stepped frontier of Tulkens in Chapter 10.

Structure of the book

The rest of the book therefore seeks to explore each of these aspects in explaining the source of productivity growth in turn, beginning with the description of the Thatcher miracle in Chapter 2. Lansbury and Mayes start at the macroeconomic level, setting out how productivity changed in the UK during the 1980s, how this is related to movements in demand and the factors of production. The analysis is then disaggregated first to the industry and then to the individual business level to to show where the contributions to productivity growth originate. In Chapter 3 the authors begin by looking at the decomposition of the process of change, showing the extent to which it is entry, exit or shifts in the shares of production across industries rather than continuing improvements in firms which existed through the period which contributed to the rise in productivity. They show that each of these factors is important, although none strikingly so.

In Chapter 4 Lansbury and Mayes go on to consider the extent to which growth in productivity has arisen from an outward shift in the production frontier rather than from a shortening in the tail of less efficient behaviour and a net movement towards the frontier. In common with Førsund in Chapter 14 it is the outward movement of the frontier which appears the more important step. The chapter concludes, however, by an analysis of the factors which explain the relative size of inefficiency within industries. The most important factor is openness to competition, whether facilitated by trade or restricted by concentration within the industry. Heterogeneity of the industry not surprisingly increases the spread of productivity performance compared to the frontier of best performance as does the rate of growth of the industry. This section expands on a pooled cross-section/time series basis the analysis developed initially in Mayes, Harris and Lansbury (1994) for the single year 1977 (see also Caves, 1992, for an international comparison). Although Dick Caves unfortunately could not participate in the Symposium itself, his work in putting together the international teams of collaborating researchers was crucial in providing the basis for the comparisons. He has been diligent in commenting on the work of the participants and deserves grateful recognition for his contribution to the success of the enterprise.

Chapters 2, 3 and 4 formed the heart of the Fulbright Symposium as it was the research project which led to the writing of them that was instrumental in the organisation of the symposium. The chapters were circulated to all the participants to the symposium and have benefited from their extensive comments, in being able both to eliminate errors and explore some further hypotheses. The research itself was financed by the ESRC to whom Mayes and Lansbury are grateful but neither the ESRC nor NIESR bears any responsibility for the views expressed.

Keith Cowling produced particularly extensive and constructive comments which are reproduced as Chapter 5. However, the organisers would like to take the opportunity to thank Peter Hart who made valuable com-

ments on several of the chapters and to John Barber and David Higham
from the Department of Trade and Industry whose experience in a policy
department during the Thatcher miracle was invaluable as was the accumulated experience from the department's research. The remaining chapters develop the issues and explore other methods of measuring the sources
of productivity growth, drawing in particular on evidence from other
countries.

Chapters 6, 7 and 8 complete the picture of the experience in the UK.
Chapter 6 by Mason and van Ark provides considerably more detail on
the plants to be compared. Whereas Lansbury and Mayes use every business reporting to the Central Statistical Office in the Annual Censuses of
Production for the years 1979 to 1989, a total of over 160,000 observations for 180 identified industries within manufacturing, Mason and van
Ark describe two very small-scale comparisons between limited samples
of plants typical of their respective industries. Here the emphasis is on a
detailed comparison, focusing on the sources of difference in human capital, quality and organisation which lead to productivity differentials between the UK, Germany and the Netherlands.

Mary O'Mahony also looks at comparison with Germany in Chapter
8, but this time at the industry level. Here her concern is to improve the
basis for comparison between the two countries and hence to show that
although there was a considerable catch-up by the UK in the 1980s it can
be exaggerated by inappropriate measurement and that a substantial gap
still remains. This is good news for those who are hoping that as the UK's
current recovery proceeds it will be possible to embark again on faster productivity simply by a narrowing of the gap between the two countries, with
UK firms adopting the best practice shown on the Continent.

In Chapter 7 on the other hand, Cameron and Muellbauer restrict their
analysis to the UK but explore the role of R&D in the process of the growth
of productivity. R&D capital is a direct reflection of the expansion of the
knowledge base and illustrates how an advantage can be translated into a
continuing dynamic gain and hence improvement not just in productivity
but in (un)employment through competitiveness as well. The remaining
seven chapters then extend the methodological aspects of the analysis and
show how evidence from Australia, Belgium, Canada, the USA, Sweden,
Norway and Japan can be used to support and develop the conclusions
drawn in Chapters 2–4 for the UK.

Chris Harris provides the most comprehensive study in Chapter 9, reporting on a whole series of studies undertaken by the Bureau of Industry
Economics in Canberra on relative productivity in Australia. These are in
two groups – a pair of comparisons for single products within plants be-

longing to the same company located in different countries round the world. The second half of the chapter looks at comparisons made at the industry level of productivity in transport and utilities, areas which are particularly difficult to compare, both because of the strong service element in their output and because of the strong element of monopoly in their structure. This chapter develops the data envelope approach to comparing productivity in these circumstances.

The problem of comparing service industries is developed much further at the detailed level by Henry Tulkens and Amador Malnero in Chapter 10 in the analysis of the efficiency of bank branches in Belgium. This analysis is particularly helpful in developing the framework for the study of the sources of productivity growth in two dimensions; first showing how a single measure of productivity can be derived by using an appropriate weighted index number where there are multiple inputs and outputs for each outlet and second developing a means of expressing the feasible frontier of efficient production, using only actual observed data. The net result is a frontier which rises by a series of steps as each new plant on the frontier is encountered. Hence no assumptions about the form of production functions or the derivation of hypothetical values to fill in the gaps are required. (Førsund in Chapter 14 uses a similar approach but has a faceted – piecewise linear – frontier instead of a stepped one.)

The authors of the next four chapters all have the advantage of being able to use databases of information on individual businesses from Censuses of Production which run across years. In many respects Chapter 11 by John Baldwin on Canada and Chapter 12 by Martin Neil Baily, Eric Bartelsman and John Haltiwanger on the United States are companion pieces, exploring how the behaviour of different groups of businesses contribute to the overall change in productivity levels. Both chapters employ a form of shift-share analysis to show the extent to which it is improvement within sectors or groups rather than shifts between them which account for the observed improvements in productivity.

Baily, Bartelsman and Haltiwanger show that for the period 1977–87 in the USA the major contribution to growth in productivity comes from firms whose employment is also rising. Furthermore, that group is concentrated in a fairly narrow range of industries. Small firms have the least impact as, while they may have made an important contribution to increasing employment, they tend to have below average productivity and hence reduce the rate of productivity growth for the economy as a whole. Baldwin finds exactly the same result for small firms and confirms that it is firms within the market that are gaining market share that are much more important in raising overall productivity than new entrants as these in the early years after entry at least tend to have below average productivity, largely because they are small.

Førsund (Chapter 14), Wilfridson and Hjalmarsson (Chapter 13) and Tybout (1994) (also presented and discussed at the symposium) extend this decomposition in a number of further directions. Wilfridson and Hjalmarsson are particularly helpful as they introduce dynamics to the process, explaining how a partial adjustment model can be incorporated and underutilised capital accounted for. By looking at total factor productivity as well as labour productivity they are able to isolate the influences of changes in capital and material inputs as well. Førsund's sample of industries in Norway covers the years 1976–88 and shows how the contribution of technology to productivity growth varies considerably over the period. Because he computes a frontier we can see that in some cases, particularly small firms, some of the participants actually diverge from the frontier over time. James Tybout's analysis lumps together movement in the frontier and efficiency movements relative to it in a single residual. These movements prove to be more important than either increases in the scale of operation or the increase in the shares of plants with above average productivity. Although this may be a feature specific to Mexican industry, over the years that he studies (1984–90) it conforms quite strongly to the UK experience of Chapter 4. Since Tybout also uses translog functions there is considerable similarity in the method of the two chapters.

The book is completed with an attempt by Akio Torii to reconcile the conflicting definitions of allocative, technical and X-inefficiency, which are widely used by authors even though they are inconsistent.

Taken together these chapters serve to emphasise the complexity of the sources of productivity growth but they also show that there is very considerable similarity across countries. Hence where these foreign studies use more developed methods or full databases of businesses over time, they provide a pointer to the sorts of conclusions that are likely to be obtained for the UK. That said, therefore, it is clear that the Thatcher 'miracle' reflected not so much unique forces in the UK but an extreme example of them because of the depth of the recession and the extent of the ensuing recovery. The greater depth meant that there was a larger contribution to increasing productivity growth from the exit of the least efficient. The extent of the restructuring meant that there was a considerable contribution from new entrants. The degree to which a gap had opened up between the UK and its competitors meant that the frontier of best performance could advance particularly rapidly. The growth of existing successful firms played an important role but the degree to which firms moved nearer to the frontier of best performance was rather limited.

All in all, therefore, a much more complex picture is painted once one can look at the detail of the 15–20,000 individual businesses in manufacturing, recorded in the Annual Censuses of Production, than is apparent simply from the analysis of aggregate or industry-level data. If and when the proposed business database comes on stream, like its counterparts in Canada, the United States, Norway and Sweden used in this book, it will be possible to develop much more accurate insights, especially if direct estimates of the capital stock become available.

2 Productivity growth in the 1980s

MELANIE LANSBURY AND DAVID MAYES[1]

Extravagant claims have been made about the success and failure of economic policy to improve the structure of industrial competitiveness in the UK during the 1980s. However, one fact which stands out is the striking improvement in labour productivity in manufacturing industry. Between 1980 and 1990 net output per head in 1985 prices increased by almost 60 per cent. This compares with 35 per cent and 17½ per cent over each of the two previous decades and hence is a substantial improvement over what had gone before.[2] Although small by Pacific Asia standards, it also represents a clear improvement in the UK's position compared with its major competitors (table 2.1).

However, this striking growth covers a period when manufacturing output contracted rapidly by 14 per cent between 1979 and 1981 and then rose to only 12 per cent above its 1979 value by 1990. Employment fell throughout from 6.8 million in 1980 to 5.1 million in 1990. The good productivity performance is therefore likely to be not the result of an all round improvement but a combination of the loss of the less efficient activities, the improvement in performance of existing activities and the starting of new more efficient enterprises. Insofar as the improvement was due to contraction the performance is not so impressive unless there was offsetting expansion elsewhere.

Various hypotheses have been advanced to explain this surge in productivity (Crafts, 1988; Muellbauer, 1991). Many of these focus on changes in the labour market. There is a group of 'industrial relations' hypotheses which relate to the changes in the powers of trade unions and management over the 1980s. Metcalf (1993), for example, suggests that unionisation is negatively associated with financial performance or profitability. Further evidence from Nickell et al. (1992) suggests that between 1979 and 1984

Table 2.1 *Relative labour productivity (output per worker-hour) (UK=100)*

	USA	Germany	France	Japan
1960	255	110	90	50
1962	255	115	95	57
1964	252	112	95	65
1966	235	112	100	68
1968	235	120	107	75
1970	220	122	110	88
1972	220	125	112	97
1974	190	120	110	96
1976	195	130	120	110
1978	195	145	140	120
1980	180	135	140	125
1982	165	125	138	125
1984	170	120	130	125
1986	175	125	125	120
1988	170	120	122	125
1990	172	126	128	133

Source: O'Mahony (1993).

productivity growth was higher in unionised firms. Productivity growth has also been associated with changes in working practices over the 1980s. Ingram (1991) suggests that the combination of increased competitive pressures, brought on by the scale of the recession in the early part of the decade and the abolition of incomes policy encouraged an increase in wage negotiations involving a productivity element.

A second group of hypotheses relates productivity growth to plant closures over the decade, suggesting that actual closure induced different responses from those stemming from marginal variations in output. After 1979 there was a marked rise in the number of liquidations, in particular voluntary closures as firms reassessed their ability to survive. This upward trend continued throughout the decade (Bowden *et al.*, 1992). It has been argued that if these exits were the least productive firms this could, at least partly explain the productivity growth. However Grant (1985) has suggested that those firms with higher levels of debt were more likely to go under in the early 1980s due to the high interest and exchange rates.[3] The decade also saw a change in the size distribution of manufacturing plants (Oulton, 1987). Between 1979 and 1984 manufacturing experienced a fall of 39 per cent in the number of large plants and a resulting fall in the proportion of labour employed in them, by 43 per cent.[4] However, Oulton found no evidence to support the view that these exits were the most inefficient and even some to the contrary – that large plants that closed may have had above average productivity but below average profitability.

The role of the capital stock is emphasised in explaining the 1980s productivity growth in a third hypothesis. A vintage capital model can be used to explain both the slowdown in the 1970s and the recovery in the 1980s (Muellbauer, 1986; Darby and Wren-Lewis, 1988; Price et al., 1990). The authors argue that during the slowdown in the 1970s firms lowered the rate at which they introduced new technology. Since workers were using older and less technically advanced capital, of presumably lower productivity, labour productivity fell. After 1979 an unexpected fall in demand brought on by the recession, sharp rises in exchange rates and interest rates and a tight fiscal policy caused firms to scrap old capital prematurely thus causing the sudden surge in labour productivity. A symmetric line of argument (Darby and Wren-Lewis, 1988) has been that over the 1970s manufacturing firms consistently held too high demand expectations and therefore hoarded excess labour. The combination of a switch in economic policy and a recession in 1979–80 helped shatter these expectations and resulted in a shake out of excess labour and the resulting rise in productivity.

A fourth explanation that has been offered is that the growth in productivity is related to a bounce back from the severity of the previous recession (Englander and Mittelstädt, 1988; Crafts, 1991). Supporters of this theory argue that, owing to the extent of international competition and the diffusion of technologies and work practices, levels of productivity for similar countries should converge. Since during the 1970s UK manufacturing productivity fell relative to its main competitors, the 1980s were a period of 'catching up'.

A further approach is to relate the productivity rise to the boom in new technology over the decade, in particular to the increasing usage of computers. However, although this technology boom clearly occurred, it does not explain why countries such as the UK, the USA and Japan experienced improving productivity growth when in others, such as Germany and France, productivity growth continued to slow well into the 1980s. It has also been argued that, although the best firms in the UK are world class competitors, overall performance has been hampered by the long tail of less efficient firms.

We seek to provide new evidence to test some of these hypotheses. We use data on 30,000 businesses drawn from the Annual Censuses of Production to explore the degree to which the productivity growth of the 1980s was due to

- a rise in productivity in a specific group of industries rather than across manufacturing as a whole
- a shift in activity from lower to higher productivity industries
- a shift from industries with lower productivity growth
- the loss of the least efficient businesses
- the entry of new more efficient businesses
- an improvement in best practice
- an improvement in the performance of continuing businesses relative to best practice.

Our data do not allow us to explore all the hypotheses we have set out in any detail. For example, there is no information recorded in the Annual Census of Production on R&D or labour relations and working practices at the level of the individual business. Even though we have data on investment and output we cannot determine the technologies embodied in the particular equipment that has been purchased nor establish changes in the quality and composition of output (or inputs for that matter). Some of these issues are dealt with in other chapters, in the individual plant sample studies of Mason and van Ark in Chapter 6 for example, or the more aggregate study of R&D by Cameron and Muellbauer in Chapter 7. This does not mean that our work is not an important step forward, even if it does not paint the total picture.

Previously most exploration of the problem has had to occur at a macroeconomic, or at best industry, level if it hopes to be comprehensive. Alternative investigations in more detail have looked only at comparisons of a limited number of plants, in particular industries. (Mayes *et al.*, 1994, explores these different approaches in more detail.)

We have divided our study into three parts. In the remainder of this chapter we examine the changes in the structure of productivity growth over the 1980s, showing, for example, that the improvement in productivity was widely spread and that only a relatively limited proportion of the growth can be explained by a shift in production towards high productivity or high productivity growth industries. However, while the growth of productivity was spread over the whole decade its composition varied markedly between the years of recession and the years of output growth. In the former many of the slower growing and less competitive industries contracted sharply, achieving the productivity growth more by shedding labour and closing the least productive plants.

One advantage of having this time series of data is that our analysis can also contribute to the debate about the relationship between the rate of growth of output and the rate of growth of productivity exemplified by the controversy over Verdoorn's Law (Kaldor, 1966, 1975; Gomulka, 1971; Cripps and Tarling, 1973; Rowthorn, 1975, 1979).

In Chapter 3 we move on to consider sources of productivity growth which can only be considered at the level of the individual business. We explore whether the distribution of productivity has changed, with a reduction in the tail of less productive firms, and whether foreign ownership affects productive performance. However, the bulk of the chapter is concerned with exploring the extent to which productivity growth is due to the efforts of continuing businesses, the exit of the less productive or the entry by new more productive enterprises. The composition of businesses in each industry changes substantially over the period as a whole and considerably even from one year to the next.

While the switches between industries may have had little impact on productivity for manufacturing as a whole the exit of the less efficient and the entry of more efficient business is an important contribution to productivity growth.

Finally in Chapter 4 we also use the Annual Censuses of Production in a separate exercise to explore the extent to which the improvement of productivity represents an increase in the general efficiency of industry compared with what was technically achievable in each year, rather than the result of technical progress in what could be achieved. In the main we do this by extending the single year estimation of inefficiency by reference to stochastic frontier production functions (described in Mayes *et al.*, 1994) to estimates over the whole of 1980 to 1990 for a breakdown of some 182 industries within manufacturing. However, we also explore the changes in the shape as well as the mean of the distribution of labour productivity for each business over the decade.

There is little indication that there has been much in the way of a reduction in the tail of inefficient businesses within each sector.[5] The whole distribution of productivity and technical efficiency has moved upwards, with only minor reductions in spread or skewness. The increase in external competition has helped reduce inefficiency but much of the variation in performance reflects product and service diversity within industries.

Taking the three chapters together, considerable scope remains for improvement of labour productivity in the UK even within existing technologies. Work by colleagues at NIESR suggests that a substantial proportion of this scope lies in improving training, skills and work organisation (Prais, 1993).

A cautionary note on the definition of productivity

In the foregoing discussion we have already used two measures of labour productivity: net output per head and value added per head. Our subsequent analysis is couched largely in terms of value added per head, not because this is a better measure than any other but because this was the variable which could be extracted from the Annual Census of Production which was comparable with parallel analyses which have been undertaken in Australia, Canada, Japan, South Korea and the United States.[6]

Each measure is likely to give differing results and some are more relevant to particular purposes than others. There are two primary choices that have to be made:

1 whether to use a measure of gross or net output,
2 whether to measure labour on a per capita or person-hour basis.

If gross output is used then it is necessary to consider all inputs, including materials and bought-in services, in forming an explanation. Using net output or value added effectively deducts these inputs from both sides of the equation.[7] The use of hours rather than numbers of employees is likely to be more accurate (as we explain below), since it eliminates differences between hours worked, but it was not available to us.

Secondly, although labour input is measured in physical units, output is more likely to be in terms of current values than in volumes. Hence comparisons across time or between countries require that these values be deflated to a common base. Furthermore, unless products and processes are very closely defined, both outputs and inputs show considerable heterogeneity. Little, if anything, may be known about the differences in composition across either time or space. Where the components are very different such compositional variation may come to dominate all other aspects of the comparison. Although our analysis may appear very detailed, dividing manufacturing into only 182 sub-industries will still leave it open to major problems from composition. We address these where possible as the discussion develops but remain aware of the drawbacks the particular measures pose. As all these issues are well known we do not develop them further here.

Once one starts to unpick the components and sources of the rapid productivity growth of the 1980s, most lines of argument suggest that the degree to which that increase is due to the more efficient use of existing inputs is relatively small. We can approach this from a number of directions. In this chapter we begin by considering the contribution of factors other than labour to the increase in labour productivity. We move on to explore how much the increase is due to a change in the structure of manufacturing industry rather than to improvements within each individual sector.

Accounting for growth – the contribution of labour, capital and other inputs

The work of Oulton and O'Mahony (1994) provides a helpful background for our analysis. Working at the industry (rather than the business) level, they explore the determinants of the growth of manufacturing output up to 1986, using a growth accounting approach. They are able to show that most of the output growth is due to increases in inputs and only some 5 per cent is due to productivity over 1979–86. While labour productivity increased by 4 per cent a year the capital–labour ratio increased by 6 per cent a year. This increase in the ratio occurred because the labour input fell over the period while the capital input remained almost unchanged in total. Output fell during this period by 2 per cent a year. By focusing on total factor productivity growth in this manner they are able to show that in aggregate the period is characterised by a switch between labour and capital, a switch which mainly involved a shakeout of labour. This discussion of the aggregate figures disguises the fact that output and capital increased in some industries while decreasing in others. Throughout the period capital will have been renewed with older capital being scrapped and new investment coming on stream. In the same way some workers will have retired and others started their careers. Even with an unchanged level of unemployment some of those of working age will have entered unemployment and others left the unemployment register to return to work or take up other activities. The composition of the two variables will thus have changed markedly. Unfortunately we cannot provide an easy match between these data and our own, not just because they do not cover identical time periods but because Oulton and O'Mahony use SIC(68) rather than our choice of SIC(80).[8]

This finding that much of the growth in labour productivity can be explained by an increase in the relative quantity of capital even if that new capital has a productivity only equal to the average of the existing capital stock is disheartening. One would have expected that the productivity of new capital was above average and that the retirements from the capital stock tended to be below average over the course of the the period. Thus, even if there were no technological change observed capital productivity would rise. Since we know there was considerable technical improvement over the period, this is likely to imply that the productivity of existing capital actually fell.[9]

Unfortunately we cannot pursue this interesting comparison as we do not have matching estimates of the capital variable. Oulton and O'Mahony, rather than using the estimates published by the CSO, construct their own. They use some external information but their estimates generally involve a change in the assumptions which are used in the official estimates. These estimates are compiled using the Perpetual Inventory Method (PIM) (Mayes and Young, 1994). PIM uses the annual estimates of investment recorded as part of the Annual Census of Production, depreciates them according to their age and assumptions about likely asset life and the likelihood of premature scrapping (through damage, wear and tear and obsolescence) and then revalues them to current prices. Oulton and O'Mahony question the official estimates of expected life lengths and the shape of the distribution of retirements from the stock. With these uncertainties over the measurement of capital the individual results must be interpreted with caution. We have recently completed a further analysis of our own to help the CSO improve the official estimates of the capital. The retrospective estimates will allow us to repeat the Oulton and O'Mahony calculations, although these new estimates will be on SIC(92) rather than our SIC(80) or Oulton and O'Mahony's SIC(68).

Output per employee and output per employee-hour

Most of the previous discussion has dealt with output per employee. Employees do not of course form a homogeneous input. The quality of employees can vary markedly over time, not so much because of innate ability but because of the extent of relevant education and training that they have received. However, even for identical quality it is not a unique measure of the quantity of labour as the number of hours worked can also vary. A fall in the number of hours without a fall in the number of people employed would give the mistaken view that labour productivity has fallen when in fact output during each hour may have risen but not by as much as the labour input has fallen. However as Denison (1989) points out, hours are not homogeneous either. Marginal hours may be less productive than the average simply because the worker is tired. Leslie and Wise

Table 2.2 *Annual hours worked per employee in UK manufacturing industry*

Year	1979	1980	1981	1982	1983	1984
Hours	1757	1695	1686	1703	1731	1747
Year	1985	1986	1987	1988	1989	1990
Hours	1742	1743	1763	1766	1754	1754

Source: Drawn from O'Mahony (1992), appendix table 4.

(1980) suggest that the hours immediately before overtime rates apply are likely to be among the least productive as workers try to ensure that overtime is available. Longer shifts will however reduce the ratio of setup to production time so there are many sources of variation.

In present circumstances the two definitions do not cause too much of a problem as the number of hours worked remained relatively constant over much of the 1980s, with the exception of the early years when there was an element of short time (table 2.2). Productivity increased by 4.1 per cent a year between 1979 and 1989 on either definition. When it comes to international comparisons, however, the difference is much more important. Most OECD countries, with the exception of Japan, work shorter hours than the UK. Furthermore the number of hours worked reduced during the 1980s.

It is difficult to assess labour productivity relative to what could be achieved with current equipment and technologies as it is hard to establish an objective standard. We follow one approach later in the paper by estimating frontier production functions for each industry and comparing actual performance with the best of what has been achieved. Smith-Gavine and Bennett tackle this problem of a yardstick directly by using technical estimates of what can be achieved in specific tasks.[10] They have constructed an index of the percentage utilisation of labour (PUL) which records the variations in the speed of manufacturing employees' work per hour. It is based on piecework and takes account of the impact of changes in equipment and working methods before computing performance from a sample of manufacturing firms. The 1980s is notable for only very limited changes in this index. There was a small fall in 1980 and a rise up to the end of 1988 before the index fell back to its value at the start of the decade. In part this is a problem with the construction of the index which makes major departures from its trend values difficult. This evidence of little change, however, fits in well with the Oulton and O'Mahony (1994) estimates from total factor productivity and our own finding that the distribution of efficiency shows no trend over the decade.

Accounting for quality

One of the main factors weakening the value of productivity comparisons is the poor treatment of quality and the characteristics of technology. Over the past twenty years there have been major quality improvements in durable goods, in particular in computers and other high technology goods. Using unit prices as a deflator therefore tends to understate real output change as some of the price will reflect the change in quality. The position is at its most acute in computers, where, despite leaps forward in power over a short period of time, prices have actually declined. Real output is thus likely to have been seriously understated. Research in the USA (Baily and Gordon, 1989) has estimated the extent of the distortions of real output growth caused by the rapid decline in computer prices and the increasing volume of sales. Using the base-period prices results in an overweighting of the growth of 'dynamic' industries in the years following the base year and an underweighting in the preceding years. To overcome this they separate out computers from the rest of the sector and then recompute output using year shares for the two parts. Re-computing total manufacturing output they show that this decreases the measured rate of growth by 0.5 per cent between 1979 and 1987. We can expect similar results for the UK. The further into the future the analysis is projected the greater the prospective error.

There is a second related effect which stems from the dramatic rise, most notably over the 1980s, in the usage of computers and high technology equipment in manufacturing industry. This has had a significant effect on the output produced per employee regardless of an actual improvement in individuals' efficiency. This assignment problem to the source of productivity change applies to almost all industries. Hedonic price indexes can be used to allow for such differences and to enable the calculation of a 'quality adjusted' measure of productivity. This method uses regression techniques to relate the prices of different 'models' or versions of a commodity to differences in their characteristics – 'qualities'. One can thereby discover the relative valuation of such qualities (Griliches, 1990).

Progress relative to other countries

In part we can judge the success of the UK's growth in productivity by comparison with other countries. Comparisons of growth rates alone are not particularly revealing because they ignore the difference in levels of productivity. Similarly comparisons over short periods of time may be misleading because cyclical and other shocks will result in fluctuations. Fortunately colleagues at NIESR have undertaken a series of comparisons of the UK with France, Germany, the Netherlands and the United States over recent years. Work by van Ark (1990a,b) suggests that differentials have narrowed sharply during the 1980s, although the recession at the end of the decade reversed this to some extent. Van Ark estimates that in 1979 UK productivity in manufacturing in terms of output per person hour was 40 per cent below that in Germany and 33 per cent below France. By 1990 the gaps had narrowed to 26 per cent and 18 per cent respectively.

In their inter-country comparisons of productivity O'Mahony (1992a, b) and van Ark (1992) considered productivity in both employee and employee per hour terms. The difference between the two measures in terms of the comparison with Germany is sufficiently large to have an effect on the policy implications. Taking the 1987 figures the gap on a per employee basis was only 13 per cent and, given the rate at which it was being closed, there appeared a real possibility that parity would be reached in the 1990s. (This was before there was any suggestion of the unification of Germany so the parity was with the then West Germany.) However, on an employee-hour basis the gap was 22 per cent, sufficiently large that its closure within a meaningful time horizon would not have been expected.[11] The emphasis in the analysis was on worker-hours as this took account of time lost due to sickness, holidays, maternity leave, strikes, and so on. Such inter-country comparisons, if they are not expressible in output volumes of the same product, have to take account of the differences in price levels and exchange rates among the countries to be compared. The use of simple published exchange rates or purchasing power parities based on bundles of consumer goods can be highly misleading. The authors therefore use unit value ratios derived from specific comparisons of particular products spread over the whole spectrum of manufacturing. Although around 200 comparisons are made in each case, they cover less than 20 per cent of sales, which may suggest caution in interpretation. The difference in the estimates of the gap in the case of Germany in 1987 are striking. An exchange-rate based comparison generates a difference of 45 per cent compared with 22 per cent using O'Mahony's preferred method for output per employee hour.

However, use of aggregate figures can be misleading as they do not compare like with like. In his Keynes Lecture to the British Academy, Prais (1993) shows that when similar plants are compared British labour productivity is considerably lower than the aggregate figures would suggest. This was amplified in the discussion by Maurice Scott, who pointed out that Maddison's (1991) comparison of GDP per head in 1987 using PPPs gave a ranking, with the UK as 100, of US 125, France 117, Netherlands

115 and West Germany 99.[12] The same applies when one considers plants which are typical of the industries in the UK and other countries, rather than exactly matched plants.[13] Mason *et al.* (1993) provide a particularly clear example in the case of biscuits. In 1990 the Production Censuses in the UK and Germany suggested that output (tons) per employee hour were 25 per cent higher in the UK than in Germany. However, by using their matched plants they were able to adjust the figures for differences in quality, which suggested that on the contrary output per employee hour in Germany was 40 per cent higher than in the UK. This example illustrates the problem, not necessarily the sign of the adjustment required. The selfsame adjustment to the comparison between the UK and the Netherlands for biscuits lowers the Dutch advantage over the UK industry from 40 per cent on production census data to 25 per cent when adjusted for quality.[14] The work of O'Mahony (1992a, b) and van Ark (1990a,b, 1992) also results in somewhat larger differentials when they take account of differences in the product mix and attempt a closer comparison of activities. All this leads us to be rather cautious about the extent of any 'Thatcher miracle' or alternatively to have a rather bullish view about the scope that is still available for catching up as the UK economy emerges from the recession.

We therefore do not attempt to replicate results stemming from analysis at the industry level but address problems which can only be tackled by using data on the individual businesses in manufacturing industry. The form of our analysis is driven by the data which are available, namely, the information collected as part of the Annual Census of Production over the years 1980 to 1990.[15] The most recent year available is 1990 and prior to 1980 the statistical classification was different.[16] These data are subject to the Statistics of Trade Act so access to them is strictly limited. Not only must nothing be published which could reveal any information about an individual business but access to the original data is restricted to officials in the Central Statistical Office directly involved with the collection and processing of the information. We are thus restricted to reporting only on aggregates and all analyses have to be done at arm's length, using algorithms which enable decisions to be taken 'mechanically' without examination of individual observations.

The maximum practical level for disaggregation is therefore the 4-digit 'activity level', which gives 182 separate industries which can be compared across the eleven years of our data. We were also restricted by the form in which the data are held. Unfortunately, unlike the United States or Canada, the data are not held in the form of a longitudinal database, where each business has a unique identifier and any information collected from it can be set out across the years. The data are held on separate

Table 2.3 *Real manufacturing productivity growth (1980=100)*

SIC code	Industrial sector	1981	1982	1983	1984	1985
22	Metal manufacturing	130.8	126.5	188.9	198.3	203.8
23	Extraction of minerals n.e.s.	101.8	108.0	130.5	119.4	132.6
24	Non-metallic mineral products	108.2	114.8	124.9	129.0	127.1
25	Chemicals	105.9	110.3	130.7	141.8	147.7
26	Manmade fibres	146.3	130.6	213.8	250.7	282.7
31	Metal goods n.e.s.	103.1	113.4	118.9	121.3	126.3
32	Mechanical engineering	100.3	104.7	107.8	112.4	115.3
33	Office & data processing equip't	105.0	126.5	129.0	137.7	142.1
34	Electrical engineering	105.8	120.1	123.6	131.5	131.8
35	Motor vehicles & parts	108.1	115.9	133.7	140.3	153.2
36	Other transport equipment	105.2	109.9	119.5	119.1	125.7
37	Instrument engineering	91.8	105.5	106.0	110.9	116.7
41/42	Food, drink and tobacco	105.5	108.7	112.9	105.3	116.9
43	Textiles	112.0	116.9	127.3	126.1	135.8
45	Footwear & clothing	108.4	114.1	120.3	124.2	126.3
46	Timber & wooden furniture	102.9	107.7	118.1	112.5	116.7
47	Paper, printing & publishing	103.1	102.6	106.8	112.7	114.6
48	Rubber & plastics	102.2	112.1	123.3	126.3	135.7
49	Other manufacturing	97.8	106.0	112.3	123.4	121.3
	Total manufacturing	105.9	112.0	121.4	124.5	129.9

magnetic tapes for each year with separate identifiers for each year. Creating a database would be a major exercise in its own right but one which we hope that the CSO and ESRC will undertake as a joint venture in the not too distant future.[17]

We now explore how the change in aggregate productivity for manufacturing as a whole is made up from changes in individual sectors and by the changing size of those sectors.

Sources of productivity growth by sector

Productivity, here measured as gross value added per head,[18] $G_{ijt} = Q_{ijt}/L_{ijt}$, where Q is gross value added and L the number of employees, for any individual business i in industry j in year t, is estimated by the CSO for each industry as $G_{\cdot jt} = \Sigma_i Q_{ijt}/\Sigma_i L_{ijt}$ after grossing up the variables be-

Table 2.3 *continued*

SIC code	Industrial sector	1986	1987	1988	1989	1990
22	Metal manufacturing	230.0	289.1	335.3	310.3	266.1
23	Extraction of minerals n.e.s.	123.9	127.9	129.0	122.3	124.4
24	Non-metallic mineral products	136.9	146.2	160.8	156.3	142.8
25	Chemicals	152.1	170.3	177.9	174.2	166.2
26	Manmade fibres	379.2	409.7	483.8	514.4	543.0
31	Metal goods n.e.s.	129.3	134.4	141.8	143.0	144.8
32	Mechanical engineering	116.5	121.1	128.1	136.6	134.3
33	Office & data processing equip't	182.1	212.5	220.6	227.3	224.8
34	Electrical engineering	128.8	134.4	145.9	144.1	144.9
35	Motor vehicles & parts	167.2	173.8	173.7	189.1	166.7
36	Other transport equipment	132.8	137.0	153.0	182.6	193.1
37	Instrument engineering	114.1	115.0	128.7	119.3	123.0
41/42	Food, drink and tobacco	114.8	127.6	119.9	124.7	129.2
43	Textiles	140.6	141.9	140.4	138.8	143.9
45	Footwear & clothing	125.8	130.9	131.7	137.3	148.1
46	Timber & wooden furniture	119.8	133.6	137.0	131.8	129.1
47	Paper, printing & publishing	124.7	127.9	133.4	133.9	133.0
48	Rubber & plastics	143.9	155.9	154.5	158.6	162.4
49	Other manufacturing	120.8	128.4	137.4	130.4	131.1
	Total manufacturing	134.2	143.9	150.2	153.8	152.6

cause, although the inquiry is labelled the Annual *Census* of Production it is only a census of businesses with over one hundred employees.[19] In 1990 this group represented 77 per cent of net output in manufacturing, that is, the large majority. Businesses with fewer than twenty employees are not sampled at all, those between twenty and forty-nine are part of a one in four sample and those with between fifty and ninety-nine employees are part of a one in two sample, both drawn randomly with replacement each year.[20] There is therefore not an exact match between our analysis of the published figures in this section and the results for the Census sample, corrected for suspect data, used in the next section. An exact comparison is in any case impossible as CSO has updated the aggregate estimates in the light of external information about the behaviour of industry, although the Census data remain unchanged.[21]

It is immediately apparent (table 2.3) that there have been striking differences in the changes in productivity over the period among sectors even at the 2-digit level. Manmade fibres (26) stands out as the fastest growing sector,[22] increasing by some 443 per cent over the decade. The other sectors where productivity grew at above the average rate are metal manufacturing (22), office machinery and data processing equipment (33) and other transport equipment (36).[23] At the other end of the spectrum, productivity grew slowest in instrument engineering (37) and mineral extraction (23) (although in absolute terms productivity is among the highest in this sector).

Not surprisingly variation was even greater at the 4-digit level. Within metal manufacturing, for example, productivity increased fastest in iron and steel (2210), 500 per cent, but slowest in steel wire (2234), 40 per cent. In footwear and clothing, hats, caps and millinery (4537) rose fastest, 92 per cent, while productivity in fur goods (4560) actually fell by 15 per cent. As our analysis in the next chapter shows, these changes do not necessarily imply a change in efficiency for continuing businesses.

The contribution that each sector makes to the overall change in productivity is a combination of the extent of the change involved and the weighting it has in total value added, with the usual attendant index number problems. Computing $[(G._{j90} - G._{j80})/(G._{j*})][(Q._{j*})/(Q._{..*})]$, where $*$ indicates the weighting basis, would isolate the contribution of each industry to the overall productivity change. It is, however, more common to use employment rather than value added weights $[(L._{j*})/(L._{..*})]$ a practice we repeat here.[24] Since the original industries are not of equal size, this exercise reflects the nature of the statistical classification as well as the nature of the change.

Figure 2.1 abstracts from the weighting and separates the change into the two dimensions of productivity growth and initial productivity level, that is, productivity in 1980.

What is particularly striking is the existence of two sectors

(25) chemicals

(33) office machinery and data processing equipment

which show both above average productivity at the outset and above average productivity growth, thereby increasing the disparities in the system. Only one industry (23), extraction of minerals, which had productivity substantially above the average, has regressed towards the mean.[25] Since this industry is dependent upon particular locations there is a considerable natural barrier to entry. Hence if businesses are closed rather than taken over this gives good scope for increasing productivity while cutting output and employment. The largest group of industries lies at the lower

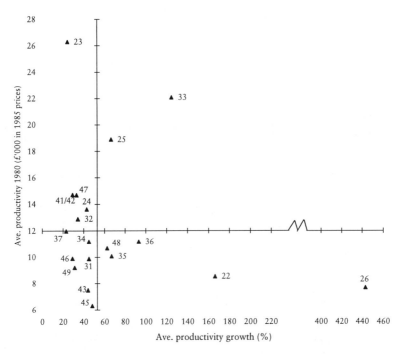

Figure 2.1 *Manufacturing productivity levels vs growth, 1980–90*
Note: Numbers on graph are 2-digit industry codes, see table 2.3 for definition.

end of the spectrum, with a lower than average productivity starting point and a lower than average productivity growth, thus helping to widen the range of behaviour. Of the industries whose productivity growth is moving them into the top right-hand quadrant, manmade fibres (26) and metal manufacturing (22) make a substantial impression with respective productivity growth of roughly nine and three times the average.

If we look at this transformation in more detail it is the EDP component (3302) of (33) which is the dramatic performer with productivity rising from twice the average for manufacturing in 1980 to three times the average in 1990 (with an average which itself rose by 50 per cent over the decade). Employment also rose in this sector, increasing its share of manufacturing by 88 per cent. The dramatic rise of manmade fibres, which we noted earlier, is however accompanied by a halving of its employment share. Iron and steel also saw a major fall in employment as the industry was restructured both before and after privatisation in 1988. Here there was considerable closure of plants as well as restructuring

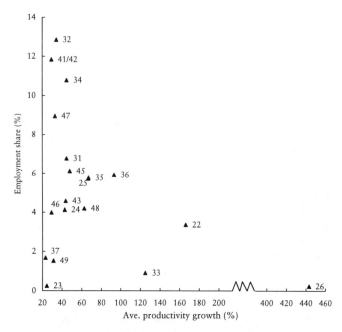

Figure 2.2 *Employment share vs productivity growth, 1980–90*

of the remaining plants. (We can see from our data on entry and exit in the next chapter that the number of businesses recorded as in existence within the sample at the end of the year fell from 189 in 1981 to 83 in 1990.[26] However, during the same period there were 91 new entrants and 167 exits. Sampling variation means that the various components of this picture do not add up exactly.) By the end of the decade its share of manufacturing employment had fallen by 53 per cent. Within metal manufacturing only 2235, miscellaneous drawing, cold rolling and cold forming of steel, increased its employment share (by 24 per cent). There is good reason to think that this is also a result of the closure of other activities in the sector, as these processes could easily be a minor activity in a business whose principal product was iron and steel. Cold processing can take place outside a steel mill.

Chemicals as a whole appears a clear success story. Although much of the analysis of the industry tends to focus on pharmaceuticals, in fact twelve out of the twenty 4-digit activity headings in this sector increased their employment share during the decade, six of them by more than a third,

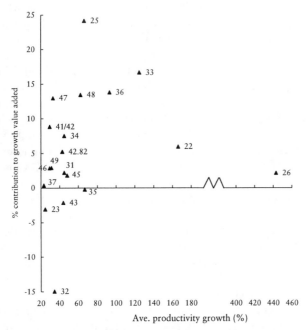

Figure 2.3 *Growth of value added, share vs productivity growth, 1980–90*

giving an increase of 11 per cent for the sector as a whole. Formulated pesticides (2568) shows the most striking changes, with productivity levels seven times the average in 1984.[27]

Interestingly enough, what figure 2.2 shows is that industries at both ends of the spectrum in terms of growth of productivity tend to have a relatively small share of manufacturing activity.[28] Most of the more important sectors in terms of their weight in total activity (more than 5 per cent) (mechanical engineering (32), food, drink and tobacco (41/42), electrical and electronic engineering (34), paper, paper products, printing, publishing (47), metal goods (n.e.s.) (31), footwear and clothing (45)) are bunched near the mean. Chemicals (25), motor vehicles (35) and particularly other transport equipment (36) have both above average productivity growth and a weight in excess of 5 per cent. The overall result is thus dominated by the larger sectors with near average performance.

The contribution of each sector to the overall growth of value added in manufacturing is shown in figure 2.3 (the higher up the vertical axis the greater the contribution). Chemicals (25) is the sector which makes the

largest contribution to value added growth over the decade, nearly 25
per cent. Of the other sectors only four contributed more than 10 per cent:
office and data processing equipment (33); other transport equipment (36);
paper, paper products, printing and publishing (47); and rubber and plastics (48). Of these only paper, paper products, printing and publishing
is below average productivity growth. With the exception of metal manufacturing (22) and manmade fibres (26) all those sectors with low contributions to value added growth (below 10 per cent) had average or below
average productivity growth. Footwear and clothing were the lowest
productivity sectors during the decade at about half the manufacturing
average, although productivity growth was near the average for UK manufacturing. With the exception of soft furnishings (4555), whose employment share doubled over the decade, activity moved out of the sector.
Textiles (43) showed a similar picture, with a productivity level some 60
per cent of the average. However, here again there was an exception –
carpets, rugs and mats (4345) where productivity more than doubled
through the decade reaching a level 50 per cent above the manufacturing
average by 1990. Matching this was an increase of some 130 per cent in
the activity's employment share.

Two other low productivity sectors, timber and wood furnishings
(46) and other manufacturing (49), also saw a fall in their employment
shares, with the exception of miscellaneous wooden articles (4650), shop
and office fittings (4672) and miscellaneous manufacturing (4959). From
their definition we can expect these residual categories to show marked
differences in performance. They can be the categories where new products, not easily classifiable within the existing system, appear.

However, if we take the general pattern of these industries together at
both the high productivity/high productivity growth and low productiv-
ity/low productivity growth ends of the spectrum we can see that there
has been a clear tendency for UK manufacturing to move towards these
higher performing activities and out of the lower performing ones, without simultaneously causing a regression towards the mean. The sectors
with both below average productivity and productivity growth represented
43 per cent of value added in 1980 but their share had fallen to 38 per cent
by the end of the decade.

However, overall the implications of this shift are very limited as is
shown in table 2.4. If 1980 industrial weights had been maintained throughout the decade, productivity would have increased by 54 per cent instead
of the 53 per cent recorded. Actual productivity increased every year until 1990. Indeed, one of the striking features of the table is the consistency
of the rate of growth of productivity over the period compared with

Table 2.4 *Comparison of actual manufacturing productivity growth during the 1980s with that using 1980 employment shares as weights*

	Actual productivity	Using 1980 employment data
1980	100.0	100.0
1981	105.9	105.1
1982	112.0	110.8
1983	121.4	120.5
1984	124.5	124.2
1985	129.9	130.3
1986	134.2	134.9
1987	143.9	145.8
1988	150.2	152.7
1989	153.8	156.7
1990	152.6	153.7

Note: Productivity measured as value-added per employee.

the strong variations in the rate of growth of manufacturing output. Between 1981 and 1982 productivity grew rapidly (figure 2.4); indeed 1982 was the year of maximum productivity growth. Furthermore, value added fell in 1980 and 1981 before four years of steady growth, as opposed to productivity, which took a sharp downturn between 1982 and 1983. Beyond that point there is a clear comovement with value added. Taking these two points together we might infer that although the 1980s do appear consistent with the Verdoorn Law of comovement of output growth and productivity growth, the early part of the decade did show greater productivity growth than might otherwise have been expected, allied with a heavy loss of unemployment, thus adding credence to the hypothesis of a shake out of surplus labour.

The profile of change

One of the most intriguing features of productivity growth is its distribution over the cycle of economic activity. The 1980s provided fertile ground for such an observation with the strongest economic cycle since the war. The years 1979–81 saw a 3.2 per cent fall in GDP, while 1987 had the fastest rate of growth, 4.2 per cent, since the 7.4 per cent of 1972. Yet by the end of the decade GDP had begun to slow again with growth of only 0.8 per

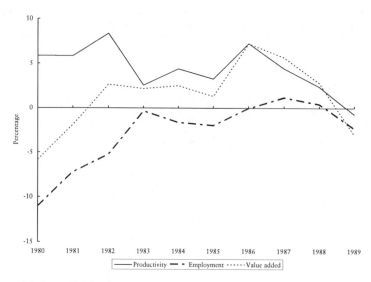

Figure 2.4 *Annual growth rates*

cent in 1990. Manufacturing industry has always shown a larger cycle
than the economy as a whole, partly because its products are not in the
main necessities and partly because its products have an extended life
and are storable. It is therefore possible to postpone purchases when conditions are difficult and advance them later. Similarly the stock cycle enables firms to accentuate the output cycle by deliberately running stocks
down in a recession after building them up involuntarily at the end of the
upturn when demand tends to be overforecast.

This pattern is repeated in 1979–81 for manufacturing but with much
greater amplitude as output fell by 14.2 per cent. The eventual recovery
was also stronger with output rising by 7 per cent in 1987 alone. However, the recession at the end of the 1980s was rather different in character
and affected the whole of the economy much more evenly than its pred-
ecessors, both in terms of its impact across industries and in its regional
impact. The 1979–82 recession exaggerated regional disparities and had
a disproportionately adverse impact on manufacturing (and construction).
The recent recession on the other hand has shown a smaller discrepancy
between services and manufacturing (table 2.5), although manufacturing
still showed over twice the contraction. The construction cycle, however,
has been deeper after a delayed start.

Productivity also tends to follow a cyclical path but with a lag (see
Englander and Mittlestädt, 1988). When output falls workers are put on

Table 2.5 *Output growth 1990–92 (1985 prices, annual percentage change)*

Sector	Weight	1990	1991	1992
Agriculture	19	5.1	2.7	2.4
Fuels and water	106	0.0	3.8	0.2
Manufacturing	238	-0.1	-5.0	-1.2
Construction	59	1.0	-8.7	-5.4
Services	578	1.2	-2.2	-0.1
GDP(O)	1000	0.6	-2.5	-0.4

Source: Oxford Economic Forecasting, *UK Industrial Prospects*, September 1993.

short time or have their overtime reduced before redundancies are contemplated. Hence productivity is likely to fall as demand eases off. Once it is clear that there is a recession and demand will not pick up quickly firms cut costs harshly and commence the path of redundancy. In this period productivity rises markedly. It only slows when bottlenecks begin to emerge.

It is argued (Darby and Wren-Lewis, 1989) that the recession of the early 1980s was so deep that redundancies were brought forward, shaking out many people who were underemployed, who had been allowed to continue because the problems in trying to increase their work rate were too great. Productivity hence started rising more vigorously and earlier than might have been expected. Employment in manufacturing industry fell by 24 per cent between 1979 and 1983 – further and longer than the fall in output (see figure 2.5). Indeed, as the recovery in output continued to improve, employment continued to fall, resulting in a further 7 per cent decline over the period 1983–90. The recent recession has, however, indicated that the pattern of employment and labour market behaviour has altered. Not merely has manufacturing largely maintained its share of activity in the recession but the shake out of labour came earlier as did the recovery in employment. This implies that the 1980s did indeed represent not just a change in economic structure away from manufacturing but also a change in economic behaviour. Labour has become more sympathetic to the needs of the firm as articulated by the management, firms have been able to be more flexible with their workforce both inside and outside the workplace. Treu (1992) argues that internal flexibility has become more developed than external flexibility and hence it is now rather easier for firms to respond to shocks by internal reorganisation. As a result less job loss is required to achieve a given change and lags during which some of the labour force are unemployed while the process of external adjustment takes place are shortened.

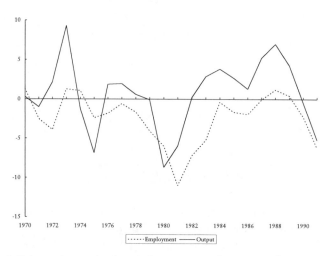

Figure 2.5 *Annual growth of manufacturing employment and output*

Hence productivity has not had to face such a dramatic cycle (see figure 2.4). The distribution of inefficiency can similarly be expected to vary on a cyclical basis (although as is apparent in what follows this variation is very limited). As inefficient businesses get shaken out in the downturn we might expect the spread of industry to narrow and the tail of inefficient enterprises to shorten. In an upturn two phenomena are likely to permit a greater spread in efficiency. First of all the increased demand is likely to reduce the pressures on firms and hence permit the less efficient to survive. Second, the process of growth will itself involve greater investment in a more productive capital stock, hence shifting the production function. During that process of transition different businesses will be operating on the new or old functions, giving an increased spread of behaviour round the compromise function which will tend to be estimated under the structure of our methodology.

If we make a comparison of the two extreme periods, the recession of 1980–82 and the rapid growth of 1985–9, the different sectors of manufacturing make somewhat different contributions to the growth of productivity and to value added (tables 2.6 and 2.7). While manmade fibres (26), office machinery (33) and metal manufacturing (22) have the fastest growth of productivity in both periods, the above average growth sectors in the two periods are, in declining order,

Table 2.6 *Productivity growth in the upturn and downturn*

SIC code	Industrial sector	Productivity growth (% increase)	
		Downturn (1980-82)	Upturn (1985-89)
22	Metal manufacturing	26.5	52.2
23	Extraction of minerals n.e.s.	8.0	-7.8
24	Non-metallic mineral products	14.8	23.0
25	Chemicals	10.3	18.0
26	Manmade fibres	30.6	82.0
31	Metal goods n.e.s.	13.4	13.3
32	Mechanical engineering	4.7	18.5
33	Office & data processing equip't	26.5	59.9
34	Electrical engineering	20.1	9.3
35	Motor vehicles & parts	15.9	23.4
36	Other transport equipment	9.9	45.2
37	Instrument engineering	5.5	2.2
41/42	Food, drink and tobacco	8.7	6.7
43	Textiles	16.9	2.2
45	Footwear & clothing	14.1	8.7
46	Timber & wooden furniture	7.7	13.0
47	Paper, printing & publishing	2.6	16.8
48	Rubber & plastics	12.1	16.9
49	Other manufacturing	6.0	7.6
	Total manufacturing	12.0	18.4

downturn: electrical engineering   *upturn:* other transport equip't
               textiles   non-metallic minerals
               motor vehicles and parts
               non-metallic minerals
               footwear and clothing
               metal goods n.e.s.

In the decline therefore some slow growing sectors like textiles, footwear and clothing improved their productivity markedly, an experience not repeated in the upturn. The distribution of productivity growth rates was also more skewed in the upturn with other transport, whose productivity growth was unspectacular as becomes a high performer.

Table 2.7 *Percentage contribution to growth of value added*

SIC code	Industrial sector	Productivity growth (% increase)	
		Downturn (1980-82)	Upturn (1985-89)
22	Metal manufacturing	4.5	6.7
23	Extraction of minerals n.e.s.	0.4	-0.4
24	Non-metallic mineral products	4.1	8.4
25	Chemicals	5.3	13.9
26	Manmade fibres	0.8	1.1
31	Metal goods n.e.s.	7.7	5.0
32	Mechanical engineering	31.6	6.2
33	Office & data processing equip't	0.3	9.0
34	Electrical engineering	-0.2	3.9
35	Motor vehicles & parts	12.3	5.9
36	Other transport equipment	-1.2	8.9
37	Instrument engineering	1.3	0.7
41/42	Food, drink and tobacco	5.1	5.8
43	Textiles	3.2	-0.7
45	Footwear & clothing	3.8	0.5
46	Timber & wooden furniture	2.4	4.1
47	Paper, printing & publishing	13.2	11.4
48	Rubber & plastics	3.7	8.1
49	Other manufacturing	1.8	1.6
	Total manufacturing	100.0	100.0

Table 2.7 enables us to disentangle an improvement in productivity alone from an improvement in economic performance, contributing to the growth of value added. In the downturn almost one third of the total growth comes from mechanical engineering, the next two largest growth sectors are motor vehicles (35) and paper, printing and publishing (47), with contributions of 12 per cent and 13 per cent respectively. When it comes to the upturn the contribution to the growth of value added is much more evenly spread. Only chemicals and paper, printing and publishing contribute more than 10 per cent. The two periods are thus clearly different in the character of the structural change involved.

On the basis of an analysis of the data at the 4-digit industry level it therefore appears that, despite substantial shifts in the proportion of activity taking place in various sectors, this is not an important contribution to the rapid growth in productivity during the 1980s. Productivity in the large majority of sectors grew by between a quarter and two thirds over the decade compared with the 50 per cent growth for manufacturing as a whole. Neither the very rapidly growing sectors like manmade fibres, metal manufacturing, office machinery and data processing equipment and other transport nor the sectors with slow productivity growth – instrument engineering and mineral extraction – had sufficiently large changes in weights over the decade to have a major impact on the average.

Only chemicals, office machinery and data processing equipment and other transport equipment had both productivity growth well above average and sufficient output growth to make a major contribution to growth over the period as a whole. The process of productivity growth over the decade was thus widely based.

However, this general growth hides two rather different contributions if we split the period into phases of overall output growth and recession. In many of the less well performing industries, in productivity and output terms, the major productivity growth came during the periods of recession. Textiles, footwear and clothing in particular made a marked contribution to productivity growth in the recession years.

There is thus more than one force leading to good aggregate productivity performance. There are some leading industries whose productivity has grown very rapidly. There have been sharp improvements in declining industries. Although there is some relationship between productivity growth and output growth there has not been a strong movement in the economy towards the high growth sectors in either sense.

However, all the foregoing describes the pattern of change at the industry level. The more interesting questions which our dataset allow us to answer relate to the individual businesses within the industries. Does the growth in productivity in an industry stem from a general rise in productivity in all businesses, from a more than average rise in the productivity of the businesses which initially had above average levels or from a more rapid rise in the productivity in businesses which were initially below average? These would represent very different patterns of behaviour. Is it the best which are improving their performance still further or are the less productive moving up towards the performance of the best? Is the productivity growth concentrated in small businesses or large businesses?

Moreover, concentrating on existing businesses may be missing the source of productivity growth altogether. It may very well be that much of the growth comes not from changes within businesses but from the exit of poor performers and the entry of more productive and more dynamic new firms. We tackle these questions in the next chapter.

Appendix table 2A.1 *Definition of industries*

SIC(80)	Industry
2210	Iron & steel industry
2220	Steel tubes
2234	Drawing & manufacture of steel wire & steel wire products
2235	Miscellaneous drawing, cold rolling & cold forming of steel
2245	Aluminium & aluminium alloys
2246	Copper, brass and other copper alloys
2247	Miscellaneous non-ferrous metals & their alloys
2310	Extraction of stone, clay, sand & gravel
2396	Extraction of miscellaneous minerals
2410	Structural clay products
2420	Cement, lime & plaster
2436	Ready made concrete
2437	Miscellaneous building products of concrete, cement or plaster
2440	Asbestos goods
2450	Working of stone & other non-metallic minerals
2460	Abrasive products
2471	Flat glass
2478	Glass containers
2479	Miscellaneous glass products
2481	Refractory goods
2489	Ceramic goods
2511	Inorganic chemicals except industrial glass
2512	Basic organic chemicals except specialised pharmaceutical chemicals
2513	Fertilisers
2514	Synthetic resins & plastic materials
2516	Dyestuffs & pigment
2551	Paints, varnishes & painters' fillings
2552	Printing ink
2562	Formulated adhesives & sealants
2564	Essential oils & flavouring materials
2567	Miscellaneous chemical products for industrial use
2568	Formulated pesticides
2570	Pharmaceutical products
2581	Soap & synthetic detergents
2582	Perfumes, cosmetics & toilet preparations
2591	Photographic materials & chemicals
2599	Chemical products, not elsewhere specified
2600	Production of manmade fibres
3111	Ferrous metal foundries
3112	Non-ferrous metal foundries
3120	Forging, press & stamping
3137	Bolts, nuts, washers, rivets, springs & non-precision chains

Appendix table 2A.1 *continued*

3138	Heat & surface treatment of metals, including sintering
3142	Metal doors, windows, etc.
3161	Hand tools & implements
3162	Cutlery, spoons, forks & similar tableware; razors
3163	Metal storage vessels (mainly non-industrial)
3164	Packaging products of metal
3165	Domestic heating & cooking appliances (non-electrical)
3166	Metal furniture & safes
3167	Domestic & similar utensils of metal
3169	Finished metal products, not elsewhere specified
3204	Fabricated constructional steelwork
3205	Boilers & process plant fabrication
3211	Agricultural machinery
3212	Wheeled tractors
3221	Metal-working machine tools
3222	Engineers' small tools
3230	Textile machinery
3244	Food, drink & tobacco processing machinery; packaging & bottling machinery
3245	Chemical industry machinery; furnaces & kilns; gas, water & waste treatment plant
3246	Process engineering contractors
3251	Mining machinery
3254	Construction & earth moving equipment
3255	Mechanical lifting & handling equipment
3261	Precision chains & other mechanical power transmission equipment
3262	Ball, needle & roller bearing
3275	Machinery for working wood, rubber, plastics, leather & making paper, glass, bricks & similar material; laundry & dry cleaning machinery
3276	Printing, bookbinding & paper goods machinery
3281	Internal combustion engines & other prime movers
3283	Compressors & fluid power equipment
3284	Refrigerating machinery, space heating, ventilating & air conditioning equipment
3285	Scales, weighing machinery & portable power tools
3286	Miscellaneous industrial & commercial machinery
3287	Pumps
3288	Industrial valves
3290	Ordnance, small arms & ammunition
3301	Office machinery
3302	Electronic data processing equipment
3410	Insulated wires & cables
3420	Basic electrical equipment
3432	Batteries & accumulators

Appendix table 2A.1 *continued*

3433	Alarms & signalling equipment
3434	Electrical equipment for motor vehicles, cycles & aircraft
3435	Electrical equipment for industrial use, not elsewhere specified
3441	Telegraph & telephone apparatus & equipment
3442	Electrical instruments & control systems
3443	Radio & electronic capital goods
3444	Components other than active components, mainly for electronic equipment
3454	Electronic consumer goods & other electronic equipment, not elsewhere specified
3460	Domestic-type electrical appliances
3470	Electric lamps and other electric lighting equipment
3510	Motor vehicles & their engines
3521	Motor vehicle bodies
3522	Trailers & semi-trailers
3523	Caravans
3610	Shipbuilding & repairing
3620	Railway & tramway vehicles
3640	Aerospace equipment manufacturing & repair
3710	Measuring, checking & precision instruments & apparatus
3720	Medical & surgical equipment & orthopaedic appliances
3731	Spectacles & unmounted lenses
3732	Optical precision instruments
3733	Photographic & cinematographic equipment
3740	Clocks, watches & other timing devices
4116	Processing organic oils & fats
4122	Bacon curing & meat processing
4123	Poultry slaughter & processing
4130	Preparation of milk & milk products
4147	Processing of fruit & vegetables
4150	Fish preparation
4160	Grain milling
4196	Bread & flour confectionery
4197	Biscuits & crispbread
4213	Ice cream
4214	Cocoa, chocolate & sugar confectionery
4221	Compound animal feeds
4222	Pet foods & non-compound animal feeds
4239	Miscellaneous foods
4240	Spirit distilling & compounding
4270	Brewing amd malting
4283	Soft drinks
4290	Tobacco industry
4310	Woollen & worsted industry

Appendix table 2A.1 *continued*

4321	Spinning & doubling on the cotton system
4322	Weaving of cotton, silk & manmade fibres
4336	Throwing, texturing, etc. of continuous filament yarn
4340	Spinning and weaving of flax, hemp & ramie
4350	Jute & polypropylene yarns & fabrics
4364	Warp knitted fabrics
4370	Textile finishing
4384	Pile carpets, carpeting & rugs
4395	Lace
4396	Rope, twine & net
4398	Narrow fabrics
4399	Other miscellaneous textiles
4410	Leather (tanning & dressing) & fellmongery
4420	Leather goods
4510	Footwear
4531	Weatherproof outerwear
4532	Men's and boys' tailored outerwear
4533	Women's & girls' tailored outerwear
4534	Work clothing and men's & boys' jeans
4535	Men's & boys' shirts, underwear & nightwear
4537	Hats, caps & millinery
4538	Gloves
4539	Miscellaneous dress industries
4555	Soft furnishings
4556	Canvas goods, sacks & other made-up textiles
4557	Household textiles
4610	Sawmilling, planing, etc. of wood
4620	Manufacture of semi-finished wood products & further processing & treatment of wood
4630	Builders' carpentry & joinery
4640	Wooden containers
4650	Miscellaneous wooden articles
4663	Brushes & brooms
4672	Shop & office fittings
4710	Pulp, paper & board
4721	Wall coverings
4722	Household & personal hygiene products of paper
4723	Stationery
4724	Packaging products of paper & pulp
4725	Packaging products of board
4728	Miscellaneous paper & board products
4752	Printing & publishing of periodicals
4753	Printing & publishing of books

Appendix table 2A.1 *continued*

4812	Miscellaneous rubber products
4832	Plastics semi-manufacture
4834	Plastic building products
4835	Plastic packaging products

4910	Jewellery & coins
4920	Musical instruments
4941	Toys & games
4942	Sports goods

Appendix table 2A.2 *Manufacturing productivity (ratio of original estimates to published ACOP)*

	Industrial sector	1980	1981	1982	1983	1984	1985
22	Metal manufacturing	0.940	1.030	0.973	1.105	1.150	1.109
23	Extraction of minerals n.e.s.	0.764	0.818	0.776	0.776	0.796	0.856
24	Non-metallic mineral products	0.945	1.053	1.026	1.026	0.986	0.977
25	Chemicals	1.037	0.986	1.044	1.036	1.073	1.031
26	Manmade fibres	0.911	0.861	0.761	0.973	0.976	1.094
31	Metal goods n.e.s.	0.972	1.001	1.014	1.001	1.006	1.015
32	Mechanical engineering	1.021	1.042	1.037	1.008	1.013	0.999
33	Office & data processing equip't	1.075	1.102	1.250	1.019	1.138	1.217
34	Electrical engineering	1.005	1.025	1.065	1.047	1.038	1.036
35	Motor vehicles & parts	1.018	1.083	1.078	1.232	1.081	1.108
36	Other transport equipment	0.941	0.970	0.996	1.053	0.981	0.983
37	Instrument engineering	1.002	1.005	1.073	1.022	1.037	1.023
41/ 42	Food, drink and tobacco	1.030	1.046	1.071	1.035	1.058	1.013
43	Textiles	0.996	1.016	0.997	0.992	0.982	0.985
45	Footwear & clothing	0.977	0.996	0.989	1.005	0.999	0.975
46	Timber & wooden furniture	1.014	1.030	1.032	1.055	1.014	1.008
47	Paper, printing & publishing	1.065	1.087	1.093	1.057	1.077	1.073
48	Rubber & plastics	1.016	1.007	1.036	1.036	1.042	1.025
49	Other manufacturing	0.933	1.058	1.101	0.930	0.969	0.962
	Overall	0.993	1.013	1.028	1.028	1.026	1.010

Appendix table 2A.2 *continued*

	Industrial sector	1986	1987	1988	1989	1990
22	Metal manufacturing	0.935	1.474	1.142	1.139	1.062
23	Extraction of minerals n.e.s.	0.821	0.949	0.809	0.912	0.782
24	Non-metallic mineral products	0.877	1.062	1.011	1.069	1.028
25	Chemicals	0.958	1.224	1.205	1.173	1.183
26	Manmade fibres	1.043	1.248	1.271	1.345	1.170
31	Metal goods n.e.s.	0.916	1.074	0.926	1.020	0.969
32	Mechanical engineering	0.904	1.075	0.894	1.096	0.970
33	Office & data processing equip't	1.059	1.357	1.314	1.260	1.430
34	Electrical engineering	0.908	1.085	0.952	1.018	0.989
35	Motor vehicles & parts	0.736	1.297	0.876	1.194	0.995
36	Other transport equipment	0.960	1.066	0.957	1.524	1.211
37	Instrument engineering	0.997	1.073	1.032	0.975	0.970
41/ 42	Food, drink and tobacco	0.943	1.077	0.961	1.118	1.071
43	Textiles	0.857	1.055	0.882	0.916	0.922
45	Footwear & clothing	0.928	1.064	0.939	1.040	1.007
46	Timber & wooden furniture	0.859	1.158	0.992	1.020	1.028
47	Paper, printing & publishing	0.943	1.118	1.047	1.125	1.112
48	Rubber & plastics	0.928	1.184	0.982	1.066	1.020
49	Other manufacturing	0.824	1.065	0.956	0.987	1.027
	Overall	0.893	1.110	0.972	1.094	1.034

3 Entry, exit, ownership and the growth of productivity

MELANIE LANSBURY AND DAVID MAYES

This chapter uses the detailed data on individual business to explore the extent to which the distribution of businesses' productivity, entry, exit and foreign ownership have contributed to productivity growth. In the first instance we explore whether the shape of the distribution of productivity within each industry has changed over the period.

Changes in the distribution of productivity

A simple means of exploring whether the character of the industries is changing is to examine not just the means of the distribution of productivity in each industry but also the higher moments. If it is the case that the process of change during the 1980s eliminated many of the least efficient plants and encouraged those which continued to move closer to best practice one would expect that the variance of productivity might fall. There are of course other factors which might lead it to rise over the same period if, for example, product heterogeneity increases because of technical change over the same period.

Figure 3.1 shows that the distribution of variances has only changed slightly between 1980 and 1990.[1] In so far as it has changed it is the lower range of variations that have increased, although the mode of the distribution has actually fallen. There is no clear tendency for the number of higher variances to fall.[2] Looking just at summary measures of the distribution of coefficients of variation of productivity from each of the 182 industries within manufacturing (table 3.1) we can see that, if anything, there has been a tendency for variation to rise right across industry. However, this shift in the mean of the distribution has been accompanied by little

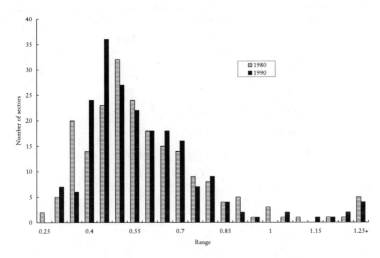

Figure 3.1 *Coefficients of variation of productivity in UK manufacturing industry 1980, 1990*

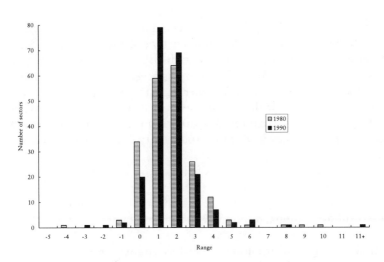

Figure 3.2 *Skewness of UK manufacturing industry productivity 1980, 1990*

Table 3.1 *Distribution of productivity*

	Coefficient of variance		Skewness	
	Mean	Standard deviation	Mean	Standard deviation
1980	0.5653	0.2811	1.240	1.557
1981	0.5659	0.2292	1.028	1.533
1982	0.5828	0.2943	1.320	1.728
1983	0.5690	0.2595	1.361	1.515
1984	0.6134	0.2531	1.475	1.762
1985	0.5700	0.2582	1.362	1.672
1986	0.5905	0.2680	1.374	1.616
1987	0.5698	0.2507	1.259	1.126
1988	0.6265	0.7255(a)	1.177	1.469
1989	0.6199	0.3359	1.333	1.240
1990	0.5510	0.2083	1.184	1.436

Note: (a) This is caused by an outlier in the data. In shipbuilding and repair, SIC 3610, average productivity fell by roughly a half in 1988.

change in the variety of experience among industries. There is a slightly clearer shift in the skewness of the productivity distributions (figure 3.2). As is to be expected, even in 1980, most distributions which show any skewness have a positive skew. That trend is accentuated between 1980 and 1990 with an increase in the number of sectors with a small positive skew but a fall in those with a higher positive skew. However, looking across the period as a whole (table 3.1) there is no clear trend in either the extent or variation in skewness of the productivity distributions across industry.

Since productivity within industries will vary for many reasons including scale it might be expected that there may be some increase in the number of below average businesses as the most competitive plants improve their international position, with a greater bunching of the rest of plants.[3]

In her work on the distribution of productivity within industries over the period 1963–79, Sheryl Bailey (1992) found that the within-industry coefficients of variation did not show any significant linear trend over time in most cases (only 31 out of 128 industries showed a coefficient deemed to be significant at the 5 per cent level).[4] However, looking across all the industries the average trend was upwards – variation was increasing over the period (by 0.1 per cent a year). Bailey did not have access to the original plant data but to distributions of productivity by size class.[5] Therefore her work is not directly comparable even allowing for the difference in industrial classification.

However, her work has a more important link with the present analysis as she attempted to explain the variation in the dispersion of productivity over 1963 to 1979 using a set of explanatory variables similar to those used in the other studies in Caves (1992) as set out in Chapter 4.[6] In the light of our previous work we feel that this question should be dealt with rather differently. Labour productivity as such is the product of a wide range of factors. If we want to address the questions posed at the outset (to what extent is the improvement in productivity during the 1980s due to the improvement in the efficiency of businesses compared to what can be achieved, and to what extent is it due to technical progress and the advance in frontier of feasible production?), then we need to establish what that frontier is and have a plausible behavioural model which explains how businesses transform inputs into output. This is the subject of Chapter 4 in which we also explore the determinants of the distribution of technical inefficiency in each of the industries relative to that frontier. First, however, in this chapter we consider the contribution of continuing businesses, the entry of new businesses and the exit of others to the process of productivity growth.

Contributions of continuing, exiting and entering firms to the growth of productivity[7]

As is clear from the work of Baldwin (1990), one of the most important features explaining the behaviour of productivity and efficiency lies in the 'churning'[8] of businesses within and between industries. The competitive process involves not just the development of existing firms but new entrants who challenge the incumbents, often bringing with them new ideas for products and processes of production. These new entrants can be totally new firms, new lines of business for existing firms which are likely to specialise in related industries, or new plants for existing firms in the same industry. Thus some entrants will be the result of restructuring and hence part of the process of internal change within the company.[9] Churning also involves changes in ownership of existing plants, a facet not separately distinguished in our analysis.

Table 3.2 *Number of 'births' relative to the total number of businesses (per cent)*

Industrial sector	1981	1982	1983	1984	1985	1986	1987	1988	1989	1990
Metal mfg.	3.96	3.21	2.97	6.35	5.41	6.84	11.43	9.44	4.76	3.96
Extraction of minerals n.e.s.	4.29	13.41	2.45	4.97	7.88	10.00	22.22	22.39	3.58	10.85
Non-metallic mineral products	4.96	4.47	3.75	5.35	6.87	6.93	11.46	9.02	8.69	7.66
Chemicals	3.22	3.00	4.21	5.79	5.06	6.31	8.83	6.73	9.56	7.57
Manmade fibres	0.00	6.67	0.00	12.90	3.33	9.38	0.00	5.88	9.38	0.00
Metal goods n.e.s.	2.86	3.91	2.24	7.96	4.13	7.44	7.04	6.62	8.54	6.22
Mechanical eng.	3.55	3.85	3.45	6.45	5.08	5.17	5.53	7.78	9.43	7.81
Office & data processing equip't	18.18	8.39	20.86	15.22	9.59	6.94	29.38	15.07	14.13	16.05
Electrical eng.	4.59	4.37	3.06	6.90	5.31	4.41	7.92	4.86	9.65	8.65
Motor vehicles & parts	3.17	3.25	3.42	3.59	2.64	4.28	9.07	5.91	4.95	12.32
Other transport equipment	2.34	2.84	3.92	6.26	5.90	2.97	6.02	4.35	6.04	11.71
Instrument eng.	7.74	4.57	4.53	6.39	3.40	5.81	12.70	10.37	5.74	10.22
Food, drink and tobacco	4.64	2.70	3.86	10.79	3.94	4.11	8.26	11.05	10.83	6.38
Textiles	2.71	2.42	2.16	4.48	3.50	3.07	4.26	3.72	4.79	3.35
Leather goods	1.83	2.76	2.55	8.61	4.08	4.44	2.94	8.94	3.33	2.72
Footwear & clothing	3.05	3.50	3.33	7.77	4.50	6.13	7.36	4.80	7.54	5.03
Timber & wooden furniture	3.38	3.81	4.03	7.61	6.63	6.38	10.73	8.32	10.14	7.21
Paper, printing & publishing	3.99	2.92	4.30	6.43	4.85	6.38	10.41	8.98	9.57	7.08
Rubber & plastics	3.05	1.95	3.53	7.17	4.44	6.72	9.59	9.01	11.46	6.67
Other mfg.	4.15	3.34	3.67	24.75	3.41	11.31	17.45	10.04	12.46	7.51
Total mfg.	3.88	3.58	3.60	7.35	4.90	5.75	8.89	7.97	8.97	7.28

By and large we would expect that the greater the churning in an industry the more competitive it is. Low churning is likely to be a feature of
industries which are not readily contestable because of high entry or
exit costs – particularly those which involve heavy capital investment
in physical plant (a point explored explicitly in the next section). Entry
and exit is also heavily affected by the economic cycle. Tables 3.2 and 3.3
show that, contrary to the general impression from bankruptcy statis-

Table 3.3 *Number of 'deaths' relative to the total number of businesses (per cent)*

Industrial sector	1980	1981	1982	1983	1984	1985	1986	1987	1988	1989
Metal mfg.	10.10	7.79	6.58	10.00	8.51	6.34	7.22	5.23	3.28	5.05
Extraction of minerals n.e.s.	3.83	7.06	4.88	9.31	4.35	9.70	7.65	4.70	2.32	10.76
Non-metallic mineral products	5.66	6.87	3.75	4.98	5.47	6.26	6.59	4.77	3.48	7.94
Chemicals	6.55	7.82	5.76	5.98	6.07	5.31	6.55	6.04	5.94	5.39
Manmade fibres	17.78	8.82	6.67	0.00	6.45	3.33	0.00	3.45	14.71	3.13
Metal goods n.e.s.	5.73	6.53	4.93	6.45	5.05	4.70	3.75	4.56	5.80	4.33
Mechanical eng.	6.98	6.80	4.55	6.90	5.12	4.13	7.07	7.67	6.50	4.10
Office & data processing equip't	8.16	18.75	11.61	12.27	19.57	6.16	8.33	8.47	10.96	11.90
Electrical eng.	6.10	8.43	6.73	3.79	5.81	5.46	6.29	4.69	11.52	7.18
Motor vehicles & parts	6.68	5.86	3.94	5.08	5.22	11.21	6.93	5.86	4.30	4.95
Other transport equipment	3.94	4.69	6.06	3.71	7.69	3.63	6.18	5.59	9.73	7.55
Instrument eng.	6.65	5.30	3.78	7.48	5.71	4.46	6.28	6.15	10.19	5.29
Food, drink and tobacco	4.99	6.32	4.07	8.68	5.65	5.66	7.11	6.27	7.79	6.27
Textiles	9.99	7.78	6.47	6.42	4.74	5.53	4.24	5.23	5.50	6.34
Leather goods	8.38	10.98	4.13	1.27	2.39	4.76	2.22	8.09	13.82	7.33
Footwear & clothing	10.69	7.82	8.46	6.40	5.99	4.79	4.83	3.77	6.26	6.94
Timber & wooden furniture	6.19	4.95	7.19	5.56	5.47	7.13	5.63	4.92	6.32	8.51
Paper, printing & publishing	5.31	4.37	4.46	4.86	4.87	5.73	4.61	4.13	5.70	5.29
Rubber & plastics	4.75	3.73	3.80	2.71	5.38	5.40	4.21	5.34	4.43	4.86
Other mfg.	10.36	7.80	2.74	4.52	5.63	3.66	4.11	3.77	3.49	5.69
Total mfg.	6.75	6.64	5.26	6.03	5.57	5.56	5.82	5.36	6.37	6.02

tics (Bowden *et al.*, 1992, Robson, 1992),[10] exits have remained a relatively stable share of the number of businesses over the whole of the 1980s. The range has been only 1½ percentage points, between 5¼ and 6¾ per cent. Entries on the other hand vary much more procyclically, with a range nearly four times as large, from 3½ to 9 per cent.   This gives a clear procyclical pattern for the net change in the number of firms (table 3.4).

Table 3.4 *Net new entrants as a percentage of the total number of firms in an industry, 1981–9 (UK manufacturing industry)*

1981	1982	1983	1984	1985	1986	1987	1988	1989
-2.76	-1.68	-2.43	1.78	-0.66	-0.07	3.53	1.60	2.95

Note: The correlation between net new entrants and the rate of growth of manufacturing output over the period 1981–9 is 0.82.

Table 3.5 *Cumulative net exits 1981–9 as a proportion of end of period businesses*

Industrial sector	
Metal manufacturing	0.17
Extraction of minerals n.e.s.	-0.45
Non-metallic mineral products	-0.14
Chemicals	0.01
Manmade fibres	0.24
Metal goods n.e.s.	-0.06
Mechanical engineering	0.04
Office & data processing equipment	-0.31
Electrical engineering	0.06
Motor vehicles & parts	0.15
Other transport equipment	0.11
Instrument engineering	-0.07
Food, drink and tobacco	-0.06
Textiles	0.34
Leather goods	0.21
Footwear & clothing	0.18
Timber & wooden furniture	-0.11
Paper, printing & publishing	-0.16
Rubber & plastics	-0.20
Other manufacturing	-0.45

However, table 3.4 also emphasises the decline in the number of firms in manufacturing over the period as a whole. This is much more graphic when shown at a sectoral (2-digit) level (table 3.5). Over the period ten industries experienced an increase in the number of businesses and ten a decrease but of these increases, two are by almost a half, mineral extraction (23) and other manufacturing (49) and one by a third, office machinery

(33). No other industries experience a rise in the number of businesses of over 20 per cent. Three industries also showed a fall in the number of businesses by over 20 per cent: textiles (43), manmade fibres (26) and leather and fellmongery (44). Thus manmade fibres is not merely showing the fastest growth in productivity but is concentrating on a smaller number of businesses. While in a related sector textiles is contracting the number of businesses and growing more slowly. Office machinery represents a third combination of rapid growth in productivity, businesses and output.

This process of complex structural change in manufacturing industry is thus not dominated by a single paradigm but reflects a combination of strikingly different experiences. A note of caution needs to be taken when looking at the more extreme values in this analysis as, in the case of manmade fibres for example, they appear in an industry group where the number of businesses is relatively small.

Entry and exit provide a helpful insight both by looking at the total numbers of entries and exits (table 3.6) and at their difference (table 3.7), described as gross and net 'churning' in the respective tables. Gross churning can be on an immense scale with at least a third of the businesses in data processing equipment changing in 1981, 1983, 1984 and 1987. No other industries show anything like this level of business turnover, although other manufacturing shows a change of nearly a third in its businesses during 1984. The net figures make it clear that with the exception of four largely isolated instances net churning does not exceed 10 per cent in any one year. Indeed in over 60 per cent of cases net churning does not exceed 3 per cent in any year. The process of development is thus characterised by change in businesses rather than by the process of net increase. (It must be remembered that mergers and takeovers are excluded from this analysis.) Churning here entails that the same activity was not undertaken on the same location in consecutive years. Thus in one sense it is an overestimate as a business may shift between industries with only a relatively small change in the composition of output, while it will be an underestimate where a new firm restarts production in a failed enterprise within the year on a particular site.

In theory it should be a straightforward task to decompose the total increase in productivity, $\Delta G_{.jt} = G_{.jt} - G_{.jt-1}$ into its three components, $\Delta^c G_{.jt}$, $\Delta G^b_{.jt}$, $\Delta G^d_{.jt}$, where the superscripts c, b and d refer to the continuing, entering and exiting businesses respectively, by weighting each of them according to their contribution to value added in the industry. In practice it is more difficult because any business can be in one of eight circumstances in the two years t and $t-1$:

Table 3.6 *Gross churning (entries + exits)/total businesses*

Industrial sector	1981	1982	1983	1984	1985	1986	1987	1988	1989
Metal mfg.	11.75	9.80	12.97	14.86	11.75	14.07	16.67	12.72	9.81
Extraction of minerals n.e.s.	11.35	18.29	11.76	9.32	17.58	17.65	26.92	24.71	14.35
Non-metallic mineral products	11.82	8.21	8.73	10.82	13.13	13.52	16.23	12.50	16.63
Chemicals	11.05	8.76	10.20	11.86	10.37	12.86	14.87	12.67	14.95
Manmade fibres	8.82	13.33	0.00	19.35	6.67	9.38	3.45	20.59	12.50
Metal goods n.e.s.	9.39	8.84	8.68	13.01	8.83	11.20	11.60	12.41	12.86
Mechanical eng.	10.35	8.40	10.35	11.57	9.21	12.24	13.20	14.28	13.52
Office & data processing equip't	36.93	20.00	33.13	34.78	15.75	15.28	37.85	26.03	26.02
Electrical eng.	13.02	11.11	6.85	12.71	10.77	10.70	12.61	16.39	16.83
Motor vehicles & parts	9.03	7.19	8.50	8.80	13.85	11.21	14.92	10.22	9.90
Other transport equipment	7.03	8.90	7.63	13.95	9.52	9.15	11.61	14.08	13.58
Instrument eng.	13.03	8.35	12.01	12.10	7.86	12.09	18.85	20.56	11.03
Food, drink and tobacco	10.96	6.77	12.53	16.44	9.60	11.22	14.56	18.84	17.10
Textiles	10.48	8.89	8.58	9.23	9.03	7.31	9.49	9.22	11.13
Leather goods	12.80	6.90	3.82	11.00	8.84	6.67	11.03	22.76	10.67
Footwear & clothing	10.87	11.95	9.74	13.76	9.28	10.95	11.14	11.06	14.48
Timber & wooden furniture	8.33	11.01	9.60	13.08	13.76	12.01	15.66	14.64	18.66
Paper, printing & publishing	8.36	7.38	9.16	11.30	10.58	10.99	14.53	14.68	14.86
Rubber & plastics	6.77	5.75	6.24	12.55	9.83	10.93	14.93	13.44	16.31
Other mfg.	11.95	6.08	8.19	30.38	7.07	15.42	21.23	13.54	18.15

	t	$t-1$
1	present and sampled	present and sampled
2	present and sampled	present not sampled
3	present not sampled	present and sampled
4	present not sampled	present not sampled
5	not present	present and sampled
6	not present	present not sampled
7	present and sampled	not present
8	present not sampled	not present

Table 3.7 *Net churning (entries – exits)/total businesses*

Industrial sector	1981	1982	1983	1984	1985	1986	1987	1988	1989
Metal mfg.	-3.83	-3.36	-7.03	-2.16	-0.93	-0.38	6.20	6.17	-0.29
Extraction of minerals n.e.s.	-2.76	8.54	-6.86	0.62	-1.82	2.35	17.52	20.08	-7.17
Non-metallic mineral products	-1.91	0.72	-1.23	-0.12	0.60	0.34	6.69	5.54	0.76
Chemicals	-4.59	-2.77	-1.76	-0.28	-0.24	-0.24	2.79	0.79	4.17
Manmade fibres	-8.82	0.00	0.00	6.45	0.00	9.38	-3.45	-8.82	6.25
Metal goods n.e.s.	-3.68	-1.02	-4.21	2.91	-0.57	3.69	2.48	0.82	4.21
Mechanical eng.	-3.25	-0.69	-3.45	1.34	0.95	-1.90	-2.15	1.28	5.33
Office & data processing equip't	-0.57	-3.23	8.59	-4.35	3.42	-1.39	20.90	4.11	2.23
Electrical eng.	-3.84	-2.36	-0.73	1.10	-0.16	-1.88	3.23	-6.66	2.46
Motor vehicles & parts	-2.70	-0.70	-1.65	-1.63	-8.56	-2.65	3.21	1.61	0.00
Other transport equipment	-2.34	-3.22	0.21	-1.43	2.27	-3.20	0.43	-5.38	-1.51
Instrument eng.	2.44	0.80	-2.95	0.67	-1.06	-0.47	6.56	0.19	0.44
Food, drink and tobacco	-1.67	-1.37	-4.82	5.14	-1.72	-3.00	2.03	3.26	4.56
Textiles	-5.06	-4.05	-4.25	-0.26	-2.02	-1.16	-0.97	-1.78	-1.55
Leather goods	-9.15	-1.38	1.27	6.22	-0.68	2.22	-5.15	-4.88	-4.00
Footwear & clothing	-4.76	-4.96	-3.06	1.78	-0.29	1.30	3.59	-1.46	0.60
Timber & wooden furniture	-1.58	-3.38	-1.53	2.15	-0.50	0.75	5.81	2.00	1.62
Paper, printing & publishing	-0.37	-1.54	-0.56	1.56	-0.88	1.77	6.28	3.27	4.28
Rubber & plastics	-0.68	-1.85	0.81	1.79	-0.96	2.51	4.25	4.58	6.60
Other mfg.	-3.66	0.61	-0.85	19.11	-0.24	7.20	13.68	6.55	6.77

Clearly we have no information on Cases 4, 6 and 8. They can only be estimated by grossing up according to the sampling proportions on the basis that those businesses outside the sample are distributed in the same way as those inside it. We do, however, have estimates for Cases 1, 2, 3, 5 and 7. Case 1 gives us the estimate of the change in productivity for identified continuing firms, Case 5 the level of productivity for those who exited and Case 7 the level of productivity for new entrants. The sum of Cases 1 to 3 gives a second estimate of the change for continuing

Table 3.8 *Percentage births/deaths above and below average productivity*

	Births above average productivity	Deaths below average productivity
1980		59.9
1981	61.1	61.9
1982	61.4	55.8
1983	68.3	55.0
1984	87.1	57.7
1985	57.7	49.0
1986	62.7	55.6
1987	51.3	60.8
1988	52.5	58.7
1989	60.4	49.4
1990	64.7	

businesses – without taking account of matching estimates, while Case 1 + Case 2 gives a fuller estimate of the level of productivity for continuing firms in year t and Case 1 + Case 3 the corresponding estimate for year $t - 1$. The appropriate weighting system is therefore more complicated as we have to use the sampled data to estimate for the unsampled.[11]

It is immediately clear from table 3.8 that the productivity of most new entrants is higher than that of the sample as a whole in all years, although that difference was negligible in 1987 and 1988. Similarly in most years most exits had a lower productivity than the sample as a whole. Our initial hypothesis that churning would contribute to the increase in productivity is therefore borne out, although it appears that the effect is greater for entry rather than exit. The numbers of entrants and exits are small so attempting any grossing up for the businesses not sampled is decidedly hazardous. Weighting the observations by value-added suggests that exits were below average productivity in every year. Entrants on the other hand may have been somewhat below average during the recession years at the beginning and end of the decade. This switch is somewhat surprising as it implies that the larger entrants were below average productivity in the recession years. Since we can only compare consecutive years we are not able to replicate the analysis of Baldwin and Gorecki (1990a, b) where they show that the contribution of entrants improves as they mature. This is a typical example of a learning curve.

Table 3.9 *Percentage growth of productivity, 1981–90*

	FOEs	DOEs
22	74	103
24	31	31
25	50	60
26	442	267
31	53	41
32	35	37
33	487	36
34	57	43
35	52	54
36	17	90
37	60	35
41/42	56	24
43	56	42
45	36	37
46	36	25
47	65	32
48	54	51
49	25	41
Total	59	41

Baldwin and Gorecki find that after ten years the average shares of value added accounted for by the new entrants have risen by 50 per cent. Hence in a sense our measure underestimates the impact of new entry if the Canadian experience is repeated in the UK because it looks purely at the short run impact. It would also be interesting to examine the productivity performance of these new entrants during subsequent years to see if they continued to move up the productivity distribution as they did in Canada. This must wait for a longitudinal database to be constructed in the UK.

The role of foreign ownership

There is relatively little information about the characteristics of individual businesses available from ACOP apart from their inputs and outputs but one exception is ownership. We do know if businesses are domestically or foreign owned.

In 1991 foreign owned manufacturing firms employed 15 per cent of total manufacturing employment and produced 18.3 per cent of GVA. Throughout the decade the importance of foreign owned enterprises (FOEs) increased slightly and by 1990 they employed 16 per cent of UK manufacturing employees and produced 21.7 per cent of total GVA. FOEs had both higher productivity and higher productivity growth. At the beginning of the period FOEs were 25 per cent more productive than DOEs (domestically owned enterprises), by 1990 this had increasd to 45 per cent. Thus over the decade the productivity of FOEs had risen by 59 per cent as compared to 41 per cent for DOEs (table 3.9). This experience is general. In 1981 at the 2-digit sector level the productivity of FOEs exceeded that of DOEs in all sectors except office machinery and data processing equipment (33) and instrument engineering. Even then FOEs in sector 33 experienced productivity growth far in excess of their domestic counterparts.

Over the period 1981–90, productivity growth of FOEs exceeded that of DOEs in nine of the eighteen sectors while the reverse was true for only five sectors, the remaining four having approximately equal growth rates. Office machinery and data processing equipment stand out with productivity of FOEs rising by 487 per cent, compared with just 36 per cent for DOEs. Furthermore FOEs in this sector increased their share of total value added by 48 per cent over the decade and their share of employment by 37 per cent. (The other high productivity growth sector was man-made fibres. In this sector FOEs increased their productivity by two-thirds more than DOEs. Here there was little change in the shares of FOEs' employment and value added.)

We cannot conclude from this that foreign ownership *per se* is responsible for higher productivity or productivity growth. Foreign investors naturally choose sectors where they expect above average returns because of the extra costs and risks of foreign investment. Nevertheless the extent of their better performance is striking and a simple shift-share analysis suggests that they contributed to increasing the rate of productivity growth over the decade by some 11.5 per cent.

This initial study of the individual businesses has revealed that there has not been a great change in the distribution of productivity within industries. If anything variance in productivity increased over the decade. While many of the more extreme examples of industries with long tails of lower productivity businesses eliminated much of the tail (by exit or improvement in relative productivity) there was actually a slight increase in skewness of the distribution of productivity within industries over manufacturing as a whole.

We can put more than one interpretation on this. Viewed one way round, the businesses with the highest productivity may be advancing even faster. Viewed from the other perspective those with lower productivity are slipping relative to the best. The more favourable view seems more appropriate when we combine this finding with the general rise in productivity across all businesses. The reduction in the more extreme 'tails' of low productivity but some increase in the number with more moderate skewness (and consequent fall in the numbers with little or no skew) would be consistent with a simultaneous elimination of poor performance and some increase in diversity as industries develop and change their structure markedly over a period of such striking change in performance. Clearly further study of the detail is required to come to a firm view.

What is clear, however, is that entry and exit have made an important contribution to the growth of productivity. It is of course a normal experience that businesses which are performing poorly will tend to fail and that new entrants will expect to have more to offer than many existing incumbents, if only because they have to overcome the costs of entry. Since we do not have matching data on entry and exit for other periods we cannot tell whether their contribution is unusually large during the 1980s. What is clear is that both entry and exit are important across the whole period, whether it is a period of recession or rapid output growth. If anything it appears that the impact of entry is rather greater than that of exit.

One other facet that comes across clearly is that foreign owned businesses tend to have above average productivity and productivity growth. This is not, of course, necessarily the result of foreign ownership as foreign investment itself tends to focus on businesses where the rate of return is likely to be highest and performance best, given the difficulties associated with operation in other countries.

4 Shifts in the production frontier and the distribution of efficiency

MELANIE LANSBURY AND DAVID MAYES

In previous chapters we have looked purely at the question of the distribution of productivity, distinguishing the sources of the overall change in manufacturing productivity by shifts between sectors, shifts within sectors and then decomposing those within-sector shifts into changes emanating from entry and exit and change due to the action of existing businesses. We noted also that there had been some change in the shape of the distributions of productivity, with the reduction of the 'tails' of many of the most skewed distributions. Simply looking at the aggregate distributions does not tell us how individual businesses have performed compared with the best performance of businesses of the same size in terms of labour, capital or other inputs. In this chapter therefore we seek to extend the analysis by enquiring how far the change in performance is due to an improvement in what can be achieved by the technology available, given the inputs employed, and how far it is due to a reduction in the level of technical inefficiency, compared with that frontier, of what could be achieved.

This is best explained diagrammatically. Figure 4.1 denotes by I_t the minimum combinations of labour and capital that can be used to produce a given quantity of output.[1] Any firm producing on that frontier, say at A or B, would be operating at maximum possible efficiency. The firm f_t is however clearly below maximum efficiency. The ratio Of_t/OB gives an idea of the extent of that inefficiency (technical efficiency in the Farrell, 1957, terminology, as it takes the factor ratio as given). The following year technical change enables firms to operate more efficiently and use fewer inputs to produce the given level of output as denoted by the line I_{t+1}. The typical firm is likely to have invested during the year, its labour force will have gained more experience and hence its position will have changed to, say, f_{t+1}. Inefficiency in this second year is then measured by Of_{t+1}/OC.

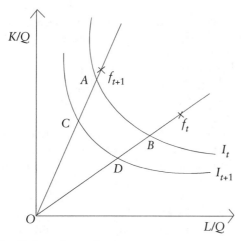

Figure 4.1 *Inefficiency in production*

Technical progress between the two years can be measured by ratio of the two curves along any factor ratio, that is, OB/OD or OA/OC. There is of course no reason to expect the shift in the curve to be homogeneous so that the two ratios are identical. Thus while $(Of_{t+1}/OC)/(Of_t/OB)$ would show the improvement in efficiency, it is necessary to use some weighting of OB/OD and OA/OC to show the improvement in performance due to technical change. The geometric average is commonly used (see Tulkens, 1989, for example).[2]

There are many ways of approaching this empirical problem in practice (Mayes *et al.*, 1994). In our analysis we have opted for estimating a stochastic translog production function rather than pursuing, say, a programming approach (as do Färe *et al.*, 1985, Färe, Grosskopf and Li, 1992, for example). It is easy to debate the relative merits of this way forward, which include the grounding in economic theory, the ease of comparison across years, the flexibility of the translog form, and so on.However a major determinant of our choice was simply consistency with our earlier work, which formed part of a large international project. Choosing the same approach permits direct comparison with our own results for the UK in 1977 (Mayes *et al.*, 1994) and with similar work in five other countries: United States, Japan, Australia, Canada and South Korea, reported in Caves (1992).

The form of the translog function is well known

$$\ln Q = a_0 + \tfrac{1}{2}a_1(\ln K)^2 + \tfrac{1}{2}a_2(\ln L)^2 + a_3 \ln K +$$
$$a_4 \ln L + a_5 \ln L \ln K + \Sigma_{i=0}^{n}a_{i+6}Z_i + v$$

although our specification adds a set of further variables, Z_i, which help account for other sources of variation in the inputs (see Caves and Barton (1990) for a discussion).[3] The Z_i used in the present case relate only to labour:

Z_1 operatives as a percentage of employment

Z_2 per capita wages and salaries of operatives

Z_3 per capita wages and salaries of administrative, technical and clerical employees

owing to lack of available data. Other possibilities were either poorly determined or impossible to measure. The three variables included an attempt to give a closer insight into the quality of labour used in the business. If firms pay their workforce rather higher then the inference is that either they have a higher value added product or they have some degree of residual protection in their markets. The higher the skills level again the more likely that this is to be reflected in the sophistication of the product and the complexity of after sales service.

Secondly, in order to permit the use of a frontier and establish a means of estimating efficiency, we need to make some assumptions about the residuals v_i. We assume that as in so many cases the reported error contains two components, the first is the myriad of small issues which between them allow policymakers to declare that their sum represents a result which is normally distributed and hence permits the use of standard statistical methods in analysis. Secondly it is hypothesised that there is a second asymmetric component representing inefficiency, whose frequency of occurrence falls the greater is the level of inefficiency. According to convention this distribution is given a straightforward form, usually half normal or exponential to ease estimation. Mayes *et al.* (1994) reports on the use of the truncated normal but following our earlier extensive exploration of the consequences of this choice we opted for the half normal.[4]

The use of a stochastic frontier places a particular meaning on the word 'frontier' as random variation can take observations outside it. The frontier is set by actual revealed performance, it is not heavily affected by any extreme observations. Hence it is not a measure of some theoretical maximum performance and therefore may reflect absolute inefficiency in the sense that all firms in UK industry may be performing less efficiently than those in the same industry in other competitor countries. In this sense therefore our measure of inefficiency might be thought to underestimate the extent of the poor performance.

Efficiency and the frontier are estimated for each industry by a form of maximum likelihood, suggested by Torii (1992a, b), which he labels modified corrected ordinary least squares.[5]

Table 4.1 *Summary statistics of average technical inefficiency*

	Mean	Standard deviation	Minimum	Maximum
1980	0.3594	0.2309	0.0367	1.1559
1981	0.3995	0.2647	0.0820	1.6442
1982	0.4183	0.2814	0.0218	1.4555
1983	0.3733	0.2816	0.0662	1.9508
1984	0.4217	0.2397	0.0769	1.2248
1985	0.3412	0.2252	0.0120	1.2803
1986	0.3266	0.2244	0.0126	1.2263
1987	0.3366	0.2306	0.0701	1.3999
1988	0.3626	0.2606	0.0582	1.4377
1989	0.4039	0.2769	0.0799	1.5910
1990	0.3422	0.2221	0.0717	1.2073

Table 4.2 *Correlation between measures of inefficiency*

	ATI/SKEW	ATI/λ	ATI/σ_e	SKEW/λ	SKEW/σ_e	λ/σ_e
Total	-0.8046	0.3371	0.8315	-0.3195	-0.3996	0.2584
1980	-0.8068	0.7426	0.8651	-0.9375	-0.4396	0.4079
1981	-0.7720	0.6733	0.8673	-0.9067	-0.3915	0.3401
1982	-0.7936	0.7359	0.8663	-0.9146	-0.4358	0.4308
1983	-0.7507	0.3133	0.8658	-0.2992	-0.3731	0.2132
1984	-0.7799	0.6509	0.7832	-0.9033	-0.3073	0.2353
1985	-0.8283	0.3123	0.8229	-0.3683	-0.4222	0.1736
1986	-0.7930	0.3337	0.7850	-0.3400	-0.3076	0.1935
1987	-0.7949	0.7871	0.7577	-0.9517	-0.3050	0.3402
1989	-0.8279	0.6203	0.8719	-0.6117	-0.4912	0.4973
1989	-0.8087	0.4740	0.7952	-0.2932	-0.3524	0.4623
1990	-0.8484	0.7740	0.8264	-0.9336	-0.4518	0.4167

As in the previous two chapters these data are drawn from the Annual Censuses of Production for the years 1980 to 1990 (see Appendix for definitions of variables used)[6] for the 182 4-digit activity headings in SIC(80).

A separate frontier and measure of inefficiency are thus estimated for each activity heading in each of the eleven years. (The data are not pooled across time because of the inability to match businesses across time in the database as mentioned above.) However, it was not possible to decompose the residuals in the required manner in eight cases because they were too unlike the hypothesised distributional shapes giving results for 174 industries.

We have not shown the estimates of the frontier functions themselves as there are 20,000 parameter values but efficiency measures derived from them are summarised in table 4.1. The measure used here is Average Technical Inefficiency (ATI) (Aigner et al., 1977, Meeusen and van den Broeck, 1977a, b), although we did in fact also estimate three other measures (the standard deviation of the residuals, σ_e, their skewness (SKEW) and the ratio of the variances of the two component distributions, λ). The estimates from these other measures have not as yet been analysed in any detail. Table 4.2 shows that there is considerable correlation between the skewness and variance measures and ATI although they are not themselves strongly related.[7]

The striking feature about the ATI estimates is that they show no strong trend over the decade. Using a simple linear regression, time appears to have had a significant, negative effect on inefficiency, although very small in size,

$$ATI = \quad 0.684 - 0.00367\, t \qquad \overline{R}^2 = 0.0016.$$
$$ (4.427)\ (-2.026)$$

The production frontiers have themselves shifted over time, often quite strikingly between individual years. With relatively constant levels of inefficiency and rising productivity the general movement in frontiers is clearly outward but this movement is also clearly correlated with the rate of growth of real value added. Many industries actually show contractions of the frontier in recession years.

We were inclined to expect this pattern of behaviour, both from the nature of the estimation method and from the results of previous time series analysis for Japan (Torii, 1993) and South Korea (Yoo in Caves, 1992). However, this does rather reduce the emphasis that can be put on the notion that the structural change of the 1980s had a marked effect on the 'tail' of inefficient industries in the UK. Rather more it was that the whole distribution advanced towards the performance of competitor countries.[8] There was a surprising similarity in the extent of inefficiency across the six countries compared in Caves (1992) for the year 1977 (see table 4.3). There is no clear logic in the ranking of the five countries compared with general economic performance either in terms of levels or rates of

Table 4.3 *Comparison of inefficiency across five countries (ATI, 1977) (standard deviation in parenthesis)*

Dependent variable	USA	Japan	S. Korea	UK	Australia
Value added	0.502 (0.156)	0.210	0.680 (0.189)	0.390 (0.141)	0.336 (0.188)

Source: Caves (1992).

Table 4.4 *Rank correlation of average technical inefficiency between years*

	Indus-try ave.	1980	1981	1982	1983	1984	1985	1986	1987	1988	1989
1980	0.541	1.000									
1981	0.572	0.393	1.000								
1982	0.604	0.286	0.423	1.000							
1983	0.563	0.221	0.375	0.435	1.000						
1984	0.652	0.327	0.315	0.375	0.322	1.000					
1985	0.541	0.209	0.207	0.265	0.272	0.271	1.000				
1986	0.615	0.305	0.219	0.207	0.283	0.401	0.291	1.000			
1987	0.585	0.281	0.168	0.219	0.190	0.337	0.339	0.482	1.000		
1988	0.614	0.229	0.306	0.255	0.174	0.301	0.422	0.423	0.411	1.000	
1989	0.573	0.341	0.154	0.204	0.292	0.242	0.378	0.366	0.321	0.384	1.000
1990	0.554	0.276	0.170	0.244	0.284	0.290	0.267	0.312	0.387	0.347	0.350

growth. Rapidly growing countries like Japan or Korea do not appear to have markedly different patterns of inefficiency from slower growing instances like the UK. In Korea also it was difficult to distinguish any trends in efficiency, merely 'a lot of variation round a stable mean' (Caves, 1992, p. 18). Thus despite the lack of correlation between years or path over time there was considerable consistency in the results for each industry viewed across the period as a whole.

The inefficiency measures are correlated weakly across consecutive years (table 4.4) so it appears that either this behaviour is subject to considerable change or the measure itself is rather unstable. Given the degree of churning which occurs within the industry with well over 10 per cent of businesses changing between consecutive years a degree of variation is to be expected. Furthermore these data have exactly the same sampling pattern as was revealed in the discussion of the productivity statistics in

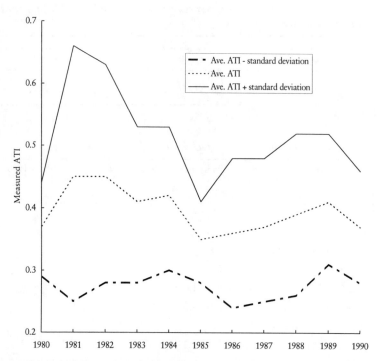

Figure 4.2 *Average technical inefficiency in the 1980s*

Chapters 2 and 3 as they are drawn from the same Annual Censuses of Production. Hence, on average, only two-thirds of the observations are likely to be common to consecutive years. Hence although this may have only a limited impact on the means of variables, measurements related to the distribution of the individual observations such as the measures of inefficiency may be much more severely affected. This is not necessarily a criticism of the method although it might lead us to put more faith on values averaged across a number of years.

While there is no prima facie link between inefficiency and the state of the economic cycle on the basis of the aggregate figures shown in table 4.1 we investigate whether the effect is any clearer at the individual industry level in the next subsection. Average ATI has low values in both recession and high growth years. More interesting perhaps (figure 4.2) is the fact that the variance of the ATI measures also varies, reflecting in the main the existence of higher, more extreme, values in some years rather than any clear trend in behaviour.

Inefficiency in industry

'Inefficiency' as we have measured it is bound to be a catch-all category and not a clinically separated measure of technical inefficiency alone. In the first place we have estimated single frontier production functions for 'industries' defined by statisticians which in fact cover quite a wide variety of activities. This misspecification will itself be captured in the residuals. While some may feature in the symmetric stochastic residual other parts will appear in the skewed residual labelled inefficiency. Before going on to estimate the extent of this misspecification and other causes of apparent inefficiency we can note from the ATI measures by industry averaged over the eleven years of estimation that (44) leather and fellmongery had the highest value of ATI (0.61) (table 4.4). Other manufacturing is indeed just the sort of hotch-potch industry we have mentioned. Extraction of aggregates, which forms an important portion of (23), is also a localised activity with high transport costs so considerable differences in efficiency could persist.

At the other end of the spectrum (43) textiles show the lowest level of inefficiency (ATI = 0.25). The occurrence of this particular industry helps emphasise the point that we are discussing relative not absolute inefficiency. Competitive pressures in the textile industry are very harsh. In some respects the scope for innovative production methods to introduce striking differences in cost structures are relatively limited. As an area of traditional UK manufacturing the definitions at the 4-digit level are quite narrow and hence assumptions of homogeneity may in this case be more appropriate.

The relation of inefficiency to productivity

Inefficiency as defined by ATI is a measure of the variability of performance within an industry relative to a theoretical production frontier. This measure is therefore not directly comparable with Chapter 2 where we examined a measure of productivity (value added per head). For example an industry may be highly productive but if the spread of firms' performance *within* the industry is large, so too will be measured ATI. Furthermore, if the production frontier has shifted out over our period of observation the average level of productivity would rise without there necessarily being a fall in technical inefficiency.

The regression analysis on the determinants of inefficiency (table 4.6) shows that an increase in productivity is associated with a higher level of inefficiency, although the effect was small. An unexpected finding in this regression was that higher *levels* of productivity were also associated with greater inefficiency across industries. Both relationships show coefficients which appear significantly different from zero, although, as the bivariate representations below indicate, the relation is weak.

$$\text{ATI} = \begin{array}{cc} 0.371 + & 0.00141 \text{ DPROD} \\ (64.4) & (3.75) \end{array} \qquad r = 0.074$$

$$\text{ATI} = \begin{array}{cc} 0.322 + & 0.00299 \text{ PROD} \\ (30.0) & (5.13) \end{array} \qquad r = 0.107$$

A look at the data on average levels of productivity and inefficiency at the 2-digit level shows that the vast majority of sectors have levels of average productivity bunched around the overall average for manufacturing industry. However a small number of industries drive the statistical relationship. At the top of the productivity spectrum we find office machinery and data processing equipment (33), extraction of minerals (23) and chemical and manmade fibres (25 and 26) (see figure 2.1). All of these high productivity sectors also have average ATI levels at or above the average for total manufacturing (see table 4.5). At the bottom of the spectrum lie footwear and clothing (45) and textiles (43) both of which have ATI levels substantially below the overall average, with sector 43 having the lowest ATI level (0.25) of all sectors. There are few counter examples so the relation is established. As we noted before, in industries with low productivity, fierce external competition may have ensured that the spread of efficiency can only be limited. Again these are relative measures of efficiency so a wide spread of behaviour can be consistent with a high average or frontier level.

Determinants of inefficiency

The variation in efficiency observed is in part a function of the structure of industry (Caves and Barton, 1990; Mayes *et al.*, 1994). Over the 1980s economic policy has deliberately attempted to remove the constraints which enable inefficiency to persist and has tried to create structures which will enhance the forces of competition. This has come from competition policy restricting market dominance and restrictive practices, deregulation, the removal of external barriers, culminating in the moves towards the single European market and a variety of other measures including those aimed at trade unions to try to increase both labour market and product market flexibility (Bollard *et al.*, 1993).

In this section we go on to explore the systematic components explaining inefficiency at the activity level and see how the changes of the 1980s have affected that explanation and the resulting behaviour.

In undertaking this analysis we have followed the pattern of our previous work on 1977 (Mayes *et al.*, 1994) and the international comparison (Caves, 1992) in taking the measures of inefficiency as the dependent variable and regressing them on a set of explanatory variables reflecting five sources of influence. These five categories can be summarised as representing:
- competitive conditions
- product differentiation and heterogeneity
- industry dynamics
- spatial disparities
- organisational influences.

The specific variables used under each of these headings are defined in the Appendix. We are heavily constrained in our choice of explanation as the data need to be at the same (4-digit SIC(80)) level of disaggregation (except for economy-wide measures of the state of the economic cycle which apply to all industries) and available for all eleven years. The data are stacked into a pooled time series/cross section set combining all 174 industries and eleven years, a maximum of 1914 observations.

The nature of the hypotheses can be summarised briefly.

Competitive conditions

We explore three simple sets of hypotheses here. First that the more concentrated an industry the greater the opportunity for inefficient behaviour (*CONC* is the five firm concentration ratio, which is published for the Annual Census of Production). However, to quite some extent the inefficiency which this can cause may be absolute rather than relative with oligopoly firms with similar levels of (in)efficiency. Indeed research in the USA and Canada (Caves, 1992) shows that the adverse impact of concentration in terms of relative inefficiency may peak before the highest levels are reached. The square of the five-firm ratio is used to explore this (*CONCSQ*).

Second, openness to foreign trade is a good indicator of the strength of competition in the industry. This can come from foreign companies in the form of the import share (*IMPORTS*) or because UK firms are able to export a large proportion of their output to other markets (*EXPORTS* – the export share). (We also try a number of hybrid variables in the form of the share of net trade, *TRADE*, exports and imports taken together,

Table 4.5 *Average technical inefficiency in UK manufacturing industries*

SIC code	Industrial sector	1980	1981	1982
22	Metal manufacturing	0.55	0.58	0.69
	(st. dev.)	0.34	0.23	0.36
23	Extraction of minerals n.e.s.	0.48	0.39	0.43
	(st. dev.)	0.20	0.05	0.17
24	Non-metallic minerals	0.41	0.44	0.49
	(st. dev.)	0.32	0.40	0.30
25/26	Chemicals and manmade fibres	0.41	0.39	0.41
	(st. dev.)	0.28	0.26	0.21
31	Metal goods n.e.s.	0.29	0.46	0.30
	(st. dev.)	0.18	0.27	0.20
32	Mechanical engineering	0.34	0.33	0.43
	(st. dev.)	0.22	0.16	0.35
33	Office machinery & data processing equip't	0.33	0.65	0.51
	(st. dev.)	0.15	0.25	0.00
34	Electrical & electronic engineering	0.34	0.39	0.34
	(st. dev.)	0.15	0.17	0.17
35	Motor vehicles & parts	0.40	0.26	0.37
	(st. dev.)	0.19	0.11	0.19
36	Other transport equipment	0.41	0.40	0.28
	(st. dev.)	0.21	0.22	0.16
37	Instrument engineering	0.22	0.25	0.30
	(st. dev.)	0.13	0.14	0.16
41/42	Food, drink & tobacco	0.41	0.35	0.40
	(st. dev.)	0.18	0.23	0.26
43	Textiles	0.27	0.26	0.27
	(st. dev.)	0.13	0.13	0.20
44	Leather & fellmongery	0.36	1.17	1.03
	(st. dev.)	0.01	0.47	0.20
45	Footwear & clothing	0.27	0.35	0.38
	(st. dev.)	0.18	0.23	0.16
46	Timber & wooden furniture	0.41	0.68	0.67
	(st. dev.)	0.27	0.24	0.32
47	Paper/paper products; printing/publishing	0.39	0.41	0.48
	(st. dev.)	0.28	0.22	0.34
48	Rubber & plastics	0.39	0.41	0.38
	(st. dev.)	0.16	0.16	0.07
49	Other manufacturing industries	0.34	0.37	0.42
	(st. dev.)	0.14	0.21	0.17
	Total manufacturing	0.37	0.45	0.45
	(st. dev.)	0.07	0.21	0.18

St. dev. is the standard deviation of the component industries under each heading.

1983	1984	1985	1986	1987	1988	1989	1990	Average
0.39	0.48	0.37	0.24	0.27	0.42	0.41	0.35	0.43
0.25	0.19	0.11	0.07	0.17	0.42	0.27	0.16	0.13
0.42	0.40	0.30	0.51	0.38	0.24	0.43	0.44	0.40
0.27	0.08	0.07	0.09	0.15	0.04	0.21	0.28	0.07
0.38	0.36	0.37	0.28	0.29	0.32	0.47	0.41	0.38
0.34	0.20	0.30	0.21	0.21	0.20	0.33	0.29	0.06
0.38	0.49	0.36	0.30	0.41	0.31	0.48	0.33	0.39
0.25	0.26	0.18	0.14	0.32	0.15	0.33	0.20	0.06
0.32	0.39	0.31	0.25	0.30	0.40	0.28	0.29	0.33
0.21	0.21	0.21	0.13	0.19	0.35	0.20	0.17	0.06
0.37	0.41	0.34	0.30	0.31	0.32	0.38	0.28	0.35
0.25	0.21	0.23	0.21	0.20	0.22	0.23	0.19	0.04
0.58	0.23	0.39	0.23	0.56	0.62	0.40	0.31	0.44
0.30	0.08	0.33	0.04	0.18	0.18	0.17	0.11	0.15
0.36	0.36	0.35	0.37	0.38	0.41	0.53	0.40	0.38
0.23	0.18	0.19	0.21	0.19	0.22	0.38	0.23	0.05
0.64	0.43	0.34	0.41	0.26	0.32	0.50	0.41	0.39
0.77	0.29	0.19	0.41	0.11	0.16	0.26	0.20	0.10
0.25	0.42	0.34	0.39	0.68	0.74	0.38	0.66	0.45
0.08	0.08	0.05	0.28	0.33	0.24	0.29	0.04	0.16
0.42	0.34	0.24	0.36	0.33	0.33	0.24	0.24	0.30
0.36	0.26	0.09	0.29	0.12	0.17	0.12	0.10	0.06
0.33	0.55	0.35	0.36	0.39	0.48	0.42	0.38	0.40
0.17	0.28	0.24	0.20	0.19	0.27	0.23	0.21	0.06
0.25	0.32	0.24	0.29	0.18	0.19	0.22	0.26	0.25
0.17	0.23	0.21	0.30	0.11	0.08	0.14	0.19	0.04
0.72	0.73	0.35	0.69	0.49	0.45	0.34	0.42	0.61
0.05	0.50	0.16	0.01	0.05	0.28	0.07	0.07	0.27
0.40	0.39	0.25	0.30	0.27	0.21	0.27	0.33	0.31
0.28	0.22	0.17	0.24	0.16	0.22	0.15	0.29	0.06
0.57	0.61	0.49	0.44	0.37	0.49	0.58	0.35	0.51
0.35	0.15	0.31	0.13	0.21	0.36	0.33	0.28	0.11
0.37	0.45	0.45	0.33	0.37	0.43	0.56	0.37	0.42
0.17	0.18	0.26	0.24	0.38	0.23	0.25	0.15	0.06
0.35	0.32	0.32	0.55	0.46	0.40	0.56	0.41	0.41
0.18	0.18	0.16	0.11	0.05	0.18	0.06	0.28	0.08
0.28	0.29	0.40	0.26	0.26	0.34	0.44	0.31	0.34
0.22	0.07	0.20	0.20	0.09	0.16	0.26	0.12	0.06
0.41	0.42	0.35	0.36	0.37	0.39	0.41	0.37	0.39
0.13	0.11	0.06	0.12	0.12	0.13	0.11	0.09	0.08

GROSTRADE, and concentration adjusted for the size of imports (*CONC2* and its square, *CONC2SQ*).)

Lastly we look at the degree of churning in the industry, looking at the ratio of entrants and exits by both number and turnover (and in total). This gives eight variables: *ENTRY, EXIT, NCHURN, GCHURN, ENTRY1, EXIT1, NCHURN1* AND *GCHURN1*, where 1 indicates value added weighted variables.

Product differentiation and heterogeneity

Here the hypothesis is straightforward, the greater the ability to differentiate or the greater the heterogeneity of the particular activity heading then the greater the scope to run businesses differently and hence the greater the potential for recording higher values of inefficiency in the way we measure it. Unfortunately only one measure was readily available, namely the proportion of total sales within each industry covered by the principal product (*SPECIAL*). Ideally we would have liked to try a wider range of measures and subsequent analysis will include the number of minimum list headings (the finest classification) within each 4-digit activity.

Industry dynamics

This is the most challenging of the explanations from the point of view of the aims of our study. The model we have described thus far is essentially static. Only current values are used in the calculation of the frontier production function. However, the problem for the firm of trying to be efficient is a dynamic one and the particular annual figures represent an interval in time over which that process of adjustment is observed. Part of the observed inefficiency is because the process of transition to the desired structure of production is incomplete. Thus switches between technologies may appear as technical inefficiency, particularly if they occur during the year of measurement. Ideally we would want to introduce the dynamism at the level of the individual business (see Piesse *et al.*, 1993 for example) but since observations cannot be related across years we are stuck with the secondhand problem of trying to introduce the dynamic factors after the event.

There are at least three ways in which we can attempt this. The first is to introduce a dynamic structure into the estimation process by including lagged values of variables or some explicit adjustment process such as error correction mechanisms. To some extent this is trying to set out the extent of the original misspecification.

Second, we can incorporate variables which themselves reflect the degree of dynamism in an industry. We have already seen the measures of entry and exit. Measures of innovation or spending on R&D were included in our 1977 study but the poor match of headings contributed to a lack of success on that occasion (Mayes *et al.*, 1994) and this problem is exacerbated in the current case where categories are narrower. The fact that the data available are not annual would also tend to make these variables act more like industry dummies than direct explanations. The variables we tried therefore related to the rate of change in the industry (ΔQ), (ΔL) and ($\Delta Q/L$).

Finally our concern was that inefficiency was affected by the pressure of the macroeconomic environment. We have therefore included the variables *DGDP* (change in GDP), *GDPFOR* (expected change in GDP),[9] *INTEREST* (interest rates) and *PRICES* (inflation rate) (table 4.8). These variables in effect act as a more behavioural representation of what in our initial formulation were annual dummies and a time trend. Since they are treated as applying equally to all industries, they impose a specific cyclical pattern on the data rather than letting the dummy variables follow a less constrained path. Here again it would be preferable to operate on the original data as then these cyclical variables could be permitted to have different effects on different industries. This is clearly what happens in practice as capital goods industries for example are far more affected by the economic cycle than food, drink and tobacco. Purchases of the former can be postponed but consumption of necessities is the last area of spending to decline under recessionary pressures. With the exception of interest rates, these macro variables appear to have a significantly positive effect on measured inefficiency. However, the size of the influence of these variables is fairly small with expected change in GDP having the largest effect on ATI, at nearly 2 per cent. It thus appears that both faster change and greater expected inflation lead to a greater spread of efficiency. However, the impact on the rest of the model is very small with the other variables being largely independent of these macro changes.

Spatial disparities

The argument in this case is simply that if production has to be heavily dispersed across the country, either because local tastes vary or transport costs or perishability demands it, then there is a good opportunity for variation in efficiency. Here again only one variable is available from the Annual Census of Production (*GEOG*) the percentage of the industry's output concentrated in the largest production area.[10]

Managerial and organisational influences

In practice a large proportion of the residual variation among firms comes from the way they organise themselves, train their employees, motivate their staff and adopt a corporate culture and market focus. Most of these items are difficult to measure and in any case relate to the individual firm and are not readily usable at the industry level to which we are confined here. The difficulty of putting an exact finger on these issues is exemplified by Leibenstein's (1966) concept of X-inefficiency. We can, however, point to some structural characteristics of the industry.

The first is the relationship between enterprises and the basic data unit of the business. We might expect that a firm running a number of different sites will ensure much more homogeneity among them than would purely independent firms at each site (*ESTENT* is the establishment/enterprise ratio).

Second, the structure of the labour force may give an indication as to the variety which can be expected from it. Industries with higher ratios of non-production workers to total employees (*ADRAT*) may have much more scope for innovation and differentiation through customised value-added. The pay of these workers (*WADH*) and even that of production workers (*WOPH*) may give an indication of the sophistication and hence possible product variety in the industry.

Lastly, as we mentioned earlier, if entry and exit costs are high, then again there will be scope for greater variation in efficiency. A firm which cannot transfer extensive assets to another use will write off its sunk costs and continue producing as long as it covers variable cost or until it needs to invest again substantially. We therefore include capital intensity (*KINTENSE*) in the model.

Estimated equations

The full set of variables is defined in the Appendix to this chapter but since some of these are different measures of the same phenomenon they were not all run together in the model. Table 4.6 sets out the principal findings after elimination of the less successful variables within each category for the static model. This process effectively involved the testing of non-nested hypotheses as in some cases the variables are substitute explanations of the determinants of inefficiency.

The most successful explanatory variables in terms of individual significance are those relating to trade, capital intensity, the geographical spread of production, the relative sophistication of the production process and the

Table 4.6 *Explanations of inefficiency using ATI as the dependent variable. Static and lagged adjustment models*

Exogenous variable	Equation number					
	1	2	3	4	5	6
LAGATI						0.250
						9.66
CONC	-0.000398		-0.000489			-0.00171
	-0.36		-0.44			-1.50
CONSQ	0.0000079		0.0000085			0.0000189
	0.63		0.68			1.46
NEWTRADE	-0.0152	-0.0149	-0.0157	-0.0163	-0.0150	-0.0144
	-2.68	-2.78	-2.77	-2.89	-2.77	-2.56
KINTENSE	0.0114	0.0112	0.0130	0.0130	0.0127	0.158
	2.28	2.20	2.28	2.24	2.22	3.44
OPRAT	-0.113	-0.097	-0.125	-0.121	-0.103	-0.105
	-2.06	-1.90	-2.29	-2.20	-2.03	-1.96
WAGE	-0.0409		-0.0581	-0.0509		-0.957
	-0.73		-1.02	-0.90		-1.67
DPROD	0.000961	0.00102	0.000944	0.00103	0.000973	
	2.31	2.49	2.26	2.53	2.37	
ESTTOT	0.000598	0.000583	0.000586	0.00576	0.00568	0.000417
	8.66	8.60	8.51	8.51	8.40	6.20
GEOG	0.00127	0.00119	0.00110	0.000980	0.00105	0.00119
	1.88	1.85	1.63	1.51	1.64	1.72
d81			0.0503	0.0509	0.0494	0.0780
			2.45	2.49	2.44	3.77
d82			0.0655	0.0657	0.0644	0.0815
			2.99	3.01	2.95	3.78
d83			0.0293	0.0294	0.0283	0.0347
			1.33	1.33	1.29	1.63
d84			0.0750	0.0749	0.0739	0.0836
			3.80	3.80	3.76	4.33
d88						0.0319
						1.62
d89			0.0414	0.0416	0.0437	0.0493
			1.95	1.96	2.06	2.38
CONSTANT	0.377	0.339	0.383	0.377	0.325	0.307
	4.92	7.44	4.95	5.08	7.19	4.02
Number of obs.	1850	1850	1850	1850	1850	1700
$\overline{R}^2$	0.085	0.086	0.095	0.096	0.096	0.158

Note: Numbers below coefficients are t-statistics.

size of the industry (all of these with the expected signs, that is, the greater the involvement in international trade (whether through imports or exports), the less capital intensive (the lower are sunk costs), the less sophisticated the nature of production, the less concentrated is its location and the smaller the industry then the less the inefficiency. This results in a significant effect in each of the four static categories of effect we have outlined. However, some of the interim results are noteworthy. In the first place measures of concentration were by and large both rather insignificant and perverse in sign, whether or not trade is included in the measure. Thus the greater the concentration the less the inefficiency, although the squared term did indicate that there was a maximum for this effect. The one exception was when the concentration ratio was weighted by the size of the market (labelled COSIZE). The larger the value added of the largest five firms then the greater the inefficiency.[11] This implies that market power has absolute as well as relative facets.

Second, our measures of churning worked rather poorly. In so far as there was a relation it was positive – the greater the churning the greater the inefficiency. There is clearly a problem here about the direction of causation. Inefficient industries are likely to be subject to greater structural change – an argument which implies the opposite sign to the idea that the more actively an industry is contested the more efficient it is likely to be. There are also clear differences among the different years. The early years 1981–4 are clearly characterised by greater inefficiency and the years 1986–7 with less.[12] This to some extent reflects the economic cycle.

Trying to explore this in a more dynamic context was only partly successful. The rate of productivity growth did have a positive coefficient suggesting that rapid change may be associated with a greater spread of efficiency but attempts to introduce other variables showing the rate of change within industries was not promising. The greater rate of change in output or employment in the industry during the year then the higher the level of measured inefficiency. Similarly the greater the rate of net investment the lower the inefficiency. However, the estimators were at best significant at the 10 per cent level and were not robust. If on the other hand we specify a simple partial adjustment model by including the lagged value of the dependent variable this works relatively well (table 4.6, last column). The coefficient is stable to changes in specification of the independent variables and holds a value of a quarter, a relatively small pass through from one year to the next. This more dynamic model is able to explain about an eighth of the total variation, not a large proportion by comparison to the exercises described in Caves (1992) but nevertheless a proportion which is not negligible in the context of cross-section studies

Table 4.7 *Dynamic explanations of inefficiency using first difference ATI (DATI) as the dependent variable fixed effects model*

Exogenous variable	Equation number		
	1	2	3
LAGLAGDATI			0.0437
			1.34
DCONC	0.00204	0.00218	0.00465
	1.08	1.14	2.30
DNEWTRADE	0.0257	0.0247	0.0321
	1.45	1.40	1.63
DKINTENSE	0.167	0.138	0.208
	2.27	1.89	2.95
DOPRAT	0.335	0.283	
	1.58	1.34	
DLAGESTTOT	-0.000396	-0.000494	
	-1.19	-1.48	
DWAGE	-0.204	-0.209	-0.185
	-1.98	-2.07	-1.74
DDPROD			0.000653
			1.29
DESTTOT	0.000786	0.000307	0.000473
	2.91	0.98	1.60
DNCHURN	-0.0849	-0.0905	
	-1.01	-1.08	
DSPECIAL			-0.00180
			-0.81
d82		0.0613	
		2.38	
d84		0.0809	0.0754
		2.94	2.48
d85			-0.0397
			-1.44
d86			0.0270
			0.97
d87		0.0458	0.0345
		1.93	1.25
d88		0.0620	0.0379
		2.56	1.40
d89		0.0739	0.0651
		2.42	2.05
CONSTANT	-0.00743	-0.0434	-0.0346
	-0.97	-3.57	-1.94
Number of obs.	1548	1548	1295
$\overline{R}^2$	0.014	0.021	0.027

Note: Numbers below coefficients are *t*-statistics.

Table 4.8 *The influence of macroeconomic factors on ATI*

Explanatory variable	Equation number			
	1		2	
LAGATI			0.259	(10.00)
CONC			-0.00133	(-1.16)
CONSQ			0.0000150	(1.16)
NEWTRADE	-0.0169	(-3.05)	-0.0149	(-2.66)
KINTENSE	0.0112	(2.06)	0.145	(3.17)_
OPRAT	-0.138	(-2.46)	-0.116	(-1.12)
WAGE	-0.0699	(-1.24)	-0.103	(-1.84)
DPROD	0.00112	(2.81)		
ESTTOT	0.000588	(8.61)	0.000418	(6.17)
GEOG	0.000693	(1.06)	0.000774	(1.11)
DGDP	0.000974	(2.42)	0.0178	(4.15)
GDPFOR	0.0185	(2.01)	0.0321	(3.34)
PRICES	0.00674	(2.43)	0.0183	(4.41)
CONST	0.332	(4.13)	0.140	(1.61)
No of obs.	1868		1720	
$\bar{R}^2$	0.086		0.153	

Note: *t*-statistics in parentheses.

for such a wide range of industries. The earlier single year study for the UK (Mayes *et al.*, 1994) relating to 1977 was rather more successful in explanatory terms but had more problems with implausible coefficient values. Looking at changes in behaviour alone (table 4.7) is not surprisingly less successful but it does indicate that an increase in concentration tends to increase inefficiency. Furthermore there is some sign that an increase in churning may reduce inefficiency. However, the peversity lost in concentration is replaced by one for trade where increases in trade seem to be associated with rises in inefficiency.

Taken together it appears that only a small proportion of technical inefficiency in the 1980s can be explained by coherent factors. Although there was relatively little change in average technical inefficiency during the 1980s the movements in the determining variables over the period show that most of the factors which assist efficiency moved in a favourable direction for manufacturing as a whole. The trade ratio increased by over a third and average capital intensity fell by a similar proportion. However the remaining shifts were relatively small (concentration, geographical concentration, operative ratio). With the exception of the ratio of operatives to total employees, changes in these influencing factors resulted in a fall in ATI. It is the size of industries which appears to have been the single most important factor lowering total manufacturing ATI over the decade. However, despite the size of some of the changes, the smallness of the coefficients means that the other determinants do not appear to have a heavy influence on ATI either singly or jointly. Many of these factors relate to the structure of industry and contribute little to the explanation of the change in performance during the 1980s, they 'merely' explain why inefficiency varies among industries.

Conclusions

If we take chapters 2, 3 and 4 together we can draw a clear set of conclusions.

1. Little of the increase in productivity during the 1980s can be accounted for by a switch from low productivity and low productivity growth sectors to those with a higher level and/or faster growth. If the sectoral distribution of manufacturing industry had been the same in 1990 as it was in 1980 productivity growth would only have been almost the same over the decade.

2. It is widely argued that one of the causes in the improvement in productivity during the 1980s was the reduction in the tail of inefficient plants. In practice however this tail of less efficient plants has been little changed in size. The major gain has been in the improvement in the whole of each industry, moving the frontier of best practice in the UK towards that achieved in its more successful competitors.

3. However, while the size of the 'tail' of inefficient plants may not have changed much its composition most certainly has. There has been substantial entry and exit in each year with over 10 per cent of businesses changing every year, rising to over a third for some industries on occasion. Entry of new plants with above average productivity and exit of below average plants has accounted for a portion of the annual increase in productivity but in absolute terms the initial contribution appears small.

4. As entries and exits can only be observed in the year of occurrence we are likely to have considerably underestimated their contribution if the evidence of more extensive studies in Canada and elsewhere also applies to the UK. New firms tend to face initial problems but those which con-

tinue to grow over the years can make a substantial contribution to productivity growth as is shown in Chapter 11.

5. The distribution of productivity within industries has shifted little in shape over the decade.

6. Although a small number of industries have shown spectacular productivity growth during the decade these have been relatively small in size, with the exception of data processing and related equipment. The important contributions to growth in manufacturing have come from more traditional industries such as food, drink and tobacco and paper, printing and publishing, which have below average productivity growth, with the exception of chemicals which has performed well on all criteria. Industries such as steel show a marked change in structure, with a dramatic reduction in the number of businesses.[13]

7. The decline of the early 1980s and the period of rapid growth later in the decade show some important differences in the growth of productivity. Although some industries make a strong contribution throughout, there is an apparent shake-out effect during the recession in industries such as textiles, clothing and footwear which otherwise exhibit poor productivity levels and relative productivity growth. In the upturn 'other transport equipment', principally aerospace, makes the most obvious contribution to the growth of manufacturing.

8. Foreign owned businesses have shown both higher productivity levels and higher productivity growth than domestically owned businesses in the same industries.

9. On average there has been a small reduction in technical inefficiency in manufacturing industry over the decade. In so far as inefficiency has fallen the main determinant identified appears to be more effective internal and external competition.

10. Implications
- there is still room for catch-up with other competitors
- the relatively weak growth scenario forecast for the rest of the 1990s suggests that the productivity gains of the 1980s are not being translated into the sorts of improvement in competitiveness that might have been expected. This will give strength both to those who argue that there is room for industrial and related policies (Britton, 1992) and to those who argue that there is scope for supply-side reform, particularly in human skills (Prais, 1993)
- there does, however, seem to be general agreement that the days of relative decline for manufacturing compared to the rest of the economy are over, at least for the rest of the decade. The changes within manu-

facturing during the 1980s are part of that explanation. However, some of it lies in the changes in the other sectors – the decline of North Sea oil, the increased openness of services markets and the restrictions on the public sector.

The analysis in these three chapters has been only partial. However, the use of detailed data at the level of the individual business has shown that the rise in productivity over the 1980s has been widely based and that many of the hypotheses advanced such as a switch in industry structure or the elimination of the 'tail' of inefficient businesses do not on their own explain much of the change. Tails of inefficient businesses remain but this does not imply that they are the same businesses each year. One of the striking features of the data is the high rate of entry and exit and change in individual performance from one year to the next.

Many hypotheses cannot be tackled with this information set. We cannot determine the role of R&D, of different management methods, labour relations or levels of training, for example. Some of this is picked up in the chapters which follow. Nevertheless, the lack of individual explanations does not deny the greatly improved productivity performance in the UK during the 1980s.

Appendix

Definitions of variables

BIRTHS = Number of new firms entering the industry in year x
DEATHS = Number of firms exiting the industry in year x
CONC = percentage firm concentration value (percentage of net output produced by the five largest producers in year x)
CONC2 = CONC × [total sales/(value of imports + total sales)]
COSIZE = CONC × total sales
EMP = Industry employment in year x
ESTTOT = Number of businesses in the industry in year x
EXSIZE = DEATHS/ESTTOT
ENTSIZE = BIRTHS/ESTTOT
ENT1 = (BIRTHS − DEATHS)/ESTTOT
PROD = Gross value added per head in 1985 prices
GEOG = Percentage of net output concentrated in the largest geographical production area
WOPH = Wages of operatives per head
WADH = Wages of administrative, clerical and technical (non-operative) employees per head
WAGE = WOPH/WADH
OPRAT = Ratio of operatives to total employees
ADRAT = Ratio of non-operatives to total employees
CAPITAL = Net capital expenditure
KINTENSE = Capital expenditure/labour cost
ESTENT = Ratio of establishments to enterprises
IMPORTS = Value of imports/total sales
EXPORTS = Value of exports/total sales
TRADE = IMPORTS − EXPORTS
NEWTRADE = IMPORTS + EXPORTS
COVERAGE = IMPORTS/EXPORTS
GROSTRAD = (exports + imports)/(sales + imports)
d(..) = Annual rate of change of variable
LAG(..) = Lagged variable

5 Productivity, quality and the production process. A comment on chapters 2–4

KEITH COWLING AND GUY VERNON

This comment focuses on the importance of issues of product quality and the nature of the production process in the context of the explanation of productivity growth in the United Kingdom in the 1980s. We argue that the Lansbury–Mayes results can only be accurately interpreted if these two issues are seriously addressed.

The issue of product quality

The authors discuss this matter early on in the context of inter-country comparisons. They mention the biscuit factory case where, in terms of output per head, the UK had a 25 per cent superiority over Germany, but when output was 'corrected' for quality, this was turned into a 40 per cent superiority for Germany (Mason *et al.*, 1993). If this sort of correction has any general resonance then clearly we have to be quite circumspect about productivity measurement and comparison which fails to take product quality seriously But taking product quality seriously is a difficult and extremely time-consuming task. Fortunately, however, we now have a systematic study of quality change in durable goods which offers for the first time an indication of its importance, product by product over an extended period, Gordon (1990).[1] Previously one-off examples of the use of hedonic techniques for adjusting specific price indices had been available going back to the original work on automobiles by Court (1939). Now we have valid comparisons across the whole economy for those goods where we expect substantial technical change over time – consumer and producer durables.

Gordon's results revealed dramatic quality improvements for durable goods: producer durables averaged 3 per cent per annum quality improvement, consumer durables 1½ per cent. If unrecognised, this implies a dramatic understatement of productivity growth within these sectors of the economy: ignoring quality appears to imply a major specification error which raises questions for productivity measurement in terms of time series validity, cross-industry comparisons and cross-national comparisons. In response the US Bureau of Economic Analysis has introduced a hedonic price index for computer systems and the UK Central Statistical Office is currently considering the adjustment of the price indices for computers and automobiles. In terms of the present study Gordon's results suggest that the industry comparisons being made cannot be adequately done without addressing this fundamental point. A number of different issues arise.

First, there is a question of the possible differential bias in the comparison of durable and non-durable goods, as well as the differential bias within durable goods.[2] Triplett (1988) has argued that the unadjusted non-durables price index is subject to a downward bias (that is, quality deterioration over time) and hence, given Gordon's results indicating an upward bias in the unadjusted price index for durables, the relative indices of productivity growth may be very significantly biased in the absence of quality adjustment.

Second, if our measures of productivity growth for durables are biased down and consumption of durables is highly income elastic, then we might expect that countries with high incomes will experience greater downward bias in measured productivity growth than lower income countries. Thus we need to be cautious in talking about the improvement of UK productivity growth in the 1980s relative to that of countries like Germany and the United States.

Third, the significance of the problem varies substantially across specific products within the durable goods sector of the economy. In the case of the United States very large rates of drift of quality adjusted price index from 'official' price index are identified for computers; telephone switching equipment; calculators; electric generating boilers and turbines; television sets; commercial aircraft; stationary air compressors; centrifugal pumps and diesel engines: but the computer industry is revealed as the case that really stands out. Gordon estimates that between 1951 and 1984 the quality-adjusted price of computer systems and processors fell by 20 per cent per annum and Scherer reports that productivity growth in the US computer industry averaged 26.8 per cent per annum over the period 1978–88 when adjusted for quality change in the product (Scherer, 1993). Excluding this industry Scherer concludes that manufacturing productivity growth in the United States was 'disappointing' over the 1970s and 1980s – less than that sustained over two centuries of English pin manufacturing!

. Fourth, in making cross-country productivity comparisons we need to be alert to differences in the quality of the typical product consumed. Consider the case of the car industry in the United Kingdom and Germany, an important comparison because of the importance of the industry and because of the suggestion that the manufacturing productivity gap between the two economies has been significantly closing over the 1980s (O'Mahony, 1992a, b). It is fairly clear that the typical German car is of higher quality than the British car: Mercedes, BMW and Audi are very prominent in the German market – quality car production is much more important in Germany. This has obvious implications for production volume per worker: labour input per car in assembly is higher, as is labour input in component production. But, of course, what is produced is quite different. We need to adjust productivity measures by the quality of the output produced. This is multidimensional and a complicated matter but if not carefully handled can introduce substantial biases in comparisons across countries. But, is there anything systemic about quality in the British/German comparison? We suspect there is and we see two ingredients. First, Germany has never fully accepted the American model of mass production – there has been a persistence of the characteristics of craft production within modern industry and these skills will be reflected in the quality of the product as well as the volume. And second, the German consumer appears more sensitive to the quality of the product, a complicated matter of taste, culture and income.

Our overall conclusions about productivity and product quality are that without adequate treatment of quality we cannot easily make time-series comparisons, nor cross-industry comparisons; we need to qualify industry results by what is known from hedonic work about quality change in the industry; computers are a special case requiring specific hedonic estimates of productivity growth; and high income per capita economies may have their productivity growth understated relative to lower income countries – part of 'catch-up' may be a problem of measurement!

The nature of the production process

Although an acknowledgement of the existence of variations over time in labour's work intensity in British manufacturing is implicit in some passages of the chapter there is no systematic consideration of the essence or nature of the production process which allows such a phenomenon to occur. Further, there is no appreciation of the (related) endogeneity of the precise form of that process with respect to macroeconomic conditions, in particular unemployment. We believe that the neglect of these characteristics of industrial production in the paper blinds the authors to significant microeconomic tendencies which can aid in the explanation of the remarkable performance of labour productivity in UK manufacturing industry in the 1980s.

It is now accepted by many researchers working in mainstream macro and labour economics that the reality of the nature of the production process is such that workers cannot generally be paid according to their (marginal) productivities as was assumed in the traditional models of labour demand.[3] Thus 'auction' labour markets constitute only one type of labour market, and not a very widely observed one at that (Green, 1988, p. 301). This is because at the level of an individual worker productivities are not usually observable continuously. Worker effort, and thus productivity, becomes an endogenous variable, influenced by the balance of power between the firm and its workers. There is an 'effort bargain', and researchers must look inside the 'black box' of the firm to understand it. This has long been recognised by those working in the Marxian tradition, developing the insights contained in the work of Marx himself (see Bowles, 1985).

Unemployment and the 'worker discipline' effect

In the models developed in both the neoclassical and Marxian traditions worker effort under a given production process is influenced by the incentive structure offered to workers by the firm, by the extent of monitoring and by macroeconomic conditions. Such a specification reflects the underlying theme that effort is determined by the relative power of firms and their employees in the workplace, and that this power is in turn determined by the costs which each party in the labour contract can impose on the other by withdrawing from it.

In such models effort thus becomes dependent on the wage paid and on labour market conditions in as much as these affect the cost of job loss to a worker (in the literature of both schools) and to the firm (in the Marxian literature).

The cost of job loss to an employee might be crudely measured by the (expected) pecuniary loss involved with the loss of the current job. This has been the approach adopted in the formal modelling of both schools. As unemployment mounts, or the closely related average duration of unemployment lengthens, the cost of job loss to a worker rises as the chances of finding alternative employment at a comparable wage decline. In a variety of models this leads to a wage-effort vector involving more effort and thus higher productivity.[4] The cost of job loss, and thus the 'disciplining' effect of the mounting unemployment on labour, is likely to rise particularly for workers with firm or industry-specific skills employed in industries in which employment is in secular rather than cyclical decline, as their chances of re-employment and/or their alternative wage fall dramatically.

Whilst the cost of job loss to a worker escalates in times of rising unemployment, the costs the firm faces in firing workers fall. By standard search theory, a replacement is less costly to find with a large pool of unemployed to choose from (Green and Weisskopf, 1990, p. 242). Moreover, for employers whose industries are in secular decline,who want to pare down workforces anyway, the cost of labour replacement does not arise at all.

Thus it is clear that rising unemployment can lead to a shift in the balance of power in the workplace towards the employer which disciplines labour, spurring it to further efforts. There is a considerable body of empirical support for the relevance of such a mechanism in manufacturing industry across Europe and in the United States. The work of Weisskopf (1987), Schor (1988) and Wadhwani and Wall (1988) demonstrates the relevance of such a worker discipline effect to the United Kingdom in particular.

The severity of the British recession of the early 1980s deserves emphasis here. Across the economy it represented the deepest recession since the war. Moreover manufacturing was hit with disproportionate severity, with output falling by 24 per cent in the years 1979–83, as is acknowledged here. It is surely difficult for those involved in abstract academic discourse to appreciate the fear which such severe and deteriorating conditions instilled in the remaining workforces of manufacturing industry.

Thus the shift of power towards the employer within the workplace may well be underestimated using the narrow pecuniary perspective on the cost of job loss to the employee as detailed above. For the costs of job loss are not merely pecuniary (Layard et al., 1991, p. 259), and workers appreciate this. Indeed their awareness of the severely debilitating psychological effects of the sack or redundancy are likely to be heightened in a period of mass unemployment as their friends and neighbours increasingly suffer. This can only lead to further increases in work intensity as fear of job loss is itself intensified.

Such considerations, then, help to explain the significant rises in labour productivity witnessed in manufacturing as a whole in the early 1980s. They are perhaps particularly relevant to those industries shedding labour rapidly, and seemingly irreversibly. The strong contribution of textiles, clothing and footwear to productivity growth against a background of very large employment falls in the industry in this period is the clearest indication that such analysis is relevant.

Mass unemployment and changes in the production process

Thus far it has been argued that the unemployment of the early 1980s undermined the power of labour in the effort bargain and thus led to an intensification of labour's work effort in the given production process. But the shift of power within the workplace has implications not only for the outcome of the current effort bargain but for the framework within which that bargain is struck – for the very production process itself.

The endogeneity of the production process with respect to prevailing economic conditions in general is implicit in the seminal Marxian contribution of Marglin (1974). A consideration of it is requested by Green (1988, p. 310). Here we are particularly interested in the implications for the production process of mass unemployment sustained over a period of several years.

Rebitzer (1988) has argued that in the presence of prolonged mass unemployment the distribution of the types of employment contracts used in the economy may be altered. He argued that when unemployment is high 'long term employment relations', featuring a climate of reciprocity in the workplace, become more costly relative to 'short term employment relations', which rely rather more on employee fear to extract effort. The firm is then encouraged to move towards a personnel policy less dependent on the carrot of high wages and more dependent on the stick of the dismissal threat. Thus he suggests one way in which the relationship between firms and their labour, the social relations of production, may be transformed by the response of employers to the emergence of mass unemployment. But it is only one possible implication of such a macroeconomic environment for the production process.

Mass unemployment weakens labour's position in the implicit bargain over the nature of the production process and thus allows the easier adoption of techniques and processes which firms favour. Thus it can make profitable innovations in production processes which would otherwise be unprofitable owing to the suspicion and resistance of labour. The workers' reluctance to see a change in the production process is dominated by their fear of job loss in the context of mass unemployment. Such a possibility is identified and investigated in Weisskopf (1987).

Thus the macroeconomic conditions of the early 1980s provided firms with an opportunity to revolutionise the production process. Some responded, doubtless, by introducing systems of production allowing management to exercise tighter control over their employees. But there were other responses too, 'Total Quality Management' (TQM) with its flexible working practices, team working and quality circles was increasingly implemented in spite of the contemporary objections of large segments of manual labour. This process can only have been eased by the impact of the macroeconomic backdrop on the self-assurance of labour.

This trend towards the introduction of elements of TQM was reinforced through the 1980s by the adverse experience of those firms seeking to raise the pace of work within the older, more hierarchical production processes, which increasingly found problems in quality control and sought to change the nature of production. Inasmuch as these changes in the distribution of production technologies used brought the expected productivity gains, these processes contributed to the rise in aggregate productivity in the 1980s.

Turning now to a specific example of the relevance of the analysis presented here it would seem that a partial explanation of the very rapid growth in productivity in metal manufacturing can be found in the dramatic employment falls in iron and steel, as detailed by Mayes and Lansbury. These can be seen as a factor which was at once a cause and an effect of the restructuring of the industry in the 1980s, a factor which of course interplayed with others to determine the shape of the industry today.

We think that the power considerations discussed here not only bring a better understanding of the processes involved in the industrial restructuring of the 1980s but also aid any assessment of the desirability of the remarkable growth in labour productivity in manufacturing.

Final remarks

We have argued that quality matters in productivity measurement and must therefore be taken seriously. We have also argued that part of the explanation of the productivity improvement in the 1980s in Britain lies within the changing nature of the production process whereby effort is extracted from labour. These two matters may be interrelated as we have already hinted. Whilst the imposition of a higher pace of work may have been successful in terms of volume of output, this may have been associated with a deterioration in terms of quality. If less time is allowed to complete a given task, and the quality of the work is subject to particular metering problems, then it is possible that quantity has been substituted for quality within the revised production processes of the 1980s. The recognition of a quality problem was indeed a central feature of British industry by the mid to late 1980s. The case of the car industry was widely cited and there began a re-evaluation of the production process emphasising greater participation of shopfloor workers in the search for better 'build quality'. The recent successes of Rover and Land Rover have represented a turning-away from the conflictual approach of the 1980s towards a more consensual approach today.[5] Whilst people in the industry were fully aware of the quality problems of the 1980s this awareness does not extend to the usual measures of productivity growth. We shall only fully understand the 1980s if and when we are able to quantify the changing nature of the product resulting from the changing nature of the production process – a difficult but ultimately rewarding task.

6 Productivity, machinery and skills in engineering: an Anglo-Dutch comparison

GEOFF MASON AND BART VAN ARK[1]

This chapter discusses a detailed comparison of productivity, machinery and skills in matched samples of precision engineering plants in Britain and the Netherlands. The work was carried out as part of a long-running programme of research on human capital formation and labour productivity at the National Institute of Economic and Social Research (NIESR) in London which has taken as its central task to examine international differences in workforce education attainments and training provision and to seek to identify the mechanisms by which such intercountry differences in human capital formation contribute to relative levels of labour productivity (Prais, 1988).

In an earlier series of comparisons of matched samples of plants in Britain and (West) Germany, three different sectors of manufacturing were investigated – engineering, furniture-making and clothing – and in all of them higher average levels of labour productivity in German plants were found to be closely related to the greater skills and knowledge of their workforces (Daly *et al.*, 1985; Steedman and Wagner, 1987, 1989). Similar results applied to a comparison in a non-manufacturing sector – hotels (Prais *et al.*, 1989).

Like Germany, the Netherlands enjoys a substantial advantage over Britain in respect of workforce qualification levels. However, in contrast to the German apprenticeship-based training system, the great majority of Dutch vocational qualifications are gained in the course of full-time schooling. In turning to the Netherlands for a new set of comparisons, we wished amongst other things to examine the impact of this very different system of vocational education and training on relative productivity performance.

The structure of the chapter is as follows: the first section outlines the methodology employed and describes the samples of plants visited in each country. In the second and third sections we summarise recent trends in engineering output, employment and industrial structure and report on comparative levels of physical labour productivity in our two national samples. We then examine the links between relative productivity performance and inter-country differences in, respectively, the age, utilisation and maintenance of machinery and workforce skills and training. A concluding section summarises the main findings of the study and draws out important implications for vocational education and training policy in both countries.

Methodology and sample selection

The main advantage of the plant-matching research method as it has been developed in successive NIESR studies is that cross-country differences in productivity performance can be related to detailed information about workforce qualifications and training programmes in each sample of plants and to many other factors affecting labour productivity, such as the age and sophistication of machinery in use, manning levels and workplace organisation, production planning and quality control methods, maintenance procedures and so on.

The difficulties of undertaking 'controlled comparisons' of national samples of plants are well known: in particular, care needs to be taken to ensure that the samples of plants are not only well-matched for product area and mix of employment-sizes but are also adequately representative of national populations of plants in respect of these and other key criteria. At the same time, an important (but sometimes misunderstood) feature of the NIESR research method is that no deliberate effort is made to match the type of production processes in use as well as the products made. The rationale for this decision is that any attempt to control for production technologies would (apart from adding to the difficulties of achieving representative national samples) simply divert attention from a key aspect of the human capital 'story', namely, the complementarities between management/workforce skills and the selection, installation and subsequent adaptation and utilisation of physical capital equipment.

The obvious limitations of the matched-plant comparisons are the narrow focus on individual sectors and the heavy costs of field work which necessitate reliance on smaller samples of plants, and shorter periods of time in each plant, than might be possible with alternative methods of enquiry. Hence the present study should be seen as complementing and amplifying other comparisons of Anglo-Dutch productivity levels based on wider statistical sources such as Production Census data for manufacturing as a whole (van Ark, 1990a, b).

Table 6.1 *Number of engineering plants visited by product area*

	Britain	Netherlands
Pumps	5	3
Valves	3	3
Spring	4	3
Total	12	9

Table 6.2 *Distribution of plant sizes in national samples of engineering plants*

Employment size group	Britain	Netherlands
	Number of plants	
1–99	2	3
100–199	6	6
200–299	2	0
300–plus	2	0
Total	12	9
	Number of employees	
Median plant size in samples[a]	260	140

Note: [a]The median size is here defined such that half of all employees are in plants above that size and half below it.

Table 6.3 *Medians and quartiles of population plant size distributions[a] in the engineering industries, Britain and the Netherlands*

	Britain	Netherlands
	Number of employees	
Lower quartile	35	30
Median	135	90
Upper quartile	455	260

Sources: BSO, *Report on the Census of Production*, 1988; CBS, *Statistiek van het Ondernemingen – en Vestigingenbestand*, 1987.
Note: [a]Refers to local units in Britain and legal units ('enterprises') in the Netherlands in the combined metal products and mechanical engineering industries (Britain SIC 1980, Classes 31 and 32; Netherlands SBI 34 and 35).

Within engineering we focused on manufacturers in three metal-working sectors: centrifugal liquid pumps, industrial hydraulic valves and cold-coiled compression springs.[2] A total of twelve plants were visited in Britain and nine in the Netherlands (table 6.1). The median employment size of all plants in the British engineering industry is substantially larger than in the Netherlands and, in the interests of representativeness, this disparity was reflected in the distribution of plant-sizes in each national sample (tables 6.2 and 6.3). Nevertheless, care was also taken to ensure a considerable overlap in the size of plants visited in each country.

Plants were initially identified through trade directories in each country. In both countries roughly three quarters of the plants who were formally asked for a visit agreed to participate. All the visits lasted for roughly half a day and interviews were conducted with production and/or personnel managers. In each case the visit included a period of time on the shopfloor and it was therefore sometimes possible to speak to production supervisors and workers as well. In addition to the manufacturing plants, we also visited machinery suppliers and vocational schools and colleges and compared vocational examinations with the help of college teachers in each country.

Approximately two thirds of the visits were made by two researchers (one from each country) and the remainder were carried out by a single researcher. In order to economise on travelling costs, the plants selected for visits in Britain were geographically clustered in the South East and Midlands. In the Netherlands, the plants visited were widely dispersed in location. All the main visits took place during 1991; some supplementary visits and telephone interviews were carried out in 1992.

Output, employment and industrial structure

Total employment in the combined metal products and mechanical engineering industries in Britain was just over 990,000 in 1991, approximately 21 per cent of all employment in manufacturing. In the Netherlands employment in the same industries – some 147,000 in 1991 – was only a slightly smaller fraction (18 per cent) of the total numbers employed in Dutch manufacturing.[3]

In recent years the metalworking industries in both countries have experienced sharp competition from mass producers of standardised goods in southern Europe and in Asia. As a result both industries have undergone substantial reorganisation and rationalisation with product ranges typically being narrowed and refocused towards small and medium-batch production of higher value added goods produced largely in response to specific customer orders rather than for stock.

This restructuring process has been particularly intense in Britain with many changes in firm ownership, plant closures and reductions in manning levels: between 1980 and 1991 employment in the combined metal products and mechanical engineering industries in Britain fell by a third. Output in these industries rose by some 17 per cent between 1981 and 1990 before a sudden, sharp decline of roughly 11 per cent in 1991. Over most of this period productivity in surviving firms increased rapidly and in 1991 was some 29 per cent higher than in 1980.[4] The economic performance of the corresponding Dutch industries has been less volatile and essentially more robust than in Britain: employment fell sharply in the early 1980s but by 1991 had returned to 1980 levels. Between 1980 and 1991 both output and labour productivity rose by an average of just over 1 per cent a year.[5]

The differing trends in employment in the two industries were broadly reflected in our two national samples of plants. In the Dutch plants we visited, total employment had actually risen by some 15 per cent in the previous five years, in some cases reflecting the absorption of activities from other plants within the same companies. By contrast, in the British sample total employment had fallen by more than 20 per cent over the same period as similar inward transfers of employees in some plants were more than offset by continued labour shedding elsewhere.

As a result of this ongoing contraction in employee numbers, the average size of British engineering plants has almost halved since the late 1970s. As noted earlier, average plant sizes in the British industry are still considerably larger than in the Netherlands but the two industries now have much more in common than in earlier decades with a substantial overlap of plants of moderate size (say, 100–200 employees) engaged in specialised small- and medium-batch production for both domestic and international customers.

This high degree of specialisation meant that finding producers of closely matched products in the two countries was not easy. Previous National Institute comparisons of engineering plants in 1983–4 in Britain and Germany encountered similar problems in matching, and it was noted that Britain tended to manufacture a lower grade of product than Germany. The impression gained in the course of our later round of visits (1991–2) was that most surviving British firms were now producing closer to the average quality levels found in other West European countries. Indeed, for many types of pump and valve, adequate levels of quality and reliability are prerequisites for survival in markets where the potential costs of equipment failure to users (such as process industries) far exceed the purchase prices of the goods themselves.

In both countries the mechanical engineering industry, in particular, is strongly exposed to foreign competition: in 1989 exports accounted for some 39 per cent of total sales by British producers and imports represented some 40 per cent of total home demand. The Dutch mechanical engineering industry is even more trade-oriented with a 50 per cent exports/sales ratio in 1989.[6] As a result several of the firms in our two national samples were in direct competition with each other, in both home and third country markets.

Comparisons of productivity levels

In spite of the recent fast growth in British engineering productivity, estimates based on Production Census data suggest that output per hour worked in the combined metal products and machinery industries was about 30 per cent higher in the Netherlands than in Britain in 1990, slightly below the estimated 35–40 per cent productivity advantage for Dutch manufacturing as a whole.[7]

In our chosen sectors of pumps, valves and springs, most plants produce goods to a wide range of physical dimensions and other specifications. It was therefore not possible to obtain meaningful physical measures of total output for each plant which could be related to total labour input (direct and indirect) in order to compare physical productivity performance in our two national samples. Accordingly we followed the method previously used in Daly et al. (1985) of comparing the direct labour inputs involved in the manufacture of similar products in each country.

Six pairs of plants making products to similar specifications were identified, two in each of the three sectors under consideration. In each case the selected products were deemed by production managers to be 'representative' of the plants in question. Detailed information was sought from each plant on actual, not planned or 'standard', output rates and direct labour inputs. Comparisons were then based on the average outputs per direct person-hour associated with specified sequences of operations, for example, the coiling and grinding phases of spring manufacture and, in the case of pumps and valves, the machining of key components and subsequent assembly of the final product.

In all the six pairs of plants yielded some twenty-three closely matching operations for which comparisons of productivity levels were feasible (with each pair of plants providing between two and five observations). As

Table 6.4 *Estimated productivity differentials for matched operations in national samples of engineering plants*

Type of operation	Number of matched operations	Average output per person-hour[a] Netherlands/UK (UK=100)
Machine set-ups	7	} 160
Set-up plus machining[b]	4	}
Machine processing	8	129
Assembly	4	127
Total:		
Unweighted average	23	143
		(9.2)
Weighted average[c]	23	136

Notes: Standard error in brackets.

[a] Direct labour productivity (output per person-hour) was measured as follows for the different types of operation:

— machine set-ups: the reciprocal of the average direct labour input per unit of production (calculated as the total set-up time in hours divided by the number of units in each batch to be machined). See note 7 for a discussion of the results if an alternative definition excluding the batch size element is applied.

— machine processing operations: for pump and valve components, the reciprocal of the required labour input per unit of output (defined as the average machining time per unit divided by the average number of machines controlled by each worker); for machining operations in the spring plants, output per person-hour was measured simply as the average throughput rate on each machine (number of springs per hour) multiplied by the average number of machines per worker.

— assembly operations (pumps and valves only): output per person-hour was again the reciprocal of the average direct labour input (in person-hours) per unit of production.

[b] In these four cases one or both of the paired plants could only provide labour input data for the set-up and machining operations combined.

[c] Estimated average productivity differentials applying to each group of operations (machine set-ups, machine processing and assembly) weighted in line with their approximate shares in total direct employment (1:2:1 respectively).

shown in table 6.4, across the full set of matched operations, the (unweighted) average difference in output per direct person-hour was 43 per cent in favour of the Dutch plants; the sampling standard error on this estimate is plus or minus 9 percentage points. The average productivity gap ranged from 27 per cent in assembly operations and 29 per cent in machining operations to a 60 per cent advantage in machine set-up times for the Dutch plants. If these results are weighted in relation to the distribution of total direct employment in each national sample, the estimated Dutch advantage reduces to an average 36 per cent.

Although our comparisons were based on direct labour inputs only, it should be noted that the ratio of direct to indirect labour was, on average, very similar in both our national samples. The overall result is consistent with Production Census-based estimates of the Dutch advantage in engineering productivity (as noted above) which relate to both direct and indirect labour inputs.

For all three types of operation which were compared, the Dutch plants' advantage in productivity levels was found to derive in the main from shorter average labour *times* required to carry out the main tasks involved. In respect of machine-setting comparisons, the productivity measure employed meant that estimated levels of output per person-hour were positively related to product batch sizes in each case (see table 6.4, note *a*). However, the great majority of batch sizes in the chosen product areas turned out to be fairly similar in the two countries.[8]

In the comparisons of machine processing operations, estimated productivity levels varied directly with average ratios of machines to operators but (as discussed further below) inter-country variation in machine-manning levels was also minimal when similar operations were being carried out.

A further comment concerns the variation in average productivity differentials between the six pairs of plants from which data on closely matching operations were obtained. Analysis of this variation showed that it was not related in any way to the complexity of the products in question or to differences in plant employment-size, rather it simply appeared to reflect the substantial differences in efficiency which exist between plants in each country (a proposition supported by our observations during plant visits).

In summary, our results point to a sizeable gap in average productivity levels in favour of the Dutch industry. In the following sections we consider how this gap is related to the age, utilisation and maintenance of machinery and to the skills and training of the workforce in each national sample.

Physical capital endowments

Age of machinery in national samples

In both Britain and the Netherlands precision engineering firms have undertaken substantial new investments in machinery in recent years. As table 6.5 shows, some 45 per cent of machines in the British plants we visited had been purchased in the last ten years. However, the compara

Table 6.5 *Age distribution of machinery and shares of CNC machines in engineering plant samples*

	Britain	Netherlands
	Employment-weighted percentage shares	
Age of machinery (years):[a]		
Under 5	25%	40%
5–10	20	30
Over 10	<u>55</u>	<u>30</u>
	100	100
Average age (years):[b]	12	8
CNC machines as percentage of all machines	20	35

Notes:

[a]Age-distributions of machinery in individual plants weighted by their respective shares of total employment in each sample; results rounded to the nearest 5 per cent.

[b]Calculated from above distributions: mid-points were taken for the two closed intervals; the top (open) interval was taken as having a mid-point of seventeen and a half years in Britain and fifteen years in the Netherlands.

ble proportion in our Dutch sample was even higher at 70 per cent. The Dutch plants were also ahead in the use of advanced computer numerically controlled (CNC) equipment which accounted for some 35 per cent of all machines in use in the Dutch sample compared to about a fifth in Britain.[9]

The faster rate of new investment in the Dutch plants can be partly attributed to the longer payback periods on which they operate: in the Netherlands new machinery was expected to pay for itself within an average of five years compared to an average of three years in the British plants. In addition, generous tax allowances have motivated many Dutch companies to bring planned capital investments forward in recent years.[10] However, apart from these factors impinging on formal systems of investment appraisal, there were also important inter-country differences in management and workforce skills which affected the speed of introduction of new technology in each sample of plants. In particular, as will be discussed further below, British managers were much less well supported by the highly qualified technical staff needed to help assess technological options and get new equipment installed and up and running smoothly.

National origin of machinery

The two samples also differed considerably in the national origins of machinery. In the British plants the 'conventional' (non-CNC) machines were primarily British-made with a minority coming from Continental (for example, German) suppliers; in the particular case of spring-coiling machines all new equipment now tends to be imported (reflecting the withdrawal of British suppliers from this field). In the Dutch sample there were very few conventional machines of domestic origin; the bulk of such equipment has traditionally come from Germany, Switzerland and other western European countries.

In the case of CNC equipment, purchases by British plants have been fairly evenly divided between Japanese and European (for example, German or Swedish) suppliers. The Dutch sample again presented a contrast in that nearly all their CNC machines were of East Asian origin (mainly Japanese or Korean) – Dutch managers cited price and availability as the main considerations in their choice.

Previous matched plant studies have suggested that companies using foreign-made machinery were disadvantaged in respect of maintenance and repair services and the supply of spare parts. However, in this study we encountered little dissatisfaction with the service provided by third country suppliers. Indeed, as will be discussed below, significant proportions of the plants visited in both countries were content to rely heavily on suppliers and/or other external agencies for all or most of their major repairs.

Machine set-up times and running speeds

It is important to note that the higher productivity levels identified in the Dutch sample relative to Britain could not simply be attributed to the more rapid replacement of conventional by CNC machines in Dutch plants, with associated improvements in changeover times and metal-cutting speeds. In our detailed comparisons of matched operations, all the paired plants were using the *same* basic type of equipment, either conventional or CNC, and yet an overall Dutch advantage in average machine set-up and processing times was still found to apply.

As noted, the differences in required labour inputs were frequently substantial: where, to take one typical example, approximately one and a half hours were needed in a Dutch plant to set up a conventional machine tool for a specified series of operations on a particular component, the average labour time required in a matching British plant was about one hour longer. In this example the sequence of tasks largely consisted of reading and interpreting technical drawings; planning the procedures to be followed;

selecting and attaching the tools, jigs and fixtures to be used; and then undertaking a 'trial run' machining the first component in the batch, making adjustments to the equipment as necessary to achieve the required specification.

In part, the differences in the average times required by setter operators in each country to carry out their allotted tasks could be attributed to differences in the age and quality of machinery and of raw materials used. In several British plants, for example, managers directly referred to the difficulty of 'holding the tolerances' on antiquated machines or of certain older machines 'always having problems'. In such circumstances longer average times were needed for setting-up, in part because of the difficulty of getting trial products to conform to specification and, in addition, running speeds had to be restricted to help monitor and maintain accuracy levels.

British managers also complained more frequently than their Dutch counterparts about the uneven quality of raw materials supplied to them, in particular, castings. In some cases this too appeared to contribute to slower average set-up times and running speeds as operators had to take special care to avoid high reject rates. Such complaints about British foundry products echoed those heard several years earlier during the previous engineering study (Daly et al., 1985) but most of the British engineering plants visited continued to rely in the main on domestic suppliers. By contrast, most Dutch plants were prepared to obtain castings from a wide variety of countries in their efforts to obtain a satisfactory combination of price and quality.

However, other factors affecting machine set-ups and running speeds in the two national samples relate primarily to differences in human capital. Nearly all the plants visited in each country were operating with a mix of machines of different ages, both conventional and CNC in nature. The efficient use of such diverse stocks of capital equipment requires high levels of management and technical support skills in process and method planning, production scheduling and materials purchasing as well as appropriate levels of workforce skill in setting-up, operation and maintenance of equipment. Most of these issues are explored in later sections of this chapter. However, some of the differences in process planning and shopfloor organisation between the two countries deserve immediate consideration.

Factory organisation

Machine operators' ability to minimise downtime depends heavily on smooth flows of raw materials and workpieces around their factory and the ready availability of appropriate tooling and work-holding equipment. In as many as half the British plants visited, managers pointed out problems of factory layout and organisation which hampered productivity, for instance, by forcing machine-setters to lose time 'wandering around' looking for the particular equipment they needed. In some cases it was suggested that 'compromises' might be necessary if the right equipment could simply not be found.

Other concerns related to difficult access or sheer distance between departments (the latter an obvious problem in the larger plants) and machines being grouped together according to their function (turning, drilling, and so on) rather than with regard to common sequences of operations. Indeed, no fewer than three of the twelve British plants were actually in the throes of upheaval during our visits attempting to improve factory layout. By contrast, in the Netherlands most such problems appeared to have been addressed some time ago and only one of the nine Dutch plants visited still had significant difficulties with shopfloor layout.

Until a few years ago such differences between the two samples might have been expected to manifest themselves in higher levels of ancillary shopfloor labour in Britain as well as higher rates of machine downtime. However, only one plant in our British sample still retained significant numbers of such employees at the time of our visit. In the other British plants with layout problems we gained the clear impression that it was mainly the pace and smooth flow of production that were adversely affected.

Manning levels

The sharp and continuing fall in British engineering employment since the early 1980s has already been noted; in large part this has reflected a reduction in 'overmanning' by British firms relative to their Continental and other foreign competitors. As one consequence we observed very similar ratios of machines to operators in both Britain and the Netherlands when similar operations were being performed.[11] As will be discussed more fully below, we did observe higher manning levels in some British machine shops where semi-skilled operators were dependent on the services of full-time setters. However, in general it was the machine shops which appeared to have borne the brunt of British managers' recent efforts to cut back on labour requirements, both through multiple machine-manning and (as just noted) by reducing employment of ancillary labour.[12]

In other departments such as assembly and the 'stores' (preparing sets of internally processed and bought-in components prior to assembly), British manning levels were frequently found to be higher than in counterpart Dutch plants. For example, in the British pump plants visited the ratio of machinists to assembly workers was approximately 1.2:1; in the Dutch pump-makers the equivalent ratio averaged 2:1. In the British sample as a whole the ratio of machine shop to stores employees was 5:1 compared to 7.5:1 in the Netherlands. The underlying reasons for such disparities will be considered below in our discussion of workforce skills and training.

Breakdowns, maintenance and repair

As in previous matched-plant comparisons the British plants were found to be experiencing higher rates of machine breakdown than their Continental rivals. Many interruptions to production were simply caused by machine parts being left unreplaced until they 'burned out' but we also heard of more fundamental problems applying to new as well as old equipment: in one case we were told of a new machine's 'teething problems' lasting as long as nine months; in another a fairly new machining centre had remained 'down' for a full three weeks and seven conventional machines had had to be brought back into production to replace it.

A much smaller incidence of breakdowns was reported or observed during our Dutch visits. As confirmed in our discussions with machinery suppliers, this reflects to a very great extent the more meticulous adherence to prescribed maintenance procedures found in Dutch plants and their greater attention to preventative maintenance in general. Full preventative maintenance programmes were established in two thirds of the Dutch plants visited compared to only one in six of the British sample. The 'emergency maintenance' approach in most British plants was usually justified on the grounds of spare capacity which allows production to be immediately transferred to another machine in the event of a breakdown. However, such transfers still cause delays, particularly if re-setting of the replacement machine is required.

The Dutch sample also had an edge in the skills and training of their maintenance personnel (all qualified to craft level or above compared to 85 per cent so qualified in the British plants). At the same time it should be noted that half the plants in each national sample employed very few (at most one or two) or even no full-time maintenance staff and were content to rely on external service contractors for all or most of their major repairs. In this context the smooth running of production greatly depends on the ability of shopfloor operators to undertake 'first-line' maintenance of equipment (inspection, routine cleaning and greasing, and so on) and to anticipate serious problems at an early stage of their development, and at shopfloor level there was a pronounced gap in Anglo-Dutch skill levels (as discussed in the following section).

Human capital endowments

Engineering skill supplies in the Netherlands and Britain

By international standards the Dutch education and training system is notable for its relatively early provision of vocational education for a significant proportion of secondary school pupils and the high rate of attendance in full-time vocational schools after the age of sixteen (see Mason *et al.*, 1992).

The majority of those acquiring engineering craft skills in the Netherlands do so by first attending full-time junior technical (LTS) schools between the ages of thirteen and sixteen and subsequently receiving on-the-job training in the course of their first employment. Other less common – but growing – means of obtaining craft-level qualifications are through formal apprenticeship programmes where trainees continue to attend college courses part-time after taking up employment, and through two-year full-time college-based courses (known as KMBO courses) which arrange work placements for trainees with local employers.[13]

At technician level the great majority of trainees acquiring qualifications do so at full-time intermediate technical (MTS) schools, with courses usually lasting four years, one of which is spent out of school on industrial training placements. At degree level about three quarters of Dutch professional engineers graduate from higher technical (HTS) colleges and a quarter from universities.

One consequence of this highly organised Dutch system of vocational education is that, at graduate and technician levels, the Netherlands produces some 35–40 per cent more qualified engineering personnel each year than does Britain and at craft level annual Dutch output is over twice as high as in Britain (Mason and van Ark, 1993, Appendix A). This disparity in skill supplies was clearly manifested in our two samples of engineering plants.

Shopfloor qualifications and training

In both national samples roughly half the workforce was in direct production (machine tool operators, assembly workers, painters, welders, and so on in pumps and valves; machine and press operators and tool-makers in springs). As table 6.6 shows, over three quarters of shopfloor workers in the Dutch plants were qualified to craft level or above compared with only 41 per cent in the British plants. In the Dutch sample the proportions so qualified were broadly the same in all three sectors; in Britain the proportion of craft-trained workers was much higher in pumps than in valves or springs but still well below that in counterpart Dutch plants.[14]

Table 6.6 *Qualifications and training in engineering plant samples*

	Britain	Netherlands
Shopfloor qualification	41% craft 59% semi-skilled	12% technician 66% craft 22% semi-skilled
Average initial training times for machine operators: Skilled	3–4 year craft apprentice	LTS plus 11 months on-the-job training training
Semi-skilled	13 months on-the-job training	n/a (New recruits need LTS minimum)
Apprentices	3% of total employment	<1% of total employment
Shopfloor supervisors' qualifications	85% craft 15% without vocational qualifications	50% technician 50% craft
Maintenance workers' qualifications	85% craft 15% without vocational qualifications	35% technician 65% craft

Note: Classification of formal qualifications in each country: Craft: British City & Guilds Part II passes or equivalent; Dutch LTS certificates and primary apprentice awards. Technician: British Higher National Certificate/Diploma and (Ordinary) National Certificate/Diploma awards; Dutch MTS certificates and advanced apprenticeship awards.

The marked disparity in craft skills between the two industries is partly the consequence of the relative distribution of initial training costs between employers, individuals and the public authorities in the two countries. The usual way for British employers to develop craft-skilled workers is to incur the full costs of a three to four year apprentice training (including wages for trainees during a first year of off-the-job training and subsequent paid day release for college attendance). By contrast, the employers in our Dutch sample had satisfied most of their skilled labour needs by recruiting holders of LTS (or in some cases MTS) qualifications and putting them through an on-the-job training programme (lasting, on average, roughly a year).

In effect, the bulk of vocational education and training costs in the Netherlands are borne by the public authorities in their provision of full-time schooling and by those individuals who forgo the possibility of paid employment to stay in full-time education past the age of sixteen. Apart from the costs associated with on-the-job training, the only additional costs to most employers in our Dutch sample arose from trainees' occasional attendance on short courses of off-the-job education and training. Fewer than 1 per cent of employees in the Dutch plants visited were registered apprentices receiving part-time day release for college attendance.

In our British sample apprentices represented some 3 per cent of total employment with six of the twelve plants making notable efforts to maintain initial training levels in the face of economic recession at the time of our visits. This commitment to traditional craft training reflected the need to preserve a core skills base in an industry where managers are aware of their dependence on the 'black arts' of experienced machine-setters able to carry out high-precision work on a range of different machines.

However, the bulk of shopfloor training in the British industry is confined to developing 'semi-skilled' workers in a narrow range of tasks, capable (as described to us) of carrying out 'repeat work' and 'scaling familiar products up or down' but poorly equipped to undertake new and complex operations on a regular basis. As table 6.6 shows, when British employers recruit individuals without prior experience as machine operators, the average time invested in their initial training even slightly exceeds the average periods of on-the-job training given to LTS-qualified recruits in the Netherlands; but – lacking theoretical education and breadth of experience – semi-skilled workers generally remain less versatile and self-reliant than fully trained craft workers.[15]

In the Dutch plants an LTS or equivalent certificate has for some time been a minimum criterion for shopfloor recruitment and the question of initial training to semi-skilled level therefore hardly ever arises. LTS pupils' prior exposure to the use of machinery, and to workshop practice in general, gives them a 'head start' over pupils from general schools in absorbing the content of initial on-the-job training programmes; this is especially true where trainees have followed courses largely based around the needs of locally important employers. Initial training programmes may also be accelerated by recruiting students from local KMBO courses (as described above) who have previously undertaken work placements at the companies in question; roughly half the plants in our Dutch sample engaged in recruitment practices of this kind.

In consequence, the Dutch industry has been able to raise a much larger proportion of its shopfloor workforce to craft standard and this has produced clear benefits for labour productivity. In Dutch machine shops, for instance, the relative abundance of craft-skilled setter-operators contributed to the lower average set-up times observed in our physical productivity comparisons and, in addition, enhanced flexibility in switching workers from one type of machine (and product) to another in accordance with diverse and rapidly changing production needs. The higher proportion of skilled mechanical fitters in the Dutch pump and valve plants was also associated with lower average product assembly times.

By contrast, the preponderance of semi-skilled workers in the British industry has negative consequences for both flexibility and the pace of production. In some British plants semi-skilled operators have to be supported by full-time setters and production time is lost if one of these setters is not immediately available every time they are needed. In other cases semi-skilled workers in Britain are trained to set as well as operate some machines but, as we were told during several of our visits, they are likely to be confined to simpler and/or a smaller number of machines than are craft-trained workers and are also more likely to stay within a single area (for example, drilling) rather than learn a range of different operations.

In the words of one British manager, 'you have to be patient' with semi-skilled workers: whenever they are transferred to a new machine, the initial drop in productivity is that much greater and more protracted than in the case of skilled craft workers and a greater amount of supervision or 'doubling-up' (one operator teaching or assisting another) is required. The same applies in assembly departments where semi-skilled workers are likely to need extra time and assistance in order to put together more complicated, customer-specific products. The relatively low proportion of craft-level workers in the British plants also has consequences for the delivery of more formalised updating and continuing training programmes, to which we now turn.

Updating and continuing training

The most common form of updating training for established employees in both countries is provided by the suppliers of new machinery and is likely to involve short courses of off-the-job training as well as instruction on-site during installation. In the earlier comparison of British and German engineering plants it was found that the individuals sent by British plants on these courses were frequently not well-equipped to absorb the new material and subsequently impart it to their co-workers.[16] During the present study machinery suppliers reported that this situation had greatly improved – partly as a result of accumulated experience with CNC equipment – and that most British customers now take great care to send competent personnel on suppliers' courses. However, as noted above, most of the British plants we visited faced greater difficulties than their Dutch counterparts in transmitting the competences required for new machinery to a large proportion of their shopfloor workforce – and this in turn was associated with greater problems in getting new equipment up and running smoothly.

Apart from machinery suppliers' courses, a wide variety of other ongoing training programmes were mentioned in both countries, ranging from one-day courses in Statistical Process Control techniques for nearly all direct employees to two-week courses in electronic control systems for small groups of technicians and skilled machinists. Roughly half the plants in each national sample also reported sponsoring small numbers of adult employees to attend one- or two-year college courses leading to recognised qualifications. Although it did not prove possible to gather comparable data on employer-financed on-going training in our two national samples, we formed the view that the annual volume of such training per employee in Britain exceeded that in the Netherlands. However, the difference was in no way great enough to bridge the overall gaps in workforce skills between the two samples.

Supervisors

The Dutch advantage in production workers' skills was reinforced by generally higher levels of supervisory competence. In the British plants visited some 85 per cent of supervisors were craft-trained and 15 per cent remained semi-skilled; in the Dutch plants nearly all supervisors were vocationally qualified, half of them to technician (MTS) standard and half to craft (LTS) level.

These differences in qualification levels did not manifest themselves in a markedly wider span of control for supervisors in Dutch plants.[17] Rather, the main advantage of employing MTS-qualified supervisors appeared to be their ability to discuss potential improvements in shopfloor processes and methods with production engineers and managers and to liaise effectively with technical support staff in general. Indeed, in respect of technical expertise, Dutch supervisors qualified to MTS level compare more than favourably with *Meister*-trained supervisors in German manufacturing.[18]

Technicians on the shopfloor

In addition to the supervisors just mentioned, a further 12 per cent of shopfloor employees in our Dutch sample held technician-level qualifications. They had typically been recruited for work which in the British plants was the province of craft workers, for example, CNC machine operation (and, in smaller firms, on-machine programming as well) in situations involving small batch sizes and complex product specifications.[19]

Although technicians in both countries generally possess higher-order diagnostic and programming skills than craft workers, many British employers regard the college-based education courses followed by technicians as 'too theoretical' and lacking in metal-cutting skills and knowledge. The structure and content of MTS courses in mechanical engineering – with trainees undertaking systematic workshop practice in college and gaining shopfloor experience during their year's work placement – make Dutch technicians less vulnerable to this criticism. This contrast was highlighted in the spring plants visited where, in both countries, skilled toolmakers play a critical role in the in-house development of tools, fixtures and special-purpose machines. In the Dutch plants 90 per cent of toolmakers held MTS qualifications; in the British plants the toolmakers were all craft-trained and the concept of employing technicians for this work would rarely be entertained.

In nearly all of the Dutch plants employing technicians on the shopfloor, we were told that MTS-holders aspire to positions in 'white collar' technical departments and their retention typically depends on suitable career opportunities being made available to them. Nonetheless, the production skills and experience they have gained as shopfloor workers constitute a useful background for technical support work in areas such as design and production engineering.

Managers and technical staff

Senior managers in each national sample held much the same levels of technical qualifications with some 55–60 per cent in each case being engineering graduates or technicians. This category included ten of the twelve managing or general directors in the British sample and six out of nine top managers in the Dutch plants. However, Dutch managers enjoyed far greater support from highly qualified technical staff than their British counterparts: technical support staff – defined as those responsible for research, design and development, production engineering, production planning, office-based programming and test, inspection and quality control – accounted for roughly a third of indirect workers in both national samples. As table 6.7 shows, just under 80 per cent of technical support staff in the Netherlands held technician- or degree-level qualifications against 45 per cent so qualified in Britain. The percentage without vocational qualifications in the Netherlands was only half that in Britain.[20]

As with craft skill supplies, these disparities in technical support skill levels are associated with differences in the extent to which initial training

Table 6.7 *Vocational qualifications held by technical support staff[a] in national samples (by percentage)*

	Britain	Netherlands
Graduate	11	21
Technician[b]	34	58
Craft[b]	24	5
No vocational qualifications	31	16
Total	100	100

Notes:
[a]See text for definition of 'technical support' category.
[b]See notes to table 6.6 for classification of technician- and craft-level qualifications in each country. Graduate qualifications are classified as follows: British university and polytechnic first degrees; Dutch university degrees and HTS certificates.

costs are borne by employers in each country. The bulk of engineering technicians in Britain are apprentice-trained at employer expense; by contrast the relatively large annual outflow from full-time intermediate technical (MTS) schools in the Netherlands facilitates the recruitment of prospective technicians on the open market; the main subsequent costs to Dutch employers are those associated with initial on-the-job training.[21] The resulting differences between the two industries in the proportions of technicians with appropriate qualifications for the work they perform had visible consequences for new product and process development in each case.

For instance, several of the Dutch plants visited had expanded their involvement in installing as well as supplying their products and were therefore able to make quick product improvements in response to customer feedback. The British plants in the same lines of business appeared to have a much less systematic approach to product development. In some British plants we were further told that the introduction of new equipment was being hindered by shortages of qualified production engineers. Although most British plants did not explain their relative lack of new investment in these terms, it was obvious in several cases that the only staff capable of selecting and installing new equipment were already 'over-extended' by involvement with day-to-day production and sales problems. There were few, if any, parallels to this situation in the Dutch plants visited.

In pump and valve manufacturing competitive success is enhanced if products are made to a 'modular' design which allows key components to be produced in relatively large batch sizes without compromising the ability of plants to assemble small batches of final products to customer-specific requirements. Most Dutch plants in these sectors appeared to be more advanced than their British counterparts in this respect. The benefits of 'standardising' on key components were clearly understood by most British production managers and during our visits several of them reported recent progress in simplifying product designs (cutting out needless complexity in and gratuitous differences between components). However, very few of the British plants were near to implementing a concerted policy of 'modularisation'. In one case a British manager explained his difficulties as a long heritage of product design being 'driven by the technical department ... who like starting with a blank sheet of paper every time' – a phenomenon described as 'draughtsmen's licence' in another plant.

Within the British sample, it should be noted, a small minority of plants had clearly been successful in terms of new product and process development and these were precisely the plants which possessed an 'above average' supply of technically qualified support staff (usually as a result of their own substantial investment in technician apprentice training). However, their performance remains exceptional.

These observations support a general proposition that the relative abundance of technically qualified indirect staff in Dutch engineering plants allows greater freedom for senior managers to think strategically about the inter-relationships between product design, production planning and market sales – with positive consequences for productivity performance.

Summary and conclusions

In spite of rapid growth in British engineering productivity in the past decade, our comparisons of plants making similar products suggest that output per hour worked in the British industry is still about 25–30 per cent lower than in the Netherlands. This result is consistent with estimates based on Production Censuses in both countries.

Competitive success in European metalworking industries increasingly requires firms to be able to meet highly specific customer requirements. As a result of competition from newly industrialising countries, it is now more difficult for British firms to survive in mass production of standardised goods and the majority of British plants visited were indeed engaged in specialist small- and medium-batch production. In contrast to Daly *et al.* (1985, p. 52), who carried out a similar comparison of British with German engineering plants in 1983–4, we encountered very few British firms that could be described as 'complacent' in the face of international competitive pressures. Nonetheless, the performance of most British plants relative to their Dutch rivals was still restricted by slower investment in new capital equipment and by lower average levels of workforce skills and knowledge.

The greater use of new machinery in the Dutch industry partly reflects the longer financial payback periods on which Dutch firms operate and the recent bringing forward of planned new investments in response to generous tax allowances. However, the rapid and effective introduction of new technology also requires managers to be well-supported by highly qualified technical staff and the Dutch plants were found to enjoy a decisive advantage over their British counterparts in this respect.

The larger proportions of employees qualified to craft and technician level found in the Dutch engineering industry were found to contribute positively to relative productivity performance in several ways, for example, the greater ability of craft-trained production workers (as compared to semiskilled workers) to reach demanding quality standards under the daily pressure of small- and medium-batch production and to switch flexibly between different products and tasks; and the contribution made by highly qualified technical support staff to new product design and development as well as to the implementation of process innovations. Higher skill levels in the Netherlands primarily reflect that country's widespread provision of full-time vocational education and training. As elsewhere, trainees completing full-time courses of vocational schooling still need to undergo programmes of structured on-the-job training when they first enter employment. However, the relatively high attainments of students at junior and intermediate technical schools in the Netherlands give Dutch employers a considerable 'head-start' over their British counterparts in terms of the 'trainability' of their workforce, both as new entrants to the labour market and subsequently as adult workers who may need retraining and updating.[22]

In this context Dutch employers are able to carry out training to given standards more quickly and cost-effectively than is possible in Britain, and in many cases they are able to set their training standards much higher than is feasible for their British counterparts. Indeed, as was often pointed out to us in the Netherlands, the relatively high levels of wages and accompanying social charges in that country provide sharp incentives to employers to seek the high levels of workforce skill and productivity required to succeed in high value added manufacturing.

Although our comparisons suggest that engineering employers in Britain finance a (proportionately) larger volume of initial and continuing training than is found in the Dutch industry, much of it does no more than compensate for relative deficiencies in the vocational education and training of British workers prior to their taking up employment. In consequence, a majority of British plants are still unable to aspire to average Dutch skill levels on the shopfloor or in technical support departments.

The results of this study have implications for education and training policy in both countries. Amongst other things we have shown the extent to which Dutch engineering firms have benefited from a supply of potential new recruits with qualifications from junior technical schools. However, one effect of educational reforms currently in progress in the Netherlands will be to postpone by one year the age at which specialised vocational training commences in junior vocational schools. Hence future 16-year-old leavers from junior technical schools will all stand in need of further education and training through the apprenticeship system or full-time courses at 'short intermediate' (KMBO) schools if the relatively high levels of shopfloor skills and knowledge identified in this study are to be maintained.[23]

In Britain the need for further reforms in vocational education and training policy is more fundamental in nature. In contrast to the Netherlands, the courses of state-funded full-time vocational education available in Britain cater for only a small proportion of each age cohort. The bulk of British training to craft and technician standards is financed by employers through a traditional apprenticeship system which, however, lacks the institutional and legal foundations of other, more successful apprenticeship systems in countries such as Germany.

A major implication of the National Institute's comparative studies for British policymakers is that both types of system – full-time schooling and employment-based apprenticeships – are potentially capable of delivering a relatively high-skilled workforce. A coherent set of vocational education and training reforms in Britain would attempt to strengthen and harmonise both types of provision: in the case of engineering, for instance, the volume of craft and technician apprenticeship training could be increased if first-year off-the-job training took place in full-time vocational colleges, thus delaying trainees' entry to employment and reducing the share of training costs which is borne by employers. Systematic coordination of college-based and employment-based training provision for many industries in this way would contribute greatly to the achievement of a 'high skill, high productivity' economy.

7 Knowledge, increasing returns and the UK production function

GAVIN CAMERON AND JOHN MUELLBAUER[1]

Economic growth is a complex process. Although growth of the physical capital stock and of the workforce tend to be more visible, technological knowledge of various kinds has usually been found to play a significant role in economic growth. This knowledge can be in the form of new organisational methods and production techniques, as well as of new products and of new processes. This chapter constructs a quarterly model of UK manufacturing output between 1962Q1 and 1992Q4, and attempts to assess the contribution made by domestic R&D and by technology imported from abroad (proxied by technological royalties paid to foreign firms).

The chapter is divided into six sections. The first reviews the empirical evidence on the link between knowledge and productivity. The second discusses the theoretical approach taken, and notes its limitations. The third discusses our measures of innovation. The fourth presents the results of regressions without knowledge variables. The fifth presents the results of regressions with knowledge variables and the sixth draws conclusions. A separate data appendix shows how the innovation data were compiled.

Previous studies

The seminal study by Solow (1957) found that 87½ per cent of the increase in US labour productivity between 1909 and 1949 was caused by technological change (the whole of the 'residual' was attributed to technological change). Although later researchers reduced this contribution by making allowances for changes in labour quality and correcting mismeasurements of capital and output (see Jorgenson, 1990, for a survey), the unexplained residual still accounted for around a third of economic growth.

An obvious next step was for researchers to attempt to model the residual using explicit measures of knowledge, such as R&D spending and patenting (see Griliches, 1980, for example). This raises interesting questions which are beyond the scope of the present work about whether knowledge can be measured. However, the majority of the total factor productivity studies found that R&D spending (measured in a variety of ways) made a significant contribution to productivity growth, with a 1 per cent increase in the R&D capital stock typically leading to a rise in output of between 0.05 and 0.1 per cent (see Griliches, 1988). Industry-funded R&D spending was usually found to be most significant, with government funding making only a very small contribution.

Recent developments in growth theory (for example, Romer, 1986, and Aghion and Howitt, 1992) have also suggested that innovation and learning may play an important role in explaining productivity change. A number of studies have modified the growth accounting framework to allow for externalities in capital formation (so that the capital coefficient in a Cobb-Douglas production function may be greater than capital's share in output, and so that the capital and labour coefficients may actually sum to more than one). However, econometric work by Barro and Martin (1992), Mankiw *et al.* (1992), O'Mahony (1992b) and Oulton (1992) has tended to produce coefficients on physical capital that approximate its actual share in output.

Most empirical work on the relationship between knowledge and productivity has been for the United States, largely because United Kingdom data on R&D and patenting were thought to be too unreliable. Three recent studies of the United Kingdom are worthy of comment.

Sterlacchini (1989) is a typical total factor productivity study. Sterlacchini estimates his model for each of the periods 1954–63, 1963–73, 1973–9 and 1979–84, using a panel of fifteen industries. The dependent variable is the average annual rate of growth of total factor productivity during each of the periods (value-added minus capital and labour inputs weighted by their shares in value-added: that is, assuming constant returns to capital and labour). The independent variables are a variety of measures of innovative activity (mainly industrial R&D spending, and data on the number of significant innovations in each industry from Robson *et al.*, 1988). His R&D variables are constructed by taking the ratio of intramural R&D expenditures to net output by industry, with a single year value proxying the R&D intensity for the periods considered.[2] His regressions suggest that innovation has a significant and positive effect on productivity growth for most of the period, except between 1973 and 1979. However, since each of Sterlacchini's regressions contain only fifteen observations (the number of industries in the cross-section), the study has very few degrees of freedom, and also imposes the constraint that the innovation to productivity relationship is the same in each industry. Overall, although the paper's data analysis is excellent, its econometric basis is questionable.

Budd and Hobbis (1989) estimated a long-run model of UK manufacturing productivity between 1968Q1 and 1985Q4, using a cointegrating methodology. They found that patenting by UK firms in the USA, and imports of machinery from abroad (assumed to embody the latest technology) have a significant and positive effect on productivity. However, the estimated contribution of imported machinery is very high, greater than the contribution of capital stock growth, and the authors suggest that this may be because the machinery imports variable may be picking up trending effects in output that they do not model explicitly.

Oulton (1992) considers two questions that arise from the new growth theory. First, do standard constant-returns growth accounting calculations understate the role of capital in growth by only giving it a weight equal to its share of output? Second, do increasing returns arise at the industry level? He attempts to answer these questions by using the dataset described in O'Mahony and Oulton (1990a, b), which has data on 124 UK industries (based on SIC1(68) minimum list headings) for nine years (1954, 1958, 1963, 1968, 1973, 1976, 1979, 1982 and 1986, giving eight inter-year comparisons). In general, he finds no support for the 'capital is special' view, with the weight given to capital growth in multi-factor productivity calculations being correct on average. Oulton also finds evidence against the DeLong and Summers (1991) argument that investment in plant and machinery (rather than all investment) is particularly important for economic growth.

The three papers described above all start from the assumption that knowledge is a major source of economic growth, and all use a Cobb-Douglas framework to examine this relationship. However, that is where their similarities end. The Sterlacchini and Oulton studies are on cross-section data, while Budd and Hobbis look at aggregate data. Furthermore, they all have different ways of proxying knowledge. Sterlacchini uses R&D data, Budd and Hobbis use patenting and machinery imports, while Oulton assumes that knowledge is embodied in the capital stock.

This chapter attempts to steer a middle course. We use an aggregate model, with a large number of observations (124 between 1962Q1 and 1992Q4), and we also consider a variety of variables (various measures of domestic R&D, as well as technology licensed from foreign firms) and test these variables against the competing hypotheses that productivity follows a shifting time trend (see Muellbauer, 1991) and that there are increasing returns to physical capital.

Theoretical framework

We assume a standard value-added Cobb-Douglas production function that includes knowledge capital as a separable factor of production (see Griliches and Lichtenberg, 1984).

$$Q_t = A \cdot R_t^{\gamma} \cdot K_t^{\alpha_1} \cdot L_t^{\alpha_2} \tag{7.1}$$

where Q_t equals output (value-added), R_t is the knowledge R&D capital stock, L_t is labour input, K_t is capital input, and A is a constant. In logs this becomes

$$\ln Q_t = \ln A + \gamma \ln R_t + \alpha_1 \ln K_t + \alpha_2 \ln L_t. \tag{7.1a}$$

From (7.1) we can interpret symbol γ as being the elasticity of output with respect to knowledge capital.

We assume a knowledge capital generating process as follows

$$R_t = \rho R_{t-1} + \mu + \phi RK_t \quad \text{where } |\rho| \le 1 \tag{7.2}$$

and μ is the exogenous rate of knowledge increase, ρ is a measure of the persistence of the knowledge capital stock and RK_t is knowledge created during the period.

To implement equation (7.1a) it is necessary to use a proxy variable for RK_t in equation (7.2). If we proxy RK_t with observed R&D spending (RD_t), and assume $\phi = 1$ and $\rho = 1$,[3] equation 7.2 becomes

$$R_t^* = \sum_{i=0}^{t} RD_t + t\mu \tag{7.3}$$

where R_t^* is the capital stock proxy based on the sum of past R&D spending plus a time trend. Taking logs and substituting (7.3) into (7.2) yields

$$\ln Q_t = \ln A + \gamma^* \ln RDK_t + \beta_t + \alpha_1 \ln K_t + \alpha_2 \ln L_t \tag{7.4}$$

where RDK is the sum of past R&D spending from equation (7.3), and β_t is the time trend effect of exogenous knowledge capital.

However, as Schankerman (1981) has pointed out, the labour and capital inputs of R&D are double-counted in that they also appear in K_t and

L_t. Assume that capital and labour in manufacturing (but not in R&D) are paid their marginal products (excluding learning by doing for example). In this case the only source of rents in manufacturing is knowledge, and γ^* is therefore a measure of the rents, spillovers, and risk-premia inherent in R&D.

We now assume constant returns to capital and labour (that is, $\Sigma\alpha_i = 1$). Since we have assumed that labour and capital in manufacturing are paid their marginal products, we take the α_i terms to be equal to the actual shares of capital and labour in value-added, which is the discrete-time Tornqvist-Divisia index (see Nguyen and Kokkelenberg, 1992). A measure of total factor productivity is therefore

$$\ln T_t = \ln A + \gamma^* \ln RDK_t + \beta_t. \qquad (7.5)$$

There are, however, a number of theoretical problems with Cobb-Douglas approaches of this nature, as well as empirical problems with the assumption that equation (7.5) is a good proxy of equation (7.4).

Problems with the theoretical approach

Muellbauer (1984) discusses a number of problems that arise in aggregate production functions of this nature. The first is the problem of aggregation. The second is that of capital measurement, capacity utilisation and unobserved scrapping. The third is that of measurement biases in output. To these we can add the problem of separability of capital, labour and R&D.

First, aggregation problems arise because different sectors and different firms have different capital and labour shares. A bias arises in the estimate of total factor productivity if deviations in sectoral rates of change are not distributed independently from sectoral factor shares. This is most likely to occur when productivity growth is driven by switches from low productivity and low productivity growth sectors to those with high productivity and high productivity growth, rather than by balanced growth in all sectors. Muellbauer (1984) argued that the evidence for UK manufacturing suggested that the aggregation biases over sectors are small.

Second, it seems likely that relative price changes (of labour, capital, raw materials, and knowledge creation) may cause the measured values of physical capital stock and the knowledge capital stock to systematically misstate the actual values. Consider the effect of a permanent increase in energy prices relative to labour, capital and knowledge (and call this an *oil shock*). The stock of physical capital and the body of knowledge that it embodies may be specific to a lower level of energy prices, and may thus become obsolescent. UK gross capital stock data are constructed from gross investment data under fixed service life assumptions. The assumed service lives do not vary cyclically or respond to relative factor prices. When companies become bankrupt and assets are sold abroad or simply taken out of use, no allowance is made for such scrapping. These assumptions are difficult to reconcile with the economic responses that would be expected when prices, wages, taxes and demand vary. The approach taken by Muellbauer (1991) is to fit time trends with linear splines allowing slope changes to occur at times when, on *a priori* grounds, one would expect a great deal of unobserved scrapping.

Third, there are likely to be biases in the UK measure of real value-added in manufacturing. The most serious, the 'gross output bias', arises from the CSO practice of approximating changes in real value-added by applying fixed value-added weights to changes in gross output volumes (see also Stoneman, 1992). Other biases arise because of problems with the price deflators which are used to deflate the current price data which are a major source for the output index. Respectively these are the 'domestic price bias', the 'list price bias', and the 'price control bias' discussed in Muellbauer (1984).

Last, it is unlikely that R&D is separable in the production function. Grossman and Helpman (1991) pose the helpful counterfactual question – what would the rate of growth of output have been in the absence of any investment by firms in the creation of knowledge? New growth theory (Romer, 1986, for example, as well as Scott, 1989, and Hulten, 1992) argue that it is the embodiment of new technology in capital equipment that is the most important feature of the innovative process, and studies of the diffusion of innovations, such as Stoneman (1990), tend to support this view. Denison (1989), however, argues that it is inadvisable to adjust for embodied technical change because it assigns to capital formation an effect that is better viewed as an advancement in knowledge.

Innovation variables

There can be no single, perfect measure of innovative effort. Comprehensive attempts to describe the technological performance of countries and industries have usually relied on a wide variety of partial indicators. We choose to use various measures of United Kingdom industrial R&D spending, as well as technological royalties paid to foreign firms.

R&D spending may be an inadequate measure of both the inputs into and the outputs of the innovative process (see Pavitt and Patel, 1988). Stoneman (1990) and Mansfield (1985) have argued that it is the diffusion of new technology that is more important. Along similar lines, Scott (1989) has suggested that gross investment may capture technical change more effectively than either net investment or R&D spending. Researchers, such as Griliches (1988) and Budd and Hobbis (1989) have argued that patenting is a better indicator of innovative output than R&D spending. Furthermore, Dasgupta and Maskin (1987) suggest that the increase in knowledge capital from one particular R&D programme is unlikely to be the same as that produced by a different programme with the same volume of resources.

As mentioned earlier, Schankerman (1981) has pointed out that the labour and capital components of R&D are 'double-counted' in total factor productivity regressions such as that in equation (7.5) above, because they appear once in the traditional measures of labour and capital and once again in the research and development expenditure input. This 'Excess Return Interpretation' or ERI means that the calculated elasticity of R&D is either a risk premium or a supra-normal profit on R&D investments. Schankerman also notes that another bias occurs because current R&D spending is usually counted as an expense by firms, and is therefore treated as an intermediate good in the National Accounts and subtracted from value added. Schankerman demonstrates that the effect of the excess returns interpretation is to reduce the measured contribution of R&D to output growth, while the effect of the expensing bias can be to either increase or decrease measured returns to R&D.

UK firms accrue gains when they import technology from abroad. Foreign firms are unlikely to be able to appropriate all the (social) returns occurring in the United Kingdom. This suggests that estimates of total factor productivity should account for foreign knowledge as well as domestic knowledge. However, most studies of total factor productivity have been for the United States, which is not usually considered to have been a major importer of foreign technology, although this may now be changing. For a medium-sized, open economy such as the United Kingdom, however, foreign technology, both embodied in new capital and disembodied, is likely to be of importance. For this reason, Budd and Hobbis (1989) attempt to use measures such as machinery imports and technological royalties to proxy the inflow of foreign knowledge. We will use technological royalties since we can be more certain that they represent 'best-practice' technologies. However, see Ledic and Silbertson (1986) for some discussion of the problems with such data.

There are also more prosaic problems inherent in the construction of any capital stock variable: choice of an appropriate depreciation rate, lag structure, base values and deflators. These issues are discussed at length in the Appendix. Here we present a summary of the three most important issues.

First, there is the question of the time lag with which R&D should enter the R&D capital stock. Mansfield (1985) suggests that research results leak out fairly quickly (within two years in most of the cases he studied), whereas Schott (1976) preferred to use a declining lag structure which included R&D spending up to six years in the past. Typically, researchers (such as Griliches, 1980) have assumed that R&D spending affects productivity either without a lag or with a lag of one year.

Second, most studies of R&D spending use the GDP deflator to convert current price spending into constant price spending (see Edgerton, 1993, for example). However, it is unlikely that the prices of goods and services used in R&D, such as scientific and technical personnel, scientific instruments, computer hardware and software, chemicals, and so on, rise at the same rate as prices in the whole economy. Of course, some components of R&D spending may rise more slowly in price than the GDP deflator. Jankowski (1993) recently tried to construct R&D deflators for US Business R&D and found that they differed significantly from the GDP deflator. The Appendix also discusses the construction of an R&D deflator for UK manufacturing R&D.

Third, there is some controversy over the choice of an appropriate depreciation rate (see Bosworth, 1976; Schott, 1976; Griliches, 1980; and Terleckyj, 1980, for discussion). Many researchers have chosen to use a zero rate of depreciation, while others have argued that if knowledge becomes obsolescent the knowledge capital stock must fall.

However, it is important to make a distinction between obsolescence and the rate of depreciation. The high rates of obsolescence of knowledge observed in firms by researchers such as Pakes and Schankerman (1984) merely reflect obsolescence of knowledge to individual firms. In effect, this obsolescence is a measure of technological progress, because it shows that knowledge is either being superseded or has leaked out to other firms.

The stock of knowledge in our formulation is an index of the productivity of the set of best-practice production plans. If R&D creates a new production plan that supersedes an old one, it must be more productive for it to be implemented, thus the productivity of the set of production plans increases. So, although knowledge of vacuum tube technology is obsolescent in the computer industry, the superseding knowledge of semi-conductors is more productive, and the index of knowledge is higher. Of course, if knowledge of vacuum tubes is forgotten, future research in the area (if it is necessary) may be less productive (that is, the potential rate of increase of knowledge capital will be slower, but the level of knowledge capital will be unchanged).

It seems unlikely that the stock of knowledge as we have just defined it can depreciate in the standard sense that physical capital can depreciate. Presumably, the level of total factor productivity in manufacturing could be maintained at the current level merely by replacing physical capital and labour as they wear out, even if no further research is undertaken.

Total factor productivity without innovation variables

Growth of total factor productivity slowed in all industrial countries in the 1970s. There is still no universal agreement on the causes of the slowdown except that it was not merely a short-term cyclical phenomenon. The recovery in manufacturing productivity growth from the end of 1980 is striking, even after correcting for cyclical labour utilisation effects, as shown by Muellbauer (1991).

We have updated this research to the first quarter of 1993. The method consists of fitting a production function to UK manufacturing data for 1958Q3 to 1993Q1, assuming constant returns to scale. Output is real value added. Various biases in the index of output are discussed in Muellbauer (1984). Labour input is measured by the combination of number of workers, number of weeks worked per year (which falls because of longer holidays) and *effective* weekly hours of work. As explained in Muellbauer (1984, 1986), data on overtime hours can be used to construct a utilisation index that corrects labour input for cyclical variations in utilisation.

The capital stock is measured by the CSO's gross capital stock series. The main problems with this are assumptions on obsolescence and utilisation. In particular, one would expect a higher rate of capital scrapping from 1973 because of increases in the relative prices of raw materials and fuel, and also during the 1980–81 recession. Similarly it seems plausible that in 1990–91 the further worsening of competitiveness and high real interest rates would have led to an increase in scrapping. In the equation that is estimated, shifting time trends pick up the joint effect of changes in technology, work practices, and measurement errors in the capital stock. In part these measurement errors can represent under-utilisation and, in part, permanent scrapping. The CBI capacity utilisation index is included to reflect varying utilisation rates of capital. In the next section we attempt to model the effect of technological changes explicitly.

Figure 7.1 plots total factor productivity not corrected for utilisation and the output bias against the combined effects of the split time trends. The time trends imply the following annualised rates of 'total factor productivity

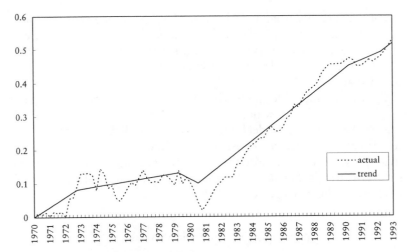

Figure 7.1 *Total factor productivity – actual and trend 1978(1)–1993(1)*

growth' (defined as changes in value-added that cannot be explained by other variables, chiefly weeks worked, number of workers, effective weekly hours of work, the measured capital stock, and the output bias terms):

1958Q3–1972Q4	3.0 %;	1973Q1–1979Q2	0.8 %
1979Q3–1980Q3	–2.4 %;	1980Q4–1990Q2	3.7 %
1990Q3–1992Q2	2.0 %;	1992Q3–1993Q1	3.7 %

There was a dramatic increase in the trend rate of growth of productivity in the 1980s. There are a number of possible explanations for this. First, capital scrapping in 1979–80 meant that from 1981 onwards, the proportionate increase in the capital stock would be substantially higher than recorded by official statistics. This would lead to an upward bias in the total factor productivity figures. Second, the 1980–81 recession led to a major shake out of labour that had been mistakenly hoarded during the late 1970s. Amongst other possible hypotheses are the weakening of trade-union power; the withdrawal of state subsidies; the shedding of below average labour and capital; increasing subcontracting; the widespread adoption of 'microchip' technologies; and simply that UK manufacturing had so much lost ground to catch up on international best-practice.

We experimented with a number of specifications in an attempt to capture the effect of the 1990–91 recession on productivity. The model that worked best, although it did not fully capture the cyclical effect, suggests that the recession temporarily reduced the trend rate of growth of total factor productivity from its 1980s rate of 3.7 per cent a year to around 2 per cent a year between 1990Q3 and 1992Q2. It is very early to draw conclusions about what has happened since 1992Q2, but we have assumed in figure 7.1 that the trend rate of growth returns to its 1980s rate of 3.7 per cent a year.

We also attempted to model UK total factor productivity by replacing the shifting time-trends with a stochastic time trend as suggested by Harvey (1989). The resulting model fitted the data less well than the shifting time-trends approach, which suggests that the changes in total factor productivity growth rates are more the result of structural breaks than smooth stochastic trends. However, this analysis did tend to confirm our choices of dates for the major structural breaks.

Total factor productivity with innovation variables

We have discussed the importance of innovation in the growth process, and suggested a number of measures of innovation. Furthermore, we have also noted that commentators such as Romer, 1987, and Scott, 1989, have argued that technology only affects output when it is embodied in capital. If we were to make the (strong) assumption that these embodiment effects are separable in the production function from the disembodied effects of our innovation measures, we could estimate a nested equation of the general form (ignoring time trends, labour utilisation measures, and output bias terms for the moment):

$$\ln Q - \alpha_L \ln L - \alpha_K \ln K = \beta_0 \ln L + \beta_1 \ln K + \beta_2 \ln RDK. \qquad (7.6)$$

Six hypotheses can be tested in this general specification if we set a_L and a_K to equal labour and capital's shares of value added respectively, and use Schankerman's (1981) Excess Return Interpretation discussed earlier to interpret the coefficient on the R&D stock, b_2, as an excess (social) return to R&D. The first is that the labour and capital coefficients are equal to their shares in value added $(b_0, b_1 = 0)$, and that any externality is captured by the R&D stock $(\beta_2 \neq 0)$. The second is that the coefficient on labour is equal to its share in value added, but that the coefficients on capital and the R&D stock sum to equal capital's share in value added $(b_0 = 0, b_1 = -b_2)$. The third is that the there is an excess return to the R&D stock, and that the coefficient on capital can differ from its value-added share $(\beta_1, \beta_2 \neq 0$, which nests hypotheses 1 and 2). The fourth is that there is an excess return to the R&D stock and that there are increasing returns to labour and capital jointly in their value-added share proportions

$(\beta_0 + \beta_1 \neq 0, \beta_2 \neq 0)$. The fifth is that there are constant returns over all three variables, with the return on the R&D stock subtracted from the value-added shares of capital and labour in equal proportions ($b_0 = -(b_0 + b_1)$). The sixth is that all three variables can have coefficients different from their value-added shares which nests all the previous hypotheses ($\beta_0, \beta_1, \beta_2 \neq 0$). We can express these hypotheses as follows:

Hypothesis (1) $\ln Q - \alpha_L \ln L - \alpha_K \ln K = \beta \ln RDK$

Hypothesis (2) $\ln Q - \alpha_L \ln L - \alpha_K \ln K = \beta (\ln RDK - \ln K)$

Hypothesis (3) $\ln Q - \alpha_L \ln L - \alpha_K \ln K = \beta_1 \ln RDK + \beta_2 \ln K$

Hypothesis (4) $\ln Q - \alpha_L \ln L - \alpha_K \ln K = \beta_1 \ln RDK + \beta_2 (\alpha_L \ln L + (1 - \alpha_K) \ln K)$

Hypothesis (5) $\ln Q - \alpha_L \ln L - \alpha_K \ln K = \beta (\ln RDK - \alpha_L \ln L - (1 - \alpha_K) \ln K)$

Hypothesis (6) $\ln Q - \alpha_L \ln L - \alpha_K \ln K = \beta_1 \ln L + \beta_2 \ln K + \beta_3 \ln RDK$.

However, there are a number of problems with the empirical estimation of these hypotheses. As we noted earlier, one of the main functions of the shifting time-trends in the model is to allow for capital mismeasurement – premature scrapping, and under-utilisation. The capital mismeasurement is such that if capital is unrestricted in a regression like equation (7.6), its coefficient is significantly negative, which is implausible.

Second, there is a problem of collinearity between the base trend and the R&D capital stock. The correlation coefficient between these two variables is 0.991. In estimation, this collinearity shows up in the expected manner. Inclusion of both variables in an unrestricted estimation typically yields insignificant t-statistics on both variables, with the base trend dominating to some extent.

We experimented with a variety of innovation variables. In practice, industry-funded BERD (Business Enterprise R&D) plus technological royalties proved best. We also experimented with various lags, base stocks and depreciation rates for our innovation variables. We found that the fourth lag, using a base stock calculated according to the Griliches (1980) method discussed in the Appendix, along with a zero depreciation rate, gave more consistent results than any other formulation.

Estimation of hypothesis 6 (not reported here), which allows all the coefficients to differ from their value-added shares, gave the clear conclusion that the coefficient on labour on the right-hand side can be validly restricted to zero (that is, the return to labour is equal to its share in value added). This allowed us to disregard the results of hypotheses 4 and 5, which both imply that the coefficient on labour is different from zero.

Table 7.1 *Regression estimates of hypotheses 1 to 3*

	$\beta \ln RDK$	$\beta (\ln RDK - \ln K)$	$\beta_1 \ln RDK + \beta_2 \ln K$
Trend 1 (0.0072)	β 0.002 (0.14)	β 0.009 (0.32)	β_1 0.405 (2.3)
			β_0 −0.797 (2.3)
	s.e. 0.009212	s.e. 0.009209	s.e. 0.009029
Trend 2 (0.006)	β 0.0070 (4.9)	β 0.144 (5.1)	β_1 0.438 (2.5)
			β_0 −0.729 (2.1)
	s.e. 0.009195	s.e. 0.009129	s.e. 0.009049
Trend 3 (0.005)	β 0.126 (8.9)	β 0.257 (9.2)	β_1 0.466 (2.7)
			β_0 −0.672 (2.0)
	s.e. 0.009188	s.e. 0.009090	s.e. 0.009071
Trend 4 (0.0045)	β 0.154 (10.9)	β 0.314 (11.2)	β_1 0.479 (2.7)
			β_0 −0.643 (1.9)
	s.e. 0.009187	s.e. 0.009080	s.e. 0.0090835
Trend 5 (0.004)	β 0.182 (12.9)	β 0.370 (13.2)	β_1 0.493 (2.8)
			β_0 −0.615 (1.89)
	s.e. 0.009189	s.e. 0.009076	s.e. 0.009097
Trend 6 (0.003)	β 0.239 (16.9)	β 0.483 (17.2)	β_1 0.521 (3.0)
			β_0 −0.558 (1.6)
	s.e. 0.0091958	s.e. 0.009088	s.e. 0.009129
Unrestricted	β 0.152 (0.8)	β 0.375 (1.8)	β_1 0.329 (1.6)
			β_0 −0.955 (2.3)
	Trend 0.00454 (1.3)	Trend 0.00396 (2.2)	Trend 0.00996 (2.4)
	s.e. 0.009231	s.e. 0.009119	s.e. 0.0090534

Note: Period is 1962Q1 to 1992Q4, dependent variable is log value-added in UK manufacturing minus labour and capital inputs weighted by their value-added shares. Details of the construction of the labour variable are in Muellbauer (1991).

We estimated a number of variants of each hypothesis, with the coefficient on the base trend restricted to a range of plausible values, or unrestricted. The restriction of the base trend, by removing the collinearity, significantly reduced the standard error of the estimated R&D coefficient.

Table 7.1 shows the results of estimation of the first three hypotheses, with the base trend restricted to various plausible quarterly values (0.003, 0.004, 0.0045, 0.005, 0.006, 0.0072). The upper bound of 0.0072 is given by the value of the base trend when the R&D variable is omitted. We also estimated a variant without a restriction on the base trend.

Note that hypotheses 1 and 2 are restrictions of hypothesis 3. Hypothesis 1 restricts the right-hand side coefficient on capital to equal zero. Hypothesis 2 restricts the right-hand side coefficient on capital to be equal in size but opposite in sign to the coefficient on R&D capital.

As we mentioned earlier, the capital coefficients in the unrestricted trend version of hypothesis 3 are significantly negative, and the base trend in the unrestricted version is implausibly high at almost 1 per cent per quarter. As shown by the following likelihood ratio tests of these restrictions, hypothesis 2 is accepted somewhat more strongly by the data than hypothesis 1.

Likelihood ratio tests for hypothesis 3, restriction $\beta_1 = -\beta_2$

Trend 4 (0.0045)	$\chi^2 (1) = 1.066$
Trend 5 (0.004)	$\chi^2 (1) = 0.586$
Unrestricted trend	$\chi^2 (1) = 2.96$.

Likelihood ratio tests for hypothesis 3, restriction $\beta_2 = 0$

Trend 4 (0.0045)	$\chi^2 (1) = 3.986$
Trend 5 (0.004)	$\chi^2 (1) = 3.634$
Unrestricted trend	$\chi^2 (1) = 5.982$.

On purely statistical grounds then, the preferred model is hypothesis 2. This implies that there are jointly constant returns of degree one to capital, labour and R&D. However, the contribution of capital is around zero, with R&D yielding a coefficient of around 0.375 per cent. These results should be taken not so much as a rejection of a role for capital in production as a symptom of the measurement errors in the capital stock data.

Table 7.2 presents estimates of the trend variables in hypotheses 1 and 2 and compares them with the values of the trend variables when the R&D capital term is omitted. The inclusion of the R&D capital term reduces the importance of the base trend, as is to be expected given their collinearity. However, the R&D capital terms also have some effect on the significance and size of the 1973Q1 trend variable, suggesting that a slowdown in the growth of the R&D capital stock may have had some influence on the slowdown of productivity growth in the 1970s.

If, however, we look at hypothesis 1, which restricts the coefficients on capital and labour to equal their value-added shares, the fit of the model

Table 7.2 *Regression estimates of hypotheses 1 and 2 (base trend unrestricted)*

	With $\beta \ln RDK - \ln K$		With $\beta \ln RDK$		Without R&D terms	
	Coeff.	t-stat	Coeff	t-stat	Coeff	t-stat
Base trend	0.00396	2.2	0.00454	1.3	0.0072	28.9
tr73q1	−0.00461	−8.1	−0.00448	−4.0	−0.0053	−12.9
tr79q3	−0.00829	−5.6	−0.00845	−5.6	−0.0088	−6.0
tr80q4	0.0154	10.5	0.016	11.2	0.016	11.2
Tren	−0.00557	−5.0	−0.00501	−4.7	−0.0049	−4.7
β	0.375	1.8	0.152	0.8		
s.e.	0.009119		0.009231		0.009271	
R^2	0.998		0.998		0.998	
DW	1.70		1.68		1.68	
ADF	−9.4[0.00]		−9.3[0.00]		−9.3[0.00]	
AC F(5,101)	1.14[0.34]		1.10[0.37]		1.03[0.40]	
ARCH F(4,98)	1.50[0.21]		1.80[0.13]		1.80[0.13]	
Normality $\chi^2(2)$	0.866		0.703		0.486	
HS F(31,74)	0.45[0.99]		0.47[0.99]		0.51[0.98]	
RESET F(1,105)	2.6[0.11]		1.1[0.29]		1.0[0.33]	

Notes: Period is 1962Q1 to 1992Q4, dependent variable is log value-added in UK manufacturing minus labour and capital inputs weighted by their value-added shares. Details of the construction of the labour variable are in Muellbauer (1991). Base trend = normal trend, tr73q1 = normal trend starting in 1973Q1 and 0 before, tr79q3 = normal trend starting in 1979Q3 and 0 before, tr80q4 = normal trend starting in 1980Q4 and 0 before. Tren = normal trend starting in 1990Q3, and constant after 1992Q2, 0 before 1990Q3.

ADF	Augmented Dickey-Fuller test, MacKinnon (1991).
AC $(M-N,T-K-M)$	F-test for nth to mth order residual autocorrelation in a model with K regressors and t observations, Harvey (1981).
ARCH $(r,T-2r-K)$	F-test for Autoregressive Conditional Heteroscedasticity of r-th order, Engle (1982).
Normality $\chi^2(2)$	χ^2 test for Normality, Jarque and Bera (1980).
HS	F-test for heteroscedasticity, White (1980).
RESET $(j,T-j-K)$	F-version of the RESET test for j powers, Ramsey (1969).

is rather worse than under hypothesis 2. The coefficient on lnRDK suggests that output has an elasticity of around 0.15 with respect to R&D capital. This is a more plausible magnitude than the estimate of 0.375 from hypothesis 2 when the base trend is not restricted. The latter is obtained at the cost of eliminating capital altogether from the production function.

The poor quality of the CSO capital stock series is the principal problem with our regressions. As we have already discussed, there are good reasons for believing that the official UK physical capital stock series for manufacturing is of poor reliability because of problems of premature scrapping and retirement. Furthermore, O'Mahony (1993) has pointed out that the service lives for physical assets assumed by the CSO (sixty years for buildings, and twenty-four years for equipment) are significantly longer than those assumed by other countries. We used two artificial capital stock series to attempt to improve the model. First, we used the data calculated by O'Mahony on the basis of US service lives (forty and seventeen years, respectively). Second, we calculated an implicit depreciation rate from the official series, and then calculated a new series based on a series of multiples of this depreciation rate (one and a half, two and three times the rate), following the approach of Haskel and Martin (1993) and Lynde and Richmond (1993) among others.

Unfortunately, the empirical results of this exercise were indifferent, with the coefficients on physical capital in unrestricted regressions remaining negative. This suggests that the main problem with the UK capital stock is premature scrapping and unobserved retirement, rather than systematically shorter service lives.

Our findings do tend to confirm the results of other work (such as Griliches, 1980; Mansfield, 1980; and Sterlacchini, 1989) which found a significant relationship between productivity growth and R&D spending. Furthermore, our elasticity estimates are similar to the recent estimates of Coe and Helpman (1993). They estimate that the elasticity of UK productivity with respect to domestic R&D capital is around 0.23.

Conclusion

As we have seen, many studies have found a significant relationship between technological knowledge and productivity. Most such studies have been for the United States, since UK data on technological performance were generally thought to be of poor quality and reliability. This study has constructed a quarterly model of UK total factor productivity between 1962Q1 and 1992Q4. We chose to use measures of UK industrial R&D

spending and technological royalties paid to overseas firms as our innovation indicators, and have discussed their construction and weaknesses at length.

Overall, there are two principal problems with our model. The first, and most important, is the poor quality of the capital stock series. The second is the degree of collinearity between the R&D capital stock and the time trends that are necessary to compensate for capital stock mismeasurement. We have attempted to correct these problems as far as practicable at this stage.

Although proxying capital mismeasurement by shifting time trends is far from perfect, the empirical evidence suggests that unrecorded scrapping increased and service flows fell from 1973 onwards, with a particularly heavy fall between 1979Q3 and 1980Q3 when UK manufacturing contracted by around 16 per cent. After 1980Q4, the trend in output improved considerably and there is little evidence that this rate of growth has slackened over the past few years, after correcting for cyclical utilisation factors.

Our model suggests that the stock of R&D capital (which represents both UK industry-funded Business Enterprise R&D as well as payments for technology imported from abroad) makes a significant contribution to productivity in UK manufacturing over the period considered. This result agrees with many other studies that have found a significant relationship between technological knowledge of various sorts and productivity. However, the role played by physical capital in our model is somewhat ambiguous, although some light has been shed on the exact nature of the capital mismeasurement problem, which seems to stem more from premature scrapping than from systematically over-stated service lives.

All this suggests that the analysis cannot proceed further without either a better capital stock measure, or by using sectoral data, and possibly excluding those sectors where capital stock mismeasurement is most predominant.

Appendix – Innovation data sources and definitions

There are several problems in compiling innovation capital stocks – the choice of deflators, appropriate lags, depreciation rates, and starting values. We deal with these in turn, but first we discuss the sources of the innovation expenditure data themselves.

Construction of a manufacturing BERD series

Official data for current prices manufacturing Business Enterprise R&D (BERD) are available from various CSO and OECD publications for the years 1961, 1964, 1966–9, and 1972–91.[4] Schott (1976) conducted a survey of BERD spending between 1948 and 1970. We spliced this data onto the CSO data to obtain a series back to 1948, and also used the Schott data to make interpolations on the CSO series for the years 1962, 1963 and 1965. We used a linear interpolation for 1970 and 1971.

Industry-funded BERD

Data on the percentage of total BERD funded by industry itself were available in the CSO publications for the years 1964, 1966–69, 1972, 1975, 1981, 1983, 1985–91.[5] We assumed that the proportion was the same for manufacturing BERD as for total BERD. The percentages of total BERD funded by industry for all other years in the period 1961–91 were interpolated. Before 1960 we assumed a constant proportion of 0.6, which is broadly consistent with a comparison of the total BERD data in Schott (1976) with the industry-funded BERD data in Edgerton (1993).

Technological balance of payments data

Data on payments by UK firms to foreign firms for technological licences were available for 1964–70 in CSO *Studies in Official Statistics* No. 21, for 1971–4 in CSO *Studies in Official Statistics* No. 27, for 1975–80 in Ledic and Silbertson (1986), for 1981–5 in OECD *Main Science and Technology Indicators*, and for 1986–90 in Cabinet Office (1993).

Capital stock measurement issues

A deflator for UK BERD

Most studies of R&D spending in the United Kingdom have used the GDP deflator to convert current price spending into constant price spending (see Edgerton, 1993, for example). However, it is unlikely that the prices of the goods and services used in R&D, such as scientific and technical personnel, scientific instruments, computer hardware and software, chemicals, and so on, rise at the same rate as prices in the whole economy. Of course, some components of R&D spending may rise more slowly in price than the GDP deflator. For example, a satisfactory deflator for durable goods should take into account quality changes, such as the increased power and

Table 7A.1 *Alternative measures of R&D costs, 1970–91*

	GDP (E) deflator	R&D deflator
1970	19	18
1975	36	35
1980	72	68
1985	100	100
1990	132	140
1991	140	149

speed of computers. Unfortunately, hedonic price indices are difficult to calculate except for specific goods (see Baily and Gordon, 1989, for further discussion of such issues).

A number of researchers have attempted to construct a deflator for R&D spending. A recent study by Jankowski (1993) is probably the most comprehensive and reliable attempt to construct R&D price indices. He used a Laspeyres weighted average of price indices for five different factor inputs (engineering and scientist salaries, support personnel, materials and supplies, plant and equipment, and other inputs) to construct deflators for twelve US manufacturing industries between 1969 and 1988. His results suggest that the use of industry-specific R&D deflators produces very different results from the use of the GDP deflator.

The latest CSO figures (CSO, 1993) suggest that wages and salaries account for around 42 per cent of total BERD spending. We constructed a weighted average of the index of average earnings of administrative, clerical and technical employees in manufacturing[6] (42 per cent) and the manufacturing producer output prices index[7] (58 per cent). Our R&D deflator has two advantages over the GDP deflator, in that it allows for the importance of wages and salaries in the R&D process, and is based on data for a more appropriate part of the economy. Table 7A.1 compares our constructed R&D deflator with the GDP deflator.[8]

Our R&D deflator is not a perfect substitute for a deflator that properly allows for all the diverse components of the R&D process. It does, though, have the virtue of more realistically approximating R&D costs than the GDP deflator, and shows the clear conclusion that real increases in R&D spending are substantially overstated by the GDP deflator.

However, empirical implementation of our R&D deflator was problematic, since GDP-deflated R&D variables were more stable and significant in our regressions on pages 130–5.

Lag structure

There are likely to be long and significant lags between R&D and productivity change. Mansfield (1985) suggests that research results leak out fairly quickly (within two years in most of the cases he studied), whereas Schott (1976) preferred to use the following declining lag structure which included R&D spending up to six years in the past:

$$RD_t = 0.23R_{t-1} + 0.27R_{t-4} + 0.2R_{t-8} + 0.14R_{t-12} + 0.05R_{t-16} + 0.02R_{t-20} + 0.01R_{t-24}$$

where RD_t is the quantity of R&D knowledge entering the capital stock at time t and R is R&D expenditure.

Some researchers (such as Griliches, 1980) have assumed that R&D spending affects productivity without a lag, while others (such as Mansfield, 1980) have noted that the ratio of R&D to output (known as R&D intensity) changes only slowly over short time periods. However, R&D intensities do change significantly over time, for example, the ratio of BERD to value added in US electronics rose from 16.3 per cent in 1973 to 23.8 per cent in 1989.

All the above discussion suggests that the R&D capital terms in our regressions should be lagged. We tried a number of specifications, first with lags up to twelve quarters, and parsimoniously testing down. In practice the fourth lag was most significant.

Depreciation

To construct a capital stock measure of technological knowledge, one needs to assume a depreciation rate.

$$RDK_t = RDK_{t-1} + RDt - \delta RDK_{t-1}$$

where RDK_t is the R&D capital stock, and RD is the volume of R&D knowledge entering the capital stock.

Most studies of the link between R&D and productivity have argued that the R&D knowledge stock does not depreciate (Griliches, 1988; Budd and Hobbis, 1989; Sterlacchini, 1989). This is usually because such measures provide the best fit in estimation. However, studies of patent renewal data such as Bosworth (1976) suggest that a depreciation rate of 10 per cent would be more appropriate (see also Pakes and Schankerman, 1984).

Base stocks

We tested a variety of base stock assumptions, either using the UK R&D capital stock as calculated by Schott (1976) or assuming that the relationship between the ratio of R&D Capital to Physical Capital over a base period followed the ratio of BERD to Gross Investment. In practice, the best solution was to follow Griliches (1980), who calculated his initial 1958 value as equal to R&D spending in 1958 divided by g, where g was the estimated rate of growth of R&D spending during 1959–64.

Conclusion

We have discussed some issues in constructing R&D capital stocks for the United Kingdom. In practice, it was left to the data to reveal the best specification of the BERD stocks. Parsimonious estimation and sensitivity analysis suggested that the fourth lag of the capital stock of industry-funded BERD (plus technological royalty payments) was most significant, along with a 0 per cent depreciation rate and a base stock calculated following Griliches (1980). Despite the better theoretical basis of our R&D deflator, we found that the GDP deflator performed more consistently during estimation.

8 Anglo-German productivity performance since 1973

MARY O'MAHONY AND KARIN WAGNER

This chapter examines the relative productivity performance of manufacturing industries in two industrial nations, the United Kingdom and Germany.[1] The focus is on comparing performance in the 1980s relative to that achieved in the period 1973 to 1979. It builds on previous research which presented measures of relative manufacturing productivity levels in these two countries in the late 1980s (O'Mahony, 1992a) and attempted to explain these by differences in various forms of capital (O'Mahony, 1992b). This chapter returns to the traditional focus on productivity growth rates by examining the productivity performance in a number of industries within manufacturing. However, it utilises the results of the earlier work by relating productivity growth rates to levels.

The chapter begins with an examination of the cross-industry pattern of productivity growth in the two countries. By relating productivity growth to productivity levels we consider the question of whether there has been any trend towards convergence of productivity levels in the two countries over time. We then ask if productivity growth is correlated with the growth of output or labour input and examine the relationship with average plant size.

Recent contributions to the theory of economic growth (for example Lucas, 1988; Romer, 1990a) emphasise the importance of the accumulation of various forms of capital in explaining cross-country patterns of productivity growth. In the second section we present data on the relative amounts of three forms of capital accumulation in the two countries – that is, fixed capital (equipment and structures), labour force skills and research and development expenditure – and we consider the relationship between capital accumulation and productivity growth.

Productivity growth, productivity levels and convergence

This section examines the labour productivity record of manufacturing industries in Germany and Britain in the 1980s and compares this with their relative performance in the 1970s. Growth rates of gross value added per worker hour are shown in table 8.1 for selected time periods. The growth rates are shown for thirty industries within manufacturing; details of the industry classifications together with data sources are available in O'Mahony *et al.* (1994).

In the period 1973–89 the productivity performance of manufacturing was not very different in either country. Over this time period the growth rate of labour productivity was also similar in Britain and Germany in aggregate manufacturing and neither country had a significant advantage in a count of the number of industries with higher productivity growth. Large differences in the productivity record in the two countries emerge when the period is further sub-divided into the years 1973–9 and 1979–89. In general, productivity growth in British manufacturing was historically low in the period 1973–9 which is notorious as a time when British industry experienced severe difficulties (eleven of the thirty industries experienced negative productivity growth). In Germany productivity growth rates remained positive in all industries but the growth rates were somewhat lower than those achieved in the previous decade (see O'Mahony *et al.*, 1994 for details).

In the decade from 1979 to 1989 British manufacturing industry showed a remarkable turnaround in terms of labour productivity performance. Only five of the thirty industries had lower productivity than for 1973–9 and eight industries showed growth rates which were higher than the 'golden age' of 1960–73 (*ibid.*). The increase was most marked in iron and steel, which showed a pronounced reduction in its labour force of 63 per cent between 1979 and 1989. The important motor vehicles sector showed a pronounced improvement where there was also evidence of a reduction in overmanning, of a little under half the 1979 workforce. This may be due in part to Japanese transplants which implemented new methods of production such as total quality control and job flexibility.

Experience in Germany during this period was very different. In general annual productivity growth rates slowed considerably from those experienced in 1973–9. Productivity growth was very low in this decade in traditional areas of German strength such as mechanical engineering and vehicles. The problems encountered by these industries are currently the subject of much press coverage in Germany.

Table 8.1 *Growth rates of labour productivity, % per annum*

	Germany			United Kingdom		
	1973–89	1973–9	1979–89	1973–89	1973–9	1979–89
Chemicals	2.97	3.00	2.96	3.02	-0.52	5.15
Mineral oil refining	2.22	4.35	0.94	0.97	-1.12	2.23
Plastic products	2.27	2.32	2.24	2.69	1.07	3.66
Rubber products	1.43	1.26	1.54	2.59	-0.74	4.58
Mineral products	2.48	3.11	2.11	2.00	-0.81	3.69
Ceramic goods	1.49	1.85	1.27	1.79	1.96	1.69
Glass	3.70	4.85	3.02	2.68	0.52	3.97
Iron & steel	3.43	3.76	3.24	5.55	-8.69	14.10
Non-ferrous metals	3.09	4.90	2.00	0.99	-1.74	2.62
Plant & steelwork	1.81	2.68	1.28	1.74	2.50	1.29
Mechanical engineering	1.96	2.69	1.52	2.07	0.70	2.89
Office machinery	6.74	11.25	4.04	7.69	10.15	6.21
Motor vehicles	2.49	4.42	1.33	3.63	0.68	5.41
Shipbuilding	1.83	0.76	2.46	3.81	0.86	5.57
Aerospace	1.87	1.75	1.94	3.51	-5.31	8.81
Electrical engineering	4.63	6.29	3.63	3.65	2.97	4.06
Instrument engineering	2.05	2.56	1.74	3.48	3.40	3.53
Finished metal products	2.45	2.70	2.29	2.59	2.43	2.68
Leisure equipment[a]	2.81	3.43	2.43	2.04	1.21	2.54
Timber	2.55	1.78	3.02	1.94	-0.74	3.55
Wood products	0.65	1.34	0.23	1.66	1.15	1.96
Paper & board	3.90	5.96	2.67	3.40	-0.28	5.62
Paper products	1.63	1.92	1.45	1.47	0.98	1.76
Printing & publishing	2.10	3.27	1.39	2.64	0.31	4.04
Leather & footwear	2.82	2.26	3.16	2.10	3.84	1.06
Textiles	4.30	6.29	3.10	3.48	2.49	4.07
Clothing	3.21	3.59	2.99	3.66	4.88	2.93
Food	2.94	3.12	2.83	2.28	-0.37	3.87
Drink	3.54	2.51	4.15	1.44	2.52	0.80
Tobacco	5.65	7.90	4.30	3.49	-0.26	5.74
Total manufacturing	2.71	3.37	2.30	2.86	0.72	4.15
Summary statistics						
Mean	2.83	3.60	2.38	2.80	0.80	4.00
Std	1.26	2.18	0.99	1.34	3.10	2.55

	1973–89	1973–9	1979–89
corr[b]	0.62	0.36	0.27
N (G > U)[c]	15	24	3

Notes:
[a]Toys, sports equipment and musical instruments.
[b]Correlation between labour productivity growth in Germany and the UK.
[c] Number of industries where productivity growth in Germany was greater than in the UK.

The correlation between relative (German minus UK) productivity growth in the two periods 1973–9 and 1979–89 was significantly negative at –0.68 so that, on average, industries where the British performance was relatively poor in the earlier period made up the deficit in the later period. From 1973–9 twenty-four industries in Germany had higher productivity growth than in Britain but in the following decade only three German industries performed better.

Table 8.1 shows that there is a similarity in the cross-industry pattern of labour productivity growth in the two countries over the entire period 1973–89. Thus in both countries higher than average labour productivity growth rates were recorded in chemicals, iron & steel, office machinery, electrical engineering, textiles, clothing and tobacco, whereas lower than average productivity growth was experienced in each country in ceramic goods, mechanical engineering and finished metal products, timber, wood products and printing. In the long run countries at similar stages of industrial development are likely to imitate each other's technological changes so that the high correlation of productivity growth rates in the two countries over long time periods is not unexpected. These correlations are, however, considerably smaller for the short time periods.

The low or negative correlation between relative labour productivity growth in adjacent time periods may reflect, among other things, a catch-up process whereby industries with a pronounced productivity level disadvantage in 1973 experienced faster relative productivity growth in subsequent decades as firms imitated technological improvements in the leading country. There is a considerable literature on the process of catch-up and convergence among industrial economies which concludes that, for the aggregate economy, these countries' levels of labour productivity have converged in the postwar period (see Baumol, 1986, Maddison, 1991). The evidence for convergence in manufacturing, however, is not as strong, although there appears to be some local convergence among European countries (see Broadberry, 1993). Convergence at the aggregate (or sectoral) level is predicted by the neoclassical theory of economic growth which assumes constant returns in the production function. Recent contributions to growth theory (for example, Romer, 1986, 1990a,b; Lucas, 1988) emphasise external benefits of capital accumulation which give rise to increasing returns at the aggregate level. In these models it is possible for one country to achieve a permanent productivity level advantage.

At the industry level the scope for increasing returns from learning by doing may be more pronounced than at the sectoral or aggregate economy level owing to a country's ability to exploit its comparative advantage in certain product areas. Thus, one country achieving an initial productivity advantage in an industry, say because of a new technological process which is protected by patent, could lead in the short run to diverging productivity levels if the industry grew rapidly in that country and there were significant productivity gains from learning by doing. There could even be a permanent effect if the industry in the laggard country was wiped out by competition. An example is the manufacturing of sewing machines in Britain where the last manufacturer closed its doors in 1979. It is interesting, therefore, to see if the observed sectoral or aggregate convergence of productivity levels across countries is replicated at the industry level. This requires estimates of relative levels of output per worker hour. O'Mahony (1992a) presents relative productivity levels for fourteen branch industries within manufacturing for 1987. In that study estimates of industries' relative producer prices were used to convert output to a common currency. This was deemed to give a more accurate picture of relative productivity levels than those using the official exchange rate since the latter is influenced by short-term capital movements and so, at any one point in time, is a poor indicator of differences in relative producer prices. The estimates of relative prices were based either on unit values of products (values divided by quantities) or on purchasing power parities collected by the OECD. These price estimates were constructed for a large number of products and so enabled the calculation of relative productivity for the more detailed thirty industries considered in this chapter (see van Ark, 1993, for a discussion of methodological issues in constructing price estimates).

The productivity levels for 1987 were based on data from each country's census of production rather than the national accounts data, used to construct productivity growth rates. The censuses report output and employment from the same firms whereas it is not clear if output and employment levels in the national accounts are consistent with each other, in particular in Britain where these data are collected by two different statistical offices. The time series data on productivity growth in table 8.1 were used to yield estimates of relative productivity levels back to 1973 and forward to 1989.

Table 8.2 shows the productivity level estimates for selected years. In 1973 German aggregate manufacturing had a clear productivity level advantage and this showed a dramatic increase between 1973 and 1979. The reversal of the productivity trends in the following decade led to a productivity gap in 1989 which was lower than in the early 1970s. In 1973, twenty of the thirty industries showed levels of labour productivity in Germany greater than in Britain; by 1979 this had risen to twenty-seven but fallen back to twenty-three by 1989.

Table 8.2 *Labour productivity levels in Germany relative to the UK (UK = 100)*

	1973	1979	1989
Chemicals	103.3	127.6	102.5
Mineral oil refining	88.2	122.5	107.7
Plastic products	117.3	126.4	109.7
Rubber products	124.5	140.3	103.5
Mineral products	84.1	106.4	90.9
Ceramic goods	131.5	130.6	125.2
Glass	99.9	129.5	117.7
Iron & steel	124.8	263.4	88.9
Non-ferrous metals	80.5	119.9	112.7
Plant & steelwork	123.7	125.0	124.9
Mechanical engineering	125.9	141.9	123.7
Office machinery	100.7	107.6	86.6
Motor vehicles	148.5	186.0	123.7
Shipbuilding	144.6	143.7	105.3
Aerospace	131.2	200.4	100.9
Electrical engineering	83.5	101.9	97.6
Instrument engineering	180.5	171.6	143.6
Finished metal products	130.0	132.1	127.1
Leisure equipment	115.4	131.8	130.4
Timber	95.3	110.9	105.1
Wood products	176.4	178.4	150.1
Paper & board	147.9	215.1	160.2
Paper products	164.9	174.4	169.1
Printing & publishing	158.5	189.3	145.3
Leather & footwear	93.3	84.9	104.8
Textiles	88.3	110.8	100.6
Clothing	133.5	123.5	124.2
Food	101.5	125.3	112.9
Drink	59.3	59.3	83.0
Tobacco	42.1	68.7	59.5
Total manufacturing	119.4	140.0	116.5

The estimates in table 8.2 show clearly the contrasting patterns of relative productivity in the period from 1973 to 1979 compared with the following decade. In the earlier period Britain's relative position showed a marked deterioration even in traditional areas of British strength such as food, textiles and chemicals. In the decade 1979–89 in some industries, most notably iron and steel, aerospace and motor vehicles, the British turnaround was remarkable, but Britain improved her relative position in almost all sectors. The only significant deterioration was in leather & footwear and drink and there was a small increase in Germany's advantage in clothing.

Table 8.3 *Regression results: convergence*
Dependent variable is $\{ln(PG_t/PG_{t-s}) - ln(PU_t/PU_{t-s})\}/(t-s)$

| | Relative productivity levels (*LEV*) (Germany/UK) | |
	1973	1979
1973–89	-0.028	–
	(7.57)	
1973–79	-0.030	–
	(1.85)	
1979–89	–	-0.059
		(3.60)

Notes: *PG, PU* = labour productivity in Germany, UK, respectively, *LEV* for each year is the log of the ratio of German to UK productivity, absolute values of *t*-ratios in parentheses, standard errors are heteroscedastic consistent estimates.

Given the estimates of productivity growth rates and levels in tables 8.1 and 8.2, we are now in a position to consider the question of whether there has been convergence of productivity levels over time. We first look at the relationship between productivity growth and initial levels of productivity by regressing the former on the latter – the results are given in table 8.3. The first column shows that relative productivity growth over the entire period 1973–89 is significantly negatively related to relative productivity levels in 1973. Thus those industries which showed a high German productivity level advantage in 1973 experienced lower rates of productivity growth in the following years, enabling some catch up of British productivity levels to those in Germany. The coefficients are all negative, implying trends towards convergence in all time periods, but the coefficient for the period 1973–9 is not significant at the 95 per cent level.

An alternative way of looking at convergence is to ask if the variation across industries in relative productivity has decreased over time. Barro and Sala-i-Martin (1991) suggest a distinction between β-convergence (a negative correlation between productivity growth rates and productivity levels) and α-convergence (a reduction over time in the coefficient of variation of relative productivity levels) and argue that neither type of convergence necessarily implies the other. Thus in an analysis of industry data we may see on average β-convergence but in a small number of industries we could also observe either country having a sustained increasing productivity advantage so that the variation across industries increases over time. The coefficient of variation of relative productivity levels increased from 0.28 in 1973 to 0.31 in 1979 but decreased significantly

Table 8.4 *Growth of output and labour input, % per annum*

			1973–89	1973–9	1979–89
Germany					
	Output	mean	0.61	0.30	0.80
		std	2.05	2.49	2.03
		N < 0	12	14	11
	Annual total	mean	-2.22	-3.29	-1.58
	hours	std	1.92	2.30	2.08
		N < 0	28	27	26
	correlation (PG,QG)		0.41	0.39	0.07
	correlation (PG,LG)		-0.20	-0.37	-0.25
United Kingdom					
	Output	mean	-0.45	-1.86	0.39
		std	2.19	3.37	3.01
		N < 0	18	23	15
	Annual total	mean	-3.25	-2.65	-3.61
	hours	std	1.87	1.56	2.67
		N < 0	29	29	28
	correlation (PU,QU)		0.52	0.89	0.55
	correlation (PU,LU)		-0.12	-0.11	-0.35
	correlation (QG,QU)		0.67	0.01	0.71
	correlation (LG,LU)		0.58	0.48	0.54

Notes: *PG, PU* = labour productivity growth, *QG,QU* = output growth, *LG,LU* = annual hours growth, *N* < 0 = number of industries with negative growth rates.

thereafter to 0.20 in 1989. Thus, on this measure, there is evidence of divergence of relative productivity levels in the 1970s but strong convergence in the 1980s yielding a much lower dispersion in 1989 than was observed in 1973.

We next examine briefly the growth of output and labour input. Table 8.4 shows summary statistics of growth in output, employment and annual hours worked in both countries. In Germany mean output growth was positive for each of the time periods whereas in British manufacturing mean output growth was lower in all periods than in Germany and was negative for the period 1973–89; this in turn was mostly due to strong negative output growth over the period 1973–9. In general more industries experienced negative output growth in the United Kingdom than in Germany. In 1979 twenty-three industries in Britain had lower output levels than in 1973 whereas the comparable figure for Germany was fifteen. In eighteen industries in the UK and thirteen in Germany output in 1989 was lower than in 1973.

In both countries mean labour input was reduced in all time periods.

Labour input was reduced at a considerably greater rate in the UK post-1979, owing to a very large reduction in employment. Manufacturing employment in Britain declined by nearly three million from 7.7 million workers in 1960 to 4.9 million in 1989 with two million lost in the decade 1979–89. There was some reduction in numbers in employment in Germany but of more importance in that country was the reduction in annual hours per worker due to both a shortening of the working week and increases in the number of paid holidays. Salter (1966) found a positive significant correlation between labour productivity growth and output growth for a cross-section of British industries for the period 1924–50. Oulton and O'Mahony (1994) found a similar correlation for a cross-section of British industries both for the period 1954–86 and the subperiods 1954–73 and 1973–86. Table 8.4 shows that these results are replicated for both countries in all time periods although the correlation between output growth and labour productivity growth is very low in Germany in the period 1979–89. Productivity growth in general is not significantly related to labour input growth over the long time period; this was also the result found by Salter and by Oulton and O'Mahony. However there is a significant negative correlation in Germany for the period 1973–9 and in the UK for the period 1979–89. The last two rows of table 8.4 show that the cross-section pattern of output growth, and to a lesser extent the reduction in labour input, is similar in the two countries. Thus, on average, industries with high growth in output tend to have high labour productivity growth and these are likely to be the same industries in both countries. The exception was the period 1973–9 where the correlation of output growth across the two countries was not significantly different from zero.

Finally in this section we consider the influence of differences in the average size of plants in industries in the two countries. Table 8.5 shows the median plant size in 1987 for the thirty industries. The median plant size is measured as the plant size for which 50 per cent of the workforce are employed in plants with more than that number of employees. It is preferable to the mean plant size since it is less sensitive to the lower tail of the employment distribution.

The median plant size was larger in Germany in aggregate manufacturing but it was not true that Germany operated at a larger scale in all industries. In fact in thirteen industries the median plant size was larger in the UK. The cross-section correlation of median plant size was 0.68, indicating a similar distribution of plant scale across industries in the two countries. Davies and Caves (1987) show that the median plant size can be interpreted as a measure of economies of scale. With this interpretation we should generally observe a positive correlation between labour

Table 8.5 *Median plant size, 1987*

	Germany	UK
Chemicals	1666	503
Mineral oil refining	533	1335
Plastic products	162	131
Rubber products	1701	430
Mineral products	61	106
Ceramic goods	158	390
Glass	440	377
Iron & steel	2116	715
Non ferrous metals	543	208
Plant & steelwork	326	225
Mechanical engineering	373	159
Office machinery	1705	536
Motor vehicles	2446	1432
Shipbuilding	1221	1961
Aerospace	2397	2337
Electrical engineering	707	502
Instrument engineering	60	184
Finished metal products	180	113
Toys, musical & sports goods	60	48
Timber & board	40	50
Wood products	36	69
Paper & pulp	596	367
Paper products	177	176
Printing & publishing	69	115
Leather & footwear	109	157
Textiles	232	178
Clothing	63	122
Food	20	345
Drink	124	309
Tobacco	659	1506
Total manufacturing	358	261

productivity growth and median plant size. But in some circumstances there may be significant diseconomies, for example Prais (1981) suggested that poor industrial relations in large plants gave rise to a negative correlation between median plant size and labour productivity in the UK. Table 8.6 shows that these correlations are positive for all time periods in Germany and mostly positive for the UK. The one exception is the period 1973–9 in Britain when the correlation is significantly negative. The correlation is positive and highly significant in the UK in the following

Table 8.6 *Correlation between labour productivity growth and median plant size*

	1973–89	1973–9	1979–89
Germany	0.15	0.18	0.08
United Kingdom	0.28	-0.35	0.49

decade. Thus the results in table 8.6 confirm Prais's result for the 1970s but show that this adverse effect of plant size on productivity was not a constraint in the 1980s.

The use of median plant size as a measure of scale economies may be misleading in practice since the optimal plant size varies across industries. For example in electrical engineering a plant employing three hundred workers is small but this would be considered large in the clothing industry. Given this it may make more sense to correlate productivity growth in each country with the relative median plant size across the two countries. We find that the only significant relationship is for the UK in the period 1979–89 and this correlation coefficient is negative. Thus in the 1980s British manufacturing growth rates were higher in industries where they had a size disadvantage with Germany. At first sight this result seems counterintuitive. But there was a considerable reduction in median plant size in Britain in the 1980s as compared with the 1970s which could be interpreted as an increase in competition (see the discussion in O'Mahony, 1992a). Lansbury and Mayes (in chapter 2), however, do not find a strong relationship between firm turnover and productivity growth.

Explanatory factors: fixed capital, human capital and R & D

This section examines the contribution of investment in various forms of capital to explaining labour productivity growth in the two countries. We will examine in turn the influence of fixed capital (plant & machinery, vehicles and structures), labour force skills and research & development expenditure. We examine the trends in these explanatory factors and some simple correlations between these and labour productivity growth. Finally we present some multiple regression results which combine the results for the influence of capital with the results on convergence and plant size discussed above.

Fixed capital

Estimates of fixed capital stocks were calculated for all years from 1973 to 1989; details of the estimation methods and data sources are given in O'Mahony *et al.*, 1994. Table 8.7 shows summary statistics on both levels

Table 8.7 *Productivity and fixed capital*

I. Levels of fixed capital per unit of labour input (1985 £ per 1000 hours worked)	1973	1979	1989
Germany			
Total manufacturing	16363	21774	27828
mean	19009	28665	37418
std	16442	31732	37004
United Kingdom			
Total manufacturing	10698	14009	21866
mean	14143	17940	30517
std	19847	22136	38106
N (G > U)	28	29	28
correlation (KG,KU)	0.94	0.98	0.96

II. Growth of fixed capital per unit of labour input	1973–89	1973–9	1979–89
Germany			
Total manufacturing	3.32	4.76	2.45
mean	4.16	5.98	3.06
std	1.44	2.40	1.58
correlation (dPG,dKG)	0.30	0.42	0.18
United Kingdom			
Total manufacturing	4.47	4.49	4.45
mean	4.83	4.66	4.93
std	1.36	1.77	1.78
correlation (dPU,dKU)	0.45	0.29	0.38
correlation (dKG,dKU)	0.36	0.20	0.26
correlation (dPG,KG)	0.11	0.17	-0.03
correlation (dPU,KU)	-0.17	-0.27	0.08

Notes: dPG,dPU = labour productivity growth, dKG,dKU = growth in capital per unit of labour, all growth rates are in per cent per annum.

and growth rates of fixed capital per unit of labour input. In aggregate manufacturing fixed capital intensity in Germany was about 50 per cent higher than in Britain in 1973 but fell back to less than 30 per cent in the late 1980s. Germany had a fixed capital advantage in almost all industries from the 1970s but in Germany there appears to have been a considerable reduction in capital intensity growth in the decade 1979–89. The cross-industry pattern of levels of capital intensity were remarkably similar in the two countries.

In general the growth in fixed capital intensity was positively correlated with labour productivity growth in all time periods but the correlations were small in some cases: in particular, in Germany during the period 1979–89. In contrast to labour productivity growth, the cross-section correlations between capital intensity growth in Germany and the UK were largely insignificant so that the two counties have not generally experienced similar cross-industry patterns of growth in fixed capital input. We also examined the correlation between the level of capital intensity and the growth rate of labour productivity. A positive correlation could occur if technical progress is embodied in capital goods leading to greater productivity growth in more capital intensive industries. Also, as suggested by David (1975) it may be easier to improve capital intensive technologies, that is, local technical progress which involves small improvements to production techniques may occur more readily the more machinery intensive is the production process. The final two rows of table 8.7 show the cross-section correlations between labour productivity growth and the levels of capital intensity, the latter measured by the average of the capital labour ratios for the end points of each time period. For the time periods considered in this chapter there is no evidence of such a relationship. The correlation is in fact negative (but insignificant) for the period 1973–9 in the UK and for 1979–89 for Germany.

Human capital

The above discussion focused on the role of physical capital. We next consider the role of human capital in explaining labour productivity. Data on the proportion of workers with various certified qualifications are available from the labour force surveys from the end of the 1970s. Table 8.8 shows the division of the workforces into those with higher level, intermediate level and no qualifications for aggregate manufacturing and summary statistics over the thirty industries for both countries.

It is immediately apparent that the proportion of the workforce with no certified skills is much lower in Germany than in the UK for both years but that the German advantage is mostly at the intermediate rather than the upper level. If we compare the UK and Germany for 1978/9 we see that only seven German industries had greater proportions of the workforce qualified at the upper level.[2] There were however some quality differences in this category. Most of the British awards were first degrees whereas in Germany the emphasis is on Masters degrees. In addition the number of employees with Doctorates in chemistry, physics, engineering and technology was higher in Germany than in Britain (Prais 1989; Mason and Wagner, 1993). In 1978/9 all thirty industries in Germany had higher proportions qualified at the intermediate level. In fact in twenty-five

Table 8.8 *Proportion of the workforce with certified qualifications*

	1978/9			1989		
	U	I	N	U	I	N
Germany						
Total manufacturing	3.6	60.9	35.5	6.6	67.0	26.4
mean	3.8	61.1	35.1	6.3	66.2	27.5
std	3.9	7.7	9.3	6.1	5.9	8.4
United Kingdom						
Total manufacturing	4.7	24.4	71.0	7.9	35.2	56.8
mean	4.9	23.2	71.9	7.7	35.0	57.3
std	3.5	10.6	12.1	5.4	12.0	13.8

Notes: U = upper level (degree and equivalent or higher degree), I = intermediate level (all certified qualifications below degree level but above general schooling included served apprentices), N = no qualifications.

industries the German intermediate proportion was more than twice the British and in eleven the ratio of German to British intermediate proportion was more than three.

The growth in skill proportions over the period 1978/9 to 1989 was similar in the two countries at the upper level but was considerably greater in Britain at the intermediate level. Thus the mean annual percentage growth rate of the proportion of the workforce with upper level qualifications was 4.6 per cent in Germany and 4.7 per cent in the UK and the corresponding growth rates for intermediate level proportions were 0.8 per cent and 4.6 per cent, respectively. At the upper level fifteen industries witnessed greater annual percentage growth rates in Britain. At the intermediate level the British growth rates were higher for twenty-nine industries, the exception being textiles. Despite this superior UK growth the German advantage in intermediate skills remained very high in all industries by 1989.

Up to now we have looked at the development of Anglo-German differences in skill proportions but it is worthwhile to consider the development in absolute numbers which shows a very diverse picture in the two countries. In Germany total employment was reduced slightly at an annual rate of 0.2 per cent over the period 1978–89. Decomposing this into skill groups shows that the reduction was concentrated in unskilled workers which declined from 3.03 million to 2.25 million or 2.7 per cent per annum. The number of workers qualified at the upper level increased considerably from 307,000 to 551,000, representing an annual increase of 5.3 per cent, whereas the number of workers qualified to intermediate level increased slightly from 5.2 million to 5.6 million or 0.7 per cent per annum.

In Britain we have already mentioned the huge reduction in employment in manufacturing of about two million workers from 1979 to 1989. This represented an annual decrease of 3.4 per cent per annum and as in Germany was concentrated among the unskilled which declined at a rate of 5.5 per cent per annum. The number of workers qualified to the upper level did show an increase from 325,000 to 389,000 or 1.8 per cent per annum but the number with intermediate qualifications was virtually static with an increase of fewer than 40,000 workers or 0.2 per cent per annum. These figures show that in Britain the improvement in the skill structure over this period was due almost entirely to the reduction in unskilled workers and is not based on a policy of improving the skills of the labour force as a whole by companies or the government.

The cross-section correlations between the skill proportions in the two countries were high, at 0.71 for upper level and 0.58 for the intermediate level in 1978/9, and these had not altered significantly by 1989. Therefore, there is some similarity in the relative skill intensity of industries in the two countries. In both countries engineering industries have the highest percentages of skilled workers followed by the intermediate goods industries with consumer goods having the lowest percentages, in particular at the upper level. On the other hand the cross-section correlations of the annual percentage growth rates in skill proportions in the two countries were insignificant: 0.06 for upper and 0.11 for intermediate levels. We now come to a consideration of the impact of skills on productivity growth. A series of publications by the National Institute (Daly *et al.*, 1985; Steedman and Wagner, 1987, 1989; and Prais and Wagner, 1988) have exemplified the impact of labour force skills on relative Anglo-German productivity. On the basis of matched plant comparisons it became obvious that skilled shopfloor employees are better equipped than semi-skilled to perform a number of functions which raise productivity. Thus skilled workers raise productivity by operating more machinery and also are better able to do fast and frequent changeovers of production processes or new products, recognise faults in machinery before serious breakdowns take place and adjust machinery to accommodate different materials. These factors not only raise output per worker but also raise the quality and complexity of products and therefore enhance their value added. In all four matched plant comparisons the matched goods showed, on average, a higher quality and complexity in the German plants.

O'Mahony (1993) shows that labour productivity levels in Germany relative to the UK are positively related to differences in skill levels. Here we are concerned to see if skills can help explain labour productivity growth rates. As for fixed capital, it may be the case that productivity

Table 8.9 *Labour productivity and labour force skills*

	1973–89	1973–9	1979–89
Germany			
correlation of labour productivity growth with:			
Upper proportion 1978	0.23	0.32	0.05
Intermediate proportion 1978	-0.25	-0.13	-0.33
No qualifications 1978	0.11	-0.02	0.26
growth in upper	–	–	0.16
growth in intermediate	–	–	0.36
growth in no qualifications	–	–	-0.38
United Kingdom			
correlation of labour productivity growth with:			
Upper proportion 1979	0.41	0.21	0.19
Intermediate proportion 1979	0.13	-0.18	0.24
No qualifications 1979	-0.23	0.10	-0.26
growth in upper	–	–	-0.10
growth in intermediate	–	–	0.02
growth in no qualifications	–	–	-0.42

growth is higher the greater the skill intensity of the industry. The implementation of new technical processes may be easier the greater the skills of the workforce. Data limitations mean that the 1978/79 skill intensities are used rather than the average of each period's end points. Table 8.9 shows that in all subperiods productivity growth is positively correlated with the proportion of workers with upper level qualifications but the relationship is very weak for Germany in the 1980s. The relationship between intermediate skills and productivity growth is less clear cut – for Germany the correlations are all negative and significantly so for the period 1979–89. The signs of the correlations are mixed for Britain, being negative in the 1970s and positive in the 1980s.

For the period 1979–89 we can examine the relationship between labour productivity growth and the change in the skill proportions. Table 8.9 shows that the correlations with the proportion of unskilled workers are significantly negative in both countries. These data therefore provide some evidence that industries whose skills proportions increased most in the period 1979–89 were those who achieved higher labour productivity growth. Dividing the growth in skill proportions into upper and intermediate levels shows a significant positive correlation only for intermediate skills in Germany.

Finally in this section we consider the possibility that different skill levels in the two countries lead to different investment patterns. In the clothing industry in the UK, which has a relatively high proportion of un-skilled workers, more modern equipment was installed than in Germany to overcome skill shortages. This included costly computer controlled grading of patterns and lay planning. Further, as more standardised prod-ucts were manufactured they were able to use more automated dedicated machinery and to buy specialised machinery. In contrast, automated machinery had disappeared in Germany, where conventional sewing machines are used for small batches of highly styled blouses and shirts.

An opposite example became clear in the furniture industry; this time it was more modern in Germany as only the computerised machinery could handle the customised production. Even small German firms used highly sophisticated computer numerically controlled (CNC) woodworking machinery. CNC edge-banders formed part of a linked CNC machin-ery unit, linked machine lines carried out to cut panels to precise sizes and do two-way edge-banding, milling and drilling. In Britain fully linked machine lines with automatic feed and automatic off-line were hardly seen because the managers feared large losses in production if one of the linked machines went wrong. Thus traditional machinery was found in Britain.

These examples suggest that there may be some connection between skill levels and investment in fixed capital. In Germany capital growth and skill levels, both upper and intermediate, were positively correlated and significant for most periods, the exception being the final decade 1979–89. In Britain the correlations were generally smaller and only signifi-cant after 1979. In terms of labour productivity growth it is interest-ing to look at the correlation with the interaction of fixed capital and skill levels measured by the product of the two. For Germany labour produc-tivity growth was found to be on average highest in industries with com-bined high levels of skills and high rates of investment for the period 1973–79 but not for the years 1979–89. In Britain a significant correlation is only apparent from 1979. In that decade we can also examine the correlation of labour productivity growth with the product of capital growth and skill growth. Here we find a significant positive relationship only for German intermediate skills.

Research and development

The final explanatory factor considered in this section is research and development expenditure. Periodic surveys of R&D expenditure were avail-able in both countries from the early 1960s. Fixed capital is measured as gross stocks derived by cumulating investment over a number of years as explained above. We use a similar procedure for research and development expenditures. The difficulty here is in choosing an average service life for these expenditures. No direct information is available on this but we do have a regression estimate of the coefficient on R&D from O'Mahony (1994) of about 0.05. The procedure adopted was to calculate for aggregate manufacturing the number of years of R&D expenditure which gives this coefficient value – this turned out to be eight years.[3]

Table 8.10 shows R&D per unit of labour input for total manufacturing and summary statistics for the thirty industries – detailed tables by industry for selected years are available in O'Mahony et al. (1994). From the early 1970s R&D intensity has remained higher in Germany than in Britain both in aggregate manufacturing and in the majority of industries. An examination of R&D intensity may, however, understate Germany's advantage since the total amount of R&D may confer external benefits which can be of use in more firms than those where the actual research is undertaken – R&D increases the general stock of knowledge available to everyone. These external benefits from R&D have been much emphasised in the recent literature on endogenous growth, for example see Romer (1990a). Since German manufacturing represents a much greater proportion of the total economy than in Britain the total level of R&D expenditure is considerably greater in Germany.

In general the cross-industry distribution has a very large variance since R&D intensity is particularly high in a small number of industries, that is chemicals, mineral oil refining, office machinery, aerospace and electrical engineering. This is confirmed by the cross-industry correlations of R&D intensity in the two countries, as shown in table 8.10, which is very high in all years. In Germany the R&D intensity of the aerospace industry is much higher than in Britain but the total research effort is similar in the two countries since employment is considerably greater in Britain. Office machinery is the most research intensive industry in Britain and in this industry Britain has a clear R&D advantage since employment is lower than in Germany. Turning to growth rates, table 8.10 shows that in aggregate manufacturing growth rates of R&D intensity in Germany were considerably higher than in the UK over the period 1973–9 but the growth rates in Britain overtook those in Germany in the final decade 1979–89. The growth in R&D intensity in Britain was pronounced in the iron and steel industry which showed the greatest turnaround in labour productivity growth. However in that decade the coefficient of variation is much higher in Britain so that even then the majority of industries showed higher growth rates in Germany. There was little similarity in the two countries in the cross-industry pattern of R&D intensity growth.

We next look at the relationship between labour productivity growth

Table 8.10 *Research and development expenditure*

I. R & D expenditure per unit of labour input.
1985 £ per 1000 hours worked

	1973	1979	1989
Germany			
Total manufacturing	1784	3332	5288
mean	2269	3670	4711
std	7011	9643	9054
United Kingdom			
Total manufacturing	2090	2446	4481
mean	2391	2771	4213
std	4215	4983	7308
$N (G > U)$	10	20	22
correlation (RDG, RDU)	0.83	0.82	0.76

II. Annual average growth of R&D per unit of labour input

	1973–89	1973–9	1979–89
Aggregate manufacturing			
Germany	6.79	10.41	4.62
United Kingdom	4.77	2.62	6.05
Sample statistics			
Germany			
mean	8.06	11.47	6.02
std	3.45	3.96	4.00
United Kingdom			
mean	2.55	-0.30	4.26
std	3.63	4.92	6.05
$N (G > U)$	25	30	18
correlation $(dRDG, dRDU)$	-0.25	0.11	-0.09

Notes: *RDG, RDU* is R&D expenditure per unit of labour input in Germany and the UK, respectively, *dRD* is the growth in R&D intensity.

and R&D. The correlations are summarised in table 8.11. In Germany the correlations are close to zero in all periods and this is true also for the UK in the 1970s. Labour productivity growth is negatively correlated with the growth in R&D intensity in Germany in the decade 1979/89 but the corresponding correlation is positive and significant in the UK. These results are not significantly altered if we include the absolute levels of R&D expenditure rather than its intensity. Thus only in the UK is there a strong link between R&D activity and labour productivity growth.

Multiple regressions

Finally we present the results of some multiple regressions showing the influence of the explanatory factors discussed above together with the

Table 8.11 *Labour productivity and research & development*

	1973–89	1973–9	1979–89
Germany			
correlation of labour productivity growth with:			
R&D intensity	-0.03	-0.06	-0.03
Growth in R&D intensity	-0.05	0.24	-0.18
Growth in R&D levels	-0.16	0.03	-0.29
United Kingdom			
correlation of labour productivity growth with:			
R&D intensity	0.44	-0.04	0.33
Growth in R&D intensity	0.43	0.14	0.31
Growth in R&D levels	0.41	0.10	0.16

productivity levels at the beginning of each period. The regressions were run for each country separately and the results are shown in table 8.12. For the long time period 1973–89 the combination of capital variables and relative productivity levels explains a significant proportion of the variance of productivity growth in the two countries. The signs of the variables are mostly as expected in the German equation but both R&D intensity and intermediate skills are negative and the significance level of fixed capital is low. In contrast fixed capital is highly significant in the UK equation.

For the subperiods the coefficient on fixed capital is generally insignificant for Germany and smaller than in the UK. The proportion of upper level skills has a significant positive effect on labour productivity growth in both countries for 1973–9 but is insignificant in the period 1979–89. The coefficients on intermediate skills proportions are generally negative and significantly so for the long period, 1973–89. This variable is also significantly negative in Germany for the period 1979–89. The poor performance of the intermediate skills variable may be because it is likely to be highly correlated with an omitted variable, namely that capturing industrial relations conditions. Intermediate skill intensity is highest in industries such as engineering which also have high proportions of the workforce who are members of labour unions. The relatively low productivity in Britain in the years 1973–9 and Germany in the years 1979–89 could be due to the effect of adverse industrial relations. The coefficient on R&D intensity is generally positive for the UK but nowhere significant, and is negative and significant in the German equations. The growth in R&D intensity has little explanatory power for either country, the exception being for the UK over the period 1973–89. The coefficient on plant

Table 8.12a *Regression results, selected time periods, Germany*
Dependent variable is annual growth rates of labour productivity

	1973–89	1973–9	1979–89	1979–89
constant	0.053	0.067	0.047	0.044
	(4.09)**	(2.53)*	(5.43)**	(1.93)
dKL	0.149	0.063	0.125	0.083
	(1.35)	(0.33)	(1.30)	(0.81)
dRDL	0.068	0.107	0.044	0.055
	(1.40)	(0.97)	(1.21)	(1.74)
KL	-0.005	-0.007	0.002	-0.003
	(1.26)	(0.78)	(0.42)	(0.69)
RD	-0.011	-0.018	-0.004	-0.004
	(4.18)**	(4.51)**	(2.09)*	(2.21)**
U	0.233	0.421	0.085	0.101
	(3.39)**	(3.00)**	(1.46)	(2.03)
I	-0.066	-0.096	-0.048	-0.046
	(2.82)**	(1.93)	(2.87)**	(1.16)
dU	–	–	–	0.059
				(1.16)
dI	–	–	–	0.064
				(0.18)
PL	0.054	0.086	0.057	0.058
	(1.87)	(1.32)	(1.56)	(1.65)
LEV	-0.023	-0.026	-0.019	-0.018
	(5.46)**	(2.45)*	(3.56)**	(2.97)**
adjusted R^2	0.60	0.45	0.34	0.30

Notes: KL is capital per unit of labour input; U and I are proportions of workers qualified at upper and intermediate levels, respectively; RD is R&D intensity; PL is median plant size; and LEV is the log of the ratio of German to UK productivity levels at the beginning of each time period. d preceding a variable denotes a growth rate. Absolute values of t-ratios in parentheses, standard errors are heteroscedastic consistent estimates, * significant at 5 per cent level, ** significant at 1 per cent level.

size is always positive in Germany but negative in the UK for the periods up to 1979. The productivity level variable is the correct sign in all equations and is mostly significant with the exception of the UK equations up to 1979. The equations perform particularly badly for the UK in the period 1973–9 and for Germany in the years 1979–89. In the latter period we also could include the growth in both higher and intermediate skills. These variables have positive signs in the German equation but their inclusion does not improve the explanatory power of the equation. The growth in both types of skilled labour has a negative sign in the UK equation.

Table 8.12b *Regression results, selected time periods, UK*
Dependent variable is annual growth rates of labour productivity

	1973–89	1973–9	1979–89	1979–89
constant	0.002	0.005	0.008	0.019
	(0.32)	(0.25)	(0.62)	(0.96)
dKL	0.462	0.207	0.264	0.338
	(2.84)**	(0.62)	(1.26)	(1.25)
dRDL	0.127	0.065	0.113	0.117
	(2.36)	(0.60)	(1.36)	(1.19)
KL	-0.020	-0.049	0.012	-0.008
	(5.77)**	(1.74)	(0.96)	(0.52)
RD	0.002	-0.013	0.005	0.012
	(0.29)	(0.53)	(0.44)	(0.78)
U	0.193	0.513	0.052	-0.070
	(2.88)**	(2.23)*	(0.31)	(0.30)
I	-0.043	-0.065	-0.033	-0.050
	(2.35)*	(1.28)	(1.05)	(0.98)
dU	–	–	–	-0.064
				(0.66)
dI	–	–	–	-0.077
				(0.38)
PL	0.075	-0.107	0.190	0.163
	(2.31)*	(0.69)	(2.46)*	(1.44)
LEV	0.012	0.001	0.035	0.037
	(1.81)	(0.08)	(2.93)**	(2.74)*
adjusted R^2	0.63	0.13	0.47	0.41

Notes: See table 8.12a.

Conclusion

There is a general belief that the productivity performance of German
manufacturing industry has been vastly superior to that in Britain since the
early 1960s. This chapter has shown that at the level of individual manufacturing industries Germany does not so clearly dominate Britain,
except in the period 1973–9. On the other hand the British performance
was superior in the final decade of the study from 1979 to 1989. Both countries have industries which have performed relatively well in some time
periods. The chapter shows that industries which perform relatively badly
in one period on average make up the deficit in subsequent periods. In attempting to explain relative productivity growth we have concentrated
on capital accumulation variables both because these variables are those
most often used in traditional growth accounting exercises and the

recent emphasis on capital differences in the new growth literature. German manufacturing had an advantage in all three forms of capital by the end of the 1980s and a pronounced advantage in workforce skills. Soskice (1993) suggests that this German superiority in skills is a consequence of some broad institutional differences with the UK which include cooperative industrial relations and a financial system which enables firms to take a more long-term perspective. He concludes that these institutional differences make it difficult, and probably undesirable, for Britain to imitate the German training system. Differences in the rates of capital accumulation cannot, however, explain much of the differences across the two countries in productivity performance in the 1980s relative to the 1970s. There appears to be a deterioration in productivity performance which is common to all industries in Britain in the period 1973–9 and in Germany in the 1980s. Much work remains to be done to explain these differences.

9   Productivity at the plant and industry levels in Australia

CHRIS HARRIS[1]

As in several other English-speaking countries, residents of Australia have been concerned in recent years about their current and future prosperity. These concerns relate not just to the issue of unemployment, currently at around 11 per cent, but also to the issue of growth in income per head, general living standards, and the competitiveness of its exporting and import-competing industries.

A major determinant of economic growth is productivity growth, which includes effects from technical change and innovation, investment in human and tangible capital, the exploitation of scale economies, and improved technical and price efficiencies.[2] In recent years, government agencies such as the Industry Commission (IC) and the Economic Planning and Advisory Council (EPAC) have argued that international comparisons reflect unfavourably on Australia's economic performance. For example, EPAC (1993) suggests that Australia's real per capita growth has been below the OECD country average for the entire twentieth century.[3] Moreover, the East-Asian economies have achieved double the rate of GDP growth in the OECD during the 1980s.

A better indicator of residents' standards of living than GDP per capita uses purchasing power parities, which in effect express expenditures in different countries at the same set of international prices. On this basis, Australia ranked sixth in 1990, some 15 per cent below the levels in the USA and Canada, but quite close to the levels of the other higher-ranked countries: Japan, Germany and Hong Kong (IC, 1993a, Appendix C). However, the IC commented that Australia's ranking at around sixth might not be retained, given current trends of considerably faster rates of economic growth in the East-Asian countries.

Dowrick and Quiggin (1993) suggest that it would be desirable, if difficult, also to take account of differences in environmental conditions, to distinguish welfare-enhancing consumption from protective consumption (for example, policing services), and to account for differences in the quality of leisure. Moreover, they find that GDP rankings are very sensitive to the unit used in the denominator – population, workforce or hours worked – and argue that more meaningful international comparisons can be made by assessing GDP in terms of the expenditures made by a representative consumer (with appropriate adjustments for trade).

Australia's productivity performance

The IC (1991, Appendix 4) observed that total factor productivity (TFP) growth in Australia for the business sector has been slower over both the five- and the twenty-year periods to 1990 than in other major OECD countries (West Germany, UK and Japan), whereas Australia was well towards the lower end of TFP growth in a wider comparison which included many Asian countries (IC, 1993a, Appendix A).

In addition, the major components of the Australian economy other than the agricultural and mining sectors have low levels of productivity compared with their foreign counterparts. Similar findings have been reported recently by Chand et al. (1993) for the Australian manufacturing sector between 1970 and 1985. Using a Tornqvist index of TFP for Australia and twelve other countries, Australian productivity at the beginning of the period was well below that of the USA. There was some catch-up to the USA by the end of the period, reflecting Australian manufacturing's high rate of TFP growth over the period relative to most of the other countries in the sample (mainly developed countries, plus Korea). However, the US productivity level remained more than 50 per cent above that of Australia in 1985.

The (labour) productivity level in the mid-1980s of the government-dominated electricity, gas and water sector in Australia was even lower than that of Australian manufacturing, at roughly half the level of the average achieved by the USA, West Germany, the UK and Japan (IC, 1991, Appendix 4). The disaggregated results for plants and industries presented in the second and third sections suggest a broadly similar picture.

The potential gains to the economy from reforms to and improved performance in the government-dominated sectors are substantial. The IC (1990, chapter 2) identified reforms in transport, rail, communications, water services and electricity supply, and contracting out part of public sector activity concerned with catering, maintenance and capital works

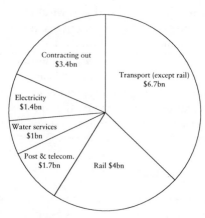

Figure 9.1 *Annual output gains from certain microeconomic reforms*
Source: IC, 1990, chapter 2)

which in the longer run could produce annual GDP gains of $A18 billion (Figure 9.1) and reduce the price level by 7 per cent. The gains from such reforms would amount to around 5 per cent of GDP annually, even though they do not include the substantial gains that could accompany general labour market reform.

The OECD (1992a, p. 86) observed that although the system of highly centralised wage fixing in Australia delivered stable nominal wage increases, a high degree of real wage flexibility at the aggregate level and an excellent job creation record in the 1980s, progress in implementing workplace reform and lifting productivity levels was elusive. Indeed, Dowrick's (1990, p. 19) econometric analysis confirms that Australia's TFP growth has been below the OECD average, particularly since 1984. However, the apparent slowdown of 0.3 percentage points a year relative to the OECD average between the periods 1979–84 and 1984–9 is small, and not significant statistically.

Until 1987, the Prices and Incomes Accord between the federal Labor government and the Australian Council of Trade Unions caused much potential bargaining about productivity and work practices to be put on ice, as had been the case in the UK during the 1970s under incomes policies (Metcalf, 1989).[4]

The March 1987 National Wage Case decision of the Industrial Relations Commission could be seen as an attempt to break the ice, as it established a link between wage increases and productivity and efficiency.[5] A similar approach was adopted by the IRC in its decision of August 1988.

It combined a 3 per cent wage rise with a 'second tier' of $A10 a week, providing the parties were committed to discussing 'award restructuring'. Award restructuring aimed to encourage the parties to examine their awards with a view to, among other things, establishing skill-related career paths; eliminating impediments to multi-skilling; creating appropriate relativities between different categories within the award and at the enterprise level; and ensuring that working patterns and arrangements enhance flexibility and meet the competitive requirements of industry.

However, commentators such as Norris (1989) and Spooner (1989) question whether the August 1988 National Wage Case decision actually resulted in significant restructuring. They point out that workers could achieve wage increases virtually automatically, although negotiations over award restructuring and efficiency and a commitment to a no-further-claims undertaking were required. The IRC Review of award restructuring concluded in May 1989 that, 'progress in some areas is considerable but in the majority it is minimal' (IRC, 1989). In 1991, the IRC accepted the need to provide for workplace bargaining and announced the introduction of an enterprise bargaining principle. The key feature of the principle is that it provides for wage increases to be negotiated between unions and employers in return for productivity changes at the workplace level.[6]

This provides a mechanism by which the pressure on industry, particularly manufacturing, can be partly alleviated as tariff and quota protection is wound back (figure 9.2). As noted by Clark (1993), the development of Australia's industrial relations system went hand in glove with industry policy. At the turn of the twentieth century, assistance was granted to manufacturers on the condition that they pay a minimum, 'fair and reasonable' wage to their employees. This principle, embodied in the Harvester Basic Wage judgement of 1907, laid the foundation for an unofficial nexus between wage fixation and protection policy, which survived for around three-quarters of a century. Governments apparently only realised in the 1980s that such policies were counter-productive. For example, in commenting on the notion that infant industries need tariff protection until they can compete, the Minister for Trade, Senator Cook, is reported to have warned (Earl, 1993):

'The trouble is that the infants never grow up – they keep demanding mother's milk for years and years. What they learn is how to protect their privileged position, not how to become vigorous children, teenagers and adults.'

In addition, there have been moves to change the operating system in government enterprises that provide goods and services to the public. The

Per cent

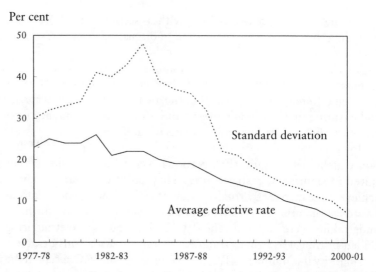

Figure 9.2 *Average effective rates of assistance and standard deviations for the manufacturing sector, 1977–8 to 2000–01*
Sources: IC (Annual reports, various years).
Note: The effective rate of assistance is defined as the percentage increase in returns to an activity's value added per unit of output, relative to the hypothetical situation of no assistance. Effective rates and standard deviations for 1993–4 to 1996–7 and the estimate for 2000–01 are projections.

focus has changed to a degree from processes and inputs to outcomes, with considerable emphasis on the need to become, and benefits from becoming, more competitive in world markets and moving towards best practice. Such benefits include not just the higher national income arising from improved efficiency in government business enterprises (GBEs) themselves, but also the beneficial (or less adverse) effect on their customers, the potential for higher income growth emphasised by new growth theory (BIE, 1992d), and the better opportunity to allocate scarce resources to environmental values, education, health care and income redistribution programmes (Baumol *et al.* 1989, p. 23).

A range of other possible benefits to Australia from an improved productivity performance has been suggested:

• improvements to its attractiveness as a host for foreign investment (BIE, 1993d, AFR, 1993), which can add to the productive base and allow employment growth to be accompanied by an increase in real wages (IC, 1993a, Appendix A);

- improvements to the efficiency of investment, which can reduce demand on national savings (OECD, 1992a, p. 83) and the foreign debt to GDP ratio (Clark, 1992)[7];
- a lower price level (IC, 1990, chapter 2) and improved competitiveness (BIE, 1994) (to the extent that the improved competitiveness is not fully offset by an appreciation of the currency and a decline in terms of trade).

Although such benefits could arise from improved productivity in particular circumstances, they might better be considered as attractive by-products rather than as objectives to be met via a strategy of an improved productivity performance. Indeed, Baumol *et al.* (1989, p. 10) suggest that:

> growth in productivity matters less for such important but transitory issues as inflation, international competitiveness of particular industries in an economy, and the associated availability of jobs. Ultimately, we shall maintain, productivity policy is not the ideal instrument to deal with these problems. Rather, what productivity policy does contribute to effectively is real wages and the economy's general standard of living.

The following sections examine Australia's productivity performance in particular industry sectors, drawing on the results of published and forthcoming work by the BIE, beginning with the findings of two micro-level studies of the major contributing factors to productivity differences between Australian plants and similar plants in other countries. The detailed results are presented in BIE (1990, 1991). These studies were motivated by the perception that while aggregate studies can expose the role of macroeconomic variables, an understanding of the microeconomic factors that affect productivity and unit cost performance requires analysis at a more detailed level.

A summary of the Bureau's benchmarking findings for the performance of a range of Australian infrastructural industries follows. The benchmarking project began following the Prime Minister's statement of 12 March 1991, 'Building a Competitive Australia', in which the Bureau was directed to identify the contribution of infrastructure services to industry costs, develop relevant performance measures, and to publish these on a regular basis. The project is being jointly sponsored by the Business Council of Australia. The results of this work are presented in six BIE reports (BIE, 1992a–c, 1993a–c). In addition, an overview of these reports was published in early 1994 (BIE, 1994).

The final section outlines some implications drawn from the preceding empirical work.

Plant level studies

Although it is difficult to compare productivity levels between countries, there is a widely held view that Australian firms are generally less productive than similar firms overseas. Various reasons put forward to explain these differences include: lack of economies of scale; inefficient work and management practices; the age, technology, flexibility and utilisation of the capital stock; poor training and skill formation; government regulation; bad industrial relations and inadequate quality control. The notion here is that there could be scope for cheap, if not free, lunches from better use of resources in the economy through reforms in areas such as the labour market; and the wage determination, training and education, and taxation systems.

The approach adopted for the research is a series of case studies involving different industries. An attempt has been made to reduce the complexity of the analysis by comparing plants with similar final products and, where possible, similar production processes. Kodak (Australasia) agreed to be the first case study (BIE, 1990). The product was Ektacolor paper, which is the paper onto which colour photographs are printed. The countries compared with Australia were Brazil, Canada and the United Kingdom.

The second case study (BIE, 1991) involved the water heater operations of S.A. Brewing Holdings Limited (SABH, now Southcorp Holdings). At the time of the study, water heaters were manufactured by SABH in two Australian plants, Rydalmere (Sydney) and Bayswater (Melbourne), and at two overseas plants, Middleville (Michigan, USA) and Auckland (New Zealand). We are very grateful to Kodak and SABH for the high degree of cooperation which we received both in Australia and elsewhere in undertaking these studies.

The SABH case study differed from our analysis of Kodak plants in several respects. First, there were two Australian plants. This allowed an analysis of factors responsible for productivity differences between plants within Australia. Second, the manufacture of domestic water heaters is essentially a metal fabrication industry with a mature technology. Therefore, this industry is more representative of mainstream Australian manufacturing than Kodak's paper finishing operations. Third, the raw materials for water heater manufacture were sourced locally in general, rather than manufactured in-house. Fourth, water heaters are currently not highly traded internationally, although there is a potentially lucrative market to the north of Australia. Finally, government regulation of water heater product characteristics, coupled with relatively high shipping costs, have provided substantial 'natural protection' to domestic producers. However, the latter factors could also have reduced the prospects for exports from Australia.

Our approach involved the collection of quantitative data on items such as outputs, inputs and utilisation rates and qualitative information on management practices, work organisation, management–labour relations and work practices. This involved detailed questionnaires and personal interviews with a large range of management and employees in the production areas as well as interviews with related areas such as training, maintenance and trade union representatives. Country data also were collected and discussions were held with employer, labour and government organisations to understand the economic and institutional environment where each of the plants operated.

The plant comparisons relate to a particular production year and therefore give a snapshot of each plant. The performance of any plant in that year could have been affected by events that distorted the results. Where possible, we have drawn attention to the influence of such factors. For example:

• the Australian Kodak plant had a relatively high standby time and low operating time during 1988, reflecting the size of the market allocated by the parent company. Market allocation depends largely on the cost of output produced by the plant; whereas

• the outputs of the water heater plants in the relevant 'snapshot' year were above normal, with the exception of the New Zealand plant which operated in an economy characterised by slow growth since the mid-1980s.

Product and market characteristics

PAPER FINISHING

Photographic paper is a light-sensitive product that requires careful handling. It is made by coating paper with an emulsion which has a silver halide (chloride or bromide) as the primary component. The emulsion is bonded to the paper with hardeners and gelatin.

The process of paper finishing is that of converting photographic paper from its bulk roll stage to a finished product, slit, spooled and packed ready for marketing. Kodak has plants all over the world to carry out this operation. The four processing plants considered in this study are located in Australia (Coburg), Brazil (São Jose dos Campos), Canada (Toronto) and the UK (Harrow).

The water heaters considered in this study consist of an inner steel water tank, the inside of which is coated with vitreous enamel; either a gas or electric heating unit in the base; and an outer sheet steel casing which contains the inner tank and its surrounding insulation. The insulation material is usually either polyurethane foam or fibreglass.

Within this broad product description there is considerable variation. For example, the US plant manufactured over 600 water heater models in 1989, with models differing as to volume, energy source, energy efficiency, shape and other characteristics. The number of models produced by the US plant decreased in later years with the phasing out of less efficient, fibreglass-insulated models that did not meet new US energy standards. A smaller range of models was produced by the other plants involved in this study.

Findings

OVERVIEW

Box 9.1 *Performance of the Kodak plants*

Variable	Australia	Brazil	Canada	UK
Unit cost	High	Very low	Medium	Low
Unit labour cost	High	Very low	High	Medium
Unit capital cost	High	Medium	Low	Low
Unit maintenance cost	Medium	Low	High	High
Hourly labour and maintenance cost	Medium	Low	Medium	Medium
Cost of capital	High	Low	Medium	Medium
Hourly labour productivity	Low	Medium	Medium	High
Hourly capital productivity	Low	Medium	High	High
Plant operating time	Low	Low	Medium	Medium
Machine setup performance	Poor	Poor	Poor	Good
Unproductive hours	Medium	Low	Low	Medium
Impact of product mix	Medium	Low	Very low	Low
Input waste	High	Low	Medium	Medium
Multi-skilling	Medium, restricted by trade	Low	Low	Medium and increasing
Demarcations (between trades)	Strong	Moderate	Moderate	Strong but decreasing
Number of unions	Three	One	One	Two
Employment of temporaries	Very restricted, by award	Not used	Some restrictions	Reduced restrictions

Box 9.2 *Performance of the SABH plants*

Variable	Melbourne	Sydney	US	NZ
Unit cost	Medium	High	Low	High
Unit materials cost	Medium	Medium	Low	Medium
Unit labour cost	Medium	Medium	Low	Medium
Unit capital cost	Low	High	Very low	Medium
Unit inventories cost	Low	High	Low	n.a.
Unit maintenance cost	Low	Very high	Low	n.a.
Hourly labour and maintenance cost	Medium	Medium	Medium	n.a.
Material prices	High	High	Medium	High
Cost of capital				
– plant and structures	Medium	Medium	Medium	Medium
– inventories	Very high	Very high	Medium	High
Hourly labour productivity	Medium	Medium	High	Low
Hourly capital productivity	Medium	Low	High	n.a.
Inventories productivity	Medium	Low	Medium	n.a.
Unproductive hours	Medium	High	Low	Low
Multiskilling	Low	Low	Low	Low
Demarcations (between trades)	Moderate	Strong	Moderate	Moderate
Number of unions	Three	Five	One	One
Overtime arrangements	Available in each plant, substantial cost premium			

The performance of the Kodak and SABH plants is summarised in boxes 9.1 and 9.2 respectively. The top row in each presents information on the relative performance of the plants in terms of the overall performance measure, the unit cost of production. The performance of the plants in terms of a range of quantitative and qualitative measures that affect the unit cost of production are shown elsewhere in the boxes. The main finding for the Kodak plants was that unit costs were higher (figure 9.3), and productivity in the Australian plant was lower (box 9.1) than in competing plants in Brazil, Canada and the UK.

Some reasons for this poor performance are product mix (determined by market demand, increasing unit cost by around 12 per cent) and low operating time of the plant (determined by the parent company's allocation of markets, based largely on production costs). However, analysis of the Australian and overseas plants has identified a range of areas in which performance could be substantially improved in line with better practices abroad. These areas lie within the broad categories of work and management practices, multi-skilling, and the adverse effects of inflation on the returns required from investments.

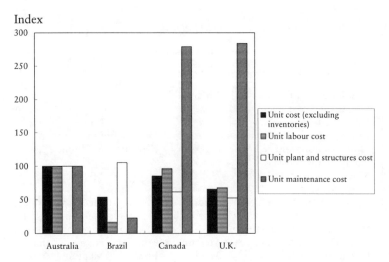

Figure 9.3 *Unit cost indices for total, labour, capital and maintenance, Kodak plants*
Note: The data are indexed relative to the Australian plant. The analysis of unit costs excludes the cost of holding inventory, material input cost, and overhead costs allocated by Kodak to the paper finishing department. The former are not taken into account due to the effect of inflation on inventory costs for Brazil. The others are omitted because of data deficiencies.

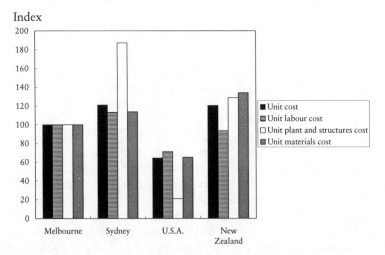

Figure 9.4 *Unit cost indices for total, labour, capital and materials, SABH plants*
Note: The data are indexed relative to the Melbourne plant. The denominator of the cost data is the level of output, expressed in terms of the 125 litre electric standard water heater.

The US facility was the best performing water heater plant, having the lowest unit costs overall and for each input (box 9.2, figure 9.4). The small New Zealand plant generally lagged behind the performances of the other plants. The main factors underlying the US plant's lower unit costs were its superior productivity and the lower materials prices available to it.

PRODUCTIVITY

The fundamental concept underlying all productivity measures is the quantity of output produced per unit of input. Two inputs are considered here: labour and capital (in terms of plant and structures).

Two measures of labour productivity were derived as indicators of the performance of the plants. The first relates output to the employment level, whereas the second allows for the number of hours employees were paid for during the year. The Australian Kodak plant ranked last according to both measures, but was not far behind the Brazilian and Canadian plants on an hours-adjusted basis (figure 9.5).

The productivity gap between Australia and the other countries was less in terms of output per hour than in terms of output per person. This outcome reflects the fact that Australian employees on average were at work for fewer hours than their counterparts abroad. One reason why the UK's performance was superior to the other plants by a substantial margin is that it was able to dedicate one machine to rolls of the same width. Thus, time was not lost in adjusting the machine to slit different widths of paper.

Two measures of capital (plant and structures) productivity were derived also for the Kodak plants. The first relates output to the value of plant and structures employed in the process, whereas the second allows for the number of hours of production for 1988 (figure 9.6). Note that whereas the capital productivity adjusted for hours of operation in Australia was the lowest, the unadjusted measure was higher than for the Brazilian plant. This outcome reflects the 2-shift operation in Brazil during 1988, versus the 3-shift operation of the Australian plant.

The performance of the Australian water heater plants fell between those of the US and New Zealand plants, generally somewhat nearer to the New Zealand end of the spectrum. This outcome was due to their lower productivity (figures 9.7 and 9.8) and the higher materials prices that they faced (see section on input costs, page 179). The relatively poor productivity performance of the Australian plants reflected their levels of unproductive hours (figure 9.9), and poor work and management practices, particularly in the case of the Sydney plant.

Index

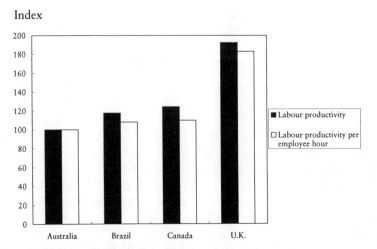

Figure 9.5 *Labour productivity, Kodak plants*
Note: The data are indexed relative to the Australian plant. Total employment in paper finishing is expressed in terms of direct labour equivalents. That is, the labour variable takes account of the difference in relative annual total cost and (presumably) productivity between direct production workers and the other categories of labour (Griliches and Ringstad, 1971; BIE, 1988). It is calculated as the sum of the number of direct production workers, and the number of employees in the other categories converted into direct production worker equivalents. The conversion involves dividing the annual cost of each other labour category by the annual standard cost of direct production workers.

Index

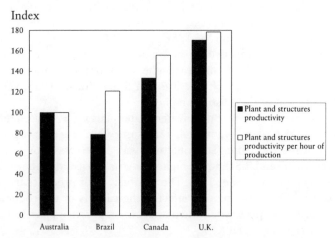

Figure 9.6 *Capital (plant and structures) productivity, Kodak plants*
Note: The data are indexed relative to the Australian plant.

Index

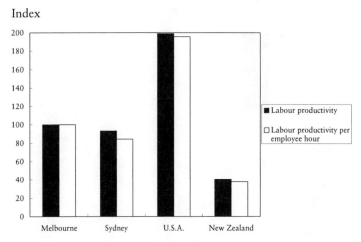

Figure 9.7 *Labour productivity, SABH plants*
Note: The data are indexed relative to the Melbourne plant. Total employment in water heater production is expressed in terms of direct labour equivalents (see note to figure 9.5), except for the NZ plant. NZ labour productivity data are derived as the ratio of unweighted output during 1989–90 to unweighted total employment in June 1990, owing to limitations in the data.

Index

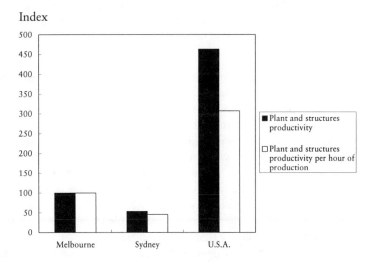

Figure 9.8 *Capital (plant and structures) productivity, SABH plants*
Note: The data are indexed relative to the Melbourne plant. Data were unavailable for the NZ plant.

Per cent

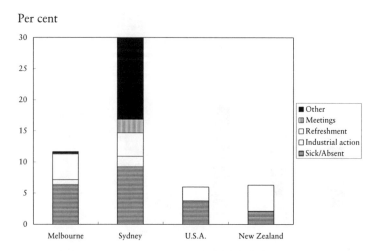

Figure 9.9 *Ratio of unproductive hours to paid hours for direct production work-*
ers, SABH plants
Note: Wash periods at each plant are excluded from the analysis. All employees at
the Australian plants are assumed to receive two paid refreshment breaks for each
workday (totalling twenty and twenty-two minutes a day for the Melbourne and
Sydney plants respectively). Consistent with information provided by workers at
the Sydney plant, direct and indirect production workers are assumed to take additional time off as follows: five, ten and thirteen minutes a day at morning tea,
lunch and afternoon tea respectively; they start work ten minutes late and finish
work ten minutes early; and they take two, thirty-minute 'toilet' breaks per day.

Differences between the two Australian water heater plants in many ways
provide more insights than comparisons between them and the US plant.
In terms of both productivity and unit cost measures, the Melbourne plant
ranked ahead of the Sydney plant. This was despite the Melbourne plant's
smaller output and less mechanised capital stock. The differing industrial
relations environments at the two plants were the main reason for the relatively poor performance by the Sydney plant during 1989–90.

The main quantitative evidence to support this conclusion was the relatively high proportion of unproductive hours (that is, hours which employees are supposed to work but do not) at the Sydney plant (figure 9.9). Much
of the 30 per cent of paid hours that were unproductive at that plant reflected work practices not sanctioned by the relevant award, such as over-
long meal and refreshment breaks, lengthy toilet breaks, starting work late
and finishing work early. These practices were a legacy of past management acquiescence and poor management–labour relations. A related

factor was the relatively high number of hours per employee lost at the Sydney plant due to sickness/absenteeism, a phenomenon that was evident for the Australian Kodak plant also (5 per cent, versus 3 to 4 per cent at the other Kodak plants).

US employees receive one paid ten-minute refreshment break each workday. This break is taken near the midpoint of the initial (five-hour) work period, in accordance with the agreement between the firm and the local branch of the union.

Data for injuries and meetings are unavailable for the NZ plant. A sickness/absenteeism rate for this plant is calculated on the basis that employees are absent for five work days per year. All employees in New Zealand are assumed to receive two paid ten-minute refreshment breaks per workday.

INPUT COSTS

Labour   Labour costs per hour in the Australian Kodak and SABH plants were broadly in line with those for plants in the other developed countries (Canada, the UK and the USA). This outcome has been assisted by a considerable period of wage restraint in Australia. Thus, a major factor behind the relatively high labour costs per unit of output in the Australian plants (figures 9.3 and 9.4) is relatively low labour productivity per paid hour (figures 9.5 and 9.7).[8] However, the levels of payroll taxes disadvantage the Australian plants relative to those abroad. In addition, workers compensation premia in some states of Australia do not seem to relate closely to the injury performances of individual workplaces.

Capital   An important factor in the magnitude of the costs associated with plant, structures and inventories is the cost of capital. This can be defined as the pre-tax real rate of return on an investment required to achieve a given rate of return after company tax. The pre- and post-tax returns differ according to the company tax rate, the relative rates of allowed and economic depreciation, the taxation arrangements for inventories, inflation, and the effect of inflation on these variables. The methodology and parameters employed for the SABH study are outlined in BIE, 1991, Appendix 1.

Taking both assets into account, the cost of capital was highest during 1988 for the Australian Kodak plant. This was due to a high rate of inflation relative to the other developed countries and less favourable depreciation provisions.

In contrast, the costs of capital for plant and structures during 1989–90 were quite similar for each of the water heater plants (figure 9.10). These

Per cent

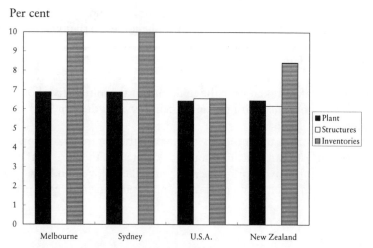

Figure 9.10 *Costs of capital for plant, structures and inventories, SABH plants*
Note: The cost of capital data exclude the impact of dividend withholding tax in the country that hosts the investment and personal tax on unfranked dividends paid by the parent company to Australian resident individuals from foreign source income. Such taxes are irrelevant to an investment funded from retained earnings because they must ultimately be paid whether or not the retained earnings are invested. The cost of capital data shown here are net of depreciation, so that estimates for assets with different lifetimes (such as plant and structures) can be analysed on a comparable basis. The gross of depreciation data are used in the calculation of capital and total costs.

outcomes occurred despite relatively generous depreciation provisions in the USA, and despite statutory rates of corporate tax in the USA (34 per cent) and New Zealand (33 per cent) which were low relative to that prevailing in Australia (39 per cent at the time, since reduced to 33 per cent). The Australian results reflect the offsetting effect of a real discount rate that was lower than in the USA, owing to a higher Australian rate of inflation in 1989–90.[9] The influence of the lower real discount rate on the New Zealand data was offset by depreciation provisions that were the least generous of the countries considered here.

The cost of capital for inventories in the USA was relatively low, owing to the availability of last in/first out valuation provisions for tax purposes. These provisions alleviated the taxation of higher inventory values that were due solely to inflation. The inflation component was taxed in Australia and New Zealand owing to the lack of a stock valuation adjustment and positive rates of inflation in these countries. The outcome is that the cost of

Per cent

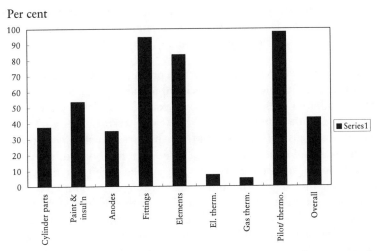

Figure 9.11 *Materials price disadvantages faced by the Australian SABH plants vis-à-vis the US plant*
Note: The data by category presented here are derived from the ratio of the simple averages of prices within each category for the Sydney and US plants. The overall figure is based on a weighted average of the price margins by category, with weights derived from materials used by the Sydney plant during 1989–90. US prices are converted to Australian currency using an exchange rate of $US0.769 per $A, the simple average of the quarterly exchange rates for 1989–90.

capital for inventories in Australia and New Zealand was high relative to other assets, and the holding of stocks was discouraged in these countries relative to investment in plant and structures. Although the annual rate of inflation in Australia had declined to around 2 per cent in 1993, the potential adverse effect of inflation on the cost of capital for inventories remains a feature of the Australian taxation system.

In summary, the reasons for relatively high capital costs per unit of output at the Australian Kodak and SABH plants are low capital productivity (figures 9.6 and 9.8) and Australia's high inflation at the time of the studies relative to the other developed countries.

Materials   The differing quality and cost of material inputs was a major theme of the SABH study (such data were not available for the Kodak study). The production of water heaters is a materials intensive process. Much (but not all) of the unit cost advantages enjoyed by the US plant reflected its access to less costly (figure 9.11) and higher quality material inputs. Since the acquisition of the US plant by SABH, management has become more aware of the extent to which material prices in Australia differ from world prices. Detailed price comparisons between Australia and the USA have been used to persuade some suppliers to lower their prices, and to keep subsequent price increases below the rate of inflation.

Reduced protection against imports in product markets accompanied by supporting microeconomic reforms in input markets can lead to increased competition, and pressure to improve workplace efficiency and to lower prices. A secondary measure would be for assessments of anti-dumping applications to give greater weight to the impact of such actions on downstream users and consumers of final products. In addition, regulation in support of competitive outcomes may need strengthening in some oligopolistic industries. The aim of such regulation would be to discourage anti-competitive behaviour by increasing the likelihood that it would be detected, and by increasing the penalties that apply to such behaviour. Further, consideration could be given to promotion of competitive outcomes by changing the merger test under the Trade Practices Act from one of market dominance to the weaker 'substantial lessening in competition' criterion. Underlying this proposal by the Trade Practices Commission is the view that domestic competition is more beneficial for Australia's economic welfare, through outcomes such as lower prices and more efficient work and management practices, than potential gains from industry mergers and rationalisation. The merits of various approaches to promoting competition are discussed in the report by Hilmer (1993), which is being considered currently by the heads of Australian governments.

Concluding comments

Kodak's Australian plant faced substantial competition, not only from other companies producing abroad but also from Kodak plants abroad, with growing pressure for improved quality and competitiveness. The outcome for paper finishing at the Australian plant was the loss of export markets and state of the art machinery to Brazil, and reduced shifts and employment at the Australian plant.

The Australian SABH plants currently compete with each other and with another producer (Hardie Dux) in the Australian market. The extent of competition that they face from imports is likely to increase in the future, owing to excess production capacity in the USA, the acquisition of US production facilities by SABH, and some reform of shipping and waterfront inefficiencies in Australia. Given the substantial gap between the productivity and cost performances of the Australian and US plants, the future viability of the Australian plants could be in question without significant improvements in performance.

Best manufacturing practice, as identified by the MIT Commission on Industrial Productivity (1989) involves six crucial patterns to be a successful manufacturer. These are:

- simultaneous improvement in quality, cost and delivery;
- staying close to the customer;
- closer relations with suppliers;
- using technology for strategic advantage;
- flatter and less compartmentalised organisations;
- innovative human resource policies.

Kodak and SABH are adopting policies and practices in all these areas to improve their manufacturing performances. They are strong in some areas such as close relations with customers and suppliers, quality, and the use of technology. Some aspects of performance, such as the price and quality of purchased inputs (reflecting factors such as lack of effective competition in input markets and the unavailability of imports at world prices due to tariff protection, anti-dumping actions and low productivity on and reliability of supply through the waterfront) and the high cost of capital for inventories, are largely outside the control of the plants. Government reform in these areas could improve the plants' competitiveness and benefit the consumers of their products.

In addition, greater competition from imports in the water heater market would be expected to yield welfare gains for consumers. Such competition would constrain the extent to which firms and unions could enter work practice/remuneration arrangements similar to those prevailing at the Sydney plant during 1989–90.

It is evident that considerable potential productivity gains could be achieved at the Sydney water heater plant from reform of work practices and 'time-keeping'. Other areas that could be improved include the degrees of labour inflexibility, overstaffing and limited job rotation. Indeed, the productivity performance of all water heater plants could be improved by the removal of demarcation barriers between production workers, fitters, electricians, storemen and forklift drivers. Such barriers meant that production workers were not permitted to remove hooks used on a paint line or to replace them after cleaning, to load final product into trucks, to be trained to drive a forklift, to undertake maintenance, or to work in a stores area. Job rotation even within production was limited at the Sydney plant.

Similar factors were evident at the Australian Kodak plant, with decreased productivity due to inter-union demarcations between production workers and areas such as transport, maintenance and the packing of containers. For example, production workers in the Australian plant were not permitted to use a spanner to tighten a bolt, or to load or unload either a truck or a pallet. Such demarcations:

- contributed to work inefficiencies and reduced productivity;
- removed the incentive to management to extend the training of groups across current skill barriers; and
- resulted in less multi-skilling and less interesting and varied work for employees.

The influence of industrial relations systems in Australia and New Zealand on opportunities for enterprise bargaining and productivity outcomes emerged in the late 1980s as a key issue in microeconomic reform in Australia, as it has been in the UK for more than a decade. Reforms directed at the development of a less centralised system with greater emphasis on enterprise bargaining have been instituted in the UK and New Zealand, and are in progress in Australia.

Such reform reflects the view that the previous system in Australia left little scope for flexible outcomes owing to factors such as craft-based union structures (which result in a multiplicity of unions at the enterprise level, increase disputes and prevent the realisation of the full benefits from multi-skilling) and institutional and attitudinal constraints (which support work practices that limit workplace flexibility and substantially reduce productivity).

Of course, enterprise bargaining is not a panacea for poorly performing firms. Although the US water heater plant has an enterprise agreement, the Melbourne water heater plant achieved a similar degree of labour flexibility within Australia's centralised system owing to the relatively harmonious relations at the plant, its small size, and the recognition by employees that their welfare was linked to the success of the employer in meeting competition from other plants. However, enterprise bargaining does provide a greater opportunity for direct bargaining between a firm and its employees over work practices, wages and conditions. There are potential gains for the parties to the bargain, and for consumers through lower prices. Moreover, wage flexibility at the enterprise level can encourage skill formation, which has been a policy priority in Australia for some years. Firms that wish to undertake a lot of training need to be able to offer lower start/higher finish career pay profiles (as in Japan and Germany) than firms that do little training (Blandy, 1989). The reason is that the wage profile in training-oriented firms needs to ensure that the costs and benefits are shared sufficiently between employees and employers, so that their joint investments are protected from piracy by other firms.

To a significant degree, it is the forces of competition in product markets that ensure firms do not grant wage rises which are inconsistent with productivity and conditions in their labour market. However, enterprise bargaining creates considerable risks for firms and employment outcomes in circumstances where unions are strong and firms operate in a competitive market. Indeed, the management of the Sydney water heater plant suggests that the historical experience there is such that the Australian Industrial Relations Commission (IRC) has a vital role to play in enterprise bargaining, in order to ensure that enterprise agreements are not the result of industrial pressure for unreasonable conditions, and that agreements are complied with. These issues were addressed by the enterprise bargaining principle announced by the IRC in October 1991.

Since 1989–90 there have been significant improvements to work and management practices at the Sydney water heater plant. Management has shut one of its production areas, improved the layout and reliability of the other production area, and reduced the level of overstaffing and unproductive hours. Additional reforms were delayed by the complexity and time required to negotiate an enterprise agreement with the five unions on site.

Finally, in November 1991, agreement was reached between the parties for wage rises of $A15 a week for workers at the plant, based on changes in work organisation and the achievement of a productivity target. A further wage rise of $A18 a week was to be paid when the plant reached its next productivity target, which would further close the gap between the Sydney and US plants. The IRC ratified the agreement as a consent award under the enterprise bargaining principle.

Unions and management in Kodak have moved since 1988 towards changes to lift the productivity and cost competitiveness of the Australian plant. These changes include a reduction in the number of unions in the total manufacturing plant from the previous eighteen, a decrease in the number of awards from twenty-two to one or two, and fewer inefficient work practices. The paper finishing department has been amalgamated; the management, equipment and workflow have been changed; and the employment level has been substantially reduced. Enterprise bargaining has been useful for Kodak and its employees in achieving improved outcomes, although some unions have yet to recognise the need for change.

However, further substantial reforms are possible and desirable at the plants. To some extent, progress with such reform seems to have been delayed by the time consuming nature of the processes associated with enterprise bargaining within the Australian system, and the presence of multiple unions on site. Reforms to the industrial relations framework would support more decentralised union structures, facilitate enterprise unionism where favoured by employees, encourage multi-skilling across current demarcations for all workers at the plants, and improve the framework for the prevention and settlement of disputes.

However, it is also apparent that legislative/regulatory reform alone is unlikely to be successful in promoting better outcomes. As demonstrated by the differing performance of the Melbourne and Sydney SABH plants, the Australian and US SABH plants, and the Australian and Canadian plants, relationships between employers and employees, and attitudes to work and the organisation of work and production processes, are also critical to the process of achieving advances in productivity and cost performance.

Indeed, the second enterprise-based pay system negotiated during 1993 by management at the Sydney plant and the unions was rejected by the workforce. The Water Heater Division General Manager commented that: 'An enterprise agreement by itself doesn't change a culture.' The proposed agreement included a new skills-based career path, and a commitment from the company that there would be no redundancies. However, the workers wished to retain promotion on the basis of seniority, and some apparently were banking on generous redundancy offers (Bolt, 1994).[10]

Industry level studies

The underlying rationale for the Bureau's benchmarking project is the view that the competitiveness of Australian enterprises in international markets is determined in part by the costs of inputs and services of Australian infrastructure, the provision of which is dominated by government business enterprises. Significantly, a proportion of these infrastructure inputs and services is obtained from enterprises which are not directly subject to competitive pressures. Many of these enterprises operate in industries which have some monopoly elements and are characterised by regulatory and institutional barriers to competition. In such cases, incentives for sound performance are weakened and actual performance may depart significantly from best practice. Where this occurs the development of international performance measures offers a way of indirectly introducing competitive pressures by comparing actual performance to international benchmarks.

The performance measures developed for the project have two objectives. The first is to compare the performance of Australia's infrastructure services against that of its international competitors from the perspective of users of those services. In particular, the project addresses whether Australia's traded goods sector is disadvantaged by the performance of domestic infrastructure service industries. The international comparisons developed for this part of the study focus on customer-oriented indicators of price and service quality. The results show Australia's competitive position in relation to other countries.

The second objective is to measure the operating efficiency of Australia's infrastructure service industries relative to their overseas counterparts. These comparisons indicate the extent to which efficiency can be improved. The key questions are how does Australia rate against world best practice, and to what extent can performance be improved?

The role of infrastructure services in the Australian economy is outlined below. It is followed by a review of the methodology used by the Bureau in assembling the performance indicators and a summary of the Bureau's results to date. A discussion of the Bureau's results using the method of data envelopment analysis (DEA) is then followed by some concluding comments.

Role of infrastructure industries in the economy

In Australia, as in other advanced economies, the service industries dominate economic activity, contributing around 70 per cent of national income. Infrastructure services are an important part of the services sector, providing energy supply, transport and communications. Though also consumed by households, infrastructure services are mainly used by businesses. Infrastructure services are in general not directly traded, but contribute to costs in all industries and so influence the international competitiveness of Australian firms.

The gross product, employment and investment of the main infrastructure industries are presented in table 9.1. Infrastructure services in total account for around 12 per cent of Australia's gross domestic product; this in turn is almost one-fifth of the total production of services. These industries employ around half a million people – around 8 per cent and 6.4 per cent of total services' and all sectors' employment, respectively. Road freight transport with associated services is the largest infrastructure industry in both output and employment. The public sector dominates investment in infrastructure, contributing around 85 per cent of the total.

Infrastructure services are often provided by government enterprises operating under natural or legislated monopolies. They have not, therefore, been subject to the same competitive pressures to achieve best practice as other sectors. As a result, the scope for reform in infrastructure service industries is likely to be greater than elsewhere in the economy.

The attainment of best practice in infrastructure services would provide a significant boost to the Australian economy. The Industry Commission (1990) estimated that gains from infrastructure reform would increase output by $A15 billion annually in 1988–9 dollars. By comparison, the removal of agricultural and manufacturing assistance measures and the implementation of contracting out by governments for the provision of some

Table 9.1 *Significance of infrastructure and other services in the Australian economy*

	Gross product 1992-3 ($bn)	Proportion of GDP 1992-3 (%)	Persons employed Aug 1993(a) ('000)	Public investment 1991-2 (b) ($m)	Private investment 1991-2 (b) ($m)
Infrastructure					
Electricity	8.8	2.2	52.6		
Gas	1.2	0.3	11.0	4167	67
Water	3.3	0.8	32.3		
Road construction	2.4	0.6	19.7	2840	n.a.
Road freight transport and services	11.8	2.9	134.3		
Rail transport	1.8	0.5	59.6		
Water transport and services	1.9	0.5	22.7	5734	2250
Air transport and services	4.8	1.2	42.1		
Telecommunications	8.1	2.0	72.2		
Post	2.3	0.6	43.0		
Other services					
Construction	27.8	6.9	559.3		980
Wholesale and retail trade	70.9	17.7	1600.5	n.a.	5192
Finance, property and business services	49.0	12.2	858.1	1457	5869
Public administration and defence	12.8	3.2	375.9	8808	n.a.
Community services	47.8	11.9	1488.9		1133
Recreation, personal and other services	17.6	4.4	615.2	n.a.	2596
Total services	272.3	67.9	6096.4	22821	18087 (c)
Total all industries	401.4	100.0	7684.9	27838	32839 (c)

Sources: ABS Cats. 5206.0, 5221.0, 6203.0, and BIE estimates.
(a) Not seasonally adjusted. (b) Gross fixed capital expenditure. Public includes government trading and financial enterprises and general government. (c) Excludes ownership of dwellings. n.a. = not applicable.

Per cent

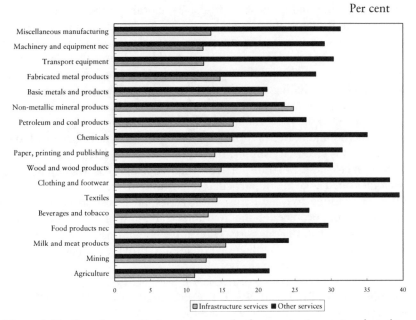

Figure 9.12 *Cost shares of infrastructure and other service inputs in selected industries*
Source: BIE calculations using the industry input–output data published by the ABS (1990).

other services and inputs would, together, achieve an increase only half this size. The sectoral impacts reported by the IC (1990) and extended by Yetton *et al.* (1992) show that benefits could be spread across all sectors of the economy.

All industries use infrastructure services in production. The contribution of the costs of infrastructure service inputs to those of final output varies between industries from around 10 per cent to almost 25 per cent. This relationship as well as the contribution of other (non-infrastructure) service industries to costs of output is illustrated in figure 9.12.

The industries requiring the greatest input of infrastructure services are the minerals processing industries – basic metals and products (extraction of metals from ores) and non-metallic mineral products (glass and clay manufactures). These industries together with chemicals processing and petroleum and sugar refining account for nearly three-quarters of energy use in the Australian manufacturing sector. The food processing industries, as well as being energy intensive through cooking and sterilisation activities, are large users of transport infrastructure. In general, industries producing more highly finished products – clothing and footwear; printing and publishing; transport equipment; machinery and equipment; and miscellaneous manufacturing industries – have the lowest requirement for infrastructure. At the same time as value adding dilutes their infrastructure requirements, most of these industries develop a high requirement for other services, including financial and wholesale and retail services.

The performance of a total of eight key infrastructure industries is being examined in the BIE benchmarking project. The three most important infrastructure industries in terms of costs to industry have been included in the study – electricity supply, road transport and telecommunications. In addition to these, rail transport, the waterfront and coastal shipping have been identified as being of particular importance to major export sectors. Of the remaining two industries in the series, air transport is a growing industry of importance for the 'invisible' trade in tourism – now among the largest of Australia's exports. Gas supply is an infrastructure service in its comparative infancy with good potential to provide an increasing proportion of energy needs in the near future.

To date the performance of five key infrastructure industries has been examined by the BIE: electricity (BIE, 1992a), rail freight (BIE, 1992b), telecommunications (BIE, 1993b), road freight (BIE, 1992c) and the waterfront (BIE, 1993c). The remaining three infrastructure industries – coastal shipping, aviation and gas supply – will be reported on in 1994. The studies will be updated to monitor the progress of reforms introduced and the pace with which performance gaps are being narrowed. An update has been published for rail freight (1993a), and the Bureau expects to publish an electricity update in early 1994.

Performance indicators

The need for international performance indicators for infrastructure provision might be considered greatest in those areas subject to the least competition. Many of Australia's infrastructure industries are in the process of being transformed from being dominated by government monopolies, at both the state and commonwealth level, to a situation of increased competition. International performance monitoring provides an important means of assessing the success of reforms introduced to improve the efficiency with which infrastructure services are provided, particularly where opportunities for competition are either limited or precluded by government legislation.

The principal criteria for choosing a set of performance measures are that they be comprehensible, comprehensive, timely and usable. The main requirement for the set of measures to be **comprehensible** is that they be relatively few in number. It is no use having hundreds or even dozens of measures presented as no one will be able to distil the essential information on the enterprise's overall performance. This reinforces the need for identification of key indicators and the importance of **comprehensive** summary measures. While detailed measures may provide important information on specific aspects of operation, it is important to obtain an overall indication of how the enterprise is performing relative to its peers or comparable organisations in other industries and countries.

Timeliness is of the essence in any performance measurement exercise to provide feedback as close to the event as possible. Equally important, however, is the consideration that the measures be **usable**. This means that the measures must be understood by the intended audience. This points to the need for relatively simple measures which are easy to interpret and for which the audience will understand what actions would lead to observed improvements. In practice, pragmatic considerations such as data availability will also have an important bearing on the choice and development of performance indicators.

In the five studies summarised in this section, a broadly similar approach has been adopted in terms of the choice of performance indicators. In all cases these have focused on the broad categories of:

- **customer-oriented** measures, which include the price paid by industry for various infrastructure services and the quality and reliability of those services; and

- **operating efficiency** measures, which encompass typically a range of partial productivity measures including labour productivity, capital productivity and utilisation as well as comparisons with what might be considered international best practice input usage in providing that service. Operating cost comparisons also have been derived where feasible (rail freight, coastal shipping).

However, given the characteristics of each industry and data availability, the detailed customer-oriented and operating efficiency measures have varied. Consequently, it has not been possible to adopt a completely standard set of indicators across all of the infrastructure industries. This applies particularly to operating efficiency measures relating to capital where the technical characteristics of, say, electricity supply are very different from those relating to telecommunications. However, even on measures of service quality the particular characteristics important to users are quite different. For instance, the main concern in electricity supply is an absence of interruptions to supply and the avoidance of power surges whereas for rail transport the important considerations are on-time delivery and a low loss or damage rate to freight.

While partial productivity indicators provide useful insights, they have to be interpreted with caution when looked at in isolation. By concentrating on the productivity of one particular input a misleading impression of overall performance may result. This points to the need for overall measures to obtain a true picture of performance. The first such measure is total factor productivity (TFP), which measures total output relative to all inputs used. A second measure is the overall technical efficiency of production. In general terms, technical efficiency refers to the extent that maximum output is produced from a given set of inputs. The Bureau has used TFP and technical efficiency (derived using data envelopment analysis) indicators in those international performance studies where sufficient data have been available.

Another important choice which had to be made in the studies was which **countries** to include in the international comparison. Considerations of which countries were regarded as having best practice in the field, which had operating environments relatively similar to that applying in Australia, and data availability were all important. In some cases the range of services provided by a particular overseas infrastructure provider was also an important consideration.

Results to date

The key result emerging from the BIE's International Performance Indicators project for Australian infrastructure is that while progress has been made in this important area of microeconomic reform, much remains to be done. Recent reform initiatives have tended to narrow performance gaps between Australian infrastructure industries and observed international best practice, but in some cases these performance gaps remain wide.

The size and importance of the various infrastructure industries also needs to be taken into account in evaluating the significance of divergences between Australian performance and world best practice. Given the importance of electricity, road transport and telecommunications to all sectors of the economy, the savings to be gained from closing even relatively small performance gaps in these infrastructure industries will be large.

PRICE

The ratios of the best and worst Australian prices relative to the cheapest international price observed for the same infrastructure service are shown in figure 9.13. A value of 1 for the best Australian price would thus indi-

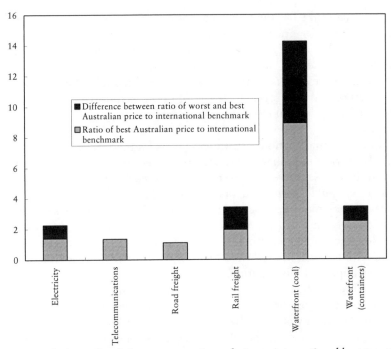

Figure 9.13 *Australian infrastructure prices relative to international best practice*
Note: A higher ratio means the Australian price is higher than the cheapest world price by that order of magnitude.

cate that it was the cheapest observed world-wide, whereas a value of 10 would indicate that the best Australian price was ten times higher than the cheapest price observed internationally.

The ratios are highest for the waterfront and rail freight. Australian port authority and ancillary coal handling charges, in particular, were over eight times higher than those of the cheapest competitor, Richards Bay in South Africa, in July 1992. Port authority and ancillary charges for containers at the most competitive port, Fremantle, were around two-and-a-half times higher than those applying in Singapore, but container charges at Melbourne were nearly 40 per cent higher again than those in Fremantle.

Rail freight charges were also nearly twice as high on average for the most competitive rail system, Australian National, compared to best practice US charges in 1992. The price range within Australian rail systems varied by over 50 per cent. Australian rail freight charges tend to be further above world best practice for bulk commodities such as coal and grain than for general freight, where there is more competition from road transport.

Australia ranked as the fourth cheapest OECD country in terms of industrial electricity prices in 1990. Although the cheapest Australian state for industrial electricity prices, Victoria, had prices 40 per cent higher than the lowest observed international price (those of TransAlta Utilities Corporation of Alberta, Canada), Victoria had the third lowest price of any thermal system. At the other end of the spectrum, Western Australia had average industrial electricity prices 60 per cent higher than those of Victoria.

For telecommunications, Australia's tariffs for business were close to the OECD average in January 1992, before the recent entry of OPTUS. Australian businesses were, however, subject to relatively high domestic telephone and public switched data network (PSDN) prices, but relatively low international, mobile and leased line charges. A composite basket of business charges in Australia was over one-third more expensive than in Sweden, the country identified as best practice for Australia. The intense competition which has followed the entry of the new supplier is expected to have improved this situation.

The infrastructure industry where Australia compared most favourably to international best practice in prices was road freight. Vehicle operating costs in Australia were only 10 per cent higher for long haul freight in recent years than those of the USA, the cheapest observed. When road-related taxes and charges were excluded, Australia performed marginally better than the USA.

RELIABILITY

The ratios of the best and worst Australian reliability figures relative to the best reliability performance observed world-wide are shown in figure 9.14. A value of 1 for the best Australian reliability would thus indicate that it was the best observed world-wide, whereas a value of 10 would indicate that the best Australian reliability was ten times worse than the best practice observed internationally.

Australia's strong performance in road freight carries over to reliability, a key measure of service quality for business. Australia was almost equal to the world-leading US figure for on-time delivery and equalled observed world best practice for the loss and damage rate. Reliability performance for rail freight, on the other hand, was very mixed, with one Australian system equalling best international practice for on-time running but the same system being worst in terms of the loss and damage of freight.

Electricity average outage times per customer were considerably higher in Sydney than in Tokyo or London, although the reporting area for Sydney also included a substantial rural component. In rural areas the dura-

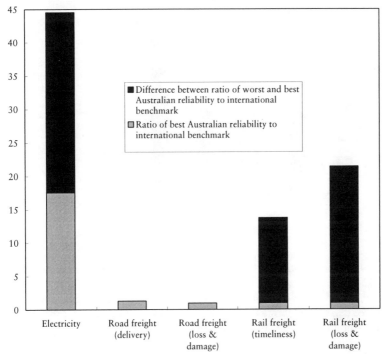

Figure 9.14 *Australian infrastructure reliability relative to international best practice*
Note: A higher ratio means worse reliability relative to world best practice.

tion and frequency of outages rose dramatically, reflecting Australia's harsh non-metropolitan environment and geographic remoteness. Although information on telecommunications reliability was sketchy, rates of call failure in Australia were significantly worse than for Canada, a country with broadly similar characteristics.

OPERATING EFFICIENCY

The proportions of observed international best practice labour and capital productivity achieved by the Australian industries are shown in figures 9.15 and 9.16 respectively. A value of 100 per cent for the best Australian performer would thus indicate that it was achieving world best productivity performance, whereas a value of 50 per cent would indicate that the best Australian performer was only half as productive as the world's best performer on that measure.

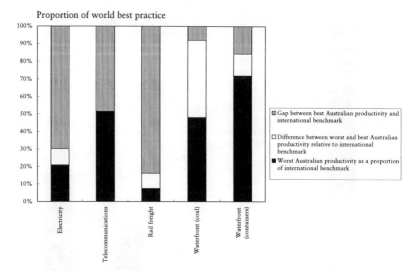

Figure 9.15 *Labour productivity performance of Australian infrastructure industries relative to international best practice*
Note: The labour productivity measures employed are annual gigawatt hours per employee (electricity), annual revenue deflated by the OECD's composite basket of telecommunications tariffs, per employee (telecommunications), net tonne kilometres per freight employee per year (rail freight), and tonnes per employee per year (waterfront).

Operating efficiency performance gaps appear to be largest for the rail freight and smallest for the road freight industries. Electricity, the waterfront and telecommunications appear to lie in that order between the two performance extremes of rail freight and road freight.

Rail freight performs poorly in terms of both labour and capital productivity and the gap between Australian unit costs and achievable world best practice was 27 per cent in 1991–92. Labour productivity in the best performing Australian system, Australian National, was only 16 per cent of that of the best US system, whereas the best Australian wagon productivity was only 30 per cent of the best US figure. The implied efficiency gaps are large, even when allowance is made for differences between the systems.

In some cases comprehensive summary measures such as total factor productivity and operating cost comparisons are also available. The Australian electricity supply industry has narrowed the gap between its total factor productivity (TFP) performance and that of the United States investor-owned electric utilities by 2.3 per cent over the two years to 1991–92

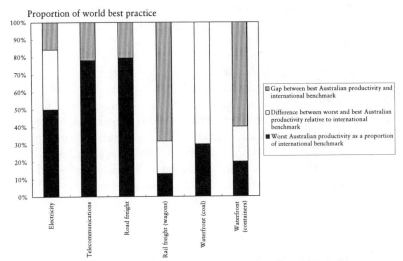

Figure 9.16 *Capital productivity performance of Australian infrastructure industries relative to international best practice*
Note: The capital productivity measures employed are the ratio of electricity generated in the year to effective plant capacity (electricity), annual output per main line (telecommunications), net tonne kilometres per vehicle per year (road freight), net tonne kilometres per freight wagon per year (rail freight), tonnes per berth metre (waterfront, coal) and twenty-foot equivalent units per berth metre (waterfront, containers).

to 26.9 per cent. For labour productivity Queensland performed best with 2.6 gigawatt hours per employee, compared to the world best of 8.6 obtained by TransAlta. The Australian industry performed better with regard to most aspects of capital productivity, with Queensland being only 15 per cent behind the highest capacity factor observed.

The performance of Australia's waterfront industry remains mixed. For some commodities, particularly coal and wheat, much of the Australian waterfront is performing at or near international best practice. For other items, such as containers, there remain significant gaps between Australian productivity performance and that of similar-sized overseas ports handling similar cargoes.

The overall productivity performance of telecommunications in Australia was at least 13 per cent below international best practice in 1990. The performance gap in terms of labour productivity was considerably larger. These results applied to the situation before the entry of OPTUS into the Australian telecommunications market.

Reliable labour productivity figures could not be obtained for international comparisons of the road freight industry. However, the Australian road freight industry has achieved capital productivity performance about 80 per cent of that found in the USA and, as noted earlier, in terms of operating costs the Australian road freight industry is the world leader when road-related taxes and charges are excluded.

Figures 9.13 to 9.16 show that for electricity, rail freight and the waterfront there are large differences between the best and worst performing Australian suppliers, as well as large differences relative to international best practice. While attention needs to be focused on performance relative to international best practice, closing the gap in domestic performance may be a useful interim target for Australia's worst performing infrastructure providers.

RECENT DEVELOPMENTS

This section summarises recent developments in issues that affect the performance of the rail freight and road freight industries and the waterfront. Analogous developments for the electricity and telecommunications industries are also discussed.

Rail freight   The rail freight industry in Australia is dominated by government enterprises. Their operations have historically not been provided on a commercial basis; there has been much uncertainty surrounding the objectives and costs of community service obligations, extensive political interference and (particularly for bulk commodities) little competition from other transport modes for market share (although coastal shipping has provided limited intermodal competition for a few cargoes).

The outcomes include substantial operating deficits and performances that are inferior to world best practice, whether on the basis of price, operating efficiency or reliability. However, the Australian systems are undertaking reforms so as to narrow the gap between their performances and world best practice. These reforms have involved reductions in the rail freight workforce and in rolling-stock fleet numbers, and workplace reforms involving multi-skilling and a greater customer focus.

Analysis for the BIE by Travers Morgan suggests that Australian systems, while making headway in reducing the performance gap relative to best practice operating cost levels, will not reach world best cost levels until 1998–9, assuming they maintain their current rate of progress in reducing costs (annual reductions of around 4.4 per cent) and that world best practice remains unchanged at its 1991–2 level. Put another way, Australian rail systems would have to almost double their current rate of improvement to reach world best practice cost structures by 1995–6, which would require additional capital investments by each of the Australian systems.

While this rate of improvement may appear unrealistic, it should be considered in the context of the performance improvement targets of Australian rail systems. For example, the National Rail Corporation (NRC) is aiming to reduce operating costs by 45 per cent in real terms and to increase labour and capital productivity by three-fold or more by 1995–96.[11] Progress in these areas slipped owing to the protracted negotiations with the public rail freight systems and the unions. Frozen equity funds, earmarked for a wide range of investments to upgrade service to customers, were not released by the NRC's government shareholders until November 1993, following the dismissal of an appeal involving the industrial agreement negotiated by the NRC. The Electrical, Electronic, Plumbing and Allied Workers Union applied for leave to appeal against certification of the agreement, which provides that NRC workers are covered by either the Public Transport Union or the Australian Services Union (Jay, 1993).

Road freight   Road freight is largely characterised by private sector trucking operators. Competition between these operators is intense and, correspondingly, the observed performance of many key areas of the industry is very close to international best practice. However, the industry is subject to substantial government taxes and charges, and relies on road infrastructure which is provided largely by state government departments and authorities, with some coordination from the Commonwealth government. So that the relatively efficient trucking industry can realise its full potential, it is necessary to ensure that road infrastructure is provided efficiently. For this reason it is important that road user charges reflect the marginal cost of using roads, and that available funds for road construction and maintenance are allocated to those areas which will have maximum economic benefit.

The National Road Transport Commission (NRTC) is pursuing regulatory reforms in relation to the industry.[12] Of particular importance are its efforts in respect of uniform road vehicle charges, and of uniform vehicle regulations and driver standards throughout all States and Territories of Australia. There are three relevant Bills either before Federal Parliament or passed by it. The Road Transport Charges Act has passed through both houses of Federal Parliament and is awaiting adoption by the states and the Northern Territory. Uniform heavy vehicle charges are proposed to take full effect in 1995. One piece of legislation before parliament is the Road Transport Reform (Vehicles and Traffic) Bill, which is to put into place a range of regulations covering issues such as heavy vehicles standards, driver standards, traffic, and vehicle operations. Further Bills will be developed to deal with registration, driver licensing and compliance.

Gains to industry and users from the adoption of uniform vehicle regulations have been estimated by the NRTC at around $A140m a year, while gains from more optimal approaches to heavy vehicle charges are in the order of several million dollars a year. Estimates of only moderate potential gains from optimal road user charges are surprising given the intensity of the debate regarding what the appropriate methodology should be for determining road charges and the high value of annual expenditure on road construction and maintenance (in the order of $A5 billion a year). However, further analysis is being undertaken on this issue, with the Australian Road Research Board developing a lifecycle costing method for use in the future.

Waterfront   There are many factors that influence the performance of the waterfront. Various port activities are provided by a mixture of government and private organisations. For instance, port authorities dominate the provision of basic port infrastructure, but stevedoring services are provided by both private and public operators. Although there is scope for some competition between ports, their geographic separation in Australia tends to limit the scope for intense competition. From the customer's point of view, there is considerable scope for improvements in the performance of much of the waterfront, including government and port authority charges, ship and cargo turn-round times, and charges for ancillary services.

Although it has been possible to reduce the number of workers employed in stevedoring to reflect increases in output per worker through better work practices,[13] it is not as easy to realign the stocks of capital equipment, berth space, and land storage areas. This reflects the legacy of past inefficiencies in labour and capital management on the waterfront. It seems that these factors will continue to impose a cost on users in the form of higher charges than would otherwise apply.

There have been a number of important developments, of relevance to the waterfront, following the release of the BIE report (1993c). These are discussed briefly below.

The Industry Commission (IC) completed its final report on the inquiry into Port Authority Services and Activities in May 1993 (IC, 1993b). While accepting that different approaches will be necessary for different port authorities, the IC advocated refocusing their activities on core areas such as ensuring safe access and harbouring for vessels, while avoiding activities that private enterprise could effectively undertake. Port authorities should be placed in a corporate environment to provide stronger incentives for better performance. Subjecting them to the Trade Practices Act and coverage by the Prices Surveillance Authority (PSA) would aid this process. The IC also suggested that market-related tests rather than regulations be used to determine how many private operators provide particular services within ports and who they should be.

Australian Stevedores was formed in July 1993 by the merger of National Terminals (Australia) and Strang Patrick Stevedoring. Some concern has been expressed by shippers that the decreased competition arising from the merger will result in increased charges. However, rationalisation of both labour and capital, as well as economies of scale and scope, are expected to yield cost savings which offer the possibility of lower charges than would otherwise have applied. There have been some teething problems with the merger – a move to reduce the workforce resulted in the placement of work bans and limitations in some ports, and workers at Australian Stevedores' Port Botany terminal were reportedly fined in November 1993 by the union because they were working too hard. The union says that fines were levied because of unsafe work practices (Korporaal, 1993).

The PSA released its second report on the Monitoring of Stevedoring Costs and Charges in August 1993 (PSA, 1993). The Authority observed that significant reductions in the nominal and real costs of stevedoring services had continued over the six months June to December 1992. These lower charges have been made possible by productivity improvements within the industry. The Authority has indicated it will continue to monitor the industry and noted that this is especially important owing to the creation of an effective duopoly with the formation of Australian Stevedores.

Data envelopment analysis

The methods for estimating the technical efficiency of production have developed rapidly since the late 1970s. Currently, the main approaches can be classified as either:

- **statistical** techniques, which characterise the production technology via parametric methods; or
- **mathematical programming** techniques, which can characterise the technology via either nonparametric or parametric methods.

The most general of the former set of techniques is the stochastic frontier approach pioneered by Aigner *et al.* (1977) and Meeusen and van den Broeck (1977a, b). In theory, the major advantage of this approach is that it is less sensitive than other methods to extreme observations and measurement error, because the distributions of errors and efficiency are modelled. In practice, the method frequently fails to provide efficiency estimates, and the results are sensitive to model specification.[14] This method was used in previous work by the BIE on the technical efficiency of Australian manufacturing industries (BIE, 1988).

Farrell (1957) and Farrell and Fieldhouse (1962) were the first to employ the nonparametric programming method. According to this approach, the free disposal convex hull is constructed from a set of observations on factor inputs per unit of output for a group of firms or industries, by linear programming techniques.

The convex hull, supported by a subset of the sample, is an estimate of the production frontier. It represents the minimum quantities of inputs necessary per unit of output, given existing technology. The estimated frontier is based neither on an explicit model of the production function nor on a model of the relationship of the observations to the unit isoquant, other than the fact that observations cannot lie below the unit isoquant.

The method yields a frontier that is known as the 'best practice', because it is derived with respect to the units in the sample (Førsund et al., 1980). The derived measure of unit efficiencies is an upper bound to the true efficiencies, because the frontier constructed via this method is the smallest set containing all the data and satisfying some regularity conditions (Färe, Grosskopf and Lovell, 1985, chapter 9).

The principal advantages of the method are that:

- it is not parametric, and so a functional form is not imposed on the data;
- multiple outputs are accommodated readily without needing to be aggregated (using output prices, for example);
- technical efficiency measures are readily calculated.

Data envelopment analysis (DEA) was introduced by Charnes et al. (1978) and formalised further by Banker et al. (1984). It is a mathematical technique, based on the principles of linear programming theory and application, to assess how efficiently each decision-making unit (for example, firm, organisation, establishment) produces its outputs.

In summary, each decision-making unit (DMU) is compared with the other DMUs in the sample. A DMU is regarded as technically efficient if the ratio of its weighted outputs to its weighted inputs is no less than similar ratios for all other DMUs, subject to certain constraints. The constraints include that weights are non-negative, and that no producing unit can be more than 100 per cent efficient with the same weights. Each DMU's 'objective' is to choose the set of weights that maximises its efficiency, subject to these constraints.[15]

A technical efficiency frontier for the sample consists of a lower envelope of linear combinations of efficient DMUs. Those DMUs which are not on the frontier are inefficient in proportion to their distance from the frontier. Moreover, DEA indicates for such DMUs a subset of efficient DMUs (the efficient reference set) and associated multipliers that enable the researcher to construct a hypothetical efficient DMU which uses less of each input but produces at least as much output as the inefficient DMU. The technical efficiency of an inefficient DMU is calculated as the ratio of its actual output to the weighted output of DMUs in the efficient reference set. Similarly, the surplus inputs of an inefficient DMU are calculated as the difference between its actual inputs and the weighted inputs of DMUs in the efficient reference set.

It is possible for a DMU to lie on the frontier and appear technically efficient because it is an outlier in its inputs or outputs, perhaps because of errors in the data. In the work reported here, a DMU is only considered to be technically efficient if it appears in the efficient reference set of at least one inefficient DMU.

In addition to its advantages, the method has several disadvantages.

- A convex hull is an unduly pessimistic estimate of smoothly curved efficiency frontier isoquants (Førsund and Hjalmarsson, 1974). This reflects the non-parametric nature of the method.

- The estimated frontier and derived measures of inefficiency are particularly susceptible to extreme observations, measurement error and misspecification (Førsund et al., 1980). This reflects the characteristic that the frontier is deterministic, and is defined by the innermost 'outliers' in the sample.

- As a non-statistical method, there is no clear, statistical way to assess the relative strengths of different model specifications.

Given these disadvantages, it is advisable to combine DEA with other techniques to reduce the extent to which erroneous conclusions might be drawn from data which are typically 'noisy' at best. This issue is expected to be addressed in subsequent work by the BIE.

Other disadvantages of DEA are shared with alternative approaches. For example, it is assumed typically that particular inputs (such as labour) and outputs are homogeneous, and the extent of price efficiency is not addressed (Farrell, 1957). In addition, results vary with the number and composition of inputs and outputs. Further, neither the specific reasons (for example, work practices, past managerial decisions) responsible for measured inefficiency nor the optimal future reform path are identified explicitly.

RESULTS

Information on the data for the three industries analysed with DEA by the BIE (1993b) for telecommunications and by Bell (1993) and Whiteman

(1993) for gas and electricity are presented in table 9.2. Following consultation with industry representatives, two outputs and three inputs were selected for both the electricity and gas industries, whereas two inputs were employed for the telecommunications industry. The two outputs were distinguished to allow for differences in the best practice production of each. For example, retailing of a quantity of electricity or gas to a large number of households requires a different mix and level of resources from those employed in wholesaling the same quantity of electricity or gas.

Electricity   The electricity industry is dominated by government monopolies, particularly at the state level. Results to date from DEA for these Australian utilities are summarised in table 9.3. The technical efficiency of the Australian electricity supply industry in 1991–2 is determined to be 88 per cent. This overall figure is derived by aggregating the results obtained (which range from 66 to 100 per cent) for the six Australian states and the Northern Territory.[16]

The results for the electricity industry in 1991–2 suggest that its output (defined in terms of sales and customers) could be improved by 14 per cent overall (from 88 to 100 per cent technical efficiency) using the same thermal and other capacity.

Moreover, the number of employees could be decreased by 15 per cent of the current level in the process. Of course, the potential for improvement varies from system to system within Australia, reflecting system efficiencies, input–output configurations and scales.

This analysis suggests somewhat higher labour and capital productivities for Australian utilities relative to best practice than those obtained via the direct comparison of utility productivities (figures 9.15 and 9.16). The main reasons for such differences are that the DEA results distinguish between technical and scale efficiencies, and allow for labour slacks, whereas the direct comparisons do not.

The finding of considerable labour slack is consistent with changes in the industry since the period covered by this work. Employment in the industry has fallen by 6.6 per cent or over 4000 persons to nearly 58,000 employees. For some utilities the reduction in employee numbers has been even larger. For instance, the Electricity Trust of South Australia reduced its operation and maintenance staff by over 20 per cent between June 1991 and June 1992. Since embarking on a major restructuring in 1989, the State Electricity Commission of Victoria has reduced its workforce by 42 per cent, from 21,500 to a level of 12,500 by early 1993 (Bates, 1993).

Current reforms in the electricity industry are aimed at creating a more competitive market. Increasing the degree of competition between suppli-

Table 9.2 *Inputs and outputs for DEA*

Utility	Inputs	Outputs	Observations
Electricity	1. Thermal capacity (MW) 2. Other capacity (MW) 3. Employees	1. Sales (GWh) 2. Customers	45 utilities from Europe, N. America, Japan, S. Africa, Thailand & Australasia.
Gas	1. Transmission mains (km) 2. Distribution mains (km) 3. Employees	1. Sales (GJ) 2. Customers	51 utilities from Britain, N. America, Japan & Australasia
Telecom-munications	1. Main lines ('000) 2. Employees	1. International traffic (minutes) 2. National traffic (minutes)	20 utilities from the OECD

Note: Data for the Australian electricity utilities are for 1991–2, as published by the Electricity Supply Association of Australia in its annual compilation of data (ESAA, 1993). Data for Japan come from published sources, mainly annual reports, and pertain to 1991–2. Data for TransAlta Utilities Corporation (Canada) and EGAT (Thailand) also are for 1991–2. The remaining data (mainly for European utilities) come from published sources for 1989–90.

Data for Australian gas utilities are for 1991–2 from their annual reports, and from the statistical compilation of the Australian Gas Association (1993). Data for overseas utilities come from various published sources, mainly annual reports, and generally are for 1992. The employment data have some limitations. First, some gas utilities offer appliance sales, installation and repairs as part of their service. This factor would tend to inflate their numbers of employees relative to utilities which do not offer such services. Second, some utilities contract out repairs, maintenance and installation of services, which would impart a negative bias to their employee numbers. Third, staff involved in capital works, including the expansion and upgrading of utilities' networks, should be excluded from utilities' employee numbers, as such upgrading is not included as an output. Employee numbers of Australian utilities have been adjusted to allow for such circumstances, but appropriate corrections were not possible for utilities abroad.

The data for telecommunications utilities are for 1990, from the OECD (1990, 1992b), and the ITU (1992). International output is measured as the number of minutes of international traffic for each country. National traffic is measured as residual revenue (after deducting the value of international traffic), deflated by the OECD's composite basket of tariffs. The labour input includes operating, technical and 'other' employees. Data are unavailable for the USA.

Table 9.3 *DEA results for Australia*

Utility	Technical efficiency	Ratio of actual to best practice capital productivity	Ratio of actual to best practice labour productivity	Labour slack
Electricity (1991-2)	88	88	75	15
Gas (1991-2)	79	79	79	0
Telecommuni- cations (1990)	90	90	64	29

Sources: BIE (1993b), Bell (1993), Whiteman (1993).
Note: The best practice reference sets identified by the DEA are used to derive potential capital and labour productivities for each non-frontier utility. The estimates are derived with returns to scale unconstrained. The detailed results are discussed in BIE (1993b) and Bell (1993).

ers of electricity is expected to encourage suppliers to minimise their production costs and to permit users to buy from the cheapest source of supply. Organisational arrangements for the interstate electricity network covering New South Wales, Victoria, Queensland, South Australia, Tasmania and the Australian Capital Territory were initiated at the July 1991 Special Premiers' Conference with the decision by relevant governments to form the National Grid Management Council (NGMC). The NGMC recommended that the transmission network be separated from generation to facilitate the operation of a competitive market, which would be expected to increase the pressure on transmitters and generators to control costs and improve quality factors such as supply reliability.

In June 1993, the Council of Australian Governments (COAG) agreed to have the necessary structural changes put in place to allow a more competitive electricity market to commence from 1 July 1995. The structural changes are to include the establishment of an interstate electricity transmission network covering New South Wales, Victoria, South Australia and Queensland. Competition is to be based on a Multiple Network Corporation (MNC) structural option. Under this option, the transmission elements of existing electricity utilities are to be separated from generation and placed in separate corporations which may be state- or region-based.

A paper trial of the new market arrangements was to be undertaken in November 1993. The objective was to allow participants to gain experience with a competitive market. All customers (10 MW and above), distributors and generation utilities were invited to participate in the trial.

Victoria agreed to participate in the trial with its generators split into several separate units. However, New South Wales challenged the need for including intra-state competition during the six month computer simulation and entered its utility as a single entity instead of as the three generating units originally envisaged.

It is understandable that individual governments will look to their own interests, for individual states can be made worse off (at least in the short term) by participating in reforms that are in the interests of Australians generally (IC, 1993a, p. 12).[17] In such circumstances, given the danger of failing to achieve the full benefits from reforms, the IC has suggested the option of qualified majority voting for some issues at COAG meetings.

Considerable scope remains for refinements to the DEA analysis. The number of inputs could be expanded to include fuels (for example, gas, coal, hydro flow, nuclear materials), the capital measures could be further disaggregated, the analysis could be extended to include data for more than one year, customer density (for example, residential customers or connections per kilometre) could be allowed for, and categorical variables (Banker and Morey, 1986) could be employed to allow for other relevant characteristics (such as degree of private ownership, extent of government regulation).

Gas   The gas industry in Australia is characterised by a mixture of government and private suppliers. Some of the government suppliers of gas are in the process of being privatised. Initial DEA results suggest that the technical efficiency of the Australian gas supply industry overall in 1991–2 is slightly lower than that for electricity, at 79 per cent, but with no labour slack (table 9.3). The results suggest that its output (defined in terms of sales and customers) could be improved by 27 per cent overall (from 79 to 100 per cent technical efficiency) using the same thermal and other capacity. As for electricity, the potential for improvement varies within Australia, reflecting system efficiencies, input–output configurations and scales. Future refinements to this work might further disaggregate the capital measures, extend the analysis to include data for more than one year, allow for customer density (for example, residential customers or connections per kilometre), and allow for other relevant characteristics (such as degree of private ownership, extent of government regulation).

Telecommunications   The DEA results for the telecommunications industry in 1990 suggest that its output (defined in terms of national and international traffic) could be improved by 11 per cent (from 90 to 100 per cent technical efficiency) using the same transmission inputs. Moreover, the number of employees could be decreased by 29 per cent of the current level in the process. The best practice reference set for Australia is Sweden and the UK, with Sweden accounting for 92 per cent of best practice. Sweden has a similar output configuration (mix and level) to Australia but considerably lower prices, whereas the UK output level is at least 200 per cent larger than Australia's. Sweden has one of the densest telephone networks in the OECD, and the highest density of cellular mobile phones in the world.[18]

The analysis suggests somewhat higher labour and capital productivities for Australian telecommunications relative to best practice than those obtained via the direct comparison of utility productivities (figures 9.15 and 9.16). As for the electricity industry, the main reasons for such differences are that the DEA results distinguish between technical and scale efficiencies and allow for labour slacks, whereas the direct comparisons do not.

The finding of considerable labour slack in Australian telecommunications is consistent with changes in the industry since the late 1980s. Employment in the industry has fallen by an average of 5000 employees (around 6 per cent) a year over the last five years, in preparation for and as a result of competitive pressures.[19]

The move towards competition in the industry accelerated in September 1990, with an announcement by the government of three major streams of reform:

- the merger of Telecom Australia and the government's international carrier, OTC, into the Australian and Overseas Telecommunications Corporation;
- the licensing by the end of 1991 of a competitor to AOTC, through the sale of the government's domestic satellite operation AUSSAT, and a third mobile only operator in 1993; and
- the revision of the Telecommunications Act to permit full competition from 30 June 1997 and to specify transitional regulatory arrangements.

The second carrier, Optus Communications Pty Limited, was selected in November 1991 and became Australia's alternative carrier on 1 February 1992. The government has adopted an industry specific regulatory regime to monitor and control the progressive transition from a government-owned monopoly to full competition in telecommunications. The regulator, the Australian Telecommunications Authority (Austel), is a statutory body, independent of the carriers and subject to ministerial direction only in certain special cases specified in the Act. Austel monitors and reports to the Minister on the performance of the carriers including the efficiency with which services and facilities are supplied, and obligations met. Austel also administers price cap and price control mechanisms.

The principal features of the new regulatory and structural framework for the Australian telecommunications industry are:

- a duopoly (to end in 1997) in the fixed (non-mobile) telephone network, with the two carriers, Telecom Australia and Optus, licensed to supply the full range of domestic and international services, using any available technologies;
- three mobile telephone licensees: Telecom, Optus, and Vodafone, which began operations in October 1993;
- full resale of domestic and international telecommunications services, voice and data, and full competition in public access cordless communications services under an Austel class licence;
- a 'universal service obligation' to be shared among carriers on an equitable basis, currently involving compensating Telecom for provision of a standard service to remote areas and payphones; and
- a robust enforcement regime, incorporating sizeable pecuniary penalties for failure to carry out lawful instructions of the Minister or Austel.

Benefits from competition are expected to include: improvements in quality and variety of telecommunications products; increased attention to consumer needs; improvements in operational efficiency through adoption of appropriate technologies; and community-wide savings through better resource allocation.

To date, there have been significant price reductions in the long distance call market. The average price for a three minute, 320 kilometre long distance call fell 8.1 per cent in real terms during 1992, without including bulk and incentive discounts (NUS International, 1993). During 1993, prices for many long distance calls continued to decline, with reductions of up to 9 per cent coming into force on particular capital city routes from 6 May 1993, while at the same time customers on lower traffic, long distance routes also benefited from price reductions (Telstra Corporation, 1993). Price cap regulations requiring Telecom to reduce the real price of calls in each of its long distance categories by a minimum of 5.5 per cent annually still apply.

A price cap also applies to international calls, for which average prices of Trans-Pacific calls have fallen by 4.3 per cent in real terms during 1992 (NUS International, 1993). Prices for international calls through Telecom reduced by an average of 10 per cent during 1992–3, both through reductions in rates to commonly called countries and through the extension of off-peak periods to thirteen hours a day on weekdays and twenty-four hours a day on weekends (Telstra Corporation, 1993). Optus offers similar discounts for calls between Australia and nominated overseas destinations.

Cheaper call prices in both these important categories would at least partially offset a 2.8 per cent rise in the real cost of exchange lines for businesses (NUS International, 1993). Nevertheless, the average price level for the standard telephone service reduced by 3.6 per cent during 1992–3 (Telstra Corporation, 1993).

The local call service continues to be quarantined from competition at present, and licensing provisions prohibit time charging of these calls. An implicit cross-subsidy persists in favour of users of long duration local calls, keeping average prices higher than necessary. Recent survey evidence suggests that Australian local call prices, based on three minute comparisons, are the highest of all industrialised countries (NUS International, 1993). As around 75 per cent of all local calls made in Australia are less than three minutes in duration, timed local calls would be likely to benefit most users, including business.

Optus has made customer service a key feature of its business. Telecom, in its transition to the competitive environment, has also adopted measures to improve customer service, including service guarantees, simplified customer access, work practice improvements, tariff restructuring and network modernisation, in an effort to retain market share. These initiatives have achieved tangible results for customers, such as extended service hours, customer appointment schemes, and standardisation and enhancement of complaints handling. In April 1993, a digital mobile network was launched in Australia; only the second in the world outside Europe.

Concluding comments

The key result emerging from the BIE's International Performance Indicators project for Australian infrastructure is that while some progress has been made in this important area of microeconomic reform, there remains much to be done. It is important that the momentum not only be maintained but increased, and that there be ongoing monitoring of infrastructure performance to ensure that reforms in fact deliver real benefits to Australia. The updates being undertaken as part of the project will make an important contribution to this process.

FACTORS INFLUENCING PERFORMANCE

From a policy perspective it is important to know whether the causes of the observed performance gaps are industry specific, or whether there are some common impediments to sound performance. In the latter case, there would be important lessons to be learnt for maximising the benefits from future reform initiatives.

The results obtained to date suggest that the degree of competition within an infrastructure industry is a key determinant of infrastructure performance, as it was for the plant level studies discussed earlier. The infrastructure industry where Australia's performance is closest to international best practice – road freight – enjoys by far the greatest degree of competition. Rail transport in contrast, the industry where the performance gap is largest, suffers from the lowest degree of competition and the highest degree of government involvement and subsidisation. The other infrastructure industries examined – electricity, telecommunications and the waterfront – lie between the extremes of these two industries in terms of both performance and the degree of competition.

Governments often determine the degree of competition permitted in infrastructure industries, both through their roles as owners of infrastructure utilities operating in legislated monopolies, and as industry regulators. A clear implication of our results is that an absence of competition detracts from industry performance relative to international best practice. In contrast, increasing competitive forces are expected to lead to improved infrastructure performance. The National Competition Policy recommended by Hilmer (1993) is an important initiative in this regard.

It should also be noted that the history of the reform process in the various industries differs substantially. For example, of the industries dominated by government monopolies and government regulations, the electricity industry was among the first to embark upon widespread reforms to work practices and organisation. This has been reflected in a significant improvement in that industry's productivity over the last decade, due largely to a change in management culture within what remains mainly a government-dominated industry. In contrast, progress has been much slower in the rail freight industry, reflecting factors such as competition between unions for members and the delayed recognition of changed objectives for the industry by some of the parties involved.

Industry-specific factors such as the regulatory and institutional environments (for example, the electricity industry has been organised on the basis of state government monopolies, but with some vertically integrated and others separated by function) can have an important bearing on performance. In addition, the measured performance of the electricity supply industries may reflect inefficiencies not only in the operation of the existing electricity supply system, but also inefficiencies in constructing major projects such as power stations in Australia. Consequently, microeconomic reform efforts should continue to be focused on the construction industry.

Rapid technical change in telecommunications, and the adoption of a new regulatory and structural framework for the industry, have forced the major infrastructure supplier to improve the price and quality of its products and to improve its customer service. Another example of industry-specific influences on performance was found in the road freight industry.

That industry has performed well by international standards, despite being burdened by taxes and charges that appear relatively high by international standards. However, there remains considerable debate over what constitutes an appropriate system of charging road users for externalities such as noise, congestion and the damage caused to pavement, and over the appropriate extent of the indirect tax on this business input.

Most governments have argued that a necessary precondition for increased competition and, perhaps ultimately, privatisation of currently monopoly government suppliers, is increased commercialisation and corporatisation of government enterprises. This process has typically led to improved operating efficiency within the enterprises concerned. However, efficiency improvements often have turned the government enterprises from loss-makers which require subsidies from the taxpayer to potentially significant sources of government revenue. Consequently, some governments have been inclined to extract increasingly large dividends from these industries, rather than allowing a larger proportion of the benefits from reform to be passed on to users in the form of lower charges and higher quality service.

For example, Haynes (1993) illustrates the degree of reform which has occurred within the New South Wales electricity supply industry, but notes that electricity prices to users have remained virtually constant while the state government has increased its dividends from the electricity supply industry substantially. As pointed out by the IC (1993a, Appendix K), the practice of governments using those government business enterprises (GBEs) which have some monopoly power to meet revenue needs could have serious implications for the efficiency of public enterprises, possibly causing prices to the users of their services to be higher than they otherwise would be. Indeed, the IC commented that:

> it could be suggested that reform programs for GBEs which focus on administrative reform and financial targets but neglect efficient pricing and the need to promote competition are more likely to lead to taxation of consumers through dividend policies than to improvements in economic efficiency.

There is an incentive for governments to use their more efficient utilities as revenue raisers and to exploit their monopoly positions, rather than to allow the entry of competitors. The issue of pricing of infrastructure services and the distribution of taxation receipts in Australia is a priority issue for further work. An additional issue which bears scrutiny is the extent to which improved operating efficiency in business enterprises which have some monopoly power is extracted by their employees, rather than being passed on to consumers. Increased competition (for example, by removing barriers to competition, vertical separation, intermodal competition), significant labour market reform and performance monitoring with public disclosure of the results can contribute to attenuating the extent of such outcomes.

Many of the reforms introduced recently to increase competition in the provision of infrastructure services do so only to a limited extent. Although there may be significant adjustment costs in rapidly increasing the degree of competition faced by many former government monopolies, too slow a reform process imposes significant costs on the Australian community. A managed transition to competition also runs the risk of the process becoming captured by existing vested interest groups, including relatively powerful government monopolies and their employees.

Moreover, experience in other cases of deregulation, particularly aviation and banking, points to the power which incumbent firms have relative to new entrants to the industry. This factor too points to the need for improvements in competition policy, plus general monitoring of the pricing and terms of access to infrastructure, if the wider benefits from increased productive efficiency are to be realised.

Another important lesson which has emerged is that while attention is focused initially on the areas of greatest inefficiency and those appearing to be causing the greatest impediments to improved performance overall, improvements in performance in those areas can be captured by groups elsewhere in the industry which face little effective competition.

For example, one of the reasons that waterfront charges have not fallen in line with improvements in operating efficiency is that waterfront labour and key stevedoring operators have been in a position to appropriate the benefits, as they face little effective competition. This outcome highlights the need to widen the focus of reform efforts through time. Reforming only one part of an industry or one link in a transport chain runs the risk of merely redistributing rents in the industry, with less benefit resulting to users of the service and the Australian economy in general. In recognition of this issue, the PSA will be monitoring the distribution of the benefits from reforms to coastal shipping and the waterfront (including stevedoring, tugs and pilots).

IMPROVING ALLOCATIVE EFFICIENCY

The main focus of microeconomic reform of infrastructure services is currently on reducing operating costs and improving productivity levels within government organisations supplying these services. Studies by the Bureau have shown that there are potentially large savings available to the Australian economy from continuing this reform process until achievable world best practice is reached. However, significant benefits can also accrue from better initial investments in these infrastructure industries (for example, roads, power stations and port interfaces).

Better decision-making can come from consistently employing an economic methodology, having more flexible funding arrangements (including procedures to allow private sector investment) and from involving state, territory and commonwealth governments and key users in a framework which identifies those investments that provide the highest payoffs, and which better integrate the various transport and other infrastructure modes.

THE ROLE OF BENCHMARKING

The current project has played an important role in focusing attention on the performance of Australia's infrastructure industries relative to international best practice. This process has highlighted the potential gains available to the Australian economy from reforming these industries, and has provided a framework for assessing the success of reforms introduced to date.

Many difficulties have to be overcome in any benchmarking study. For example, differences in outputs produced, inputs available, operating conditions and regulatory frameworks can impact on performance and make comparisons between facilities more difficult. Limitations on data availability can reduce the scope of studies to a focus on a number of partial indicators and aggregate performance.

It should also be noted that benchmarking is not a substitute for continuing reforms, particularly the introduction of increased competition. However, the limited nature of competition introduced to most of these industries to date and continuing heavy government involvement indicate that there will be an ongoing role for public performance monitoring of these industries relative to international best practice. International performance monitoring provides an impetus to maintain reform initiatives. It provides information to assess progress, the extent to which the benefits of reforms are being passed on to users, and to identify emerging issues and obstacles to performance improvements.

Data envelopment analysis and statistical techniques can make a useful contribution to this monitoring process. They can yield a single, comprehensible measure of technical efficiency for each unit in the industry under scrutiny, and separate information on the influence of scale economies on the performance of units in the industry. In addition, DEA can yield separate estimates of labour, capital and other input slacks, and information on best practice actually achieved by relevant other units. Such techniques can also be extended to examine the effect on efficiency of factors such as the institutional and regulatory environment, and changes in best practice over time, which can make the results more usable for industry and policymakers. With additional information, the extent of price efficiency can be examined also. These refinements are being considered by the BIE for use in future work in this area.

Implications of the studies

The key issues that emerge from the BIE's plant and industry level studies summarised earlier in the chapter are the role of competition policy in product markets, and the role of labour market reforms.

Competition

Issues regarding competition have already been discussed, and are therefore addressed here only briefly. Effective competition in product markets keeps costs down, ensures that the benefits are passed on to consumers, provides strong incentives for production to match evolving consumer requirements, and disciplines areas that fail to perform in these respects (IC, 1990, chapter 3).

Competition has an important role to play in achieving improved performance in both the private and public sectors in Australia. The phased reductions in protection during the 1980s (figure 9.2) enhance the exposure of many industries to foreign competition, whereas changes to government regulations are increasing competition within Australia in sectors such as electricity, gas, aviation and telecommunications. As noted earlier, international performance monitoring provides an impetus to maintain reform initiatives. It provides information to assess progress, the extent to which the benefits of reforms are being passed on to users, and identifies emerging issues and obstacles to performance improvements.

Additional reforms to increase competitive pressures have been proposed by Hilmer (1993). His committee recommended changes including:

- the removal of regulatory restrictions, including legislated monopolies for public utilities, statutory marketing arrangements for many agricultural products, and licensing arrangements for various occupations, businesses and professions;
- the restructuring of public monopolies and, if need be, the provision of third party access rights; and
- the adoption of a set of principles aimed at ensuring that government-

owned businesses comply with certain competitive neutrality arrangements when competing with private firms.

The recommendations are being considered by the Heads of Australian Governments.

Labour market

Labour market reforms would complement initiatives taken to enhance competition in product markets, reduce the extent to which the benefits from improved operating efficiency were extracted unduly by employees rather than being passed on to consumers, and could lead to improved outcomes in the labour market generally.[20]

The Prices and Incomes Accord between the Federal Labor Government and the ACTU was implemented in 1983. It was intended initially to provide centralised wage fixation with automatic six-month adjustments corresponding to movements in the consumer price index. Since then, there have been several versions of the Accord in response to the requirements of economic policy.

The results according to some researchers include lower real wages and higher employment and profit shares than those which would have occurred otherwise. Assessed against other criteria, however, Australia's performance relative to other OECD countries during the Accord period to 1988 has been no better than middling (with respect to the level of and change in unemployment, and change in inflation) or towards the tail of the field (with respect to the level of inflation, and level of and change in the current account deficit) (Wooden, 1990).[21]

Moreover, there is some evidence that the *quid pro quos* required under the Accord to ensure union compliance, such as additional social welfare benefits, forgone tax increases (particularly in the area of indirect taxes) and income tax cuts, have reduced the effectiveness of fiscal policy as a policy instrument. As a result, the government had to rely on an indirect policy instrument, monetary policy, to combat what it saw as the problems of unsustainable growth in domestic spending and a deteriorating current account deficit. The end result was a lengthy recession, from which the Australian economy had not emerged fully by end-1993.

Reflecting these and other concerns, there is considerable agreement in Australia currently that enterprise bargaining is fundamental to micro-reform of the labour market. The move to a a less centralised wage-fixing system is expected to lead to improved work practices and productivity at the enterprise level, with employees benefiting from factors such as increased wages, broader skills and more varied and interesting employment.

The approach is consistent with the available empirical data, which suggests that neither the Accord nor the previous indexation period resulted in significant increases in productivity (Lewis and Kirby, 1988). The latter outcome could, *inter alia*, have reflected union stewards acting in the 'interest' of their members by negotiating non-wage elements of the workplace bargain as partial substitutes for the higher wages that were unattainable under the centralised wage-fixing system. The non-wage elements could have included featherbedding agreements and agreements for reduced work intensity. Such arrangements were prevalent during 1989–90 at the Sydney SABH plant considered above.[22]

To a significant degree, it is the forces of competition in product markets that ensure firms do not grant wage rises which are inconsistent with productivity and conditions in their labour market. However, as the Metal Trades Industry Association of Australia (MTIA) (1991) emphasises, enterprise bargaining creates considerable risks for firms and employment outcomes in circumstances where unions are strong and firms operate in a competitive market. The possible dangers from decentralisation of wage fixing in the Australian context are emphasised by experiences in the 1960s and early 1970s, and again in 1981–2, which showed that the generalising effect of flow-ons produces an excessive overall wage movement.

Some interest groups suggest that these experiences indicate that the IRC needs to retain tight control over possible wage increases, until reforms are introduced that deal with issues such as lack of competition in some product markets, union power, legal delays in response to industrial action, and the multi-enterprise structure of unions and awards.

The move in Australia towards enterprise bargaining took a substantial step forward when the commonwealth government decided to support a revised wages system with a greater emphasis on facilitating improvements in productivity. In late October 1991, the IRC announced its decision in the 1991 National Wage Case. From then on, the IRC was prepared to ratify enterprise bargaining agreements made between parties under Sections 111 (consent awards) and 115 (certified agreements) of the Industrial Relations Act, subject to certain requirements being met.

The requirements retained relatively tight control by the IRC, in an attempt to deal with concerns such as the prospect of unsustainable wage flow-ons and lack of productivity improvement, given the structure of the Australian labour market. With respect to these concerns, for example, any wage rises were to be based on actual implementation of efficiency measures designed to effect real gains in productivity, and agreements were to set out the specific efficiency measures and wage rises agreed.

The move in Australia towards greater reliance on enterprise bargaining, subject to tight control by the IRC and the achievement of improved productivity, can be seen as an attempt to move to more favourable productivity and perhaps employment, competitiveness and efficiency outcomes than were possible under the previous Accord process.

Given apparent difficulties with the implementation of Section 115 agreements, the Minister for Industrial Relations announced in October 1991 that the commonwealth government would legislate to define more clearly the certified agreement provisions under Section 115 of the Industrial Relations Act and to separate them from the conciliation and arbitration system (Davis, 1991). Under the changes introduced in the 1992 legislation, Division 3A certified agreements, which do not require the IRC to apply the public interest test except in the case of multi-employer agreements, replaced Section 115 agreements. They require union involvement. Section 111 consent agreements, in contrast, are subject to the public interest test. In practice, they require the formal participation of unions.

Further changes were unveiled in October 1993 to facilitate enterprise bargaining. Key aspects were that:

- employers would not be able to dismiss most employees without valid reason, and minimum periods of notice were set, ranging up to four weeks for an employee with more than five years' service;
- strikes and lockouts would be legal in a 'bargaining period', but the IRC would be able to terminate the period if a party were not bargaining in good faith;[23]
- the secondary boycott provisions of the Trade Practices Act dealing with industrial action would be transferred to the Industrial Relations Act;
- a pre-litigation conciliation period, of a maximum seventy-two hours, would be required if unions broke laws against secondary boycotts, although the IRC might allow immediate access to the court if conciliation would not resolve a dispute or if serious damage were occurring;
- unions would be able to scrutinise but not veto non-union enterprise flexibility agreements;
- the IRC would, on application, be able to establish minimum wages for employees with no access to compulsory arbitration (as in Victoria) and to make orders to ensure that male and female workers received equal remuneration, including over-award payments, for work of equal value;
- employers must provide twelve months unpaid parental leave;
- an Industrial Relations Court would absorb the industrial jurisdiction of the Federal Court; and
- court registrars would be able to deal with unfair dismissals and small claims.

As noted by Smith (1993), the proposed legislation hands unions a raft of protections deriving from international law, while they retain considerable buffers from the chilly winds of competition in labour markets. According to Sloan (1993), the legislation makes little difference to the way in which large companies with heavily unionised workforces conduct their industrial relations, nor does it facilitate industrial relations change in the many smaller and less unionised companies (for to do so would attract the scrutiny of the unions). However, it: 'significantly erodes employers' capacity to withstand union blackmail through secondary boycotts', according to the Chairman of an Australian transport company, Mayne Nickless (Corrigan, 1993). Moreover, the scope for enterprise bargains to feed back into awards has the potential to generate rapid and excessive flow-ons, thereby creating an upward bias to wage rises (Sloan, 1994).

In addition to such issues, there is also the Australian tradition of craft-based trade unions, which limit the scope for realising gains from enterprise bargaining arrangements.

• A craft-based union structure is associated with rigid work demarcations that discourage multi-skilling and moves to more flexible and efficient work practices.

• Craft or occupation-based unions have opposed changes in individual firms, even when they have been supported by and offered potential benefits to their members, on the grounds that the changes might set bad precedents for members working in other firms.

• Firms can be reluctant to negotiate changes in one award in a multi-award, multi-union plant because of fear that such changes would bring demands from the other unions for similar changes. The time and effort required to negotiate change in multi-union firms may also act to discourage management from seeking change.

Most of these problems would be alleviated by a move to industry unions, as proposed by the ACTU and federal government. But only branches of unions with substantial autonomy at the firm level or enterprise unions, with their workplace focus, would seem to deal with the second issue.

Further reform could include lifting the trade union monopoly over certain categories or classes of employment. The key regulatory changes required to achieve this end include the abolition of the 'conveniently belong to' rule, the minimum size requirements, the coverage rules of existing unions, and the closed shop and preference-to-unionists award clauses where they are undemocratically imposed. Under this more competitive model, existing unions would have to perform to survive and those able to offer different or superior services would be well placed to expand. This approach would increase the incentive for unions to provide an effective collective voice in the workplace, and is consistent with the conclusion of Freeman (1986) that unions, like other institutions, need competition to keep them doing their best.

Also, bargaining outcomes could be improved with a move to relatively autonomous local branches of unions at the enterprise level, advised by officials from head office when required, as is the practice in the USA. Legislative amendments would be necessary for union locals to have the power to sign enterprise agreements in Australia. An extension of this process would involve the possibility of enterprise unions with complete autonomy or a system of voluntary agreements between employers and workers, as implemented in New Zealand.

Even with reform in these areas, union–firm bargains could result in higher wages but lower employment, profits and investment than those in a more competitive labour market. Such outcomes might be ameliorated by the implementation of power-reducing, enfranchising, employment-promoting and demand management policies, depending on particular circumstances.

To the extent that the market power of employed 'insiders' is judged to be a major factor that distorts employment, wage and investment outcomes, policies directed at the reduction of such power deal directly with the distortion and are 'first best'. In summary, policy could be directed at restricting the imposition of the closed shop, at decreasing the likelihood and effectiveness of various forms of industrial action, at decreasing insiders' reservation wages (which are influenced by factors such as alternative minimum wages and unemployment benefits) and at changing job security laws by reducing the opportunities to challenge firms' hiring or firing decisions.

While power-reducing policies can result in additional employment, they typically leave insiders worse off, owing to a decrease in their wages. On this basis the implementation of power-reducing policies could be expected to be resisted by privileged insider groups. Nevertheless, the successful implementation over time of the microeconomic reforms already adopted by the commonwealth Labor government shows that it is possible to persuade interest groups that change is necessary. A different course would be to implement substantial reform while making it clear to insider groups that protests would have no effect on the extent or pace of change. The success of such an approach would, in part, be governed by whether such policy announcements by government were perceived as credible.

In contrast, some enfranchising policies directed at improving the chances that outsiders will gain employment are unlikely to be resisted by insider groups. Such policies include training programmes and support for profit-sharing and employee share-ownership schemes. The lack of resistance to these policies could reflect the expected outcome of higher compensation for employees, but an uncertain impact on employment. Other policies in the enfranchising category include two-tier wage systems and measures that reduce the barriers to entry of new firms. Insiders are likely to resist the implementation of such policies, because they could be expected to result in downward pressure on wages.

Employment-promoting measures are intended to make insiders, entrants and outsiders more profitable for firms to employ. This policy category includes initiatives such as government investment in infrastructure and decreases in the rate of payroll tax. The expected outcomes from these policies are an increase in real wages, but an ambiguous change in employment. In contrast, measures to open the economy to greater foreign competition and to promote greater domestic competition by removing regulatory barriers to competition could have favourable effects on the level of employment, as well as having beneficial effects on the supply side of the economy.

Demand-side policy includes government employment policies, and those that affect aggregate demand in the product market. The former category tends to increase both employment and real wages, whereas the latter policy category tends to have an uncertain effect on employment outcomes where nominal wages and prices adjust rapidly to government policy. Of course, any beneficial direct effects of such policies could be offset by the adverse indirect effects on the economy of taxation measures to finance the policy initiatives.

Apart from the implementation of initiatives to promote greater domestic competition in product markets, the extent to which the commonwealth government has implemented policies to reform the labour market and thereby expand employment has been limited. As the Secretary to the Australian Treasury commented recently (Dwyer, 1993):

> If we are today looking for innovative solutions for reducing unemployment, that is partly because, over the last two decades, we have found innovative ways of creating unemployment.

Such views have even more weight, given the context of high levels of total (around 11 per cent) and long-term unemployment (around 350,000) in Australia, of limited growth in overall productivity and real wages over the Accord decade, and of several years of slow or negative GDP growth associated with 'the recession we had to have'.

While reduced protection against imports and a recent, lengthy recession have brought home to most Australian management that improved firm performance via approaches such as changed attitudes to customers and improved work practices is vital to firm success, the slow, incremental pace of labour market reform in Australia continues to diminish the extent of that success and that of the economy generally. Perhaps only a climacteric, like a rapid increase in the rate of unemployment (to 15 per cent, for example) following external shocks to the Australian economy will do the trick, as it did in the UK in the early 1980s (Metcalf, 1989).

10 Nonparametric approaches to the assessment of the relative efficiency of bank branches

HENRY TULKENS AND AMADOR MALNERO[1]

The analysis in this chapter is devoted to the 'production' aspect of the activities of a multibranch bank, that is, to the relation between the physical resource usage and the number of operations performed in each branch, per unit of time. This limited point of view prevents one from deriving an overall evaluation of the bank's performance, because the financial values involved in these operations are of paramount importance when this is the objective.

There are nevertheless good reasons for paying some attention to the strictly productive aspects of this service activity. On the one hand, for given financial values, a high productive efficiency is obviously more desirable than a low one. On the other hand, while it is clear that operations apparently inefficient from a production point of view may sometimes be explained and justified by the high financial yield they provide, it would be of interest to enable the management to identify separately these two components of the overall return. To that effect, a rigorous methodology to capture each of them is called for.Here, we provide tools for dealing with the former, leaving for a future occasion an integration with financial analysis.

For assessing the physical productivity of bank branches, we make use of what is known today as 'efficiency analysis', a technique based on the notions of a production set and of the frontier of such a set. In the case of our bank branches, a common production set is assumed to be attainable by all branches, and efficient branches are those whose activities correspond to points belonging to the frontier whereas the activities of inefficient branches belong to the interior of the production set.

The frontier itself is determined from the statistical data that describe the activities in terms of inputs and outputs, a task for which quite a variety of techniques have been developed in the literature (Lovell, 1993, provides an excellent survey of them, including their connection with productivity measurement). Our choice of frontier is the so-called 'Free Disposal Hull' (FDH), whose basic properties are expounded and discussed in Tulkens (1993a), including its relations with the alternative 'Data Envelopment Analysis' (DEA) frontiers developed by Charnes *et al.* (1978), after Farrell's (1957) initial contribution.[2]

The present application bears on a large panel of data relating to bank branches, described in the first section. We then experiment with the assessment of frontier efficiency over first time and then space, that is, per region of operation. It will be seen that taking account of both the time and the space components of the data raises specific methodological problems to which there are hardly standard answers. We shall thus have to devise some of our own.

Previous studies of bank branch efficiency and/or productivity that we are aware of are of limited help in that respect, either because of the paucity of the data they use, or because they do not involve time and space elements. Thus, in the pioneering study of Sherman and Gold (1985), the efficiency of a single cross-section of only fourteen branches of an American bank is evaluated, on the basis of branch data aggregated over one year. Nonparametric DEA frontiers are used. The same methodology is used in Vassiloglou and Giokas (1990) for analysing twenty branches of a Greek bank (all branches located in Athens). In Giokas (1991), the results of this last study are compared with those of a log-linear parametric model, applied to data concerning seventeen branches of the same bank. Finally, in Tulkens (1993a, Section 3) single cross-sections of more than eight hundred branches of two banks – a private and a public one – are studied by means of both DEA and FDH frontiers, yielding an interesting comparison of efficiency performance in the private and the public sectors. As the results on this issue appeared to be sensitive to the choice of frontier, arguments were presented that support the FDH ones.

Data and notation

We have available a panel of data bearing on the monthly operations taking place in each one of 663 branches of a major bank in Belgium. The panel extends over the eleven-month period February–December 1987. For each branch $k = 1,2,...,n$ $(n = 663)$ at time $t = 1,2,...,m$, $(m = 11)$, the data consist of a vector $y^{kt} = (x^{kt}, u^{kt})$ of the monthly quantities $x^{kt} = (x_1^{kt},...,x_i^{kt},...,x_I^{kt})$ of I inputs used and $u^{kt} = (u1_j^{kt},...,uj_j^{kt},...,u_J^{kt})$ of J outputs achieved during that period. We thus denote the dataset as

$$Y_0^{KT} = \{(x^{kt}, u^{kt}) \mid x^{kt} \in R_+^I, u^{kt} \in R_+^J, k = 1, 2, \ldots, n; t = 1, 2, \ldots, m\} \cup \{(0^I, 0^J)\},$$
$$(10.1)$$

where $(0^I, 0^J)$, , the origin of the $(I + J)$-dimensional space, is added for reasons explained below.

The list of outputs that we shall use is as follows:

1. Operations on demand and short-term deposits
2. Operations on opening of new accounts and issuance of bank cards
3. Operations on long-term deposits and earning assets
4. Operations on loans
5. Miscellaneous transactions.

This is a five-dimensional aggregate of the fifty-three different kinds of operations on which each branch reports monthly to the bank's headquarters. The criteria used for aggregation were (i) to put in the same category all operations of the same nature (for example, all operations relating to all kinds of loans, for category 4), and (ii) with the exception of those operations which, on the basis of time and motion studies, take much more time than the average in the category: those operations are included in the Miscellaneous category, which also contains items relatively less frequent such as issuance and payment of traveller's cheques, financial transfers to foreign countries, and so on.

Our aggregation procedure is admittedly coarse. As our main purpose here is the methodology of treatment of panel data, rather than an in-depth study of the actual performance of the bank, we leave for another occasion the discussion of output aggregation.

On the input side, our data file is limited to only one input, namely labour. It is expressed in terms of the number of hours of work accomplished in each branch, per month. Table 10.1 gives a summary of our data for the month of February, and figure 10.1 shows the frequency distributions of the averages of our input and output data over the eleven months of the observation period. Taking labour as a size indicator, figure 10.1a reveals that small branches obviously dominate: 414 branches (62 per cent) total less than 500 hours per month on average; counting one worker for approximately 150 monthly hours, that makes 414 branches with three or fewer employees. Furthermore, only 85 branches (13 per cent) total more than 1000 hours (about seven employees).

Table 10.1 *Summary statistics of the data for the month of February*

	Labour (hours)	Short-term deposits	Accs & cards	Long-term deposits	Loans	Misc.
Minimum	146	7.00	358.00	0.00	24.00	62.00
Maximum	3369	1302.00	18247.00	259.00	1167.00	7298.00
Average	586	200.30	3928.94	26.94	255.63	688.17
Median	414	143.00	3074.00	19.00	185.00	517.00

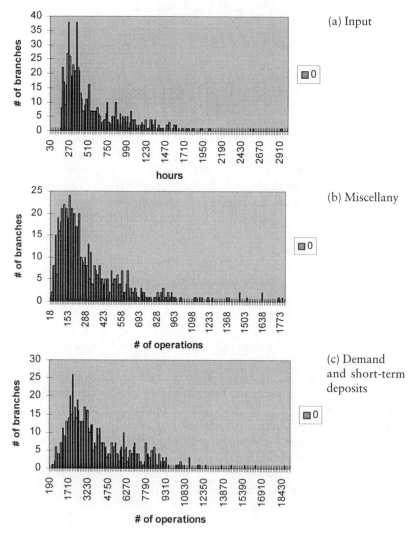

(a) Input

(b) Miscellany

(c) Demand and short-term deposits

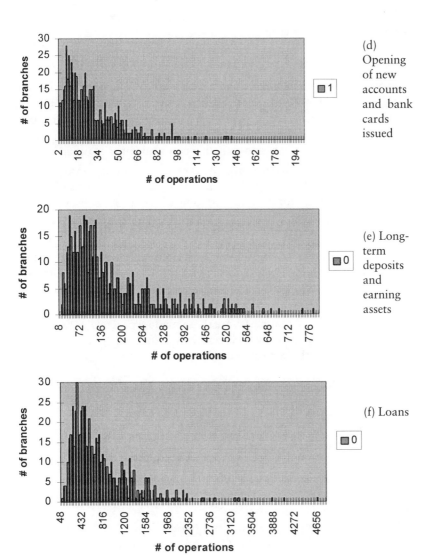

Figure 10.1 *Frequency distributions of average levels of input and outputs*

Assessing efficiency over time

Defining contemporaneous, sequential and intertemporal frontiers

We proceed here along a three-way line initiated in Tulkens (1986, section 6) and re-exposed in Tulkens and Vanden Eeckaut (1993) (sections 3 and ff.). According to this approach, efficiency analysis of panel data is made in terms of three successive estimates, respectively called 'contemporaneous', 'sequential' and 'intertemporal', that complement each other. In brief,

(*i*) *contemporaneous* efficiency estimates are those made separately at each point in time t in reference to the data observed *at that time only*: thus, using at each $t = 1,2,...,m$ the corresponding observations subset

$$Y_0^{Kt} = \{(x^{kt}, u^{kt})^t \,|\, k = 1,2,...,n\} \cup \{(0^I, 0^J)\} \tag{10.2}$$

as reference observations set. The successive reference technologies – that is, the series of production sets constructed from the monthly data and used for efficiency assessment are, in this case, assumed to be unrelated to one another.

(*ii*) *sequential* efficiency estimates are those made separately at each point in time t in reference to the data observed *up to that time only*: thus, using at each $t = 1,2,...,m$ the corresponding observations subset

$$Y_0^{K(1,t)} = \{(x^{ks}, u^{ks}) \,|\, k = 1,2,...,n; s = 1,2,...,t\} \cup \{(0^I, 0^J)\} \tag{10.3}$$

as reference observations set. The successive reference technologies, in this case, are assumed to be nested into each other, later ones always containing earlier ones.

(*iii*) *intertemporal* efficiency estimates, finally, are those made only once, using the whole observations set Y_0^{KT}, defined in (10.1), as reference observations set. The reference technology, in this case, is assumed to be invariant over time.

'Window analysis', as proposed by Charnes *et al.* (1985) is actually a special case of (*ii*), with elements of (*iii*): on the one hand, within the 'window', an intertemporal-type of computation is being made; the size of the window, on the other hand, remains constant whereas with (*ii*) it increases over time.

Finally, the convention that the origin $(0^I, 0^J)$ be an element of the reference observations set is a natural one to make, and we use it in the efficiency computations by means of FDH frontiers that we shall do below. Notice however that in the 'variable returns to scale' version of the alternative DEA frontiers, the reverse convention must be made, as explained in Tulkens (1993a).

Measurement formulae

EFFICIENCY MEASURES

Each one of the estimates mentioned above can be made using as reference technology any nonparametric or parametric frontier. As mentioned in the introduction, we shall use FDH frontiers. Although the efficiency measures can be made either in input or in output terms, we limit ourselves to input measures.

Our method of computation is conveniently summarised in terms of the following well-known optimisation problem. Specifically, for any observation (x^{kt}, u^{kt}), its efficiency degree in input is obtained as the value θ^{kt*} of the objective function at the optimal solution of the mixed integer programme:

$$\min\{\theta^{kt}, \gamma^{hs}, (hs) \in \overline{Y}_0\} \theta^{kt}, \text{ subject to}$$

$$\sum_{(hs)\in\overline{Y}_0} \gamma^{hs} u_j^{hs} \geq u_j^{kt} \quad j = 1,\ldots,J$$

$$\theta^{kt} x_i^{kt} - \sum_{(hs)\in\overline{Y}_0} \gamma^{hs} x_i^{hs} \geq 0 \quad i = 1,\ldots,I$$

$$\sum_{(hs)\in\overline{Y}_0} \gamma^{hs} = 1 \text{ and } \gamma^{hs} \in \{0,1\}, (hs) \in \overline{Y}_0,$$

where

(a) $\overline{Y}_0 = \{(hs) \big| (x^{hs}, u^{hs}) \in Y_0^{Kt}\}$

or

(b) $\overline{Y}_0 = \{(hs) \big| (x^{hs}, u^{hs}) \in Y_0^{K(1,t)}\}$

or

(c) $\overline{Y}_0 = \{(hs) \big| (x^{hs}, u^{hs}) \in Y_0^{KT}\}.$

The alternative definitions of the sets $\overline{Y}_0$ correspond to the alternative treatments of time that our three-fold distinction implies. Indeed, if (a) applies, then $\theta^{kt*} (\leq 1)$ measures the *contemporaneous* FDH-efficiency degree, in input, of observation (x^{kt}, u^{kt}); if (b) applies, then θ^{kt*} measures the *sequential* FDH-efficiency degree, in input, of this observation; and if

(c) applies, $\theta^{kt}*$ measures the *intertemporal* FDH-efficiency degree, still in input, of the same observation.

DECOMPOSED MALMQUIST PRODUCTIVITY INDICES

As both the contemporaneous and the sequential approaches allow for shifts over time of the monthly reference frontiers, one may be interested in measuring such shifts. This can be done by means of the Malmquist productivity index (introduced by Caves *et al.*, 1982), in the ingeniously decomposed form proposed by Färe *et al.* (1989). Typically, the latter authors express, for a given unit k, the Malmquist index $M^{k(t,t+1)}$ of its productivity change from time t to time $t+1$ as as the product of two indices: one that measures the efficiency change of that unit (that is, the degree of its 'catching up to the frontier'); this index is denoted below as $C^{k(t,t+1)}$ – and another one that measures the extent to which the frontier (used to measure efficiencies at t and at $t+1$) shifts (that is, technical progress); this index is denoted below as $S^{k(t, t+1)}$.

Thus, for branch k, observed at times 1 and 2, one has:

$$M^{k(1,2)} = C^{k(1,2)} \times S^{k(1,2)},$$

where the values taken on by the three indices involved imply, respectively:

—   for $M^{k(1,2)}$, productivity growth (if > 1), or decline (if < 1) of branch k;

—   for $C^{k(1,2)}$, branch k lying closer to (if > 1), or farther away from (if < 1) the contemporaneous frontier at time 2 than it was at time 1 with repect to the time 1-frontier;

—   for $S^{k(1,2)}$, an upward shift (if > 1), or downward (if < 1) of the frontier at time 2 *vis-à-vis* the one at time 1.

The precise formulae for computing these indices when FDH reference frontiers are used can be found in Tulkens and Vanden Eeckaut (1993, section 5.4).[3] Let us just point out here that, interestingly enough, they all are combinations and/or extensions of the mathematical programming problem presented above.

Applying the above to bank branches

EFFICIENCY MEASURES

Table 10.2 and the accompanying diagrams in figure 10.2 synthesise the numerical results obtained from an application to our dataset of the three efficiency measures defined above. We observe the following:

— *Contemporaneous* efficiency estimates yield average efficiency scores that fluctuate within the rather narrow band [0.92, 0.95], as well as a percentage of observations being efficient that fluctuates between 48 per cent and 61 per cent of the total. This suggests good stability of efficiency over time, although both ways of counting show a slight decrease during the two summer months, followed by a return, during the last four months of the year, to the efficiency levels of the early months.

— *Sequential* estimates modify this picture, however, showing: (*i*) a summer decline that is much more pronounced; and (*ii*) that the recovery in the last months is simply not there any more.

— *Intertemporal* estimates show a further modified picture, which is actually the reverse of the first one: there is now a peak in efficiency performance during the summer months and a lower performance in both the early and the later parts of the year.

These apparently contradictory results reveal that the overall productivity performance of the branches might have a time profile quite different from the stable one initially suggested by the successive contemporaneous efficiency estimates. But what time profile?

Let us first remember that the differences in the results come, of course, from the fact that different observations sets are used for reference in each case: gradually larger sets with the sequential estimates, as compared with the constant size sets used with the contemporaneous ones, and finally the full dataset with the intertemporal estimate. Next, considering the latter, it is clear from the two next-to-last lines of table 10.2 that the summer months play a dominant role in the determination of the position of the intertemporal frontier: 45 per cent of the branches are intertemporally efficient in July whereas the proportion is much lower for all other months. Finally, by looking at the time profile of the data, we noticed that during the summer months the aggregate output was lower (owing to less business activity in the country), and the input level too (owing to holidays of the bank's personnel). We therefore interpret the intertemporal results as suggesting that the latter is reduced *more* than the former: hence efficiency increases in these months. The seasonal personnel reduction thus induces a productivity increase that is not maintained, however, in the rest of the year.

DECOMPOSED MALMQUIST PRODUCTIVITY INDICES

In terms of contemporaneous frontiers, the above finding could mean that the successive frontiers of this type shift upward during the summer months, and downward in the spring and autumn. This conjecture happens to be confirmed by the further results, presented in table 10.3, of a computation of decomposed Malmquist productivity indices.

Indeed, one notices from the values taken on by the Malmquist indices in the top third of the table (in particular, from the line labelled 'average') that a significant change in productivity occurs in July (a 10 per cent increase with respect to June); it is followed in the three months thereafter by three successive decreases, with the most severe one in August with respect to July. Now, the two other parts of the table show that in both cases the productivity changes are essentially due to frontier shifts: indeed, the average values of the frontier shift index are very close to those of the productivity index, and – consistent with that – the catching up index does not vary noticeably from 1.

We thus identify a marked seasonal pattern in productive performance, characterised on the one hand by a rather stable efficiency performance vis-à-vis contemporaneous frontiers, and on the other hand by upward shifts of these frontiers in the summer, compared with the rest of the year.

Admittedly, this is by itself only a modest achievement. It may be of interest, however, to report that in a similar experiment done with data from eight hundred postal offices in Belgium extending over twelve months of 1983, Tulkens (1986) also found a seasonal pattern, but of exactly the reverse shape: there, outputs and inputs were reduced too in the summer, but the input was actually reduced by *less*: inefficiency thus prevailed during the summer months, reflecting a lack of flexibility in labour. The picture is thus quite different, in spite of the fact that here also, successive contemporaneous efficiency estimates had initially yielded what appeared to be a quite stable monthly efficiency performance.

More generally, it is clear that the methods used here to bring to light these time varying efficiency-productivity performances could also be exploited to characterise longer periods, extending over several years, for example. Here technical progress or regression could be identified and its sources and causes sought.

Finally, there are further by-products one can obtain from these kinds of analyses, that lie at the level of the individual units. Table 10.3 reports individual indices for a sample of ten units, each of which is thus characterised in terms of its own productivity change, of its 'catching up' in efficiency, and of the frontier change whereby it is concerned. Similarly, the efficiency scores used to construct table 10.2 are in fact individual ones (not shown here) whereby each unit can be evaluated over time. These very detailed results are naturally more destined to managerial uses: they could be used, for instance, in the design of rewarding schemes for the units' managers, based on their productive performance so measured.

Table 10.2 *Efficiency scores*

	2 Feb.	3 March	4 April	5 May	6 June	7 July
Contemporaneous						
no. obs.	663	663	663	663	663	663
no. eff	401	358	407	377	349	336
% tot.	60	54	61	57	53	51
eff. ave.	0.95	0.94	0.95	0.94	0.94	0.92
Sequential						
no. obs.	663	1326	1989	2652	3315	3978
no. eff.	401	318	339	282	302	328
% tot.	60	48	51	42.5	45	49
eff. ave.	0.95	0.92	0.93	0.91	0.92	0.92
Intertemporal						
no. obs.	7293	7293	7293	7293	7293	7293
no. eff.	182	151	120	118	171	300
% tot.	27	23	18	18	26	45
eff. ave.	0.85	0.82	0.82	0.825	0.85	0.91
	8 Aug.	9 Sept.	10 Oct.	11 Nov.	12 Dec.	ef.pt.t.
Contemporaneous						
no. obs.	663	663	663	663	663	70
no. eff.	319	358	353	374	392	10.5%
% tot.	48	54	53	56	59	
eff. ave.	0.92	0.94	0.94	0.94	0.94	
Sequential						
no. obs.	4641	5304	5967	6630	7293	8
no. eff.	208	76	61	63	113	1.2%
% tot.	31	11	9	9	17	
eff. ave.	0.87	0.76	0.74	0.77	0.81	
Intertemporal						
no. obs.	7293	7293	7293	7293	7293	5
no. eff.	208	75	61	63	113	0.7%
% tot.	31	11	9	9	17	
eff. ave.	0.87	0.76	0.74	0.77	0.81	

Notes: no. obs. = number of observations; no. eff. = number of efficient observations; % tot. = proportion of efficient branches; eff. ave. = average efficiency score; ef.pt.t. = number of branches efficient throughout the year.

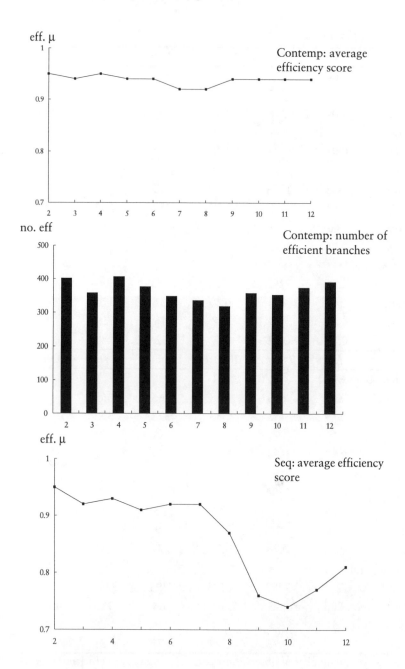

Figure 10.2 *Efficiency scores*

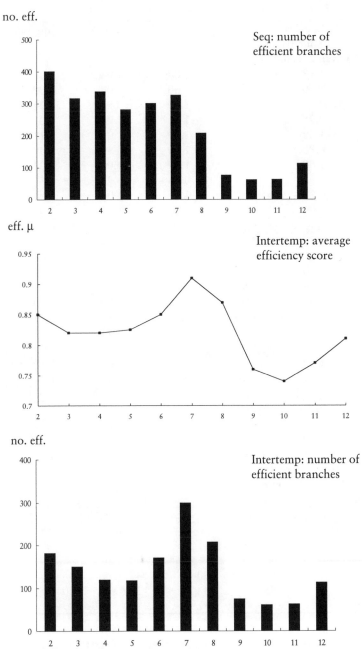

Figure 10.2 *continued*

Table 10.3 *Decomposed Malmquist productivity indices*

Branch cod.	Mar/Feb	Apr/Mar	May/Apr	June/May	July/June
Malmquist productivity index					
Sample of results at the branch level					
81013	1.13	1.00	1.00	1.04	1.06
81030	1.00	1.00	1.00	1.00	1.00
81038	0.95	1.00	1.00	0.96	1.09
81042	0.95	0.99	1.01	1.00	1.02
81044	1.00	1.00	1.00	1.03	1.11
81059	0.98	1.07	1.00	0.98	1.00
81060	1.00	1.00	1.00	1.00	1.02
81074	0.99	0.95	0.93	0.99	1.37
81077	0.98	1.00	1.12	1.00	1.00
81085	1.00	0.90	1.01	1.29	1.00

	Aug/July	Sept/Aug	Oct/Sept	Nov/Oct	Dec/Nov
81013	0.98	1.00	1.00	1.00	1.00
81030	1.00	1.00	1.00	1.00	1.08
81038	1.00	0.98	1.00	1.00	1.01
81042	0.94	0.93	0.96	1.02	0.95
81044	0.89	0.93	1.01	1.00	1.00
81059	0.98	1.00	1.00	0.82	0.95
81060	0.96	0.86	1.00	0.93	1.03
81074	1.03	0.99	1.00	1.00	1.00
81077	1.00	0.87	1.03	1.07	1.10
81085	0.71	1.14	0.95	1.00	1.01

Branch cod.	Mar/Feb	Apr/Mar	May/Apr	June/May	July/June
Summary statistics					
max.	1.68	1.47	1.36	1.65	1.75
average	1.00	1.01	1.01	1.02	1.10
min.	0.66	0.69	0.65	0.65	0.69
no of br>1	187	241	228	266	407
no.of br=1	159	175	166	126	81
no of br<1	194	152	187	151	116

	Aug/July	Sept/Aug	Oct/Sept	Nov/Oct	Dec/Nov
max.	1.91	1.52	1.49	1.65	1.81
average	0.96	0.91	0.97	1.02	1.02
min.	0.59	0.51	0.64	0.56	0.71
no of br>1	142	90	137	246	255
no.of br=1	95	43	124	150	166
no of br<1	299	492	317	139	123

Table 10.3 *continued*

Branch cod.	Mar/Feb	Apr/Mar	May/Apr	June/May	July/June
Frontier shift index					
Sample of results at the branch level					
81013	1.13	1.00	1.00	1.00	1.05
81030	1.00	1.00	1.00	1.00	1.00
81038	0.95	1.00	1.00	1.04	0.99
81042	0.97	0.96	1.06	1.00	1.02
81044	1.00	1.00	1.00	1.02	1.11
81059	1.00	1.00	0.99	0.98	1.00
81060	1.00	1.00	1.00	1.00	1.02
81074	0.99	0.95	0.97	1.15	1.19
81077	0.98	1.00	1.12	1.00	1.00
81085	1.00	1.27	0.85	1.08	1.00
	Aug/July	Sept/Aug	Oct/Sept	Nov/Oct	Dec/Nov
81013	0.98	1.00	1.00	1.00	1.00
81030	1.00	1.00	1.00	1.00	1.08
81038	1.00	0.94	1.00	1.00	1.00
81042	0.95	0.93	1.11	1.02	1.02
81044	0.89	0.93	1.01	1.00	1.00
81059	0.98	1.00	1.00	1.10	1.06
81060	0.96	0.86	1.00	1.13	1.13
81074	0.97	0.99	1.00	1.00	1.00
81077	1.00	0.87	1.03	1.02	1.10
81085	0.92	0.88	1.06	1.00	1.01
Branch cod.	Mar/Feb	Apr/Mar	May/Apr	June/May	July/June
Summary statistics					
max.	1.35	1.64	1.44	1.38	1.55
average	1.01	0.99	1.02	1.03	1.10
min.	0.76	0.73	0.71	0.77	0.88
no of br>1	244	179	266	300	490
no.of br=1	156	176	168	126	77
no of br<1	140	213	147	117	37
	Aug/July	Sept/Aug	Oct/Sept	Nov/Oct	Dec/Nov
max.	1.18	1.08	1.21	1.24	1.47
average	0.96	0.89	0.97	1.02	1.02
min.	0.63	0.61	0.75	0.80	0.78
no of br>1	123	9	105	253	264
no.of br=1	93	43	124	152	166
no of br<1	329	573	346	130	114

Table 10.3 *continued*

Branch cod.	Mar/Feb	Apr/Mar	May/Apr	June/May	July/June
Malmquist productivity index					
Sample of results at the branch level					
81013	1.00	1.00	1.00	1.00	1.00
81030	1.00	1.00	1.00	1.00	1.00
81038	1.00	1.00	1.00	0.92	1.09
81042	0.98	1.04	1.00	1.00	1.00
81044	1.00	1.00	1.00	1.00	1.00
81059	0.95	1.03	1.01	1.00	1.00
81060	1.00	1.00	1.00	1.00	1.00
81074	1.00	1.00	0.96	0.86	1.15
81077	1.00	1.00	1.00	1.00	1.00
81085	1.00	0.71	1.19	1.19	1.00
	Aug/July	Sept/Aug	Oct/Sept	Nov/Oct	Dec/Nov
81013	1.00	1.00	1.00	1.00	1.00
81030	1.00	1.00	1.00	1.00	1.00
81038	1.00	1.00	1.00	1.00	1.00
81042	1.00	1.00	0.95	1.05	1.00
81044	1.00	1.00	1.00	1.00	1.00
81059	1.00	1.00	1.00	1.00	1.00
81060	1.00	1.00	1.00	1.00	1.00
81074	1.06	1.00	1.00	1.00	1.00
81077	1.00	1.00	1.00	1.00	1.00
81085	0.78	1.28	0.90	1.11	0.79
Branch cod.	Mar/Feb	Apr/Mar	May/Apr	June/May	July/June
Summary statistics					
max.	1.66	1.66	1.68	1.56	1.63
average	0.99	1.01	0.99	0.99	0.99
min.	0.60	0.64	0.58	0.62	0.54
no of br>1	110	185	129	128	150
no.of br=1	266	272	281	250	235
no of br<1	164	111	171	165	219
Total no. of obs.	545	568	561	543	504
	Aug/July	Sept/Aug	Oct/Sept	Nov/Oct	Dec/Nov
max.	1.94	1.91	1.55	1.55	1.97
average	1.01	1.01	1.01	1.01	1.01
min.	0.62	0.57	0.71	0.50	0.58
no of br>1	165	234	176	163	128
no.of br=1	216	226	246	247	279
no of br<1	155	165	156	125	137
Total no of obs.	536	625	578	535	544

Assessing frontier efficiency by region of operation

Defining regional frontiers

The 663 branches of the bank under study being scattered across the entire country, they are organised into 'regions', each of which is headed by a regional director, in charge of supervising the branches located on the territory of his region. The idea then naturally emerges of evaluating each branch's efficiency relative only to those belonging to the same region. To this effect, one constructs a specific and distinct frontier for each region, and measures on that basis what we shall call 'within region inefficiencies'. When this is done, an interesting further analysis can be made, comparing the regional frontiers thus obtained, so as to evaluate the regions (and possibly the regional directors) vis-à-vis each other.

These two analyses are set out in this section. Our bank comprises the following ten regions (the number of branches in each appears in parentheses):

Region

1 BRUSSELS (105)	6 LIMBURG (46)
2 ANTWERP (107)	7 LIEGE (53)
3 VLAAMS BRABANT (68)	8 NAMUR & BRABANT WALLON (39)
4 OOST VLAANDEREN (80)	9 HAINAUT (79)
5 WEST VLAANDEREN (73)	10 LUXEMBOURG (13)

Measurement formulae

REGIONAL FRONTIERS COMPARISON

On the one hand, measuring efficiency within each region, at each time t, is done by means of the same model as above, except for the proviso that in each case the range of the index k in the definition of $\overline{Y_0}$ is restricted to the number of branches within each region.

On the other hand, measuring the distances *between* regional frontiers requires specific techniques. The particular one we use here[4] is inspired by those presented in Tulkens and Vanden Eeckaut (TVE) (1993) for measuring progress and regress with panel data. We substitute for the comparison between two frontiers at different moments of time, a comparison between regional frontiers at the same moment in time. Specifically, we apply the algorithm developed in section 5.2b (pp. 20–25) of TVE.

DOMINANCE EVALUATION ON A REGIONAL BASIS

A by-product of FDH frontiers is that every inefficient observation can be characterised by referring to the units that 'dominate' it: that is, units that produce more output with less input. This approach, whose general properties are developed in Tulkens (1993b), can also be applied at the regional level, leading one to distinguish between dominances occurring within a region and those occurring with units outside of the region to which the dominated unit belongs.

Application to bank branches

COMPARING REGIONAL FRONTIERS

The method mentioned above essentially yields pairwise comparisons of frontiers, some of which are illustrated in figure 10.3, for the month of February, 1987.[5]

Each diagram shows, for the input levels of each regionally efficient branch of the region quoted first (for example, Region 2: Antwerp in figure 10.3a) a measure of the distance between this branch and the frontier of the region quoted second (Region 1: Brussels in the case of figure 10.3a). If that measure is less than 1, the (Antwerp) regionally efficient branch in question lies 'below' the other (Brussels) regional frontier; if that measure is larger than 1, it lies 'above' the other frontier; if the distance is measured as equal to 1, the two frontiers coincide for this level of input.

From figure 10.3, it turns out that for the month of February, 1987, the frontier observations of Region 2: Antwerp, and of Region 3: Vlaams Brabant, lie either on or below the frontier of Region 1: Brussels. Furthermore, one can see from figure 10.3c that the frontier of Region 3 lies above that of Region 2 for input levels smaller than five hundred.

This analysis can be pursued further in the same terms but it is quickly becoming fastidious and unclear, simply because the number of pairs of regions is large. A synthetic presentation is needed, that we suggest with tables 10.4 and 10.5.

We present there, respectively for small branches (that is, with an input level under 500 hours) and for large branches (with an input level over 500 hours), a matrix of pairwise dominance between regional frontiers, as measured by the average of the efficiency scores just used.[6] Only half of the matrix is needed since if region a dominates region b, region b is dominated by region a.

The implications are summarised in table 10.6. On the one hand, Region 1: Brussels clearly dominates the rest of the regions in the country; on the other hand, the relative positions of the frontiers for the other regions are quite different for small and large branches.

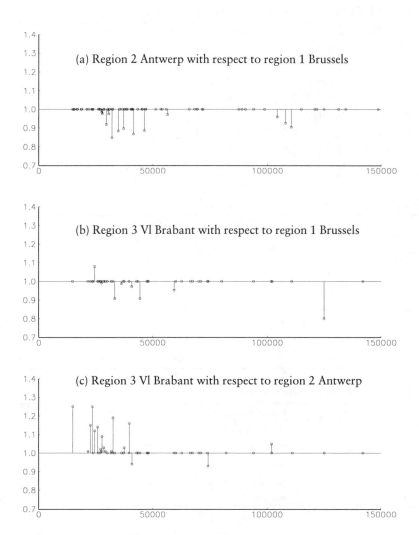

Figure 10.3 *Regional frontiers compared*

As only the result for the Brussels region is clear cut, it is worth seeking an explanation. One could argue that it is due to the fact that many people living outside the city come to Brussels to work and make mainly withdrawals, a quite routine operation indeed (often made with ATMs). Another possible explanation, offered in discusssion with one of the bank's managers was that, in Brussels, the bank had met difficulties in recruiting

Table 10.4 *Small branches (less than 500 hours worked)*

Evaluated frontier	Reference frontier (Region)						
	1	2	3	5	4	6	9
Region 2	0.98						
Region 3	0.994	1.045					
Region 5	0.987	0.986	0.961				
Region 4	0.996	1	0.965	1.008			
Region 6	1	1.019	1.005	1.015	1.002		
Region 9	0.99	1.025	0.994	1.02	1	0.993	
Region 7	0.998	1	0.989	1.003	1	0.99	0.988

Table 10.5 *Large branches (more than 500 hours worked)*

Evaluated frontier	Reference frontier (Region)						
	1	2	3	5	4	6	9
Region 2	0.998						
Region 3	0.985	1.045					
Region 5	0.987	1.021	1				
Region 4	0.996	1	1	0.985			
Region 6	1	1	1	1	1		
Region 9	0.99	1.025	1	0.995	0.985	0.991	
Region 7	1	1	0.995	0.995	1	0.98	1

Table 10.6 *Relative frontier positions*

Frontier position	Small branches	Large branches
Highest	Regions 1 and 6	Region 1
	Region 3	Region 5
	Region 9	Region 4
	Regions 2, 4 and 7	Region 9
Lowest	Region 5	Region 2

bilingual employees, a quality absolutely necessary there. The resulting manpower shortage should therefore have driven the efficiency levels of the activities in this region upwards.

Some problems arise, however. First, in the case of small branches, there is no detected dominance between Region 9 and Region 4; but this is in contradiction with the fact that Regions 2 and 7 coincide with Region 4 *and* are dominated by Region 9. Second, in the case of large branches, we could not rank Regions 3, 6 and 7 because of an almost total absence of domination relations with other regions. One explanation for these problems could be the relatively small size of our regional samples (the three unranked regions in the case of large branches have fewer than twenty observations). Another possible explanation lies in our use of average indices calculated over too wide a range of the input.

EVALUATING DOMINANCE ON A REGIONAL BASIS

The breaking down of the results can also be considered from the more managerial viewpoint described above. Here, the focus is on *individual* performances rather than on averages, having in mind what a regional manager could do to improve bad, that is, dominated, situations.

This is the purpose of table 10.7 below. We present there, for the sixty-three branches of one region (Brussels), a summary of their domination situation on a national basis.

The top third of the table concerns the fourteen Brussels branches that are *regionally inefficient*, that is, dominated by at least some other branch of the same region (and possibly also by branches of other regions). In this case, improvement can be considered at a regional level since the regional manager is shown branches within his own region that obtain better results; these can thus be taken as 'models' for the inefficient ones. One can see that dominance by several other branches does not occur very often: only for two cases (nos. 83202 and 83556) out of the total of sixty-three. These are of course the best candidates for audit and possibly reform.

In the second third of the table, we consider eight Brussels branches that are *regionally efficient* but *nationally inefficient*, that is, dominated only by branches belonging to other regions. Here, the regional manager has to consider whether methods or techniques used in these other regions could improve the efficiency of the units under his authority. The validity of the comparision can be questioned. Is it justified, for instance, to compare bank branches of big cities and of small villages? Notice that in this case, the number of occurrences of such a kind of dominance is rather low.

Finally, the last line of the table mentions the Brussels branches that are *nationally undominated*, that is, belonging to the national frontier. This is by far the largest group within the Brussels observations (65 per cent). This – as well as the remark ending the last paragraph – is of course due to the fact that the Brussels region structurally dominates those in the rest of the country, as was seen above. Efficiency analysis has nothing more to say about the branches of this third group except that they were efficient at the time they were observed.

Table 10.7 *Breakdown of Brussels branches according to regional dominance relations*

Branch code	Number of units dominating within									
	own region	other regions								
	1	2	3	4	5	6	7	8	9	10
Nationally and regionally inefficient Brussels branches										
83202	2	2	1	2	7	0	2	0	1	0
83556	7	4	9	4	2	1	1	1	4	0
83655	2	0	2	0	0	2	1	0	1	0
83671	2	0	0	0	1	0	0	0	0	0
83672	1	0	0	0	0	0	0	0	0	0
83747	1	0	0	0	0	0	0	0	0	0
83781	1	0	0	0	0	0	0	0	0	0
83820	1	0	1	0	0	0	0	0	2	0
83853	1	0	0	0	0	0	0	0	0	0
83957	1	0	0	0	0	0	0	0	0	0
83961	1	0	0	0	0	1	0	0	0	1
83981	1	0	0	0	0	0	0	0	0	0
83984	1	0	1	0	0	0	0	0	0	0
83985	3	0	0	0	0	0	0	0	1	0
Regionally efficient and nationally inefficient branches										
83147	0	0	0	0	0	0	0	1	0	0
83149	0	0	0	0	0	1	0	0	1	0
83150	0	0	0	0	0	0	0	0	1	0
83620	0	0	0	0	0	1	0	0	0	0
83633	0	0	0	2	0	1	1	0	2	0
83816	0	0	1	0	0	0	0	0	0	0
83953	0	0	0	0	0	0	0	0	1	0
83955	0	0	0	0	0	0	0	0	1	0
Number of remaining branches (nationally undominated): 41										

11 Productivity growth, plant turn-over and restructuring in the Canadian manufacturing sector

JOHN R. BALDWIN

The competitive process leads to constant growth and decline. At the margin of an industry, firms are entering and exiting. Within the main body of the population, incumbents are in a constant state of flux. Some are gaining market share. Others are losing market share. The manner in which this process is associated with productivity growth in the Canadian manufacturing sector during the 1970s has been outlined elsewhere in Baldwin and Gorecki (1991) and Baldwin (1995).[1]

This chapter extends the earlier work by examining the relationship between productivity growth and turnover for both the 1970s and the 1980s. By doing so, it investigates whether the earlier pattern extends into the 1980s. This is meant to confirm the importance of turnover and to investigate how the productivity slowdown that has occurred in the Canadian manufacturing sector in the 1980s is related to restructuring.

Examinations of productivity change are not normally conducted at the microeconomic level. The Solow growth literature traditionally examines how input change and output change are related at an aggregate level. By focusing on issues such as the quality and quantity of inputs that are being used by all firms in an industry, it ignores changes occurring within the industrial structure that may be causing trends or cycles in productivity. These changes can take several forms. First, the intensity of competition may differ over time. The extent to which new more productive firms emerge and wrestle market share away from the less innovative may vary considerably across periods, perhaps because of the existence of long-run innovation waves. Another cause of the recent productivity slowdown may originate in basic shifts in industrial structure – but not of industrial structure as it has normally come to be defined, that is the type of industries possessed by a country. Rather the relative importance of the underlying

245

production entities may change across a wide range of industries as one type of firm begins to supplant another. Shifts in technology, which make scale and scope economies more or less important, could underlie such changes.

Since the aggregate approach is not well suited to exploring the type of structural change occurring within industries, this chapter uses micro data at the plant level to do so. Two different taxonomies are utilised in order to examine microeconomic change. In the first case, plants are divided into those gaining and those losing market share. In the second, plants are divided into size classes to examine shifts in the relative importance and productivity of different sized plants.

The first section of the chapter discusses the connection between turnover and productivity growth. The second section investigates how the intensity of turnover differs over the three periods. The third section then investigates underlying changes in structure by size class.

Growth and productivity in the manufacturing sector

Changes in real GDP and employment in the Canadian manufacturing sector since 1973 are presented in figure 11.1. Real GDP in manufacturing increases in the 1970s, declines during the major recession in the early 1980s and then resumes a strong growth in the 1980s. Employment increases in the 1970s to a peak in 1981, declines dramatically in the recession of 1982, and then grows during the rest of the decade, regaining its 1979 peak only in 1987.

For the purposes of this study, the period from 1973 to 1990 is broken into three subperiods: 1973–9, 1979–85; and 1985–90. Figure 11.2 summarises the differences in the rates of growth in real manufacturing GDP, employment, manufacturing GDP per capita and the growth in total (multi) factor productivity in each of the three subperiods. The cumulative rate of growth in real GDP declines over the three periods – from 15.9 per cent to 9.6 per cent to 5.4 per cent. Cumulative employment growth is positive in the first period (4.8 per cent), turns negative in the second (–4.8 per cent), and then grows by 5.4 per cent in the last period. Productivity growth is much slower in the third period than in the two earlier periods. GDP per capita grows by 13.1 per cent and 15.3 per cent in each of the first two periods, but only by 0.3 per cent in the last. Total (multifactor) productivity increases by 8.1 per cent and 12.7 per cent in the first two periods, and declines by 8.0 per cent in the third period.[2]

The first period then is characterised by growth in both output, employment and labour productivity. The second is dominated by a sharp reces-

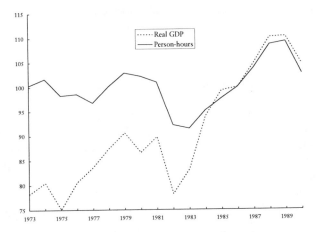

Figure 11.1 *Employment and output in manufacturing*

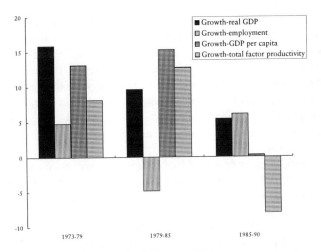

Figure 11.2 *Cumulative growth characteristics*

sion with output growing again quickly, but with employment not return-
ing to its pre-recession levels by the end of the period. The last period finds
the weakest growth in output and productivity growth.

The effect of turnover on labour productivity

Average labour productivity in an industry is simply the weighted average of the labour productivity of plants in an industry. It equals

$$\sum_{i=1}^{n} E_i \times AP_i$$

where E_i is the employment share and AP_i is the average productivity of the ith plant.

Changes in productivity can be traced to turnover to the extent that plants gaining employment share also become more productive. The size of the contribution made by producer turnover depends on the extent to which labour share is transferred from the less productive to the more productive segment and on the size of the changes in relative productivity of gainers and losers. This chapter examines the nature of this change by concentrating on two sectors. The first includes incumbents that continue throughout the period. The second contains entrants and exits.

Continuers: The population of continuing plants is divided into those that are gaining market share (growers) and those that are losing market share (decliners) over the period of study. The growers, G, are those that have found new products, new production processes and are capturing market share from those that are in decline, D. The change in market share of the growers, ΔMS_g, is just equal to the loss in market share of the decliners, ΔMS_d. Growing plants will also experience a change in their employment share ΔES_g, which need not equal the change in market share experienced, especially if their labour productivity ΔAP_g is increasing.

Declining plants will experience a change in their employment share ΔES_d just equal to ΔES_g. Since average productivity is the labour-share weighted average of the productivity of individual groups, changes in average productivity depend both on changes in the relative labour shares of growers and decliners and on changes in their relative productivity.

Denote the employment share of gainers in the final period as ES_{G2} and in the initial period as ES_{G1}, their labour productivity in the final period as AP_{G2} and the initial period as AP_{G1}; the employment share of losers in the final period as ES_{L2} and in the initial period as ES_{L1}, their labour productivity in the final period as AP_{L2} and the initial period as AP_{L1}. Then the change in productivity between the beginning (period 1) and final (period 2) is:

$$(ES_{G2} \times AP_{G2} + ES_{L2} \times AP_{L2}) - (ES_{G1} \times AP_{G1} + ES_{L1} \times AP_{L1}). \qquad (11.1)$$

This can be decomposed in a number of different but arbitrary ways. One is

$$[(ES_{G2} \times (AP_{G2} - AP_{G1}) + ES_{L2} \times (AP_{L2} - AP_{L1}) + (ES_{G2} - ES_{G1})(AP_{G1} - AP_{L1})]. \qquad (11.2)$$

Another is

$$[ES_{G1} \times (AP_{G2} - AP_{G1}) + ES_{L1} \times (AP_{L2} - AP_{L1}) + (ES_{G2} - ES_{G1})(AP_{G2} - AP_{L2})].$$
(11.3)

Decompositions such as these are mechanical. Using them to calculate the effect of turnover without carefully stating the assumptions that underlie the counterfactual that generates them can be misleading.

If it is assumed that without the competition which results in market turnover, market shares would have remained the same and only the declining sector would have had productivity growth, then it can be demonstrated (Baldwin, 1995) that the amount of productivity growth resulting from this turnover is the sum of the first and third terms of equation (11.2). Together these terms capture improvements in productivity because gainers capture market share (the third term) and because gainers improve their own productivity (term one).

If it is assumed that, without the competition associated with turnover, both gainers and losers would have experienced the same productivity growth as actually occurred, but that their shares would have remained the same, then competition and turnover would produce productivity growth as measured by the third term in equation (11.2). This term captures just the amount of productivity growth due to shifts in market share. It provides a conservative estimate of the effect of the competitive process since competition is the stimulus that creates productivity growth in the sector that gains market share and this is not included in the third term.

If it is assumed that without the competition associated with turnover, gainers would have experienced the same productivity improvement as losers and that there would have been no change in the market share of each group, then the gain from turnover can be represented as:

$$ES_{G1} \times (AP_{G2} - AP_{NEW}) + (ES_{G2} - ES_{G1}) (AP_{G2} - AP_{L2}),$$
(11.4)

where AP_{NEW} is $AP_{G1} / AP_{L1} \times AP_{L2}$. The latter assumes that the ratio of the productivity of gainers in the final period would be just the same as the ratio of gainers to losers in the first period. By doing so, we presume that the productivity growth in the losing sector is essentially exogenous, that it would have occurred irrespective of pressures being exerted on firms in the losing sector by the firms that are wresting market share from them. Since this is unlikely to be correct, this measure understates the contribution that is made by the turnover process.

The latter expression is adopted here to measure the effect of plant turnover. It consists of two parts. The first term captures the amount of productivity gain that results from gainers improving their productivity faster than losers. The second captures the portion that is derived from the replacement of losers by gainers – by the substitution of the employment share of losers with the employment share of gainers. In order to provide a benchmark for comparing the effect of turnover on productivity across periods, the value of equation (11.4) is divided by final year productivity. This ratio reveals how much productivity in the final year would have been lowered in the absence of turnover.

Entrants Assumptions regarding the nature of the effect of competition on the replacement process are just as critical for calculating the effect of entry and exit on productivity growth. Entrants are usually less productive than continuing plants. Exits are also less productive than continuing plants. If entrants are assumed to replace continuing plants, entry has a negative effect on average productivity (see Baldwin and Gorecki, 1991). If entering plants essentially replace exiting plants, then the contribution of entrants will depend on the relative productivity of entrants and exits. Earlier work suggested that the latter is a more realistic assumption, at least for the 1970s in the Canadian manufacturing sector. It will, in the first instance, be adopted here; but its continued validity for the 1980s will be examined.

Denote the market share captured by entrants as MS_{eg}, their employment share ES_{eg}, and their labour productivity AP_{eg}; the loss in market share of exits as MS_{ed}; their employment share ES_{ed}, and their labour productivity AP_{ed}. For the group of continuing plants, denote their labour share in the final period as ES_{cf}, and in the beginning period as ES_{cb}; their average productivity in the final period as AP_{cf}, and in the beginning period as AP_{cb}. Then productivity change can be written as

$$(ES_{eg} \times AP_{eg} + ES_{cf} \times AP_{cf}) - (ES_{ed} \times AP_{ed} + ES_{cb} \times AP_{cb}). \tag{11.5}$$

By assuming that entrants replace exits, we can write the change in productivity as

$$ES_{eg}(AP_{eg} - A_{ed}) + ES_{cf}(AP_{cf} - AP_{cb}) + (ES_{cf} - ES_{cb})(AP_{cf} - AP_{cb}).[3] \tag{11.6}$$

The first term captures the change that is due to the productivity difference between entrants and exits. The third term captures the effect of changes in the relative size of the group of plants that are entering and exiting. The second term represents the growth in productivity due to progress in continuing plants and was discussed above.

In order to provide a natural benchmark against which the productivity

of entrants and exits can be measured, the productivity of each will be calculated relative to continuing plants, at the end and the beginning of the
periods, respectively. Let

$$AP_{eg} = k_1 \times AP_{cf} \tag{11.7}$$

$$AP_{ed} = k_2 \times AP_{cb}. \tag{11.8}$$

Then the larger is $k_1 - k_2$, the greater will be the proportion of total change
in productivity that is accounted for by entry and exit.

Data

In order to investigate the contribution that plant turnover makes to productivity growth, plants that gain market share are divided into two groups.
The first consists of new plants. The majority of these are plants that
belong to greenfield entrants – firms that enter the industry by building
new plants.[4] The second are incumbents that gain market share. Decliners
are divided into exiting plants, the majority of which are associated with
plants exiting an industry, and incumbents that lose market share.

Changes can be measured over either annual intervals or over longer time
periods. In the short run, considerable reversals occur in plant fortunes.
Plants that grow rapidly between two adjacent years are likely to reverse
direction in the next. Therefore, this study focuses primarily on periods that
are long enough to give a sense of the amount of permanent change that
takes place, though where appropriate, the annual displacements are also
presented for contrast. Three longer-run periods are chosen: 1973–9; 1979–
85; and 1985–90. The division of plants into growing and declining segments is done separately for each of the time periods.

The data are derived from a longitudinal file of plants in the Canadian
Census of Manufactures that tracks plants over the period from 1973 to
1990 using a consistent set of SIC codes that allow market shares to be
calculated over the time period.[5] Shares are calculated at the 4-digit industry
level.[6]

Results

Market and employment share shifts

On an annual basis, over 10 percentage points of market share is transferred to gainers from losers. Figure 11.3 depicts the gain in market share

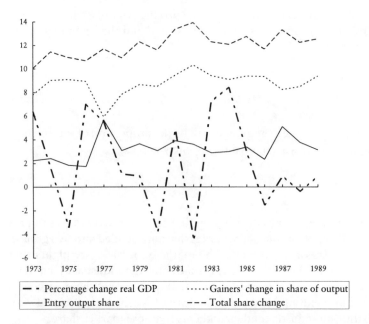

Figure 11.3 *Annual market share gains – average per industry*

that both continuing plants and new plants capture annually from 1973 to 1990. About three-quarters of the change occurs in the continuing sector. There is very little cyclical change in the amount of share that is transferred annually.

Average annual change per 4-digit industry in the three periods is presented in table 11.1. Continuing plant gainers acquire about 8 percentage points of market share but only about 4.5 percentage points of employment share on average. The difference between output and employment share change also applies to the continuing plants that lose market share, where about twice as much output share than employment share is lost. This is consistent with the hypothesis that much of annual change in output share is unanticipated or that labour is a quasi-fixed factor in the short run.

The cumulative output and employment changes for the six-year periods are presented in table 11.2. Over the longer periods, considerable market share is transferred from one group to another. Those plants gaining market share acquire upwards of 13 percentage points over each period. Plants that have entered over the period and are still in existence in the final year acquire upwards of 17 percentage points of a 4-digit industry's market share on average.

Table 11.1 *Share change (mean of annual changes in percentage points)*

Period	Continuing gainers		Continuing losers		Entrants		Exits	
	Emp.	Out.	Emp.	Out.	Emp.	Out.	Emp.	Out.
1973-9	4.1	8.2	4.3	8.6	3.3	3.0	3.0	2.4
1979-85	4.5	9.3	4.2	9.2	3.6	3.4	3.8	3.0
1985-90	4.4	8.8	4.4	8.9	4.2	3.5	4.3	3.4

Notes: Emp. = employment: Out. = output.

Table 11.2 *Share change (cumulative change in percentage points)*

Period	Continuing gainers		Continuing losers		Entrants		Exits	
	Emp.	Out.	Emp.	Out.	Emp.	Out.	Emp.	Out.
1973-9	9.6	13.6	11.5	16.1	19.5	17.8	17.6	15.4
1979-85	10.2	14.6	10.8	16.4	22.1	20.6	21.5	18.8
1985-90	10.1	16.7	14.2	19.8	28.1	25.0	24.0	21.7

Notes: Emp. = employment: Out. = output.
The figures for 1985–90 are augmented by 20 per cent to make them comparable
to the other two periods which were one year longer.

Employment shifts do not lag output shifts in the long run by as much
as they do in the short run. Plants gaining market share acquire some 10
percentage points of employment share in each period. Losers relinquish
more than 11 percentage points on average. Another major difference between the short and the long run lies in the changing relative importance
of continuing plants and entrants. In the short run, entrants gain less than
one third of the market share being acquired in total. In the longer-run
six-year periods, entrants account for more than one half of the total. In
the short run, entrants gain less than a third of all employment share
being transferred; in the long run, entrants account for two thirds of the
total gain in employment share.

Thus, the competitive process shifts over 30 percentage points of market share over each of the three periods. Figure 11.4 depicts the cumulative shifts in market share and the annual averages for each of the three
periods. The total being shifted has been increasing over time – from 31.4
percentage points in the first period to 41.7 percentage points in the last
period. Most of this increase is due to higher entry and exit.The productivity slowdown cannot be attributed to less turnover of market share in
the late 1980s compared to the earlier periods.

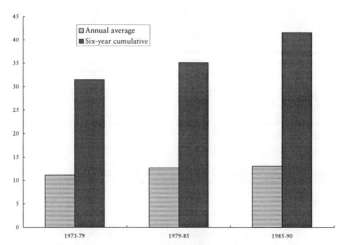

Figure 11.4 *Market share change by period*

Productivity

Entrants vs. exits in the short run Productivity gains are associated with turnover because plants that are increasing their share of the market become more productive than plants that are losing market share.

Exiting plants tend to be less productive than the population as a whole. They are eliminated by entrants, who are also less productive than the average, but are nevertheless more productive than exits. The part of the turnover process involving entrants and exits increases the productivity of the less productive tail of the plant-size distribution.

If the productivity of entrants relative to all continuing plants at the end of the period is about the same as the productivity of exits relative to continuers at the beginning, then the turnover process does not change the *relative productivity* of this segment. However, the entry and exit portion of the turnover process does increase overall average productivity to the extent that it causes the less productive tail of the plant-size distribution to increase its overall productivity as the main group of the industry advances. When entrants are relatively more productive than exits, turnover from entry contributes even more to the productivity increase experienced by the less productive plants.

In order to investigate the contribution of entry, the average labour productivity (value-added per worker) of entrants and exits and continuing plants are plotted for the period 1973–90 in figures 11.5 and 11.6. Labour productivity is calculated as the unweighted average across all plants in a

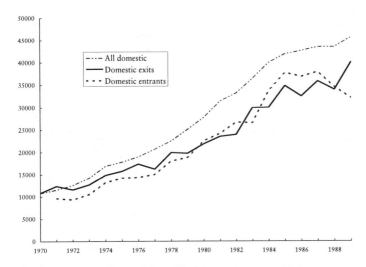

Figure 11.5 *Relative productivity of domestic entrants/exits*

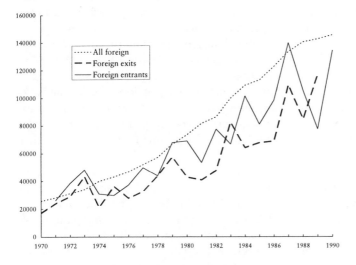

Figure 11.6 *Relative productivity of foreign entrants/exits*

category.[7] Figure 11.5 plots the productivity for domestically owned entrants and exits. Figure 11.6 does the same for foreign-owned entrants and exits. It is useful to distinguish these two groups because their characteristics are so different.[8]

Table 11.3 *Relative productivity changes over six-year periods*

	Continuing gainers/losers	Entrants/all continuers	Exits/all continuers
1973-9			
1973	0.996		81.3
1979	1.263	81.2	
1979-85			
1979	0.977		77.5
1985	1.330	84.2	
1985-90			
1985	0.946		81.3
1990	1.277	78.7	

In general, plant entrants and plant deaths are less productive than the population. The difference is less pronounced for foreign than for domestic plants. Indeed, there are several years in which average productivity of foreign entrants exceeds the average for all foreign plants. More importantly, foreign entrants are generally more productive in their first year of existence than are foreign deaths. Thus, foreign plant turnover, when considered by itself, contributes to productivity growth.

The productivity of domestic entrants, by contrast, does not as often exceed the productivity of exits. The productivity of domestic entrants does, however, exceed that of exits more frequently in the last half of the period. Nonetheless, the productivity of entrants declines dramatically in the last period, thereby suggesting that the relative productivity of new small firms was declining.

Changes in relative productivity in the longer run The relative productivity performance of both entrants/exits and continuing plants over the longer six-year periods is presented in table 11.3.[9] The first column contains the ratio of the productivity of continuing plants that gain market share relative to continuing plants that lose market share.

In each period, the gainers start at a small productivity disadvantage – the relative productivity ratio is less than one. In each period, the gainers have become considerably more productive than the losers by the end of the period – 26 per cent more productive by 1979, 33 per cent by 1985, and 28 per cent by 1990. The effect of turnover in the continuing sector on productivity is almost the same in each period. Using the formula discussed in the previous section, the productivity gain associated with turnover is calculated to have been 11.1 per cent, 13.1 per cent and 12.7 per

Figure 11.7 *Relative productivity of entrants*

cent of final year productivity. There is no indication then that the intensity of incumbent turnover, or its impact, has changed dramatically over the three periods being considered here.

Comparisons of columns 2 and 3 of table 11.3 show the longer-run effect of the entry/exit replacement process. In the 1973–9 period, the productivity of exiting and entering plants was some 81 per cent of the productivity of continuing plants. During the 1979–85 period, which was marked by a sharp decline followed by an equally sharp recovery, the relative productivity of entrants (84.2 per cent) exceeds that of exits (77.5 per cent). In the final period, the reverse occurs. The relative productivity of entrants is only 78.7 per cent of continuers while the relative productivity of exits is 81.3 per cent of continuers. The decline in the relative productivity of entrants by the last period suggests that entry began to make a lesser contribution to productivity growth by the third period.

Productivity of entrants versus continuing plants Because the performance of entrants is the one area in which divergences occur across the three time periods, the course of relative productivity of one category of entrants – greenfield entrants[10] – was investigated in more depth. The productivity of greenfield entrants relative to continuing firms for each of the first three years after birth was calculated for each of 235 4-digit industries and then averaged.[11] The results are reported for each entry cohort from 1971 to the mid-1980s in figure 11.7, along with the average wage rate of greenfield entrants relative to continuing firms. It is evident that relative productivity of entrants, which was in decline throughout the period, plummeted in

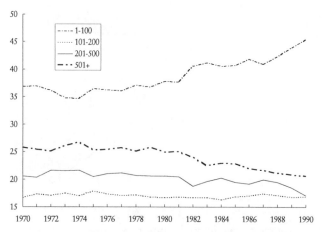

Figure 11.8 *Change distribution of employment by size class*

the mid-1980s. A major structural shift was occurring in the tail of the plant-size distribution.

Structural change in the size class distribution

Three important observations emerge from this investigation. First, turnover is increasing. Second the component that increases the most is entry. Third, there is a long-term downward trend in the productivity of entrants that accelerates in the last period.

Since entrants are smaller on average than are incumbent plants, an accumulation of new small plants via entry might be expected to have an influence on the relative productivity of small plants in general – unless entrants rapidly improved their lower initial labour productivity and wage rates relative to the population. This suggests that a major structural shift in the importance of small as opposed to large plants was taking place.

Figure 11.8 contains the relative share of employment for plants of different sizes – 1 to 100, 101–200, 201–500, and 500+ employees. Plants employing fewer than one hundred employees have increased steadily in terms of employment share over the period – from 35 per cent in the early 1970s to over 45 per cent by the end of the period. The increase was particularly rapid in the last period.

This change is not the result just of a shift of employment to sectors with relatively small plants. To demonstrate this, the manufacturing sector was divided into five major sectors – the natural resource, the labour intensive,

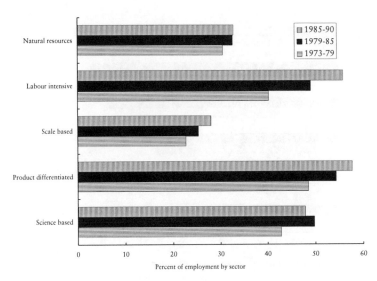

Figure 11.9 *Industry breakdown of small-firm growth*

the scale-based, the product-differentiated and the science-based industries. The five groups are defined on the basis of the primary factors affecting the competitive process. For the resource-based sector, the primary factor affecting competition is access to abundant natural resources. For the labour-intensive sector, it is labour costs. For scale-based industries, it is the length of production runs. For differentiated goods, it is tailoring production to highly varied demand characteristics. For science-based industries, it is the rapid application of scientific advance.

The five classifications were initially taken from a taxonomy developed by the OECD (1987) to investigate structural change. The OECD concordance was verified and modified with a discriminant analysis that used some fifty industry characteristics to test the validity of the classification scheme as it applied to Canada.[12] Industries are assigned to this classification based on characteristics such as natural-resource inputs, wage rates, the degree of scale economies, and advertising and research and development expenditures.

The proportion of total employment in plants with fewer than one hundred employees for each of these groups is reported in figure 11.9 for the three time periods. The proportion of employment accounted for by small plants is lowest in the scale-based industries where they have less than 30 per cent of total employment. Small plants are most important in the

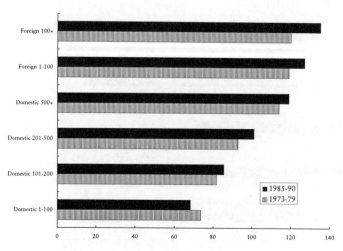

Figure 11.10 *Relative labour productivity by size class*

labour-intensive industries where they have over 50 per cent of the total by the third period. Nevertheless, in all five sectors their share increases over the three periods – by some 5 percentage points in the natural-resource sector, 9 percentage points in the labour-intensive sector, 5 percentage points in the scale-based sector, 16 percentage points in the product-differentiated sector, and 3 percentage points in the science-based sector.

By itself, this shift in the relative importance of smaller plants would have slowed down the rate of increase in average productivity. Labour productivity of domestic plants in the smallest size class was about 74 per cent of the average in the first two periods. But as figure 11.10 demonstrates, average productivity of the smallest class fell in the last period to about 68 per cent of average at the same time as the relative labour share of this size class increased. The relative labour productivity of the other size classes increased over the same period.

The increase in the relative importance of small plants and their relative productivity decline are important explanations of the productivity slowdown that the Canadian manufacturing sector experienced in the late 1980s. An increase in the relative employment share over the entire period from about 28 per cent to 35 per cent combined with a decline in productivity relative to the entire population from 74 per cent to 68 per cent would have dragged labour productivity down by 5 percentage points. This has to be set against the drop in labour productivity growth rates from an average of 14.2 per cent in the first two periods to only 1.1 per cent in the last period.

Summary

This chapter asks how firm and plant turnover contribute to changes in productivity and whether there are discernible differences in the amount of turnover over the three periods. It finds that the normal growth and decline that occurs in incumbents has not changed appreciably over the three periods, nor has its effect on productivity. In contrast, the entry and exit process is characterised by several marked differences. First, it has become much larger. Second, the share of entrants now exceeds that of exits. This means that entrants are now supplanting not just exits as they did in the earlier period; they are also supplanting incumbents (at least for the purpose of calculating average productivity). Third, the relative productivity of entrants, which has been declining throughout the period, declined markedly in the last period.

There are two interpretations of the causes of turnover – of the shifting importance of different groups of plants. In the first, plants that become more efficient, or that become more productive, supplant those that are less productive. At the margin of an industry, new plants supplant exiting plants. In the main body of an industry, incumbents who find better ways of producing products take market share away from others. The superior production techniques and the better products of the former are all reflected in improved productivity and, therefore, turnover is associated with improvements in productivity.

But this is not the only dynamic force at work that can cause shifts in production activities from one group to another. Changing international comparative advantage may cause the eclipse of one group of producers and the rise of another. Competition for resources, of course, still takes place and facilitates the shifts of employment from one group to another. However, in this scenario, employment may not necessarily shift from low productivity to high productivity, from low wage to high wage plants.

Of course, the two forces may operate simultaneously. If the comparative advantage of a country should improve in high value-added industries, plants that expand will also be the more productive. But the opposite may also occur.

The evidence that has been adduced herein strongly suggests that a restructuring phenomenon has been occurring in the Canadian manufacturing sector, with small less productive plants gaining employment share at the expense of the more productive. The reasons for this adjustment are not yet clear. They may be related to the popular fear that good manufacturing jobs are being shifted outside Canada. They may be the result of new technologies which allow small plants to compete with large plants by using less capital-intensive technologies. The sudden increase in the importance of small plants in the late 1980s may lie in the undervalued dollar of the early 1980s which could have induced small, primarily domestic plants to expand unduly. If it is the latter, a major correction in the plant-size distribution should emerge from opposite movements that occurred in the Canadian exchange rate in the late 1980s and in the recession of the early 1990s which would have hit small plants especially hard. In any case, the reason for the rise of the small plant segment and the extent to which it is related to a change in the importance of different industries bear further investigation.

12 Downsizing and productivity growth: myth or reality?

MARTIN NEIL BAILY, ERIC J. BARTELSMAN
AND JOHN HALTIWANGER[1]

Productivity growth in the manufacturing sector of the US economy has been rapid over the past decade, and has been accompanied by a substantial reduction in employment. This has engendered the conventional belief that rising productivity in manufacturing and decreasing employment are inextricably linked through some microeconomic mechanisms. Some hold the view that technological progress leads to layoffs because of mismatches between newly desired labour quality and the skills of existing workers, or because of rigidities in wages and prices (for a recent review, see Johnson, 1994). Others hold the alternative view that productivity growth happens as a result of downsizing, or re-engineering, with its concomitant layoffs. Large-scale employment reductions by major companies are routinely reported in the media as part of this downsizing trend, and applauded by market analysts for improving productivity and making the company 'lean and mean.' The expansion of international trade is often seen as a source of the competitive pressure that has led to downsizing.

The conventional wisdom that productivity growth and downsizing are connected has some basis in fact. Figure 12.1a depicts annual output and employment for the period 1958–89 for the total manufacturing sector and figure 12.1b depicts the annual growth rate in labour productivity over this time. During the 1960s and 1970s, output and employment fluctuated cyclically around a growing trend with modest growth in productivity. In the 1980s, the pattern changed with output recovering robustly from the recession in the early 1980s and employment never fully recovering. Consequently, average labour productivity rose sharply over much of this period. We focus on this period of rising productivity and falling employment using plant level data for the Census of Manufactures in 1977 and 1987. Over this interval, total employment in manufacturing establish-

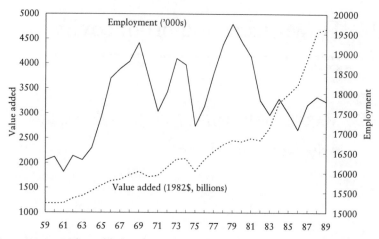

Figure 12.1a *Value added and employment, total manufacturing, 1959–89*

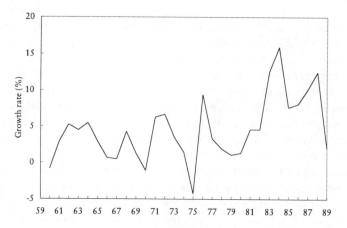

Figure 12.1b *Average labour productivity growth, total manufacturing, 1960–89*

ments fell by 4.5 per cent over the period 1977–87 even as productivity (measured by value added per worker) rose by 33 per cent.[2] Thus, it would appear that our sample of plant level data is consistent with the conventional wisdom.

It turns out, however, that it is quite misleading to draw inferences from these aggregate data to characterise what has been happening at the micro level to individual plants. Baily *et al.* (1992) and Bartelsman and Dhrymes (1992) describe the effects that composition changes have on the translation of plant level productivity to aggregate productivity behaviour.

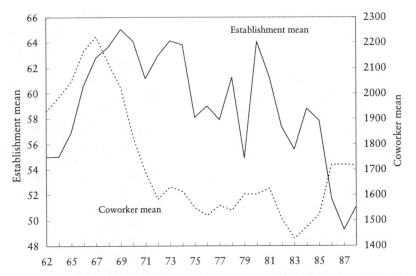

Figure 12.2 *Establishment and coworker mean, total manufacturing, 1962–88*

They find that growth in aggregate Total Factor Productivity (TFP) is mostly the result of changes in output shares between plants, rather than within plant increases in TFP.

Another related example of the pitfalls of relying on aggregate data can be found in Davis and Haltiwanger (1990). As shown in figure 12.2, the mean establishment size (as measured by published total manufacturing employment divided by total number of establishments) fell from fifty-eight workers in 1977 to fewer than fifty workers in 1987. This fact, based on aggregate data, seemingly provides evidence of significant downsizing over this period. However, the size distribution of plants is very skewed – while the typical plant is small, the typical worker works for a large plant. Davis and Haltiwanger define a summary statistic denoted the coworker mean, which is the employment-weighted average size of an establishment and thus represents the size of the plant for the typical worker.[3] The coworker mean is more than an order of magnitude larger than the mean plant size; the typical manufacturing worker in 1987 is employed at a plant with more than 1700 employees. More telling for our story is that the coworker mean, shown on the right axis of figure 12.2, fell in the late 1960s and early 1970s, before the full impact of international trade was felt. It actually has increased slightly from 1977 to 1987.

The finding that the size of the establishment for the typical worker has not declined in recent years is striking in light of the conventional wisdom on downsizing. This turns out to be just the first glimpse of the noisy, complex process of employment, output and productivity growth at the plant level. Recent work using plant level data (for example, Dunne *et al.* 1989; Baldwin and Gorecki, 1990a, 1991; Davis and Haltiwanger, 1990, 1992; Baily *et al.* 1992; Bartelsman and Dhrymes, 1992) presents a picture of a disperse distribution of output, employment and productivity growth rates that varies in both location and shape over time. We have learned from this work that when the aggregate economy grows, for example, this is accounted for by some plants growing and others contracting with the gross rates of change very large relative to the net change. This chapter continues in that tradition with a focus on the connection between employment growth and productivity growth at the plant level and the associated implications for aggregate employment and productivity growth.

As with prior studies, we find there is substantial heterogeneity among plants and industries. While layoffs often receive more publicity than do employment increases, there are in fact many manufacturing establishments where productivity growth accompanies increases in employment. Overall, plants that added workers contribute about the same to aggregate productivity as plants that downsized. Similarly, while downsizing is associated with increases in productivity, there are in fact many establishments where a reduction in employment accompanies productivity losses. Further, there are striking differences by sector (defined by industry, size, region and ownership type) in the allocation of plants in terms of whether they upsize or downsize and whether they increase or decrease productivity. While the detailed industry, region, size, ownership type and wage characteristics of plants do provide statistically significant information on the probability that a given plant is a downsizing productivity gainer, we find that most of the cross-sectional variance of productivity and employment growth rates cannot be explained by observable plant characteristics. Thus, the allocation of plants in terms of whether they upsize or downsize, increase or decrease productivity, is largely driven by idiosyncratic factors.

The data

Our primary dataset consists of all manufacturing plants that were in operation in both 1977 and 1987 as reported to the Censuses of Manufacturers (the 'continuers'). There are about 140,000 such plants. We will also present some information about those plants that were in operation in 1977, but that had shut down by 1987 (the 'exiters'); and also for the new plants that started between 1977 and 1987 (the 'entrants'). Because of the difficulty of matching plant identification numbers there is some error in allocating plants to the continuers, exiters and entrants, but we believe that this error is small.[4]

In our investigation, we consider both gross output and value added based measures of labour productivity. Gross output for our plants is measured as shipments adjusted for inventories, deflated by the 4-digit deflator for the industry in which the plant is classified. Labour input is the total employment of the plant; labour productivity, using the gross output method, is the ratio of the two. Value added is constructed for our plants by subtracting the real cost of materials from the gross output measure. The real cost of materials is measured as the dollar cost of materials deflated by a 4-digit material deflator. The value added measure of labour productivity is accordingly the ratio of plant level value added to plant level employment. In all cases, the results are reported in terms of 1982 dollars. We specifically chose the midpoint of our sample to minimise the distortions associated with using a fixed weight price index in this context.[5] Most of our results are presented in terms of the value added measure of labour productivity. We do this for a number of reasons. First, this is the conceptually preferable measure of labour productivity. Second, in spite of concerns about measurement error in both the plant level materials data as well as in the materials deflators, we find that the results are very similar with the gross output based measure.[6]

There are a number of relevant measurement concerns, given our data and methodology, that should be noted in interpreting our results. First, even for our value added based measure, we do not include the effect of purchased services. This is a concern since there is some evidence that the manufacturing sector has increased its outsourcing, particularly its purchases of services; our value added measure will capture increased outsourcing if it is in the form of intermediate physical inputs but will not capture changes in the role of purchased services. In addition, our labour measure – establishment level employment – neglects employees in auxiliary establishments such as head-office and R&D facilities. Note that Siegel and Griliches (1991) investigate the role of both of these measurement issues and conclude that they do not have much of an effect on the measurement of manufacturing productivity for the period 1977–82 (one half of our sample period). This provides some reassurance that these measurement concerns are not likely to have a serious impact on our results.

We recognise as well that our focus on labour productivity rather than total factor productivity affects the interpretation of our results. The role of capital deepening and biases in technical change cannot be well understood by the behaviour of labour productivity alone; for example, invest-

Table 12.1 *Summary statistics for Census of Manufacturers*

	1977	1987	Change (a)
Labour productivity			
All	53	73	3.87
Continuers	56	75	3.39
Entrants		67	
Exiters	44		
Employment ('000s)			
All	17850.791	17051.302	-0.45
Continuers	12776.966	12679.236	-0.08
Entrants		4372.066	
Exiters	5073.825		
Value added (1982, $ millions)			
All	938	1242	3.25
Continuers	716	952	3.29
Entrants		291	
Exiters	222		

Note: (a) Average growth over ten years, not at an annual rate.

ments in labour-saving equipment which increase labour productivity may not be successful from a TFP point of view.

Table 12.1 gives summary statistics of productivity, employment and output for all of manufacturing, for our primary sample of 140,000 continuing plants, and for the exiters and entrants. The results in table 12.1 are based on the value added measure and are restricted to plants with positive value added and materials purchases in the relevant years for the different types of plants (for example, continuers must have positive value added in both years). We see that productivity grew by 38.7 per cent for the sector as a whole for the ten-year period, while the continuers had productivity growth of 33.9 per cent.[7] It follows that the plants that entered between 1977 and 1987 had lower average labour productivity than the plants that exited. Plant turnover thus has a sizeable net positive effect on productivity. As seen, the labour productivity of exiters was substantially lower than that of the continuers, while it was not the case that entrants came in at higher than average productivity – consistent with the findings of Bartelsman and Dhrymes (1992). Decomposing the relative contribution of continuing plants and net entry, the increased productivity of the net entrants accounts for approximately 30 per cent of the overall increase in productivity from 1977 to 1987.[8]

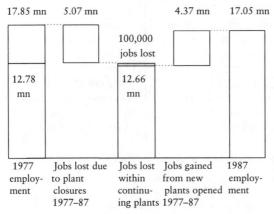

Figure 12.3 *Employment in US manufacturing establishments 1977 and 1987*
Note: Excludes plants with negative value added.

As shown in table 12.1, manufacturing employment declined by 0.45 per year.[9] Our main sample of continuers accounted for employment of 12.8 million in 1977 and (somewhat surprisingly perhaps) had just a small loss of 98,000 employees by 1987 (figure 12.3). Job destruction among the continuers thus has been almost fully offset by job creation by this same group (the job loss is only 30,000 if the negative value added plants are included). The net reduction in manufacturing employment has come about primarily from layoffs at plants that were closed which were not fully offset by hires at new plants.

The rate of output growth has been about the same in the continuers as in the whole sector. As a group, the continuers are consistent with the conventional wisdom – rapid output growth, mild employment contraction, and rapid productivity growth.[10]

Productivity and employment quadrants

In the remainder of this chapter we concentrate on the continuing plants. We have divided these continuing plants in our sample into four groups or quadrants, as illustrated in figure 12.4. Quadrant 1 consists of the 'successful upsizers', plants that were able to increase both labour productivity and employment. Quadrant 2 are the 'successful downsizers,' the plants that raised productivity but did so by reducing employment. Quadrant 3 are the 'unsuccessful downsizers', the plants that faced reductions in both productivity and employment. Finally, the quadrant 4 plants are the un-

QUADRANT II Successful Downsizers Δ Productivity > 0 Δ Employment < 0	QUADRANT I Successful Upsizers Δ Productivity > 0 Δ Employment > 0
QUADRANT III Unsuccessful Downsizers Δ Productivity < 0 Δ Employment < 0	QUADRANT IV Unsuccessful Upsizers Δ Productivity < 0 Δ Employment > 0

Figure 12.4 *Employment and productivity changes, 1977–87*

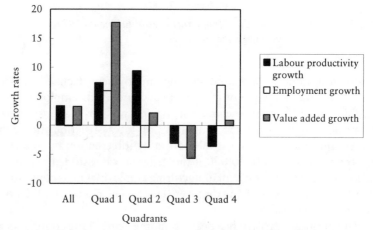

Figure 12.5 *Decomposition of MFG productivity growth, 1977–87*

successful upsizers, the plants that raised employment but at the expense of productivity.

Figure 12.5 shows the average annual percentage change in labour productivity, employment, and output for total manufacturing, and for the average plant in each quadrant. This figure illustrates clearly that productivity growth can occur by plants increasing or decreasing employment (quadrants 1 and 2), and that layoffs do not necessarily lead to successful increases in productivity (quadrants 2 and 3).

Plants can find themselves in quadrant 1 for a variety of reasons. First, the long-run increase in both labour productivity and employment is consistent with increased demand for its products combined with increasing returns technology. Alternatively, these plants could have actually moved

Table 12.2 *Summary statistics, by quadrant, 1977–87*

	All plants	DII>0 DL>0	DII>0 DL<0	DII<0 DL<0	DII<0 DL>0
Estab.	140501	44597.0	36238.0	19289.0	040377.0
pct.	1.00	31.74	25.79	13.73	28.74
Empl. pct. 77	1.00	23.91	44.79	18.80	12.49
Empl. pct. 87	1.00	38.50	28.21	11.91	21.38
Empl. growth	-0.08	5.98	-3.75	-3.71	6.98
VA pct. 77	1.00	20.22	40.50	23.38	15.90
VA pct. 87	1.00	42.26	37.01	7.66	13.07
VA growth	3.29	17.77	2.14	-5.65	0.92
Labour prod. grwth	3.39	7.38	9.43	-3.08	-3.57
productivity	4.30	7.51	10.08	-3.37	-3.22
empl. share	0.01	-0.36	0.30	0.23	0.03
cross term	-0.92	0.23	-0.94	0.06	-0.38
Contribution to labour productivity growth					
by quadrant	3.39	2.18	2.56	-0.62	-0.73
productivity		1.49	3.82	-0.72	-0.57
empl. share		-0.23	0.16	-0.17	0.24
cross term		0.91	-1.41	0.26	-0.40

their production frontier outward through technological innovation, while facing elastic product demand.

The conventional wisdom about US manufacturing over this period is captured in the quadrant 2 plants. These were the ones that raised productivity, but did so at the expense of jobs. This pattern is consistent with technological innovation combined with either falling demand or very inelastic demand (labour augmenting technical change is suggested in either case). If there were a simple way to characterise the whole manufacturing sector, then we should find that the bulk of manufacturing output and employment would be in plants in quadrant 2.

The employment and productivity behaviour of plants in the third quadrant are consistent with one of the following (i) falling demand and increasing returns to scale or (ii) negative productivity shock and elastic demand or (iii) falling demand and incomplete adjustment of employment. Based on this last interpretation, which we find the most plausible, we label these plants unsuccessful downsizers.

The final group of plants are those where falling productivity and rising employment place them in quadrant 4. The pattern here is consistent with a negative productivity shock and inelastic demand, or rising demand and diminishing returns. Alternatively, these plants could have shifted to lower quality employees, which could be observed by falling wages. We examine this hypothesis below.

Within-plant productivity growth and mix effects

In table 12.2 we show how the plants in our main group of 140,000 continuers break down into the four quadrants using the value added measure of labour productivity. There are between one quarter and one third of the plants in each of quadrants 1, 2, and 4. There are 14 per cent of the plants in quadrant 3.

Counting the number of plants may not be the most revealing way to see the relative importance of each quadrant, however, and table 12.2 also shows the employment and output shares. We see that the quadrant 1 and 2 plants make up the bulk of the sector both in employment and output. They account for two thirds or more of the sector in both 1977 and 1987. The large number of somewhat anomalous quadrant 4 plants are smaller than average.

The middle rows of the table give a decomposition for all the plants and for each quadrant separately that indicates how much of the productivity growth reflects increases within individual plants (the row labelled 'productivity') and how much comes from mix effects (the rows labelled 'employment shares' and 'cross terms'). Equation (12.1) shows the decomposition underlying these three rows in the table.

$$\frac{\Delta II_t}{II_{t-1}} = \frac{\Sigma_i \phi_{t-1,i} \Delta II_{t,i}}{II_t - 1} + \frac{\Sigma_i \Delta \phi_{t,i} (II_{t-1,i} - II_{t-1})}{II_{t-1}} + \frac{\Sigma_i \Delta \phi_{t,i} \Delta II_{t,i}}{II_{t-1}} \qquad (12.1)$$

where

$$\phi_i = \frac{L_i}{\Sigma_i L_i} 10 \quad .[11]$$

The first mix term (labelled 'empl. share') arises because of shifts in employment shares between plants. This term is positive or negative depending upon whether the plants that are above average in productivity are increasing or decreasing their shares of employment.[12] The table shows that for all plants together the term is positive, but very small. Within quadrants, this cross term is negative for the plants in quadrant 1, but positive for those in quadrants 2 and 3. It is essentially zero for the plants in quadrant 4.

The second mix effect (the row labelled 'cross term') is positive or negative depending upon whether plants that have positive productivity growth have increasing or decreasing employment shares, respectively, or vice versa. This term is negative overall, indicating that plants that have positive productivity growth do on average have decreasing employment. It alternates in sign among the quadrants (as it must given their definitions) – the quadrant 2 plants are dominating the cross term.

Although there are non trivial mix effects shown in these data, it seems that a fair general characterisation of the results is that most of the overall increase in productivity and most of the increase within each quadrant is accounted for by within plant changes. The changes in productivity over the ten-year period are not the result of mix effects. This finding is consistent with that of Griliches and Regev (1992), who look at the decomposition of labour productivity in Israeli manufacturing plants. Interestingly, it contrasts with the finding of Bartelsman and Dhrymes (1992) that TFP growth is mostly a result of mix shifts in the long run.

Contributions to overall growth by quadrant

The bottom four rows of table 12.2 treat each quadrant as a group and ask how much each group contributes to overall productivity growth. Quadrant 1 contributes almost two thirds of the overall growth. Quadrant 2 accounts for about three quarters of the overall growth. Thus, these two quadrants together account for more than the total increase in productivity as their contributions are offset by quadrants 3 and 4.

It is important to emphasize that each quadrant contributes not only through its own change in productivity, but also because its share of employment is changing. Equation (12.2) shows how this happens.

$$\frac{\Delta II_t}{II_{t-1}} = \frac{\Sigma_q \phi_{t-1,q} \Delta II_{t,q}}{II_t - 1} + \frac{\Sigma_q \Delta \phi_{t,q}(II_{t-1,q} - II_{t-1})}{II_{t-1}} + \frac{\Sigma_q \Delta \phi_{t,q} \Delta II_{t,q}}{II_{t-1}} \quad (12.2)$$

where $\phi_q = \dfrac{L_q}{\Sigma_q L_q}$, the share of manufacturing labour in quadrant

q, $II_q = \dfrac{Q_q}{L_q}$, and $Q_q = \Sigma_{i \in q} Q_i$, $L_q = \Sigma_{i \in q} L_i$.

Given equation (12.2), we see that quadrant 1 plants contribute both by the rise in productivity at each of these plants but also through the increased employment share (the positive cross term). The contribution of quadrant 2 coming from rising productivity (holding employment shares fixed) is higher than that of quadrant 1, even though the plants in these

Table 12.3 *Summary statistics, by quadrant, 1977–87, gross output*

	All Plants	ΔΠ>0 ΔL>0	ΔΠ>0 ΔL<0	ΔΠ<0 ΔL<0	ΔΠ<0 ΔL>0
Estab.	146525	43881.0	37521.0	20541.0	44582.0
pct.	1.00	29.95	25.61	14.02	30.43
Empl. pct. 77	1.00	24.22	45.40	17.78	12.61
Empl. pct. 87	1.00	38.83	28.30	11.24	21.63
Empl. growth	-0.03	5.99	-3.78	-3.69	7.11
Q pct. 77	1.00	19.59	43.33	21.01	16.07
Q pct. 87	1.00	39.03	36.45	8.96	15.57
Q growth	2.18	14.27	0.24	-4.81	1.79
Labour prod. growth	2.21	5.17	6.47	-1.76	-3.11
productivity	3.11	5.51	6.81	-2.48	-2.51
empl. share	-0.11	-0.55	0.44	0.61	-0.24
cross term	-0.79	0.21	-0.78	0.10	-0.36
Contribution to labour productivity growth					
by quadrant	2.21	1.35	1.83	-0.35	-0.61
productivity		1.01	2.81	-0.37	-0.50
empl. share		-0.28	0.08	-0.12	0.25
cross term		0.61	-1.06	0.14	-0.36

quadrants have about these same productivity growth rates, on average. This is the result of the negative impact of the falling employment shares (shown by the negative cross term) in quadrant 2.

Quadrants 3 and 4 both contribute negatively to overall productivity. For quadrant 3, much of this is due to decreases in productivity holding the employment share fixed. While this is an important component for quadrant 4 as well, the increase in employment share combined with the decrease in employment is also an important contributing factor.[13]

Quadrant decomposition using gross output measure

The analagous results using the gross output measure are reported in table 12.3. The results are strikingly similar to those obtained using the value added measure. The shares of plants, employment and output across quadrants are very similar across both measures. Of particular interest is the fact that the share of plants in quadrant 4 is about the same with both measures of labour productivity. Thus, it does not appear as if changes in the extent or nature of outsourcing is an important factor in accounting for the somewhat anomalous plants in quadrant 4.

Broadly, the respective contributions of each of the quadrants to productivity growth and the associated decompositions of these effects are also very similar with the gross output based measure. The importance of quad-

Table 12.4 *Summary statistics, by industry*

Industry	ΔII (a)	Quad. I	Quad. II	Quad. III	Quad. IV (b)
All plants	3.3895	31.18	36.53	15.37	16.92
			Deviations from above distribution		
20	0.4056	2.13	-3.99	-3.35	5.21
21	0.0087	1.47	-6.34	18.30	-13.43
22	0.1213	2.05	9.61	-5.07	-6.59
23	0.1278	0.96	3.65	-2.01	-2.60
24	0.0616	2.45	-1.55	-1.91	1.02
25	0.0169	5.26	-8.19	-1.63	4.56
26	0.1508	0.36	2.04	-2.10	-0.29
27	0.0397	3.05	-14.05	-5.99	16.99
28	0.3749	-5.55	7.97	-2.27	-0.16
29	0.2581	-7.13	20.12	-7.24	-5.76
30	0.1294	7.76	0.08	-4.54	-3.30
31	0.0157	-9.63	7.20	5.63	-3.21
32	0.0515	-5.24	1.40	3.03	0.82
33	0.1232	-15.51	21.65	3.16	-9.30
34	0.1529	-2.99	2.92	1.66	-1.58
35	0.5685	-6.91	1.41	7.68	-2.17
36	0.4019	12.10	-5.23	-2.32	-4.54
37	0.2182	1.60	-9.95	5.17	3.18
38	0.1359	-2.17	7.42	-2.52	-2.73
39	0.0270	-2.58	0.08	-0.29	2.79

Notes: I: ΔII>0, ΔL>0; II: ΔII>0, ΔL<0; III: ΔII<0, ΔL<0; IV: ΔII<0, ΔL>0.
(a) Contributions to labour productivity growth.
(b) Per cent of total employment in each quadrant.

rant 1 in accounting for the increase in productivity is slightly lower (about 61 per cent) using the gross output measure, while the contribution of quadrant 2 is somewhat larger (about 82 per cent). Thus, corrections for changes in materials usage does lower the contribution of successful downsizers somewhat which is consistent with a modest role for outsourcing in accounting for the differences in results between tables 12.2 and 12.3.[14]

Allocation of plants into quadrants, by sector

Industry and productivity

Table 12.4 presents the allocation of employment into quadrants (and the overall contribution to growth) by industry. In table 12.4 we show the division by 2-digit industry and in the Appendix describe results from the 3-digit breakdown. The first column of the table shows the contribution of each industry to the overall productivity increase of 3.4 per cent a year. By far the largest contribution to overall productivity comes from industry 35 (non-electrical machinery) and within this industry, it is 357 (office and computing equipment) that accounts for most of this. After industry 35, the next largest and roughly equal contributions come from industry 36 (electrical and electronic equipment) and industry 20 (food). Within this former industry it is 366 (communication equipment) and 367 (electronic components) that provide most of the positive impact. The growth of the three industries, 357, 366 and 367, reflects the electronics revolution. If these three were excluded from the continuers, they would reduce the overall rate of productivity growth from 3.4 per cent a year to 2.6 per cent a year. The contributions from industry 20 (food) are scattered among the different three digit elements within this industry.

The remaining columns depict the allocation of employment by quadrant for each industry, deviated from the total manufacturing shares. At the 2-digit level industries 28 (chemicals), 29 (petroleum refining), 31 (leather goods) and particularly 33 (basic metals) are the ones that have less than the average share in quadrant 1 and more than the average in quadrant 2 or 3.[15] Thus, the well-known downsizing in the steel industry with the shift towards mini-mills is reflected in these results. Overall, these industries have many plants in mature products and have reduced employment to increase productivity. However, generalisations by 2-digit industry are difficult to make since, as shown in the Appendix to this chapter, there is a wide variance of experience within the same 2-digit industry.

Region and productivity

Table 12.5 presents results for Census regions in the same format as those presented in table 12.4. New England, West North Central, South Atlantic, Mountain and Pacific regions had above average shares of their employment in quadrant 1 (successful upsizers), particularly the Pacific region. These same regions had less than average fractions of employment in quadrant 2. The sunbelt regions thus obviously were an important part of this upsizing, increasing productivity phenomenon. However, it is striking that the New England region is disproportionately represented in this group as well.[16]

Plant size and productivity

In table 12.6 we show the breakdown of the main sample by plant size, where this is measured by average employment in 1977 and 1987.[17] We

Table 12.5 *Summary statistics, by region*

Region	ΔII (a)	Quad. I	Quad. II	Quad. III	Quad. IV (b)
All plants	3.3895	31.18	36.53	15.37	16.92
			Deviations from above distribution		
New England	0.3227	5.96	-1.70	-2.62	-1.64
Mid Atlantic	0.4414	-2.82	2.16	0.36	0.30
E.N. Central	0.5642	-7.97	5.04	5.44	-2.51
W.N. Central	0.2648	1.87	-3.13	-1.87	3.13
S. Atlantic	0.5104	5.07	-0.83	-3.57	-0.67
E.S. Central	0.2798	-0.13	3.74	-0.56	-3.05
W.S. Central	0.4076	-1.32	-0.89	1.11	1.10
Mountain	0.1259	7.44	-6.44	-3.35	2.35
Pacific	0.4728	8.78	-10.27	-4.31	5.81

Notes: I: ΔII>0, ΔL>0; II: ΔII>0, ΔL<0; III: ΔII<0, ΔL<0; IV: ΔII<0, ΔL>0.
(a) Contributions to labour productivity growth.
(b) Percentage of total employment in each quadrant.

Table 12.6 *Summary statistics, by size*

Size (a)	ΔII (b)	Quad. I	Quad. II	Quad. III	Quad. IV (c)
All plants	3.3895	31.18	36.53	15.37	16.92
			Deviations from above distribution		
1-19	0.0307	0.05	-12.85	-1.40	14.20
20-49	0.1168	4.03	-9.45	-1.88	7.30
50-99	0.2196	4.37	-7.55	-2.37	5.55
100-249	0.4728	1.73	-3.36	-1.05	2.69
250-499	0.5121	0.16	-0.58	0.69	-0.27
500-999	0.6752	-1.52	3.82	0.88	-3.17
1000-2499	0.6024	-5.43	9.12	2.11	-5.80
2500-4999	0.4031	-5.82	12.62	0.86	-7.67
5000 +	0.3569	3.30	0.42	0.51	-4.23

Notes: I: ΔII>0, ΔL>0; II: ΔII>0, ΔL<0; III: ΔII<0, ΔL<0; IV: ΔII<0, ΔL>0.
(a) Average of 1977 and 1987 employment, in thousands.
(b) Contributions to labour productivity growth.
(c) Percentage of total employment in each quadrant.

find that the smallest plants did not contribute much to overall growth. But after that, the contributions come from plants of a range of sizes with the highest contribution coming from plants with 500–999 employees.

Small plants are disproportionately in quadrant 4 (unsuccessful upsizers). The quadrant 2 plants (successful downsizers) are disproportionately in the 500 to 4999 size range. These are the plants that have set the stereotype for what has happened to manufacturing over the period. Strikingly, the very largest plants (over 5000) have a larger than average fraction in quadrant 1 (successful upsizers) and only a small fraction in quadrant 4 (unsuccessful upsizers). Thus, not only do the upsizing, productivity gainers account for a large fraction of the aggregate productivity growth but they are disproportionately represented by the largest plants.

These findings are striking in light of the conventional wisdom on the importance of small businesses in the growth of the economy.[18] These results indicate that small businesses that did add employment disproportionately were likely to decrease productivity. In contrast, very large businesses that increased employment disproportionately were likely to increase productivity.[19]

Wages and productivity

Table 12.7 presents the allocation of employment into quadrants (and the overall contribution to growth) by quintiles of the level of plant real wages per worker in 1977 (in thousands of 1982 dollars per year). Downsizing plants (quadrants 2 and 3) had the highest initial real wages. Unsuccessful upsizing plants (quadrant 4) had slightly lower initial real wages than did the quadrant 2 plants while the successful upsizing plants had the lowest average initial real wages.

Table 12.8 presents the same results by quintiles of the growth in plant real wages from 1977 to 1987. The plants that increased productivity (successful upsizers and downsizers) had the highest real wage growth, with the larger increases coming from the ones that increased employment. The plants that experienced declines in productivity had reductions in real wages, with the larger decline actually occurring in the plants that raised employment.

These results raise interesting questions about the relation among wages, employment and productivity. The first possibility is that some of the wage changes observed may be associated with changes in labour quality. Under this interpretation, successful upsizers may be adding more skilled workers, successful downsizers retaining their higher skilled workers, unsuccessful downsizers retaining their less skilled workers, and unsuccesful upsizers adding less skilled workers. A second interpretation is that increases in the wages for certain types of workers may have led to capital/labour substitution, and vice versa for the plants with wage declines. A third pos-

Table 12.7 *Summary statistics, by initial wage*

Initial wage	ΔII (a)	Quad. I	Quad. II	Quad. III	Quad. IV (b)
All plants	3.3895	31.18	36.53	15.37	16.92
			Deviations from above distribution		
1st quintile	0.3721	0.49	-2.81	-2.39	4.71
2nd quintile	0.6762	1.44	-2.61	-0.96	2.14
3rd quintile	0.7961	-0.25	2.30	1.66	-3.72
4th quintile	0.9273	-1.34	3.77	0.56	-2.99
Top quintile	0.6179	-2.17	3.28	5.86	-6.97
Initial wage level		24.44	25.49	26.90	25.11

Notes: I: ΔII>0, ΔL>0; II: ΔII>0, ΔL<0; III: ΔII<0, ΔL<0; IV: ΔII<0, ΔL>0.
(a) Contributions to labour productivity growth.
(b) Percentage of total employment in each quadrant.

Table 12.8 *Summary statistics, by wage change*

Wage change	ΔII (a)	Quad. I	Quad. II	Quad. III	Quad. IV (b)
All plants	3.3895	31.18	36.53	15.37	16.92
			Deviations from above distribution		
1st quintile	-0.0216	-8.06	-12.20	5.18	15.08
2nd quintile	0.5302	-0.78	-2.36	2.71	0.43
3rd quintile	0.7802	4.54	-0.57	-0.73	-3.24
4th quintile	0.7491	0.30	5.12	-1.19	-4.23
Top quintile	1.3517	4.03	10.05	-5.99	-8.09
Mean wage change		0.69	1.86	-0.27	-0.80

Notes: I: ΔII>0, ΔL>0; II: ΔII>0, ΔL<0; III: ΔII<0, ΔL<0; IV: ΔII<0, ΔL>0.
(a) Contributions to labour productivity growth.
(b) Percentage of total employment in each quadrant.

sibility is rent sharing. Those plants that increased productivity gave (or were forced to give) a fraction of that increase to their workers. This would also lead to a positive relationship between the change in wages and the change in productivity. We are not able in this chapter to sort out these alternative possibilities. We note, however, some suggestive points. First, the magnitudes of the wage changes are much smaller than the productivity changes. If the average skill levels or the average capital labour ratios are changing, these are only a part of the reason for the productivity changes. Similarly, if rents are being shared, then only a small part of the productivity increases are being passed on to labour (as we know from aggregate manufacturing wage data). A second finding that seems clear, also, is that average wage increases are apparently not driven by the decision to expand employment. The largest wage increases came from the plants with the largest rate of employment decline. One explanation of our findings that is consistent with other trends observed in manufacturing is that skill-biased technical change has occurred in many (but not all) plants. Where it has occurred, productivity has increased and at the same time there has been a relative shift in employment to higher skilled workers (raising average wages). We hope to explore these results in future research both for understanding the evolution of the distribution of productivity and the distribution of wages.[20]

Contribution of sectoral characteristics to overall variance of employment and productivity

Tables 12.4–12.8 show that there are striking differences across plants defined by industry, region, size, and wage in the allocation of plants into the quadrants of productivity and employment growth. In table 12.9 we show the extent to which the characteristics of industry in 1977, region, size class, ownership type (plants associated with single-unit vs. multi-unit companies) and initial wage class can explain the variance of productivity change and employment change in the continuing plants.[21] This exercise should not be interpreted as yielding causal inferences but rather a sense of the connection between observable plant characteristics and the distribution of employment and productivity growth. The table shows the R statistics for regressions of the column variable on the dummy variables specified in the rows. For example, the first entry in the first column shows that only 3.1 per cent of the variance of productivity growth is explained by 2-digit industry dummy variables. The fractions of the variance that can be explained by these variables is quite small. Even when industry, region, size class, ownership type and initial wage class are simultaneously taken into account, less than 15 per cent of the overall variance in output and productivity is explained by the observable characteristics.

The last four columns of the table show the extent to which these plant-level observables can predict the allocation of plant employment into quadrants. While the explanatory power is relatively greater here, it is still small. At most, less than 30 per cent of the allocation into productivity and employment growth quadrants is accounted for by observable plant characteristics.

Table 12.9 *Percentage of variance explained by plant categories*

Dummy	ΔII	ΔL	QI	QII	QIII	QIV
2-digit ind.	3.1	1.8	1.9	2.9	1.4	2.4
3-digit ind.	9.4	3.1	8.6	8.0	5.7	5.9
4-digit ind.	13.0	4.3	12.5	11.4	9.8	10.0
Size	1.6	0.7	0.5	2.0	0.1	2.0
Region	0.1	0.3	1.6	1.0	1.0	0.5
Ownership	0.8	2.1	0.8	1.9	0.3	1.6
Initial wage	2.1	0.9	0.1	0.4	0.3	1.1
Interaction*	14.8	11.8	26.9	28.4	22.6	24.5

Note: * Includes 2-digit industry, region, size, type and wage dummies

These results provide an important caution. They tell us that the variance of employment and productivity at the plant level are dominated by idiosyncratic effects. One interpretation of these findings is that attempts to explain differences in productivity and employment performance should concentrate on such plant-specific factors as management or worker skills. A striking message is that it is possible to raise productivity and employment even within an industry that on average is lowering productivity and employment.

It may be that there are other observable characteristics that can account for the allocation of plants into employment and productivity quadrants. However, related studies also find a dominant role for the idiosyncratic component in accounting for plant level behaviour. Davis and Haltiwanger (1992) find that only 39 per cent of the allocation of employment growth into expanding and contracting plants can be accounted for by simultaneously controlling for 2-digit industry, region, size, age of plant and ownership type. This amounts to controlling for over 14,000 different sectors and even within such sectors there is substantial heterogeneity in the distribution of employment growth rates.

Concluding remarks

In contrast to the conventional wisdom, plants that raised employment as well as productivity contribute almost as much to overall productivity growth in the 1980s as the plants that raised productivity at the expense of employment. Together these two groups of plants that increased productivity account for more than the total increase in productivity growth. This is because there is an offsetting group of plants that decreased productivity over this time. Amongst the latter group, most of them are unsuccessful upsizers. That is, they increased employment but not productivity.

There are striking differences in the allocation of plants into these groups by sectoral classification. Plants in mature industries (for example, steel) were more likely to follow the conventional wisdom. That is, they disproportionately fell into the downsizing, increasing productivity group. Plants in the sunbelt regions are disproportionately represented in the upsizing, productivity increasing group. However, plants in New England are also disproportionately represented in this group. The smallest plants are disproportionately represented in the group of plants that increased employment and decreased productivity. Strikingly, the largest plants are disproportionately represented in the group of plants that increased employment and productivity.

In spite of the striking differences across sectors defined in a variety of ways, most of the variance of productivity and employment growth is accounted for by idiosyncratic factors. It is difficult to account for the allocation of plants into productivity and employment growth quadrants on the basis of observable characteristics. Thus, not only is the conventional wisdom that downsizing is the source of productivity growth incorrect but identifying who did and did not downsize and whether they were successful cannot be done with any precision on the basis of the characteristics of the plants that are reported in the Census data.

Appendix

Three-digit industry results

High fractions of employment in quadrant 1 (successful upsizers): 201 (meat products), 202 (dairy products), 225 (knitting mills), 227 (floor covering mills), 252 (office furniture), 273, 275, 277, 278 and 279 (from printing and publishing), 348 (ordnance), 357 (office and computing), 366 (communications), 367 (electronics), 376 (guided missiles), and 383 (optical instruments and lenses).

High fractions of employment in quadrant 2 (successful downsizers): 204 (grain mill products), 207 (fats and oils), 212 (cigars), 221, 222, 224, 226, 228 and 229 (textile mills), 231 (men's apparel), 261, 262, 263, and 266 (paper mills), 282 and 286 (plastics and industrial inorganic chemicals), 291 (petroleum refining), 302 and 303 (rubber), 316 (luggage), 321 (flat glass), 324 (cement), 331 and 333 (blast furnaces and primary non-ferrous metals), 346 (metal forgings), 363 and 365 (household appliances and radio-TV), 369 (misc. electrical), 385 and 386 (ophthalmic and photographic).

High fractions of employment in quadrant 3 (unsuccessful downsizers): 211 and 213 (cigarettes and chewing tobacco), 237 (furs), 245 (wood buildings and mobile homes), 266 (paper board), 304 (rubber and plastic hoses and belts), 311, 313, 314, 315 and 319 (parts of leather and footwear), 326 (pottery), 332 and 333 (iron and steel foundries and primary non-ferrous metals), 341 (metal cans), 351, 352, 353, 354 and 356 (engines and turbines, farm and garden equipment, construction machinery, metalworking machinery and general industrial machinery), 371 (motor vehicles and equipment), 374 (railroad equipment), 387 (watches and clocks), and 391 (jewellery).

High fractions of employment in quadrant 4 (unsuccessful upsizers): 205 (bakery products), 237 (furs), 253 and 254 (furniture for public buildings and partitions), 271, 272 and 274 (segments of publishing), 284 (pharmaceuticals, most likely a deflator problem), 299 (misc. petroleum products), 319 (misc. leather goods), 327 and 328 (concrete and cut stone), 372 (aircraft and parts), and 391 (jewellery).

Tables excluding industry 357

Table 12A.1   *Summary statistics for Census of Manufacturers*

	1977	1987	Change (a)
Labour productivity			
All	53	69	2.99
Continuers	56	73	2.89
Entrants		57	
Exiters	44		
Employment ('000s)			
All	17661.155	16767.332	-0.51
Continuers	12649.97	12532.558	-0.09
Entrants		43234.774	
Exiters	5011.185		
Value added (1982, $ millions)			
All	934	1151	2.33
Continuers	714	911	2.77
Entrants		240	
Exiters	220		

Note: *Average growth over ten years, not at an annual rate.

Table 12A.2 *Summary statistics, by quadrant, 1977–87, excluding computers*

	All Plants	ΔII>0 ΔL>0	ΔII>0 ΔL<0	ΔII<0 ΔL<0	ΔII<0 ΔL>0
Estab.	139985	44321.0	36049.0	19277.0	40338.0
pct.	1.00	31.66	25.75	13.77	28.82
Empl. pct. 77	1.00	23.85	44.57	18.97	12.61
Empl. pct. 87	1.00	38.18	28.16	12.04	21.61
Empl. growth	-0.09	5.86	-3.74	-3.71	6.98
VA pct. 77	1.00	20.19	40.42	23.44	15.95
VA pct. 87	1.00	41.39	36.98	7.99	13.64
VA growth	2.77	16.18	1.69	-5.64	0.92
Lab. prod. growth	2.89	6.51	8.67	-3.08	-3.57
productivity	3.82	6.92	9.21	-3.36	-3.22
empl. share	0.02	-0.30	0.28	0.23	0.03
cross term	-0.95	-0.11	-0.83	0.06	-0.38
Contribution to labour productivity growth					
by quadrant	2.89	1.88	2.37	-0.62	-0.74
productivity		1.31	3.50	-0.72	-0.57
empl. share		-0.22	0.15	-0.16	0.24
cross term		0.79	-1.29	0.26	-0.41

Table 12A.3 *Summary statistics, by industry, excluding computers*

Industry	ΔII (a)	Quad. I	Quad. II	Quad. III	Quad. IV (b)
All plants	2.8927	30.98	36.40	15.52	17.09
		Deviations from above distribution			
20	0.4076	2.33	-3.86	-3.50	5.04
21	0.0089	1.66	-6.21	18.15	-13.60
22	0.1217	2.24	9.74	-5.22	-6.76
23	0.1280	1.15	3.78	-2.16	-2.77
24	0.0617	2.64	-1.42	-2.06	0.85
25	0.0166	5.45	-8.06	-1.78	4.39
26	0.1516	0.55	2.17	-2.25	-0.46
27	0.0388	3.24	-13.92	-6.14	16.82
28	0.3781	-5.35	8.10	-2.42	-0.33
29	0.2600	-6.93	20.25	-7.39	-5.93
30	0.1297	7.95	0.21	-4.69	-3.47
31	0.0158	-9.43	7.33	5.48	-3.38
32	0.0519	-5.05	1.52	2.88	0.65
33	0.1252	-15.32	21.78	3.01	-9.47
34	0.1538	-2.80	3.05	1.51	-1.75
35	0.0577	-9.54	0.35	9.99	-0.79
36	0.4029	12.29	-5.11	-2.47	-4.71
37	0.2191	1.79	-9.82	5.02	3.01
38	0.1366	-1.98	7.55	-2.67	-2.90
39	0.0271	-2.39	0.21	-0.44	2.62

Notes: I: $\Delta II>0$, $\Delta L>0$; II: $\Delta II>0$, $\Delta L<0$; III: $\Delta II<0$, $\Delta L<0$; IV: $\Delta II<0$, $\Delta L>0$.
(a) Contributions to labour productivity growth.
(b) Percentage of total employment in each quadrant.

Table 12A.4 *Summary statistics, by region, excluding computers*

Region	Δ II (a)	Quad. I	Quad. II	Quad. III	Quad. IV (b)
All plants	2.8927	30.98	36.40	15.52	17.09
			Deviations from above distribution		
New England	0.1810	5.64	-1.66	-2.50	-1.48
Mid Atlantic	0.4194	-2.75	2.23	0.28	0.24
E.N. Central	0.5550	-7.73	5.01	5.34	-2.62
W.N. Central	0.2030	1.54	-3.14	-1.75	3.35
S. Atlantic	0.4841	5.24	-0.78	-3.67	-0.79
E.S. Central	0.2269	-0.03	3.67	-0.55	-3.09
W.S. Central	0.3896	-0.89	-1.31	1.11	1.09
Mountain	0.0903	6.58	-6.34	-3.09	2.84
Pacific	0.3432	8.47	-10.41	-4.20	6.14

Notes: I: ΔII>0, ΔL>0; II: ΔII>0, ΔL<0; III: ΔII<0, ΔL<0; IV: ΔII<0, ΔL>0.
(a) Contributions to labour productivity growth.
(b) Percentage of total employment in each quadrant.

Table 12A.5 *Summary statistics, by size, excluding computers*

Size (a)	Δ II (b)	Quad. I	Quad. II	Quad. III	Quad. IV (c)
All plants	2.8927	30.98	36.40	15.52	17.09
			Deviations from above distribution		
1-19	0.0276	0.19	-12.73	-1.53	14.07
20-49	0.1091	4.14	-9.33	-1.99	7.18
50-99	0.2054	4.44	-7.45	-2.46	5.47
100-249	0.4461	1.86	-3.33	-1.13	2.60
250-499	0.4779	0.27	-0.52	0.60	-0.35
500-999	0.5748	-1.96	4.15	0.93	-3.13
1000-2499	0.4571	-5.31	8.62	2.39	-5.70
2500-4999	0.3175	-6.33	12.88	1.08	-7.63
5000 +	0.2772	3.32	0.42	0.53	-4.27

Notes: I: ΔII>0, ΔL>0; II: ΔII>0, ΔL<0; III: ΔII<0, ΔL<0; IV: ΔII<0, ΔL>0.
(a) Average of 1977 and 1987 employment, in thousands.
(b) Contributions to labour productivity growth.
(c) Percentage of total employment in each quadrant.

Table 12A.6 *Statistics, by initial wage, excluding computers*

Initial wage	Δ II (a)	Quad. I	Quad. II	Quad. III	Quad. IV (b)
All plants	2.8927	30.98	36.40	15.52	17.09
		Deviations from above distribution			
1st quintile	0.3513	0.68	-2.80	-2.52	4.64
2nd quintile	0.5490	1.48	-2.73	-0.89	2.14
3rd quintile	0.6347	-0.32	2.24	1.69	-3.60
4th quintile	0.7960	-1.74	4.04	0.63	-2.93
Top quintile	0.5617	-1.86	3.09	5.85	-7.08
Initial wage level		24.42	25.47	26.89	25.11

Notes: I: ΔII>0, ΔL>0; II: ΔII>0, ΔL<0; III: ΔII<0, ΔL<0; IV: ΔII<0, ΔL>0.
(a) Contributions to labour productivity growth.
(b) Percentage of total employment in each quadrant.

Table 12A.7 *Summary statistics, by wage change, excluding computers*

Wage change	Δ II (a)	Quad. I	Quad. II	Quad. III	Quad. IV (b)
All plants	2.8927	30.98	36.40	15.52	17.09
		Deviations from above distribution			
1st quintile	-0.0763	-8.07	-12.21	5.10	15.18
2nd quintile	0.4343	-0.91	-2.26	2.80	0.37
3rd quintile	0.7189	4.77	-0.69	-0.82	-3.26
4th quintile	0.7001	0.45	5.05	-1.24	-4.26
Top quintile	1.1157	3.77	10.17	-5.85	-8.09
Mean wage change		0.68	1.87	-0.27	-0.80

Notes: I: ΔII>0, ΔL>0; II: ΔII>0, ΔL<0; III: ΔII<0, ΔL<0; IV: ΔII<0, ΔL>0.
(a) Contributions to labour productivity growth.
(b) Percentage of total employment in each quadrant.

Table 12A.8 *Percentage of variance explained by plant, categories, excluding computers*

Dummy	ΔII	ΔL	QI	QII	QIII	QIV
2-digit ind.	3.4	1.8	2.0	2.9	1.6	2.4
3-digit ind.	8.5	3.1	8.6	8.1	5.6	5.8
4-digit ind.	11.8	4.3	12.6	11.5	9.6	9.9
Size	1.5	0.8	0.5	1.9	0.2	2.0
Region	0.1	0.3	1.5	1.0	0.9	0.6
Ownership	0.8	2.1	0.7	1.8	0.3	1.6
Initial wage	2.0	0.9	0.1	0.4	0.3	1.1
Interaction*	14.7	11.7	26.6	28.3	22.8	24.5

Note: * Includes 2-digit industry, region, size, type and wage dummies.

13 Sources of productivity slowdown in Swedish manufacturing 1964–1989

BO WALFRIDSON AND LENNART HJALMARSSON

In the search for explanations of the productivity slowdown in the 1970s a large number of causes have been suggested – induced obsolescence of the capital stock due to the energy price shocks, energy using technical progress, convergence in technical progress between developed and less developed countries, unexpected changes in demand, government regulations, national accounting deficiencies, and so forth; for a review, see Fischer (1988).

A definite resolution of the productivity slowdown puzzle has so far not emerged. It has been suggested, for example by Berndt and Fuss (1986), that the measured slowdown is a result of using an inappropriate framework. Research has thus been directed towards the basic issue of factor demand modelling, in a search for an empirically more relevant model, and a corresponding measure of TFP growth.

The theory underlying the traditional TFP growth measure is static equilibrium theory, relying on assumptions of perfect variability of all factors of production, profit maximisation, and perfect competition. Since these are idealised assumptions, scarcely reflecting real-world conditions, one may suspect that the traditional TFP growth measure reflects not only productivity but short-run disequilibrium effects as well. This is, of course, not a new observation; methods accounting for variations in the utilisation of stocks of inputs when measuring productivity, have a long tradition. What is new in recent research are the efforts made of explicit modelling of the whole adjustment process.

The mainstream of this research is set in the framework of *temporary equilibrium*, characterised by defining a subset of inputs as quasi-fixed, and employing the restricted cost function as model of technology. Berndt *et al.* (1977, 1980) integrated the restricted cost function and the adjustment cost approach into the cost-of-adjustment (COA) model, sometimes referred to as a *third generation dynamic factor demand model*.

Using this approach, Berndt and Fuss (1986) found that 'a substantial part of the observed decline [in productivity growth] is illusionary'. As a corollary they derived an adjusted measure of TFP which differs from the traditional measure in weighting the growth of inputs by shadow cost shares instead of actual cost shares. The construction of such adjusted measures of TFP is also treated in Hulten (1986) and Morrison (1986).

Instead of the static equilibrium framework used in defining the traditional TFP measure, Berndt and Fuss suggested short-run or temporary equilibrium to be the appropriate framework. Temporary equilibrium is defined by Berndt and Fuss (1986) as 'occurring whenever the shadow value of any input and/or output differs from its market price'.

Within this framework a capacity utilisation adjusted measure of TFP growth is derived, that, when compared to the traditional measure, essentially takes the form of weighting the growth of inputs by shadow costs. The framework is thus applicable to, for example, analysis of production with quasi-fixed inputs, under non-perfect competition or regulatory environment; see also Hulten (1986) and Morrison (1986).

By treating both short-run and long-run factor demand as the outcome of explicit optimisation, the COA model states the optimising problem in a theoretically attractive form. However, in several applications of the model the results are puzzling. Notably, the estimates of short- and long-run price elasticities are often found to be of the same magnitude, even when adjustment of quasi-fixed factors is slow. Other intriguing results include estimates of short-run output elasticities (of for example labour), which in general are greater than unity (inconsistent with observed labour hoarding). The recurrence of these results indicates that the specification of the link between short- and long-run factor demand, that is the quasi-fixed factors, poses a problem.

An alternative framework for dynamic factor demand is provided by Nadiri and Rosen's (1969) interrelated *disequilibrium model* (NRIDE). Formally, the model is a set of interdependent difference equations expressing the path of inputs. The stationary part of these equations consists of the long-run factor demands, derived from a long-run cost function. The non-stationary part, representing the adjustment process towards long-run equilibrium, can be expressed as a matrix of cross-adjustment parameters, relating the adjustment of each input to the degree of disequilibrium of all inputs.The NRIDE model has been applied in several studies for example, by Craine (1975), Malcolmson (1980), McIntosh (1982), Norsworthy and Harper (1983), Kokkelnberg (1983), Asterhaki (1984), and Harris (1985).

Berndt *et al.* (1977) used the NRIDE model as a baseline for dynamic modelling of factor demand. Their finding was essentially that estimates of the adjustment parameters were highly unreliable, concluding that the problems were related to the lack of explicit specification of adjustment costs. Their COA model may, thus, be seen as a representative of a new generation of dynamic models. A practice of denoting the single-equation partial adjustment model a *first generation*, NRIDE a *second generation*, and COA a *third generation dynamic factor demand model* has emerged.

Modified versions of the NRIDE approach have been used by Hogan (1984, 1989) and Walfridson (1987). Walfridson has given special attention to the discrimination between signals with essentially different responses within the firm; rapid adjustment in output to market demand in contrast to a considerably slower rate of adjustment to input prices, due to the embodied character of factor requirements, and a dampening effect of expectation formation. The WIDE (Walfridson Interrelated Disequilibrium) model was developed as a consequence of this; see Walfridson (1989). Essentially, the WIDE model assumes non-substitution between stock and flow factors in the short run.

In Walfridson (1989), a comparison was made between the three models outlined above (COA, NRIDE and WIDE). The models were applied to Swedish manufacturing data, showing substantial differences in model behaviour. In particular, this was the case with respect to short- and long-run substitutability between variable and quasi-fixed inputs. A main result obtained for the COA model was a short-run output elasticity of labour exceeding 1.0 in all industries, while in the alternative models this elasticity did not exceed 0.5. Correspondingly, the COA model exhibited much lower substitutability between quasi-fixed capital and variable factors. These results illustrate what we consider to be the inherent problem with the COA model, that is the fact that the short-run scale properties are just a mirror of the long-run substitution possibilities. In fact, the implication of the way quasi-fixedness is defined in the restricted model is that the long-run substitution possibilities are available also in the short run. Given the specificity of capital in situ, the model's poor behaviour is not difficult to understand.

Samuelson's envelope theorem is invoked to give a theoretical justification for using quasi-fixed factors as links between the short and the long run. In the paper referred to by Berndt *et al.*, Samuelson makes a dubious statement about the empirical relevance of the model; issuing a warning that the conditions assumed are highly idealised, the model still is claimed to offer a qualitative understanding of important economic issues. The theoretical arguments presented for basing an essentially short-run model on the restricted cost function thus raises some questions about its empirical relevance.

As for the NRIDE model, the estimates indicate slow adjustment with respect to factor price ratios, in magnitude similar to those of the WIDE model. Econometric specification tests across the models also came out in favour of the NRIDE and WIDE models.

In this chapter we use the model developed in Walfridson (1989) for an analysis of productivity growth in Swedish manufacturing from the mid 1960s to the end of the 1980s. We present a decomposition of observed productivity change into components due to variations in capacity utilisation, adjustment to relative factor prices and technical change.

The WIDE model

The WIDE model integrates some elements from the COA and the NRIDE models, although the main source of inspiration is Johansen's (1972) vintage, or putty-clay approach, with its clear distinction between *ex ante* (long-run) and *ex post* (short-run) technology. Capital is assumed quasi-fixed, but its nature differs from that of the COA model in assuming short-run (or *ex post*) nonsubstitutability between quasi-fixed and variable factors. It is similar to the NRIDE model in that long-run (or *ex ante*) input substitution is represented by a long-run cost function and in that adjustment costs exist for all inputs – not only capital. It differs from the NRIDE model in its relationship between short-run factor demand and capacity utilisation and gradual substitution due to changing relative factor prices.

In Johansen's approach plant capacity is a key concept. It may be defined as the dimensioning output level or the expected output level that determines the size of a plant and, thus, the volume of real capital investment. Capital may also be a substitute or complement to other inputs, and the desired capital–capacity ratio may then be a function of relative factor prices. Additional capacity may require more of variable inputs, while a higher capital intensity may require less of at least some variable inputs. In our view, the distinction between the capacity dimension and the input substitution dimension of capital is crucial for a proper separation of short and long-run effects.

The restricted cost function represents variable costs both in the short run and in the long run, implying that it must embody properties of *ex ante* as well as *ex post* technology. Therefore, one may suspect that this approach does not disentangle short-run and long-run effects in a proper way. This suspicion is obviously confirmed by empirical results discussed above.

Long-run or ex ante properties

The long-run cost function is specified as a constant returns to scale generalised Leontief unit cost (UC) function with input specific technical change $T_i(t)$

$$UC = (\sum_i \sum_j \beta_{ij} \sqrt{P_i P_j} + \sum_i P_i T_i) \quad i,j \in \{L,E,F,K\} \tag{13.1}$$

where the P_is are input prices and L,E,F,K stand for labour, electricity, fuel and capital respectively. The long-run equilibrium values of the input coefficients, denoted by a_i, are derived by Shepard's lemma

$$a_i^*(P,t) = \frac{\partial UC}{\partial P_i} = \sum_i \sum_j \beta_{ij} \sqrt{\frac{P_j}{P_i}} + T_i, \quad i,j \in \{L,E,F,K\} \tag{13.2}$$

The unit cost function represents the optimal choice of technology *ex ante* at time t, or in long-run equilibrium, or over time if relative factor prices, P_i/P_j remain constant over the lifetime of a capacity investment. Assuming long-run constant returns to scale, the capital requirement for a plant with production capacity Q is obtained as

$$K = Q a_K^* \tag{13.3}$$

that is, at long-run cost minimisation, defined by a_K^*, the capital stock embodied in a plant represents a capacity to produce Q.

Short-run adjustment

The capacity available at a certain point of time is the outcome of investments at different times in the past at which the choice of technology from the *ex ante* production function was influenced by expected development of product demand and relative factor prices. We will here assume that technology choice at a certain point in time is made from the *ex ante* cost function at static expectations about relative prices. This means that the observed capital–capacity ratio, a_K, at a certain point of time, does not directly correspond to the actual input prices but can be regarded as the outcome of a partial adjustment process of the form

$$\dot{a}_K = \lambda_K (a_K^* - a_K). \tag{13.4}$$

The input coefficients for variable inputs at average capacity output are also assumed to be predetermined, but the rate of adjustment varies between the inputs. The assumption of predetermined capacity makes it possible to decompose the adjustment into a capacity utilisation component and an input substitution component.

We now obtain the capacity implicit in the stock of capital at t as

$$Q = \frac{K}{a_K} \tag{13.5}$$

and capacity utilisation, CU, may be defined as

$$CU = \frac{Y}{Q} \tag{13.6}$$

where Y is output. The average capacity utilisation during an extended period of time is assumed to be 100 per cent. While the capital stock is given in the short run, the utilisation of variable inputs with respect to capacity utilisation is not. We assume specific elasticities, K_i, for each input with respect to capacity utilisation, so the actual input–output coefficient for input i, a_{it} is

$$a_{it} = a_i^* \bullet CU^{K_i} . \tag{13.7}$$

We also assume that input prices are functions of capacity utilisation, for example, higher wages paid for overtime

$$P_i = P_i(CU,t) \tag{13.8}$$

and so is the rate of depreciation of the capital stock

$$\rho = \rho(CU). \tag{13.9}$$

Costs of adjustment

The capacity at a certain point of time is an aggregate of different vintages which reflects technology and relative prices when the investments were made in the past. For each input there is a distribution of input coefficients. The assumption made here is that these *coefficients may be changed* but at an *adjustment cost*. The (ideal input) coefficient is given by the long-run cost function. There are also adjustment costs due to *expansion of output* and *capacity growth*. These three adjustment costs are assumed to be separable.

$$C_{adj} = \frac{1}{2} Q(d_q \dot{Q}^2 + d_y \dot{Y}^2 + d_{ij} \dot{a}_{ij}^2). \tag{13.10}$$

Finally, we account for market imperfections by assuming a demand function for output given in inverse form

$$P = P(Y,t). \tag{13.11}$$

The econometric specification of this model is presented in the Appendix.

Data

The data set is obtained from *Statistics Sweden*. The figures are collected from industrial statistics and national accounting for the period 1964–89 covering total manufacturing, SNI 300, and SNI 31–33, 341, 342, 35–38.

Variable definitions

Production in fixed prices: Y
Volume index of production. Measured by value added at constant 1980 prices
Capital stock and capital costs: K, P_K
Since neither industry statistics nor national accounting (after 1984) report capital stock values, we have made our own calculations on the basis of investment data, using the perpetual inventory method. The rate of depreciation has been obtained from *Statistics Sweden*.

The capital stock is measured as net capital stock of building and equipment, including lease of equipment. User cost of capital is defined as

$$P_K = q_K(r+\delta)$$

where q_K is the deflator for investment goods, r the real discount rate and δ the geometric rate of depreciation for the capital stock. $r+\delta$ is approximated by the average rate of return on capital during the observation period.

Labour and costs of labour: L, P_L
Labour input is measured by an index constructed as a cost-share weighted sum of different types of labour, and labour costs cover wages and salaries including social overhead.

Electricity: E, P_E
Electricity is measured in GWh and the electricity price obtained by the ratio between electricity costs and electricity use.

Fuel: F, P_F

Fuel consumption is an aggregate measure in tons and the price of fuel is an implicit price.

Estimation results

The stochastic specification assumed includes first-order serial correlation within equations and joint normal distribution of corrected residuals. Full information maximum likelihood estimation was performed. Since the likelihood function was insensitive to increasing the maximum lag length n of (13A.3) beyond five, the results presented are obtained for $n = 5$. The parameter estimates and statistics are presented in the Appendix in tables 13A.1 and 13A.2 respectively.

Most parameter estimates have high t-values. The exceptions are the parameters representing the cross price elasticities between electricity and labour, β_{EL}, and between electricity and capital, β_{EK}. This indicates that there are no substitution possibilities between electricity and labour and electricity and capital respectively. On the other hand, fuel and capital, and electricity and fuel show up as substitutes. The estimates of the adjustment parameters, κ_i and w_0 are reasonable and significant. The κ_i-parameters reflect the variations in factor demand with respect to capacity utilisation.

Output and demand elasticities

The short-run output elasticities and the long-run demand elasticities are presented in tables 13A.3 and 13A.4 respectively. For all variable inputs and for all industries the short-run output elasticities are below one. There is substantial rigidity in the short-run input adjustment to variations in capacity utilisation.

Almost all demand elasticities are significant and of the right sign. An exception is the (low) long-run price elasticity for labour in the textile industry. This industry experienced a contraction of output and capacity of about 50 per cent during this period. In general, the differences between short- and long-run price elasticities are substantial.

Technical change

Non neutral technical change is an important determinant of long-run factor demand. The results are presented in the Appendix, table 13A.5. With a few exceptions the t-values are high. As expected, labour saving bias dominates the picture, with a reduction in labour input coefficients of about 4 per cent a year. There has also been a fairly rapid decline in input coefficients for fuel in several cases.

A decomposition of productivity change

In this section we will present the results from the decomposition of the development of total factor productivity, TFP, and labour productivity, LPRO. Since the estimated model contains residuals, caused by measurement errors, specification errors and so on, these measures will also contain residuals.

Tables 13.1 and 13.2 present a decomposition of TFP growth and labour productivity growth respectively in Swedish total manufacturing, SNI 300, between 1964 and 1989, and for different subperiods. A graphical illustration is also given in figures 13.1 and 13.2 respectively. The following notations are used:

TFP:	traditional TFP-measure calculated as a Tornqvist index
TFPCU:	change in TFP caused by variations in capacity utilisation
TFPADJ:	change in TFP caused by lagged adjustment to changes in relative input prices
TFPGD:	change in TFP caused by variations in degree days
TFPWD:	$TFP - TFPCU - TFPADJ - TFPGD$
TFPEMB	capital embodied technical change
TFPERR:	unexplained residual
LPRO:	traditional measure of labour productivity
LPROCU:	change in labour productivity caused by variations in capacity utilisation
LPROSUB:	change in labour productivity caused by adjustment to changes in relative input prices (substitution)
LPROEMB:	capital embodied technical change
LPROERR:	unexplained residual
ΔY:	change in output
ΔCAP:	change in production capacity
CU:	capacity utilisation in per cent

Thus, variations in TFP are decomposed into variations in capacity utilisation, lagged adjustment to changes in relative input prices, variations

Table 13.1 *A decomposition of total factor productivity growth, TFP, in Swedish manufacturing (SNI 300), 1964–89. Annual average changes by percentage.*

Component	1964-70	1970-75	1975-80	1980-85	1985-89	1964-89
TFP	5.07	2.57	1.36	2.81	1.84	2.86
TFPCU	1.67	-0.33	-0.94	0.99	-0.23	0.31
TFPWD	3.40	2.90	2.30	1.82	2.07	2.55
TFPADJ	0.13	0.16	0.15	0.16	0.07	0.14
TFPGD	-0.03	0.06	-0.06	-0.04	0.14	0.01
TFBEMB	2.96	2.79	2.14	1.73	2.31	2.41
TFPERR	0.34	-0.11	0.07	-0.03	-0.45	0.00
ΔY	5.56	2.78	-0.07	2.06	2.21	2.64
ΔCAP	3.34	3.13	1.39	0.63	2.59	2.25
CU	100.4	107.5	96.8	99.0	102.9	101.2

in the number of degree days, capital embodied technical change and an unexplained residual. We assume here that the change in capital stock in total corresponds to substitution and capacity change, which means that the residual in TFP is referred to an unexplained variation in variable inputs (weighted by cost-shares).

The variations in labour productivity are decomposed into variations in capacity utilisation, substitution, capital embodied technical change and an unexplained residual. The three bottom rows show annual changes in production, capacity and average capacity utilisation during the period respectively.

Since capacity in this model is defined as the long-run average production level, it is not surprising that the capacity utilisation component is close to zero for the entire time period 1964–89, while it varies considerably for different subperiods.

The variations in capacity utilisation are very large. Therefore, the major share of the variation in TFP is due to the capacity utilisation component. A calculation of variances based on all observations, 25 years × 9 industries, yields a variance in TFP of 14.9, in *TFPCU* of 14.6 and in *TFPEMB* of 0.96. The TFP-measure adjusted for capacity utilisation, *TFPWD*, has a variance of 4.9. Corresponding variances for labour productivity are 17.7, *LPROCU* 15.4, *LPROSUB* 0.35, *LPROEMB* 2.0 and *LPROWD* 10.7. Thus, variations in capacity utilisation cause a high degree of variation in both productivity measures.

When the traditional productivity measures have been adjusted for the impact of capacity utilisation and capital substitution they are close to the

Table 13.2   *A decomposition of labour productivity growth, LPRO, in Swedish manufacturing (SNI 300), 1964–89. Annual average changes by percentage.*

Component	1964-70	1970-75	1975-80	1980-85	1985-89	1964-89
LPRO	6.74	4.07	2.87	3.73	2.94	4.22
LPROCU	1.63	-0.38	-0.82	0.90	-0.19	0.30
LPROSUB	0.56	0.66	0.64	0.26	0.29	0.49
LPROWD	4.56	3.80	3.05	2.57	2.83	3.43
LPROEMB	4.08	3.84	3.00	2.60	3.53	3.43
LPROERR	0.48	-0.04	0.05	-0.03	-0.70	0.00
ΔY	5.56	2.78	-0.07	2.06	2.21	2.64
ΔCAP	3.34	3.13	1.39	0.63	2.59	2.25
CU	100.4	107.5	96.8	99.0	102.9	101.2

underlying capital embodied technical change. For the entire period 1964–89 the impact on labour productivity of capital substitution is 0.5 per cent a year, while capital embodied technical change contributes to an annual increase in labour productivity of 3.4 per cent. The substitution effect is due to the increase in capital intensity caused by the higher real wages. Therefore it varies with a lag in the changes in real wages. The slow changes in real wages during the 1980s have led to a decrease in this component with, on average, 0.3 percentage points a year, in comparison with the period 1964–80. However, the substitution as well as the technical change effect are functions of the investment rate. Thus, capital formation turns up as the driving force in productivity change.

The variations in the adjusted *LPROWD* measure are much smaller than in the non-adjusted measure. The adjusted measure shows a clear decrease in the rate of labour productivity growth during the entire period 1964–85. Not until the late 1980s is there an increase. However, it is lower than the potential created by capital formation. For annual changes, see figures 13.1 and 13.2.

No productivity slowdown puzzle

A remarkable result from the decomposition is the disappearance of the productivity slowdown in the mid 1970s: that is, the impact of the first oil price shock. For total manufacturing, traditional TFP growth fell from 4 per cent in 1974 to –2 per cent in 1975, while *TFPWD*, that is, TFP adjusted for capacity utilisation, increased from 1.5 per cent in 1974 to about 2 per cent in 1975. The same pattern holds for individual industries (see below).

The underlying capital embodied technical change was rapid during the period 1964–70, with an annual average for total manufacturing of 3 per cent. The official (that is, traditional TFP) figure for this period was 5.1 per cent a year, but the decomposition reveals that to a large extent productivity growth was due to an increase in the utilisation of existing capacity. *TFPCU* is about 1.7 per cent a year during this period. In the 1970s there are no 'windfall' gains of this kind to be exploited. Increases in production require more capacity, and TFP decreases to 2.6 per cent a year during the first part of the 1970s.

The second part of the 1970s shows a very low rate of TFP growth, about 1.4 per cent a year. The decomposition reveals, however, that about 1 percentage point of the decrease was caused by a lower capacity utilisation. The underlying capital embodied technical change was still 2.1 per cent a year.

During the first part of the 1980s, the official productivity growth figure was 2.8 per cent a year. That is more than twice the preceding five-year period, and even higher than for 1970–75. However, the capital embodied technical change, *TFPEMB*, decreases. The TFP increase is, instead, explained by the increase in capacity utilisation; *TFPCU* contributes about 1 percentage point. The cause was the large devaluation of the Swedish krona in 1982. In reality, according to *TFPWD*, this subperiod shows the smallest growth in productivity of the entire period 1964–89, 1.8 per cent a year. A potential for a productivity increase of 2.3 per cent a year, created by investments in new capacity 1985–9, is only partially realised. The official TFP figure is 1.8 per cent.

Productivity growth in individual industries

In tables 13.3a–c we present the results for the different industries. The first table shows the official TFP figures, the second table the figures adjusted for capacity utilisation and lagged adjustment to relative prices, *TFPWD*, the third table the capital embodied technical change, *TFPEMB*. The complete results are given in the Appendix, tables 13A6.1–13A6.9.

The following pattern emerges for the whole period 1964–89: Fabricated metal (SNI 380) has the highest *TFPWD* and *TFPEMB* values, exceeding 3 per cent increase per year. Textiles (SNI 320), pulp and paper (SNI 341), chemicals (SNI 350) and basic steel (SNI 370) show annual productivity increases in the range 2–3 per cent. The food industry (SNI 310) reports the lowest figures, about 1 per cent a year. The capacity in fabricated metal increased during this period by on average 3.1 per cent a year while the corresponding figure for food is 1.5 per cent a year.

Table 13.3a *Total factor productivity growth, TFP, in Swedish manufacturing (SNI 300), 1964-89. Annual average changes by percentage. Tornqvist index*

Industry	1964-70	1970-75	1975-80	1980-85	1985-89	1964-89
310 Food	2.63	1.37	0.13	1.22	-0.15	1.15
320 Textiles	7.05	2.11	-0.11	1.05	2.56	2.71
330 Wood	4.09	0.73	0.39	1.04	3.28	1.94
341 Pulp and paper	5.05	0.26	2.34	2.42	1.52	2.46
342 Printing	3.21	0.67	2.76	1.75	-0.28	1.76
350 Chemicals	8.28	2.34	1.43	1.82	2.96	3.58
360 Non-met minerals	3.90	2.05	0.79	1.31	2.15	2.11
370 Basic steel	4.41	1.34	2.63	4.52	3.16	3.26
380 Fabricated metal	5.39	4.20	1.47	3.87	1.87	3.50

Table 13.3b *Adjusted total factor productivity growth, TFPWD, in Swedish manufacturing, 1964-89. Annual average changes by percentage*

Industry	1964-70	1970-75	1975-80	1980-85	1985-89	1964-89
310 Food	1.49	1.68	0.67	1.05	0.30	1.09
320 Textiles	5.17	0.80	3.24	0.02	4.87	2.83
330 Wood	2.60	2.24	0.50	1.34	0.74	1.56
341 Pulp and paper	3.84	2.88	1.68	1.21	1.59	2.33
342 Printing	3.51	2.04	2.09	0.90	0.39	1.91
350 Chemicals	2.81	3.62	1.49	1.98	2.98	2.57
360 Non-met minerals	3.81	2.00	1.86	1.41	-0.46	1.89
370 Basic steel	3.28	2.43	3.16	2.36	2.51	2.78
380 Fabricated metal	3.73	3.65	3.20	2.36	2.70	3.17

There seems to be a strong relationship between capacity growth and TFP growth, especially regarding time-series, for an industry but also cross-sectionally across industries. There are exceptions, however. The textile industry and basic steel have had a productivity growth above average in spite of a lower than average capacity growth. Textile has even decreased its capacity by about 3 per cent a year. Non-metal minerals have had a TFP growth of 2.2 per cent a year in spite of zero capacity. It is obvious that

Table 13.3c *Capital embodied technical change, TFPEMB, in Swedish manu-facturing, 1964–89. Annual average changes by percentage*

Industry	1964-70	1970-75	1975-80	1980-85	1985-89	1964-89
310 Food	1.03	0.96	0.84	0.72	0.80	0.88
320 Textiles	3.32	2.36	2.05	1.83	2.99	2.52
330 Wood	2.07	1.74	1.05	0.76	0.88	1.35
341 Pulp and paper	2.56	2.53	1.85	1.22	1.90	2.04
342 Printing	2.33	1.69	1.62	1.45	1.88	1.81
350 Chemicals	2.98	2.73	2.03	2.02	2.17	2.42
360 Non-met minerals	4.22	1.58	1.97	0.96	1.64	2.18
370 Basic steel	4.02	3.34	2.08	1.37	1.74	2.60
380 Fabricated metal	3.34	3.67	2.79	2.27	3.12	3.05

Table 13.4 *The elasticity of the rate of capital embodied technical change with respect to capacity increases*

Industry	Elasticity
300 Total manufacturing	0.38
310 Food	0.73
320 Textiles	0.90
330 Wood	0.33
341 Pulp and paper	0.56
342 Printing	0.24
350 Chemicals	0.45
360 Non-met minerals	0.39
370 Basic steel	0.20
380 Fabricated metal	0.34

the structural change in these industries has led to substantial productivity improvements in addition to investment driven capital embodied technical change.

We have also derived the elasticity of the rate of capital embodied technical change with regard to capacity increases, presented in table 13.4. Although there is some variation between industries, the elasticities are fairly large.

Conclusions

This study is an attempt to decompose the official productivity figures for various disequilibrium effects. The main result is the large impact on official TFP figures of variations in capacity utilisation. This effect dominates the explanation for the productivity slowdown in the mid 1970s. There does not seem to be any productivity slowdown puzzle in the Swedish development.

Looking beneath the surface it turns out that Swedish manufacturing has experienced a slow decrease in adjusted productivity growth between the mid 1960s and the mid 1980s. The main reason for this is a slow increase in capital formation.

Appendix

Econometric specification

The econometric specification adopted for the present study is based on assuming separability of substitution adjustment and technical change. Substitution is thus modelled by a partial adjustment process

$$\tilde{P}_{ij} = \lambda \sqrt{\frac{P_{jt-1}}{P_{it-1}}} + (1 - \lambda)\tilde{P}_{ijt-1} \tag{13A.1}$$

By iteratively substituting P_{ij} on the right hand side of (13A.1) we obtain

$$\tilde{P}_{ij} = \sum_{s=0}^{n} w_s \sqrt{\frac{P_{jt-1-s}}{P_{it-1-s}}} + \lambda(1 - \lambda)^n \tilde{P}_{ijt-n}. \tag{13A.2}$$

To avoid putting too large a weight on a single observation $(t-n)$ we truncate after $n-1$ lags inflating all terms to insure that weights sum to unity. Then

$$w_s = \frac{\lambda(1 - \lambda)^s}{1 - (1 - \lambda)^{s+1}} \tag{13A.3}$$

where s is the number of periods before truncation.

Technical change is specified as the sum of a constant, annual percentage, capital disembodied component, and a capital embodied component, proportional to the share of new capital in the capital stock

$$T_{it} = T_{it-1} + a_{t-1}(b_{it} + b_{ie}[\delta + \ln Q(t) = \ln Q(t-1)]), i \in \{L, E, F\} \quad (13A.4)$$

where e in b_{ie} stands for embodied. Thus, the input coefficient for capital is assumed constant and technical change takes the form of reducing input coefficients of the variable inputs.

The short-run optimal input coefficients are thus specified as

$$a_i(P,t) = \beta_{ii} + \sum_j \beta_{ij} \tilde{P}_{ij} + T_{it} \quad i \in \{L, E, F, K\} \quad (13A.5)$$

where relative input prices follow a partial adjustment process with a uniform adjustment rate, λ, for all inputs.

Capacity, $Q(t)$, is defined as the ratio between the capital stock at $t-1$ and the short-run optimal capital–output ratio.

$$Q(t) = \frac{K_{t-1}}{a_K(\tilde{P}_{t-1})} = \frac{K_{t-1}}{\sum_i \beta_{Ki} \tilde{P}_{Kit-1}}, \quad i \in \{K, L, E, F\} \quad (13A.6)$$

and capacity utilisation, CU, as

$$CU(t) = \frac{Y(t)}{Q(t)}. \quad (13A.7)$$

The short-run factor demand for the variable inputs is given by

$$X_i = Y^{K_i} Q^{1-K_i} a_i(\tilde{P},t) GD^{\gamma_i} = Y CU^{K_i-1} a_i(\tilde{P},t) GD^{\gamma_i}, \quad i \in \{L, E, F\} \quad (13A.8)$$

where κ_i is the short-run output elasticity for input i, GD the number of degree days and a_i the short-run optimal input–output ratio

$$a_i(\tilde{P},t) = \sum_j \beta_{ij} \tilde{P}_{ij} + T_i, \quad i \in \{L, E, F, K\} \quad (13A.9)$$

Total factor productivity growth

Let us start from the traditional definition of TFP growth

$$\text{TFP} = \frac{\dot{Y}}{Y} - \sum_i S_i \frac{\dot{X}_i}{X_i} \tag{13A.10}$$

where $\dot{Y}/Y$ is growth in output, $\dot{X}/X$ growth in input i and S_i the cost share of input i.

Taking logarithms and differentiating with respect to time t, we obtain

$$\frac{\dot{X}_i}{X_i} = \varepsilon_{iQ}\frac{\dot{Y}}{Y} + (1 - \varepsilon_{iQ})\frac{\dot{Q}}{Q} + \sum_j \varepsilon_{ij}^{SR}(\frac{\dot{P}_j}{P_j} - \frac{\dot{P}_i}{P_i})$$

$$+ \varepsilon_{it} + \varepsilon_{ie}(\frac{\dot{Q}}{Q} + \delta) + \gamma_i \frac{\dot{GD}}{GD} + residual \tag{13A.11}$$

where

$$\varepsilon_{iQ} = \frac{\partial \ln X_i}{\partial \ln Q} \tag{13A.12}$$

and

$$\varepsilon_{ij} = \frac{\partial \ln X_i}{\partial \ln P_j} \tag{13A.13}$$

and GD is the number of degree days.

Inserting into (13A.10) TFP growth is obtained as

$$\text{TFP} = (1 - \sum_i S_i\varepsilon_{iQ})(\frac{\dot{Y}}{Y} - \frac{\dot{Q}}{Q}) + \lambda\sum S_i(1 - \frac{C_i^*}{C_i})$$

$$+ \sum_i -\varepsilon_{ie}(\frac{\dot{Q}}{Q} + \delta) + residual \tag{13A.14}$$

where C_i^* is optimal cost and C_i is actual cost.

The first component on the right hand side measures the impact on TFP of variations in capacity utilisation, while the second component measures the impact of the lagged adjustment to changing input prices. The third component measures the impact on costs of changes in the number of degree days, the fifth component the impact of the capital embodied technical change. The residual is what is left unexplained by the model.

An analogous decomposition may be obtained for the partial input productivities, AP_i,

$$
AP_i = \frac{\dot{Q}}{Q} - \frac{\dot{X_i}}{X_i} = \varepsilon_{iQ}(\frac{\dot{Y}}{Y} - \frac{\dot{Q}}{Q}) + \sum_j \varepsilon_{ij}^{SR}(\frac{\dot{P_j}}{P_i} - \frac{\dot{P_i}}{P_i})
$$
$$
+ \varepsilon_{ie}(\frac{\dot{Q}}{Q} + \delta) + residual
$$

$$(13A.15)$$

The different components have the same interpretation as in the case of TFP.

Statistical tables

Table 13A.1 *Parameter estimates, Swedish manufacturing, 1964–89. Asymptotic t-values within brackets*

Parameter	Estimate	Parameter	Estimate
β_{EE}	0.037 (4.73)	β_{Kt}	0.000 (0.14)
β_{EF}	0.010 (2.05)	β_R	-0.0286 (-11.71)
β_{EL}	0.0020 (0.40)	β_{Lt}	0.0653 (3.94)
β_{EK}	0.0004 (0.15)	β_{Kt}	0.0036 (13.03)
β_{FF}	0.043 (6.72)	δ_L	-0.1184 (-6.47)
β_{FL}	0.040 (9.98)	α_E	0.833 (7.15)
β_{FK}	-0.010 (-3.98)	α_F	0.674 (6.81)
β_{LL}	1.242 (91.10)	α_L	0.468 (6.60)
β_{LK}	0.012 (3.82)	w_0	0.207 (7.64)
β_{KK}	0.221 (131.4)		

Note: Input i and capital are substitutes if $\beta_{Kt} > 0$.

Table 13A.2 *Regression statistics, R², Durbin-Watson, autocorrelation, ρ, and log-likelihood value*

Industry		R^2	DW	ρ	Log likeli-hood values
Total manufacturing	Labour	0.975	1.43	0.22	374.5
	Electricity	0.988	1.52	0.12	
	Fuel	0.985	1.33	0.29	
	Capital	0.999	1.11	0.78	
Food	Labour	0.997	1.95	-0.33	352.8
	Electricity	0.951	1.78	0.10	
	Fuel	0.988	1.78	0.11	
	Capital	0.998	1.55	0.54	
Textile	Labour	0.617	1.51	0.10	268.5
	Electricity	0.984	1.72	-0.34	
	Fuel	0.994	1.34	0.33	
	Capital	0.789	0.96	0.68	
Wood	Labour	0.972	1.49	0.26	330.0
	Electricity	0.982	2.06	-0.16	
	Fuel	0.988	1.43	0.20	
	Capital	0.997	2.08	0.36	
Chemicals	Labour	0.967	2.23	-0.02	328.4
	Electricity	0.876	1.29	-0.02	
	Fuel	0.943	1.53	0.34	
	Capital	0.995	0.84	0.65	
Non-metal minerals	Labour	0.837	1.73	0.01	323.3
	Electricity	0.990	1.53	0.21	
	Fuel	0.999	2.23	-0.06	
	Capital	0.893	1.72	0.18	
Basic metals	Labour	0.904	1.82	0.04	318.0
	Electricity	0.958	1.28	0.39	
	Fuel	0.983	1.33	0.40	
	Capital	0.959	0.64	0.80	
Fabricated metals	Labour	0.994	1.76	0.23	343.7
	Electricity	0.934	1.95	0.14	
	Fuel	0.988	1.75	-0.27	
	Capital	0.998	1.61	0.22	

Table 13A.3 *Short-run output elasticities (capital = 0), Swedish manufacturing and main industries, average 1964–89. Asymptotic t-values within brackets*

Industry/input	Labour	Electricity	Fuel
Total	0.47	0.83	0.67
manufacturing	(6.20)	(7.15)	(6.80)
Food	0.73	0.17	0
	(4.69)	(0.92)	(.)
Textile	0.63	0.38	0
	(7.80)	(2.73)	(.)
Wood	0.05	0.97	0.51
	(0.54)	(8.12)	(3.29)
Chemicals	0.12	0.64	0
	(2.64)	(5.57)	(.)
Non-met. minerals	0.36	0.39	0.53
	(6.70)	(4.98)	(4.13)
Basic metal	0.00	0.41	0.82
	(0.42)	(6.96)	(7.99)
Fabricated metal	0.30	0.24	0
	(13.04)	(3.61)	(.)

Table 13A.4 *Short and long-run own price elasticities for inputs in Swedish manufacturing, average 1964–89. Asymptotic t-values within brackets*

Industry/ Input	Labour		Electricity		Fuel		Capital	
	Short run	Long run	Short run	Long run	Short run	Long run	Short run	Long run
Total manufacturing	-0.01	-0.03 (-6.25)	0.07	0.09 (1.25)	-0.08	-0.37 (-11.94)	-0.00	-0.01 (-2.44)
Food	-0.00	-0.03 (-5.08)	0.01	0.01 (0.06)	-0.01	-0.19 (-7.31)	-0.00	-0.01 (-1.39)
Textile	0.00	0.03 (2.31)	-0.63	-2.85 (-1.30)	-0.04	-0.36 (-14.40)	0.00	0.04 (0.82)
Wood	-0.04	0.14 (-16.67)	-0.03	-0.03 (-0.40)	-0.15	-0.57 (-13.26)	-0.03	-0.12 (-4.35)
Chemicals	-0.02	-0.10 (-10.05)	-0.22	-5.96 (1.78)	-0.13	-0.74 (-13.70)	-0.02	-0.10 (4.35)
Non-met. minerals	-0.02	-0.13 (9.29)	-0.18	-0.68 (-2.83)	-0.05	-0.31 (9.39)	-0.02	-0.13 (6.84)
Basic metal	-0.06	-0.18 (-7.50)	0.01	0.01 (0.09)	-0.15	-0.47 (-4.80)	-0.01	-0.04 (-1.82)
Fabricated metal	-0.01	-0.06 (-19.85)	-0.09	-0.28 (-1.27)	-0.05	0.23 (-4.51)	-0.03	-0.14 (-4.86)

Table 13A.5 *Percentage technical change per year in Swedish manufacturing, average 1964–89. Asymptotic t-values within brackets*

Industry/input	Labour	Electricity	Fuel	Capital
Total manufacturing	-4.20 (-3.98)	-0.06 (-3.98)	-2.86 (3.82)	0.36 (3.82)
Food	-3.04 (-3.15)	1.75 (-3.15)	-1.93 (2.77)	1.14 (2.77)
Textile	3.76 (4.31)	2.07 (4.31)	0.40 (-1.68)	2.51 (-1.68)
Wood	-2.83 (-5.71)	-0.09 (-5.71)	-0.57 (14.30)	2.02 (14.30)
Chemicals	-2.36 (0.99)	-4.10 (0.99)	1.66 (4.41)	1.39 (4.41)
Non-met. minerals	-3.17 (0.13)	3.64 (0.13)	-1.42 (4.72)	3.23 (4.72)
Basic metal	-4.99 (4.51)	-1.83 (4.51)	-2.73 (7.19)	-0.27 (7.19)
Fabricated metal	-3.64 (-3.70)	-0.49 (-3.70)	-3.64 (16.40)	1.08 (16.40)

Table 13A.6a *A decomposition of total factor productivity growth, TFP, and labour productivity growth, LPRO, in Swedish food industry (SNI 310), 1964–89. Annual average changes by percentage*

Component/ period	1964-70	1970-75	1975-80	1980-85	1985-89	1964-89
TFP	2.63	1.37	0.13	1.22	-0.15	1.15
TFPCU	1.14	-0.31	-0.54	0.18	-0.45	0.07
TFPWD	1.49	1.68	0.67	1.05	0.30	1.09
TFBEMB	1.03	0.96	0.84	0.72	0.80	0.88
TFPADJ	0.49	0.63	0.52	0.32	0.24	0.45
TFPGD	-0.01	0.03	-0.03	-0.02	0.07	0.00
TFPERR	-0.02	0.06	-0.65	0.03	-0.81	-0.25
LPRO	4.93	4.01	1.84	2.30	0.40	2.88
LPROCU	1.14	-0.31	-0.54	0.18	-0.45	0.07
LPROSUB	1.35	1.67	1.28	0.31	0.59	1.07
LPROWD	2.45	2.65	1.10	1.81	0.26	1.74
LPROEMB	1.91	1.78	1.61	1.51	1.69	1.71
LPROERR	0.54	0.87	-0.51	0.30	-1.43	0.03
ΔY	3.53	1.50	0.48	0.78	0.94	1.55
ΔCAP	2.39	1.81	1.02	0.61	1.39	1.48
CU	101.48	103.53	102.03	100.67	101.16	101.79

Table13A.6b *A decomposition of total factor productivity growth, TFP, and labour productivity growth, LPRO, in Swedish textile industry (SNI 320), 1964–89. Annual average changes by percentage*

Component/ period	1964-70	1970-75	1975-80	1980-85	1985-89	1964-89
TFP	7.05	2.11	-0.11	1.05	2.56	2.71
TFPCU	1.88	1.31	-3.35	1.04	-2.30	-0.12
TFPWD	5.17	0.80	3.24	0.02	4.87	2.83
TFBEMB	3.32	2.36	2.05	1.83	2.99	2.52
TFPADJ	0.06	0.13	0.15	0.10	0.02	0.09
TFPGD	-0.02	0.04	-0.05	-0.03	0.12	0.01
TFPERR	1.81	-1.73	1.09	-1.88	1.73	0.21
LPRO	8.78	2.99	1.49	1.78	4.84	4.13
LPROCU	1.90	1.32	-3.39	1.06	-2.34	-0.12
LPROSUB	0.65	0.87	1.03	0.68	0.46	0.74
LPROWD	6.23	0.80	3.85	0.04	6.72	3.51
LPROEMB	4.13	3.00	2.70	2.61	4.45	3.37
LPROERR	2.10	-2.20	1.15	-2.58	2.27	0.14
ΔY	-0.18	-2.07	-7.13	-2.79	-4.05	-3.09
ΔCAP	-2.08	-3.39	-3.74	-3.84	-1.71	-2.97
CU	101.52	116.46	103.02	97.73	102.43	104.20

Table 13A.6c *A decomposition of total factor productivity growth, TFP, and labour productivity growth, LPRO, in Swedish wood industry (SNI 330), 1964–89. Annual average changes by percentage*

Component/ period	1964-70	1970-75	1975-80	1980-85	1985-89	1964-89
TFP	4.09	0.73	0.39	1.04	3.28	1.94
TFPCU	1.49	-1.51	-0.12	-0.30	2.54	0.38
TFPWD	2.60	2.24	0.50	1.34	0.74	1.56
TFBEMB	2.07	1.74	1.05	0.76	0.88	1.35
TFPADJ	0.54	0.58	0.54	0.34	0.19	0.45
TFPGD	-0.02	0.05	-0.05	-0.03	0.10	0.01
TFPERR	0.01	-0.13	-1.03	0.27	-0.42	-0.24
LPRO	6.36	3.34	2.50	2.77	4.17	3.92
LPROCU	1.35	-1.32	-0.11	-0.29	2.10	0.32
LPROSUB	1.83	1.88	2.08	0.98	1.07	1.60
LPROWD	3.18	2.78	0.53	2.08	1.00	2.00
LPROEMB	2.79	2.62	1.73	1.51	1.67	2.11
LPROERR	0.40	0.17	-1.20	0.57	-0.66	-0.10
ΔY	6.24	0.96	-0.48	-1.67	3.07	1.75
ΔCAP	3.92	3.24	-0.29	-1.16	-0.56	1.21
CU	104.28	116.62	100.05	95.85	108.35	104.87

Table 13A.6d *A decomposition of total factor productivity growth, TFP, and labour productivity growth, LPRO, in Swedish pulp and paper industry (SNI 341), 1964–89. Annual average changes by percentage*

Component/ period	1964-70	1970-75	1975-80	1980-85	1985-89	1964-89
TFP	5.05	0.26	2.34	2.42	1.52	2.46
TFPCU	1.20	-2.61	0.66	1.21	-0.07	0.13
TFPWD	3.84	2.88	1.68	1.21	1.59	2.33
TFBEMB	2.56	2.53	1.85	1.22	1.90	2.04
TFPADJ	0.07	0.04	0.08	0.34	0.04	0.11
TFPGD	-0.05	0.14	-0.15	-0.05	0.23	0.01
TFPERR	1.27	0.16	-0.10	-0.30	-0.59	0.16
LPRO	8.21	2.04	4.20	3.40	3.20	4.41
LPROCU	1.29	-2.87	0.77	1.39	-0.07	0.15
LPROSUB	0.29	0.38	0.44	0.22	0.15	0.30
LPROWD	6.62	4.54	2.98	1.79	3.12	3.95
LPROEMB	4.50	4.55	3.48	2.54	4.08	3.85
LPROERR	2.13	-0.01	-0.50	-0.75	-0.96	0.10
ΔY	4.93	0.30	2.52	1.54	2.63	2.48
ΔCAP	3.47	3.56	1.65	-0.03	2.72	2.30
CU	102.57	101.56	89.18	96.22	103.64	98.59

Table 13A.6e *A decomposition of total factor productivity growth, TFP, and labour productivity growth, LPRO, in Swedish printing and publishing industry (SNI 342), 1964–89. Annual average changes by percentage*

Component/ period	1964-70	1970-75	1975-80	1980-85	1985-89	1964-89
TFP	3.21	0.67	2.76	1.75	-0.28	1.76
TFPCU	-0.29	-1.37	0.67	0.84	-0.66	-0.15
TFPWD	3.51	2.04	2.09	0.90	0.39	1.91
TFBEMB	2.33	1.69	1.62	1.45	1.88	1.81
TFPADJ	0.07	0.07	0.09	0.12	0.06	0.08
TFPGD	-0.01	0.03	-0.04	-0.02	0.08	0.00
TFPERR	1.12	0.25	0.42	-0.65	-1.64	0.01
LPRO	4.24	1.54	3.51	1.95	-0.19	2.38
LPROCU	-0.27	-1.22	0.60	0.72	-0.59	-0.14
LPROSUB	0.25	0.29	0.30	0.06	0.08	0.20
LPROWD	4.25	2.47	2.62	1.16	0.32	2.32
LPROEMB	2.88	2.13	2.06	1.96	2.48	2.32
LPROERR	1.36	0.34	0.55	-0.80	-2.16	0.00
ΔY	3.10	-0.77	2.00	1.91	1.33	1.58
ΔCAP	3.54	1.24	1.02	0.71	2.29	1.81
CU	103.50	96.26	97.20	99.60	104.38	100.16

Table 13A.6f *A decomposition of total factor productivity growth, TFP, and labour productivity growth, LPRO, in Swedish chemicals (SNI 350), 1964–89. Annual average changes by percentage*

Component/ period	1964-70	1970-75	1975-80	1980-85	1985-89	1964-89
TFP	8.28	2.34	1.43	1.82	2.96	3.58
TFPCU	5.47	-1.28	-0.06	-0.16	-0.02	1.01
TFPWD	2.81	3.62	1.49	1.98	2.98	2.57
TFBEMB	2.98	2.73	2.03	2.02	2.17	2.42
TFPADJ	0.05	0.07	0.05	0.10	0.05	0.06
TFPGD	-0.06	0.14	-0.14	-0.09	0.29	0.01
TFPERR	-0.15	0.68	-0.44	-0.05	0.47	0.08
LPRO	10.42	4.42	2.64	2.74	4.17	5.13
LPROCU	5.82	-1.37	-0.06	-0.18	-0.02	1.07
LPROSUB	0.43	0.54	0.52	0.20	0.44	0.43
LPROWD	4.17	5.25	2.17	2.72	3.75	3.63
LPROEMB	4.28	4.02	3.04	3.12	3.37	3.60
LPROERR	-0.11	1.23	-0.87	-0.40	0.38	0.03
ΔY	11.38	3.44	2.00	2.09	2.97	4.71
ΔCAP	5.56	4.81	2.06	2.27	2.99	3.64
CU	95.18	105.27	98.28	98.29	99.69	99.16

Table 13A.6g *A decomposition of total factor productivity growth, TFP, and labour productivity growth, LPRO, in Swedish non-metallic minerals industry (SNI 360), 1964–89. Annual average changes by percentage*

Component/ period	1964-70	1970-75	1975-80	1980-85	1985-89	1964-89
TFP	3.90	2.05	0.79	1.31	2.15	2.11
TFPCU	0.09	0.05	-1.07	-0.09	2.61	0.22
TFPWD	3.81	2.00	1.86	1.41	-0.46	1.89
TFBEMB	4.22	1.58	1.97	0.96	1.64	2.18
TFPADJ	0.12	0.15	0.22	0.21	0.07	0.16
TFPGD	-0.01	0.03	-0.03	-0.01	0.05	0.00
TFPERR	-0.52	0.24	-0.30	0.25	-2.22	-0.44
LPRO	6.44	4.22	3.03	2.45	1.90	3.79
LPROCU	0.08	0.02	-1.08	-0.12	2.58	0.20
LPROSUB	0.94	1.47	1.40	0.53	0.74	1.02
LPROWD	5.42	2.74	2.71	2.03	-1.43	2.57
LPROEMB	6.19	2.43	3.24	1.78	2.95	3.45
LPROERR	-0.77	0.31	-0.54	0.25	-4.37	-0.88
ΔY	3.99	-1.45	-1.74	-2.56	2.69	0.24
ΔCAP	3.88	-1.47	-0.31	-2.40	-0.73	-0.02
CU	104.05	108.24	99.14	93.13	107.25	102.23

Table 13A.6h *A decomposition of total factor productivity growth, TFP, and labour productivity growth, LPRO, in Swedish basic steel industry (SNI 370), 1964–89. Annual average changes by percentage*

Component/period	1964-70	1970-75	1975-80	1980-85	1985-89	1964-89
TFP	4.41	1.34	2.63	4.52	3.16	3.26
TFPCU	1.14	-1.09	-0.53	2.16	0.64	0.48
TFPWD	3.28	2.43	3.16	2.36	2.51	2.78
TFBEMB	4.02	3.34	2.08	1.37	1.74	2.60
TFPADJ	0.02	0.03	0.07	0.01	0.04	0.03
TFPGD	-0.03	0.05	-0.05	-0.03	0.14	0.01
TFPERR	-0.73	-0.99	1.05	1.01	0.60	0.14
LPRO	6.61	2.67	4.59	6.91	5.29	5.27
LPROCU	1.25	-1.23	-0.53	2.49	0.70	0.56
LPROSUB	0.04	0.05	0.03	-0.01	0.02	0.03
LPROWD	5.32	3.85	5.09	4.43	4.57	4.68
LPROEMB	6.58	5.35	3.43	2.59	3.53	4.42
LPROERR	-1.27	-1.50	1.67	1.83	1.04	0.26
ΔY	5.55	1.50	-0.24	1.72	1.12	2.11
ΔCAP	4.30	2.73	0.29	-0.77	0.42	1.55
CU	100.00	102.42	88.50	97.62	107.81	98.96

Table 13A.6i *A decomposition of total factor productivity growth, TFP, and labour productivity growth, LPRO, in Swedish fabricated metal industry (SNI 380), 1964–89. Annual average changes by percentage*

Component/period	1964-70	1970-75	1975-80	1980-85	1985-89	1964-89
TFP	5.39	4.20	1.47	3.87	1.87	3.50
TFPCU	1.66	0.55	-1.73	1.51	-0.83	0.33
TFPWD	3.73	3.65	3.20	2.36	2.70	3.17
TFBEMB	3.34	3.67	2.79	2.27	3.12	3.05
TFPADJ	0.03	0.05	0.06	0.09	0.04	0.05
TFPGD	-0.02	0.04	-0.04	-0.02	0.11	0.01
TFPERR	0.38	-0.11	0.40	0.02	-0.56	0.06
LPRO	6.23	5.19	2.84	4.50	3.02	4.48
LPROCU	1.44	0.47	-1.49	1.22	-0.69	0.28
LPROSUB	0.28	0.35	0.35	0.19	0.14	0.27
LPROWD	4.51	4.36	3.98	3.09	3.57	3.94
LPROEMB	4.10	4.49	3.51	3.04	4.27	3.87
LPROERR	0.40	-0.12	0.47	0.05	-0.70	0.06
ΔY	6.33	5.28	-0.59	3.65	2.57	3.60
ΔCAP	3.55	4.36	2.29	1.29	3.90	3.06
CU	99.07	109.55	96.32	100.29	102.12	101.35

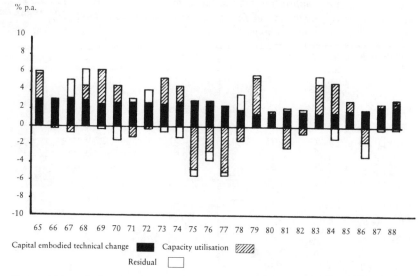

Figure 13A.1 *A decomposition of TFP growth in Swedish manufacturing 1964–89. Annual percentage change*

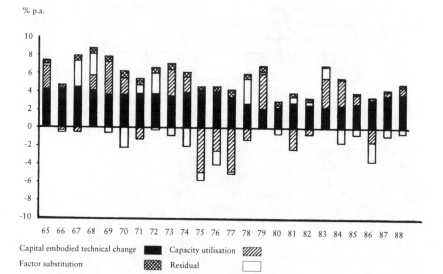

Figure 13A.2 *A decomposition of labour productivity growth in Swedish manufacturing 1964–89. Annual percentage change*

14 Productivity of Norwegian establishments: a Malmquist index approach

FINN R. FØRSUND[1]

Most studies of productivity change are aggregate in character and, at their most disaggregate, based on a production sector as a unit, focusing on estimating rates of uniform productivity growth within industries and biases of factor use (see for example Jorgenson *et al.*, 1987). Differences beween micro units, establishments or plants are averaged away, and the informational value for, say, industrial policy reduced. The average developments portrayed by aggregate studies hide the dynamics of change at the micro level, involving capacity utilisation, labour hoarding, investment and efficiency improvements when trying to catch up with market leaders.

In order to move from describing productivity developments to understanding why changes are taking place, it is necessary to base the analyses on the micro units making the decisions resulting in productivity changes. It is at this micro level that hypotheses about causes for productivity change should be formulated and tested, for example the role of labour hoarding, capacity utilisation, expectations about prices and technology, the degree of embodiment of techniques, and so on.

Ideally, such a study should be conducted within a vintage framework (see Førsund and Hjalmarsson, 1987). However, the dataset at hand is not suitable for applying a fully blown putty-clay model. We are forced to be rather descriptive, but we will stay with the data at the micro level, and develop tools for revealing productivity change that is better suited for starting to explain why these changes happen than exercises at the industry level. The basic assumption of the study is that there are efficiency differences between firms. The natural reference for technology development is then the best practice or frontier production function. The focus will be on productivity change for firms being the net effect of changes in efficiency with respect to a common frontier function for the industry and the shift in the frontier technology.

There are several alternatives for establishing the frontier production function, including stochastic and deterministic frontiers (see for example Førsund et al., 1980), but we will here explore a non-parametric approach of a piecewise linear technology, calculated by solving linear programmes rather than estimating by statistical techniques. The productivity changes are then conveniently measured by an index originating in Malmquist (1953).

The Malmquist index employed is introduced in the next section, which is followed by the set of establishment data, and then the results. Finally, some policy conclusions are suggested.

The Malmquist index

The Malmquist productivity index introduced in Caves et al. (1982) is based on binary comparisons of a production unit between two time points (or between two different units at the same point in time). The time periods to be compared are denoted 1 and 2 for short. Only quantities are involved, and at least one technology has to be known. As a convention we will compare a unit observed in period 2 with the same unit observed in period 1; that is, expressions involving period 2 observations will be in the numerator and expressions involving period 1 observations will be in the denominator. The idea of what Caves et al. (1982) termed the 'Malmquist unit 1 input-based productivity index' is to find the minimal proportional scaling of inputs for the unit observed in period 2 such that its scaled input vector and its observed output vector are just on the production surface of period 1. Caves et al. assumed the units to operate on their production functions, that is, to be efficient. Färe et al. (1989) extended the Malmquist index approach to inefficient observations like the set-up in Nishimizu and Page (1982). The extension of the Caves et al. definition is quite straightforward, substituting 'frontier technology' for 'technology'. The definitions above then have to take into consideration that a unit is no longer efficient. In order to make a meaningful comparison *both* observations must be adjusted to the frontier technology in question.

In the general setting of a cross section–time series data set the question arises of how to adapt the definitions based on two periods. One obvious way, followed by Färe et al. (1989, 1990 and 1992), is to make calculations on successive pairs of years. The reference technology then changes. One preferable property of an index covering a longer period of time is that it is possible to chain it, that is, that the index obeys the 'circular relation' of Fritsch (1936). Changing reference technology implies that the index does not chain.

The definition adopted here is based on Berg *et al.* (1992, 1993), and Førsund (1990, 1993), and is phrased in terms of Farrell (1957) efficiency measures, which express exactly the same as Shephard distance functions (see Färe, Grosskopf and Lovell, 1985). Without restricting the scale properties, efficiency may be measured either in an input-saving direction, or in an output-increasing direction (see Førsund and Hjalmarsson, 1974, 1979 and 1987). We shall assume constant returns to scale, and will therefore only refer to input-saving measures. Our generalised Malmquist productivity index, $M_i(1,2)$, for comparison between a unit for two time periods, denoted 1 and 2, with frontier technology, $F_i(.)$, from period i as reference is:[2]

$$M_i(1,2) = \frac{E_{i2}}{E_{i1}} = \frac{\text{Min}_{\alpha_{i2}}\{\alpha_{i2}:F_i(y_2,\alpha_{i2}x_2) \leq 0\}}{\text{Min}_{\alpha_{i1}}\{\alpha_{i1}:F_i(y_1,\alpha_{i1}x_1) \leq 0\}} ,i,1,2\varepsilon T \qquad (14.1)$$

where T is the set of time periods. The variables, E_{ij} $(j=1,2)$, are Farrell measures of input-saving technical efficiency for units from period j measured relative to the frontier technology for period i, and express potential input usage at the frontier relative to observed usage by a proportional movement keeping outputs constant. The numerator shows the proportional adjustment of the observed input vector of the period 2 observation required to be on the frontier function of the reference period i with observed outputs, and the denominator shows the proportional adjustment of the observed input vector of period 1 for observed outputs to be on the same period i frontier function. Note that both measures may be greater than one. If $M_i > 1$, then the observation in period 2 is more productive than the observation in period 1.

Keeping the reference technology, i, fixed implies that the index chains.[3] Using the technology of the first period as reference corresponds to a Laspeyre index, while using the last period corresponds to a Paasche index.

In the presence of inefficient observations change in productivity is the net effect of change in efficiency and shift in the frontier production function (see for example Nishimizu and Page, 1982, for such a decomposition in the parametric frontier case, and Färe *et al.*, 1989, for the piecewise linear frontier). Our generalised Malmquist productivity index, $M_i(1,2)$, $i = 1,2$, can be multiplicatively decomposed into two parts showing the catching up, $MC(1,2)$, and the pure technology shift, $MF_i(1,2)$:

$$M_i(1,2) = \frac{E_{i2}}{E_{i1}} = \frac{E_{22}}{E_{11}} \cdot \frac{E_{i2} / E_{22}}{E_{i1} / E_{11}} = MC(1,2) \cdot MF_i(1,2)$$

$$i = \text{reference technology}, \quad i,1,2\varepsilon T$$

(14.2)

We have that the frontier technology change is a relative change between period i technology and period 2 technology on the one hand, and period i technology and period 1 technology on the other hand. The distance between technology i and 2 is measured at the observation in period 2, and the distance between technology i and 1 is measured at the observation in period 1. The frontier change term measures the distance between technology 2 and 1, but it is a relative distance to the common reference technology, and the frontier term does therefore chain. If the reference technology is from either period 1 or 2 the expression for the technology shift simplifies.

We will not restrict the technology development to yield non-decreasing productivity impacts. This implies that $MF_i(1,2)$ may be less than one. One could argue that technologies cannot be forgotten, and therefore only $MF_i(1,2) \geq 1$ should be allowed (see for example Atkinson and Stiglitz, 1969). We will argue that since our frontier concept is an empirical one, a change to a less productive technology is an empirical question, maybe involving management practice, and of interest to exhibit, even though in a strict technological sense production techniques cannot be forgotten.

Efficiency scores

The Farrell efficiency score and the Malmquist index can be applied to any frontier, whether parametric stochastic or deterministic, or piecewise linear. We will explore the latter approach.[4] Farrell efficiency scores will be calculated by solving a linear programme for each unit we want a measure for. The approach originates with Farrell (1957) and was given its present form in Charnes et al. (1978), where the term Data Envelopment Analysis, DEA, was coined. The data are enveloped by the piecewise linear frontier in such a way that radial distances to the frontier are minimised. Assuming k inputs, m outputs and a benchmark sample of n units, the formal problem for unit j can most conveniently be stated as follows:

Min $_{z_j} E_j$

subject to

(a) $Yz_j \geq y_j$

(b) $Xz_j \leq x_j E_j$

(c) $z_j \geq 0$

(14.3)

where

E_j = the input saving efficiency measure for unit j,
Y = the $m \times n$ matrix of outputs in the benchmark sample,
y_j = the $m \times 1$ vector of outputs from unit j,
X = the $k \times n$ matrix of inputs in the benchmark sample,
x_j = the $k \times 1$ vector of inputs from unit j,
z_j = the $n \times 1$ vector of intensity weights defining the
benchmark unit to be compared with unit j.

The benchmark sample is the dataset which the frontier envelops, denoted i above. In our application the output and input vectors y_j and x_j of unit j are not necessarily components of the output and input matrices Y and X of the benchmark sample. The efficiency score E_j may thus exceed one, meaning that unit j is more efficient than the best benchmark we can construct. This may for example occur when the efficiency of one observation is evaluated relative to a frontier from a different year.

If we wanted to impose the restriction of not forgetting technology, the benchmark set may be defined by accumulating datasets from the first period on including the last of the two periods we are considering, in the sequential fashion of Tulkens and Vanden Eeckhaut (1993), or using the full intertemporal frontier by defining the benchmark set to be all the cross-section sets. In these cases a Paasche approach is followed. As to the frontier shift component, contemporaneous frontiers for periods 1 and 2 are compared with the accumulated frontier concepts based on sequential or intertemporal sets.

The formulation of problem (14.3) implies that the benchmark technology is restricted to constant returns to scale, since no restriction on the sum of intensity weights is introduced. By introducing such restrictions DEA can also accommodate either non-increasing or variable unrestricted returns to scale, see Grosskopf (1986). But when the performance of unit j is compared to a frontier generated from a sample excluding unit j, constant returns to scale are sufficient to ensure the existence of a solution to the LP problem in the input saving efficiency case.[5] In this chapter we shall therefore be assuming constant returns to scale.

Data

The data are based on the yearly *Industry Statistics* from Statistics Norway. The time period covered is 1976–88. Twelve 4–5-digit ISIC sectors are chosen such that all the 2-digit levels are represented, and considerations of homogeneity of products and number of units are also taken into

Table 14.1 *Data for establishments, twelve 4–5-digit sectors 1976 –88. Numbers in million Norwegian crowns, labour in 1000 hours*

	Capital				Materials			
	Min	Max	Mean	S.D.	Min	Max	Mean	S.D.
Conc.	0.2	55	7.1	7.7	0.4	53	8.5	7.8
Ferro	10.0	936	367	193	3.4	554	188	98
Hous.	0.0	269	12	26	0.2	825	24	64
Graph.	0.6	335	24	48	0.2	257	14	29
Mach.	0.0	456	33	69	0.2	281	21	49
Food	0.0	160	25	28	0.6	160	24	27
Paints	0.1	505	27	63	0.3	345	35	61
Met.	0.0	691	11	27	0.0	265	8.3	18
Paper	2.0	2534	385	491	0.5	1024	141	174
Plastic	0.8	155	27	32	0.3	138	20	23
Ships	0.0	692	30	66	0.0	714	35	72
Garm.	0.0	49	4.3	5.6	0.0	63	4.7	7.4
	Labour				Gross output			
Conc.	3.6	110	17	12	0.9	63	12	9.6
Ferro	8.0	125	420	260	3.7	822	270	147
Hous.	4.2	151	64	151	0.3	912	33	84
Graph.	2.5	977	68	119	0.6	322	23	44
Mach.	1.0	102	91	145	0.4	430	34	73
Food	1.4	452	62	72	1.2	232	36	40
Paints	3.5	125	81	161	0.4	444	45	76
Met.	1.3	896	50	80	0.4	341	14	25
Paper	7.9	131	338	310	0.7	1495	184	231
Plastic	4.9	373	63	65	0.3	165	29	30
Ships	2.1	318	167	294	0.5	1061	52	100
Garm.	1.5	553	53	60	0.1	104	8.4	12

account. The number of units vary from year to year in each sector. The sectors and some summary statistics are shown in table 14.1.

Output is measured as gross output at market prices. The three inputs are labour, measured in man-hours, and also in number of employees, materials, measured as costs of materials including energy, and capital measured by fire insurance value of buildings and machinery. The insurance values should in principle reflect replacement values of capital for observed production capacity.

All current money measures are deflated to fixed (1984) prices by using the National Accounts official price deflators.

The data have been screened for missing values and nonsensical numbers. All in all about 20 per cent of the observations have been changed in some way from the official file. In most cases units have been discarded.

Results

A problem, unavoidable by definition when working with micro data, is that there is a multitude of results to report. When attempting to condense the information one must be careful not to throw out the baby with the bathwater! The results for the twelve sectors cannot all be reported here, but we will try to give examples of the type of information this approach can give.

Average development

The broadest picture is given by the development of productivity for the (arithmetic) average unit within each sector over the total period. In figure 14.1 the Malmquist productivity index and its components are set out. The overall impression is one of productivity decline; only five of the sectors improve over the twelve-year period, and seven decline. The decomposition shows clearly that it is downward shifts in frontier technology that lead to the decline. The frontier reverses in nine sectors. In the five sectors with positive productivity development the frontier shifts outward in two of them. The catching-up term contributes positively to productivity in all but two sectors.

The development over the time periods are shown in figures 14.2 and 14.3 for the sectors paper and ships, representing industries with positive and negative development respectively. The average unit in the paper industry shows a cyclical pattern with positive productivity growth in the last years of the 1970s, then a decline in the first half of the 1980s and positive growth again in the last two years. It is interesting to note that positive frontier shifts drive the development in the two first periods, and then reverse while positive total productivity growth still continues owing to the catching-up momentum. The decline of technology continues right up to the last year, with one exception, and then technology drives the progress again. The technology reversal contributes to negative productivity growth for ships in seven of the years. When the productivity development is positive it is very modest, and driven by technology twice and by catching-up three times.

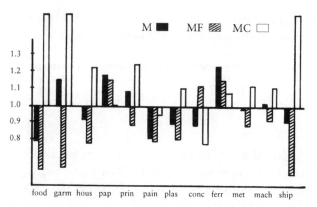

Figure 14.1 *Productivity growth average unit, 1976 reference technology*

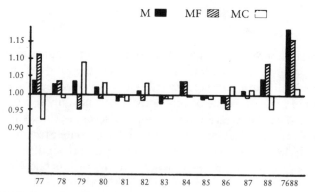

Figure 14.2 *Paper: productivity growth average unit, 1976 reference technology*

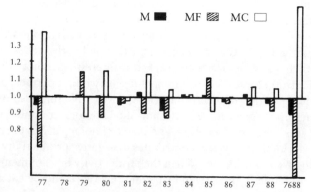

Figure 14.3 *Ships: productivity growth average unit, 1976 reference technology*

The choice of reference technology can matter for productivity development. For three of the twelve sectors the total period results are reversed from positive growth, using 1976 as base, to negative growth, using 1988 as base, but for the other sectors the results are fairly robust. The general pattern is that using 1988 as base reduces productivity growth for the early periods.

Some detailed results are set out in table 14.2 in the case of a reversal for ferro-alloys. Using 1976 as base yields a growth of 22.8 per cent shown in the last line, while using 1988 yields a negative shift of 10.8 per cent. Since catching-up efficiency is independent of the base, the difference is due to the technology part. With 1976 as the base the technology is down twice, while using 1988 the technology gets negative shifts in the area of the average unit six times. The successive frontier index is close to the 1976 base. All approaches identify the period 1979–80 as the period with a strong technology reversal.

Individual development of productivity

The complete distributions of productivity change are shown in figures 14.4 and 14.5 for paper and ships. The width of the histograms corresponds to the relative gross output in 1976. The solid horizontal lines at 1 distinguish positive from negative growth.

The total productivity distribution in figure 14.4a shows that all but two establishments have experienced positive productivity growth over the total period. The shift of the frontier (figure 14.4b) has contributed positively for all units. The catching-up effect is negative for about 40 per cent of the capacity, and most of the small units are in this group.

The most striking feature of the distribution for Ships in figures 14.6a–c is the negative impact of technology reversal. Only three units benefit from technology shifts. But most of the establishments, representing 90 per cent of output, experience a positive catching-up effect. It is worth noting that even in this industry some medium-sized and small units, having 30 per cent of total output, manage positive productivity growth.

Efficiency distributions over time

Since we have all the Farrell efficiency scores it is also of interest to follow the development of efficiency distributions over time. For the two sectors paper and ships the efficiency distributions for four years are set out in figures 14.6a–b and structural efficiency for all years in figures 14.7a–b.

The efficiency distributions are the top lines of histograms representing size of units. That information is lost when we present the distributions in

Table 14.2 *Manufacture of ferro-alloys. Average unit*

Years	Total productivity growth			Frontier productivity growth			Catching-
	Fixed reference technology	Successive		Fixed reference technology	Successive		up
	$M_{76}(i,i+1)$	$M_{88}(i,i+1)$	$M_i(i,i+1)$	$MF_{76}(i,i+1)$	$MF_{88}(i,i+1)$	$MF_i(i,i+1)$	$MC(i,i+1)$
76-77	1.038	0.880	1.038	1.013	0.859	1.013	1.025
77-78	0.999	0.950	0.987	1.091	1.038	1.078	0.915
78-79	1.019	1.008	1.040	0.916	0.907	0.935	1.112
79-80	0.881	0.868	0.882	0.887	0.874	0.888	0.993
80-81	1.102	1.037	1.117	1.105	1.039	0.998	1.120
81-82	1.038	1.011	1.029	0.999	0.972	0.990	1.040
82-83	1.035	1.079	1.057	1.018	1.061	1.039	1.017
83-84	0.990	0.997	0.980	1.036	1.043	1.026	0.956
84-85	0.965	0.967	0.973	0.938	0.940	1.028	0.946
85-86	0.991	0.966	0.981	0.999	0.974	0.989	0.992
86-87	1.054	1.042	1.049	1.035	1.024	1.030	1.018
87-88	1.116	1.111	1.094	1.134	1.128	1.111	0.984
76-88	1.228	0.892		1.150	0.836		1.067

the same diagram, so we concentrate on the shapes. The distributions for paper are close to each other and do not show any trend over time. They are all quite even starting from values of efficiency scores in the interval 0.70–0.85, implying that the units are close in an efficiency sense independent of size.

The distributions for ships, on the other hand, show positive shifts over time, especially from 1976 to 1980 and from 1980 to 1984. But one should beware of interpreting this as improvement, since the efficiency scores are relative to the current frontier, and we know that the frontier has experienced reversals. Improvement for individual units implies positive catching up. The range of efficiency scores is quite wide, starting from values in the interval 0.3–0.4.

If we want information on how the industry is keeping up with its best firms, an early article by Maywald (1957) studies the change in energy productivity of electric power plants based on an international dataset and focuses on the development of the distance between average and best practice. This distance was also suggested by Farrell (1957) as a measure of structural efficiency. Farrell structural efficiencies are defined in Førsund and Hjalmarsson (1979 and 1987) as the efficiency score of the average unit. Figure 14.7a shows that structural efficiency in the paper industry is quite high, and that it improved in the 1970s. Corresponding to the markedly more skew efficiency distributions in the shipbuilding industry,

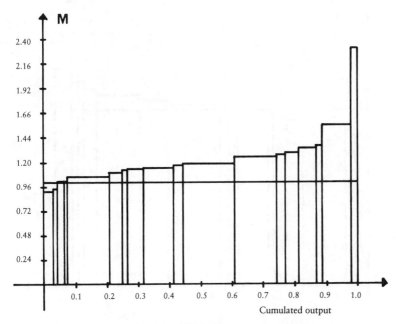

Figure 14.4a *Paper: productivity 1976–88*

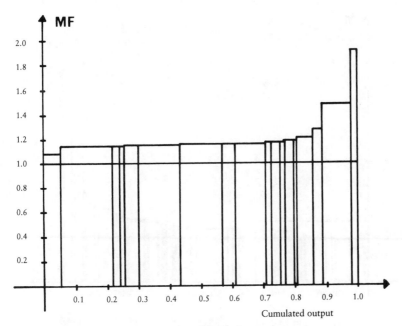

Figure 14.4b *Paper: technology shift 1976–88*

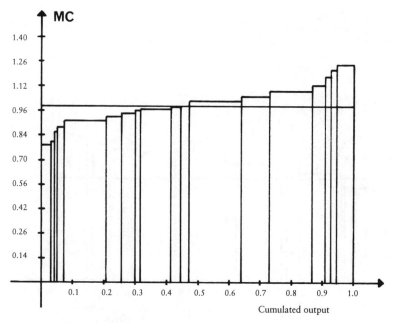

Figure 14.4c *Paper: catching-up 1976–88*

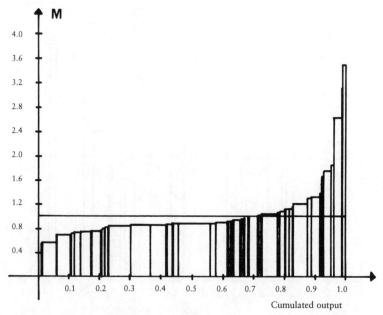

Figure 14.5a *Ships: productivity 1976–88*

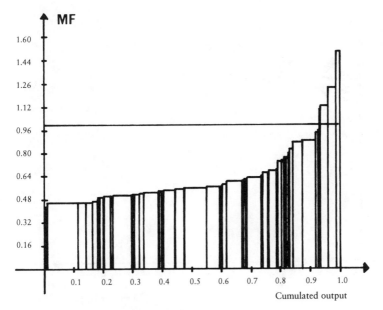

Figure 14.5b *Ships: technology shift 1976–88*

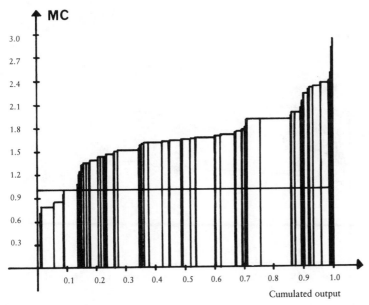

Figure 14.5c *Ships: catching-up 1976–88*

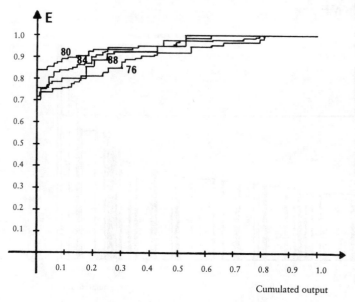

Figure 14.6a *Paper: efficiency distributions*

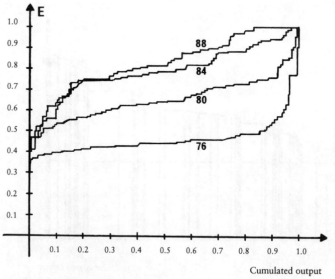

Figure 14.6b *Ships: efficiency distributions*

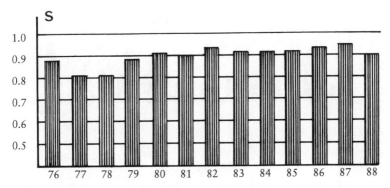

Figure 14.7a *Paper: structural efficiency*

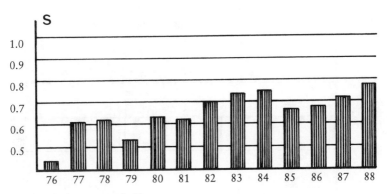

Figure 14.7b *Ships: sructural efficiency*

structural efficiencies, shown in figure 14.7b, are very low, especially at the start of the period.

Verdoorn's Law

The results presented so far have all been descriptive in nature, although yielding insights at a micro level. We will not be able to do much more, but there is one famous 'law' governing productivity development, namely Verdoorn's Law. To formulate it in popular terms, the law states that in the long run there is a positive relationship between productivity growth and output growth (see Verdoorn, 1949, 1980). This law has been subject to some discussion and empirical testing, see Rowthorn (1979), De Vries

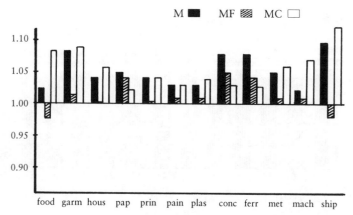

Figure 14.8a *Establishments with positive growth: unweighted mean of Malmquist index*

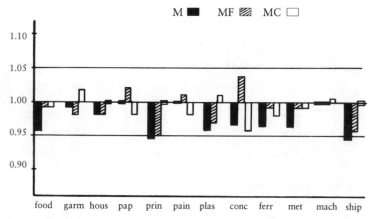

Figure 14.8b *Establishments with production decline: unweighted mean of Malmquist index*

(1980), Thirwall (1980), McCombie (1982, 1987), Fase and van den Heuvel (1988).

We will explore the law in our micro setting in an *ad hoc* fashion of casual empiricism rather than formal statistical tests. Using successive period reference technology and regarding each cross-section as a separate dataset, all the observations have been divided into two groups of positive output growth between adjacent periods. A specific unit can belong to both sets depending on the time period, we have twelve cross-sections for each sector in all.

The test of Verdoorn's Law is then simply performed by showing the (unweighted) average Malmquist indices of the two sets distributed on industries. Figure 14.8a reveals that the average values of the total index and the catching-up index are all positive for the set of units with positive output growth. Only two sectors, food and ships, have negative frontier shifts and positive output growth.

For the observations with negative output growth the covariation with the total productivity index is also overwhelming, all sector sets of negative growth in output show negative productivity change in figure 14.8b. The picture for technology shifts and catching-up is more mixed, but still showing strong correlation. These results can be confirmed to be significant by simple single equation regressions.

Concluding remarks

From the basic assumption of inefficient units insights into productivity development over the period 1976–88 are obtained, using the tool of frontier functions. Applying piecewise linear frontiers implies calculating rather than estimating, and we have no measure of degree of uncertainty of our results. However, sensitivity tests indicate that our main finding is rather robust: productivity decline has occurred for the lion's share of the establishments in the twelve industries covered. A few industries have performed well, mainly owing to positive shifts of the frontier technology. Verdoorn's Law, originally formulated at the macro level, has found support at our micro level: positive productivity growth corresponds with positive output growth.

To confirm such results further research is necessary. With the present dataset we were not able to adjust for capacity utilisation or labour hoarding. It would also be of interest to compare our detailed micro results with traditional total factor productivity measures.

15 X-inefficiency in measured technical inefficiency

AKIO TORII[1]

Technical inefficiency defined by Farrell (1957) is a calculable concept of inefficiency; a measure of distance from the production frontier. Various empirical studies have attempted to estimate levels of technical inefficiency for various industries and countries. In order to evaluate the meaning of those observed levels of inefficiency, one needs to investigate the components of the observed inefficiency. Most of the researchers who estimated technical inefficiency were interested in observing X-inefficiency. For example, Caves and Barton (1990) explicitly stated that 'technical inefficiency' in their context does mean X-inefficiency.[2]

The X-inefficiency in the mind of researchers of measured technical inefficiency is a kind of social waste distinct from allocative inefficiency as defined by Farrell. While allocative inefficiency can be defined satisfactorily, the meaning of the word *waste* is not clear. Some researchers question even the existence of the waste, claiming that what is identified is not waste and allocative inefficiency is mistaken for X-inefficiency by the problems in observation, like Stigler's (1976) argument against the existence of X-inefficiency. (See Førsund et al.,1980, for a survey paper on this scepticism from the standpoint of econometrics.)[3]

In Leibenstein's view technical inefficiency is a result of maximising behaviour and is a quite different concept from X-inefficiency, which results from non-maximising behaviour. However, technical inefficiency in Leibenstein's context is a concept defined by the cause; therefore it is a different concept from measured technical inefficiency in empirical studies. The latter is an econometric notion defined with the use of production frontiers. Consequently, the nature of measured technical inefficiency depends on the definition of the production function. In this sense it is a neutral concept. Consider the case when many possible variables constitute the set

332

of inputs for the frontier. An extreme case corresponds to Stigler's argument: every existing conduct can be explained by employing some known or unknown factor. Compare this case with that when only fundamental factors, like capital and labour, comprise the set of inputs and other factors are considered to be possible determinants of the level of X-inefficiency.

It is implausible that all the measured technical inefficiency is caused by X-inefficiency. Some measured technical inefficiency is merely superficial. For instance, even if every firm makes correct cost-minimising decisions, the technology embodied in plants can depart from current best-practice technologies. Although these discrepancies do not imply social inefficiency, they are observed econometrically as technical inefficiency. This vintage effect of investment is explained by Førsund and Hjalmarsson (1987). They maintain that: 'a dispersed structure which may be inefficient from a static point of view may be part of an optimal dynamic development' (p. 96). Thus, the existence of observed technical inefficiency is not sufficient to claim the existence of X-inefficiency.

The aim of this chapter is to investigate the relation between X-inefficiency and technical inefficiency when estimated econometrically. Does the technical inefficiency capture the X-inefficiency? What is the nature of technical inefficiency observed? To start a discussion on identifying the property of observed technical inefficiency, this chapter begins by seeking a definition of X-inefficiency from the standpoint of observability. Of course, definitions do not solve problems, but they may make clear the extent of the arguments about X-inefficiency.

A definition of X-inefficiency

Non-optimality in the definition of X-inefficiency

Confusion in controversies about X-inefficiency is due to the lack of an operational definition of it. Most of the arguments are about the optimality of conduct. However, optimality is not a good operational concept; here, to be operational, the definition must be able to categorise observed cases.

Defining non-optimal conduct in microeconomics is difficult. It is far easier to assume optimal conduct than to explain conduct which does not maximise something. If one succeeds in explaining non-maximising conduct 'rationally', then by tautology from the idea of rationality that conduct can always be justified as maximising something. One then has to define the level of optimal conduct. Optimising behaviour beyond that level is considered to be non-optimal. In this sense, non-optimality is a relative concept.

X-inefficiency is said to include both optimal and non-optimal conduct while neoclassical theory considers only optimal conduct. If the set of optimal conduct were a strict subset of conducts explained by X-inefficiency theory, the argument would be simpler. However, the difficulty is that neoclassical microeconomic theory can cover all possible conducts. Therefore although X-inefficiency theory can be expanded similarly, this set of conducts does not strictly include the set explained by neoclassical theory. Thus categorising concepts by the tool used to analyse them is not a good strategy. Even if there is an ordering among tools (tool A is a strict subset of tool B), the order relation is not reflected in the relation between the sets of phenomena explained by these tools.

Two models

To discuss the difference between technical and X-inefficiency two models are introduced. These models exhibit an asymmetric distribution of productivity, which can be observed as technical inefficiency by use of production frontiers, and helps to clarify the relation between the two concepts of efficiency.

Asymmetric distribution of cost structures

There is an infinite number of procedures for setting the asymmetric distribution. Therefore the process described below is only one possible structure, although it is typical. Consider a random variable $c(t_n)$, which represents a cost level at time t_n. The process is assumed to be generated by a Markov chain described by the transition probability:

$$P[c(t_{n+1}) = c_j \mid c(t_n) = c_i] = \begin{cases} 1 - x(c_i - c_0) & (c_j - c_i = \delta) \\ x(c_i - c_0) & (c_j = c_0) \\ 0 & \text{otherwise,} \end{cases} \quad (15.1)$$

where $x, \delta > 0$. The cost level returns to the most efficient one c_0 by the probability proportional to the distance from c_0 and the current level. Otherwise, the cost increases at the same speed. It is easy to see that the probabilistic density function of this process is half-normal if $t_{n+1} - t_n \to 0$, $\delta \to 0$, and $0 < \delta / (t_{n+1} - t_n) < \infty$ (Torii, 1992, pp. 72–5). It is assumed that an asymmetric distribution of the cost level in the distribution of these samples can be observed by ergodicity, and that the asymmetry of the regression residuals is recognised as technical inefficiency.

VINTAGE TECHNICAL INEFFICIENCY

Suppose a plant provides a product to a single market. The average cost equals marginal cost and the best current technology at time t is expressed by production cost $c_0\exp(-at)$: there is a technical progress. Plants are reconstructed with a probability which is proportional to their age, the elapsed time since their last reconstruction. To understand the rationale for this assumption, consider the ratio of breakdown or the possibility that the production technology and/or the product itself becomes obsolete as being proportional to their age. By reconstruction plants can embody the best current technology. Otherwise, the cost level of existing plants relative to current best technology increases by the rate x. Convert the current cost of the plant which is reconstructed at time s, $c_0\exp(-as)$, by evaluating relative to the current best technology $c_0\exp(-at)$. Then, this process is the same as one described in the last subsection. Therefore the stationary distribution is asymmetric half-normal and we observe technical inefficiency.

Suppose there are numerous small plants in a market. Each plant produces the same amount of output. Suppose a level of fixed cost is necessary to renovate plants. Demand is a fixed level, D, while there are N plants which serve D/N units of output. The cost of renovation of the plant is Ke^{-at}: the reconstruction cost decreases at the same rate as the production cost. Take a plant built at time s which is going to consider renovation at time t. If the renovation time is postponed by time Δt the loss caused by using a high cost plant is $(D/N)\Delta t(c_0 e^{-as} - c_0 e^{-at}) = (D/N)\Delta t c_0 e^{-at}[e^{-a(s-t)} - 1]$. On the other hand, the saving from delaying the investment is $Ke^{-at}it$ where i is the discount rate. Then the optimal renewal interval for plants is

$$t - s = \frac{1}{\alpha}\log(\frac{KiN}{Dc_0} + 1).$$
(15.2)

Note that this renewal interval is affected by variables which represent the market structure, N, K. Therefore the level of technical inefficiency is also influenced by those factors.

MANAGERIAL TECHNICAL INEFFICIENCY

Suppose a firm whose products are made by N independent processes, and N is sufficiently large. For all these processes, there are two states, H (high effort) or L (low effort). The state L causes lower production ability than state H. If M processes are in L state and $(N-M)$ are in H state, the production level is curtailed by the proportion Ma. That is, total level of performance is the product of the performance of each process. In a unit interval time, one of the processes in state H changes its state to L by opportunism or some such cause. In the same time interval, the head office examines one of these processes, which is randomly selected. The head office cannot say there is inefficiency from the observed total performance level, because there is environmental uncertainty which influences output randomly. Then the office has to examine processes directly. If a checked process is in state L, the head office will tighten the management effort and try to control cost rigidly, hence trying all processes to state H. Thus the performance of the whole process tends to become lower at a given rate, and is checked for efficiency with a probability which is proportional to the level of inefficiency (the probability that the examined process is in L state is proportional to the number of processes in state L). Therefore, the random variable, the performance of the whole process, shows the same stochastic process as the process described above, and technical inefficiency is detected by observation of this random variable.

Suppose the head office checks J processes within a time interval at a cost $C(J,Q)$, where Q is the level of production. In this case, if we also assume $N \gg M$ and $N \gg J$, then the asymptotic distribution of M is half normal with

$$\sigma = \sqrt{\alpha N / J}.$$

Therefore the expected value of M is also proportional to the inverse of square root of J. As the total production cost is proportional to M, assume the production cost is

$$D(Q) / \sqrt{J}.$$

The head office tries to minimise the sum of the production cost and the managerial cost,

$$D(Q) / \sqrt{J} + C(J,Q). \tag{15.3}$$

If $D(Q)=D^0 Q$ and $C(J,Q) = C(J)^0 Q$ are assumed additionally, the optimal value of J, J^*, is the solution of:

$$C'(J^*) = \frac{D}{2J^{*3/2}},$$

which does not depend on Q.

Thus if $D(Q)$ and $C(J,Q)$ are proportional to Q, the size of the production level, Q does not affect the optimal managerial effort. So, the observed level of inefficiency is not affected by the size of production. Otherwise, the inefficiency level depends on production scale, and so on the market structure.

Definitions of X-inefficiency

With the aid of the two analytical models several possible definitions can be examined.

ITS CAUSE

Usually X-inefficiency is defined by the outcome of some non-optimal conduct, although the non-optimality is not a useful criterion for identifying conduct as X-inefficiency or not. The non-optimality is a kind of cause: a non-optimal conduct prevents maximising output. In *Beyond Economic Man,* Leibenstein shows several such causes, and the analyses in that book can be summarised as a definition of X-inefficiency: 'In an organisation whose function is to produce a good or a service that can be specified and measured, when that organisation cannot accomplish technically maximum output level because a strict subset of the organisation does not in a manner necessary to attain such outcomes, we call that inefficiency X-inefficiency.'

Clearly this definition contains X-inefficiency caused by prisoner's dilemma. Consider an X-inefficiency caused by the existence of an inert area. The agent who is in this inert area optimises his utility by avoiding adjustment costs. However, from the standpoint of the firm's profit, this agent has to behave more optimally. More precisely, there exists some optimal conduct which maximises the profit of the firm minus the cost of effort. From a conjecture related to the principal–agent relation, the inert area chosen by the agent may be wider than the optimal one. Then this inefficiency is X-inefficiency. The ordinary labour contract does not create sufficient incentives for this agent. If the principal struggles to create an incentive system which induces the agent to behave optimally for the firm, this incentive system costs the principal (incentive cost) and the result should be sub-optimal compared to that case without this constraint. Note that utilities are excluded from this definition of output as product specificities and measurability are necessary conditions.

By this definition, allocative inefficiency caused by monopoly is not X-inefficiency. If a monopoly firm uses obsolete or outdated assets, this does not constitute X-inefficiency. That inefficiency should be categorised as allocative inefficiency because the cause is not a conflict between some subsets of that monopoly firm but the strategy of it.

Thus, the vintage technical inefficiency is not a type of X-inefficiency. How about the managerial technical inefficiency? From its construction of the cause, opportunism, that inefficiency is a type of X-inefficiency.

Thus the definition by its cause presents us with a criterion. Nevertheless, we cannot observe the cause directly from a dataset of inputs and outputs to a firm. Then several other definitions should be examined.

CURTAILMENT OF SOCIAL WELFARE

By this definition, if a departure from a production frontier curtails social welfare we consider that departure as X-inefficiency. Even if a decision by a firm makes production of that firm depart from a technical frontier it is possible that there is no X-inefficiency. Catching up frontier technology successively is not always costless.

If we adopt this definition, it is hard to distinguish this efficiency from allocative price inefficiency, because allocative price inefficiency also causes technical inefficiency to be observed. The vintage technical inefficiency is technical inefficiency which curtails welfare but it is not X-inefficient in terms of its cause. Moreover, this definition does not help us to identify inefficiency from the observed data as the definition is in terms of the cause.

DEPENDENCY OF COST ON THE COMPETITIVE STRUCTURE OF THE MARKET

The third possible definition is the dependency of cost on the competitive structure of the market. One of the properties of X-inefficiency is the dependency of cost on the market competition condition. According to this definition, the observed technical inefficiency can be classified as X-inefficiency or not by use of inter-industry cross-section analysis, so this is an operational definition. Nevertheless, a difficulty with this definition lies in the ability to distinguish X-inefficiency from allocative inefficiency because some allocative price inefficiency also has this same tendency. Consider vintage technical inefficiency. By the criterion of the cause, that was allocative inefficiency. Two factors make the level of observed vintage technical inefficiency dependent on market structure. The first is the renovation cost, K. If there is a fixed element to K, for example by indivisibility of R&D costs or special machinery cost, KN/D is not a constant, but an increasing function of the production level. In such cases inefficiency increases as N increases. The more competitive a market is, the more inefficiency should be detected. The second factor is not explicit in the model. The more monopolistic the market, the longer the interval before renewal investment (Torii, 1992, pp. 62–7), because the monopolist lacks the incentive. The logic is very similar to the one in the analysis of the relation between R&D and the competitive structure of the market.

This definition causes another problem. Consider the model again. Although in a very atomistic industry a considerable level of technical inefficiency would be observed, it is not X-inefficient. The time interval of renewal investment is determined optimally, and the decisions have no external effect. Therefore, there is no social waste. Firms keep the renewal investment very low because it does not pay privately or socially.

Managerial technical inefficiency is embedded in X-inefficiency by its cause. However if there are no scale economies nor diseconomies for the production level Q in production cost $D(Q)$ or managerial cost $C(J,Q)$, we cannot observe any association between the level of technical inefficiency and market structure. In such cases, we cannot identify this type of inefficiency by this definition.

AVOIDABILITY OR REMEDIABILITY

This definition resembles the definition by cause, however, explaining the controllability of the level of inefficiency more explicitly. Consider managerial technical inefficiency again. Apparently this efficiency is X-inefficiency from the definition by cause. Note that the level of inefficiency can be controlled. The managerial inefficiency can be avoidable if the manager allows for the cost of some checking mechanism. That is, the manager can optimise the intensity of managerial effort taking into account its cost and effect, choosing J^* defined by:

$$\frac{\partial C(J^*,Q)}{\partial J} = \frac{D}{2J^{*3/2}}. \tag{15.4}$$

This forms relative optimality. Deciding the level of managerial effort is a maximising problem under the constraint of the relation between the effect and the cost of effort level. Neoclassical economists would not class this as X-inefficiency. If the competitive structure of a market affects that decision of the manager, that effect causes *allocative inefficiency* in the decision of the level of managerial effort. Therefore we have to admit that the problem over whether the managerial technical inefficiency is X-inefficiency or not is still ambiguous.

Note that the level of inefficiency has an implicit price because the level appears in the constraint of a maximising problem. If that constraint is effective, the implicit price should be positive. If the implicit price is zero, it shows efficiency is not controllable. In those cases the firm's headquarters should maximise the profit without regard to that uncontrollable factor. In this case, the problem disappears, and the inefficiency cannot be allocative inefficiency. Therefore, the implicit price can be employed as a criterion for identification of X-inefficiency.

Relation between X- and technical inefficiency

The discussion in the last section shows us that the definition by its cause is a possible criterion for X-inefficiency, but it has problems in observability and in the relation to optimal conduct. However, if we know the implicit price of the level of inefficiency, remediability may provide a criterion. In this section we examined the ability of technical inefficiency to test for the existence of X-inefficiency.

It is easy to see that X-inefficiency is not always observed as technical inefficiency. In order to observe technical inefficiency as a symmetric error term, we need three necessary conditions:

1. a tendency to depart from technical frontiers,
2. a checking mechanism which enables the performance level to return to frontier technology,
3. ergodicity.

The first condition is for inefficiency itself. With the second condition, some equilibrium distribution of performance levels can be constructed, which can be observed by ergodicity.

Note that X-inefficiency does not always entail an asymmetric distribution of performance. If the second condition is not satisfied, the observed performance level will be distributed symmetrically around a locus detached from the true technical frontier. Even if the cause of efficiency is apparently X-inefficiency, we will not observe negatively skewed distributions of performances: no technical inefficiency is observed.

Conversely, technical inefficiency observed by the frontier technology method embraces not only X-inefficiency but also allocative price inefficiency. Consider a concave production function, $y=f(x,z)$: y is output, x and z are inputs. x and y are observable but z is not. Also suppose there is no technical inefficiency, that is, f is a single-valued frontier function. xs are dispersed so that one can estimate a production frontier. We do not argue here why x does not take an optimised value ($f_x = p_x/p_y$, p_i s are prices determined exogenously). Allocative inefficiency or diffused firm specific factor prices are assumed. There is allocative inefficiency in the decision of the unobservable variable z. Denote the second best decision of z given the value of x as $z_0(x)$. Also suppose allocative inefficiency about z is distributed symmetrically, so that the mean of the conditional distribution of z is $z_0(x)$. We observe the correspondence between x and $y = f(x,z)$. Assume the discrepancy causing allocative inefficiency is not so large. Then by Taylor expansion of f about z we get:

$$y = f(x,z) = f[x,z_0(x) + \Delta z] = f[x,z_0(x)] + \Delta z f_z + \frac{(\Delta z)^2}{2} f_{zz} + \sigma^3(\Delta z). \quad (15.5)$$

We can observe the first term of the right side of the equation. The term is determined only by x. By assumption on the symmetrical distribution of Δ_z, the second term is a symmetric divergence from the frontier $f[x,z_0(x)]$, and the third term shows that we observe asymmetric divergence in a negative direction due to concavity of f. Thus even in the absence of technical inefficiency we observe deviations composed of symmetric and asymmetric errors. When we estimate the frontier function by observed sets (x,y) using some method to estimate a frontier production function with a composed error term, we get:

$$y = \tilde{f}(x) + v - u. \quad (15.6)$$

When the term $\sigma^3(\Delta z)$ is small enough to be neglected, observed y can be decomposed to $f^{\sim}(x)$ which is the estimate of $f[s,z_0(x)]$ the symmetric term v which corresponds to $\Delta z f_z$, and the asymmetric term u which corresponds to $(\Delta_z)^2 f_{zz}/2$. If the existence of this factor z is ignored because of a problem of observation, we get measured inefficiency from the third term by decomposition of the residuals of the regression. Therefore, unless the estimation method can distinguish between technical inefficiency caused by X-inefficiency and allocative inefficiency caused by mis-specification of the frontier model, like the third term of the last equation, we cannot tell whether genuine technical inefficiency really exists. Each inefficiency is called G-inefficiency (properly observed X-inefficiency) and P-inefficiency (allocative inefficiency, but observed as technical inefficiency) for the purposes of this chapter.

Thus the technical inefficiency observed by econometric method is neither a sufficient nor a necessary condition of the existence of X-inefficiency, a priori. In the next section, an identification of X-inefficiency from the observation of technical inefficiency is discussed.

X-inefficiency in the measured technical inefficiency

In this section it is shown that not all technical inefficiency observed in an empirical study of Japanese manufacturing industries is allocative. At least a part is due to X-inefficiency. Consider again the model of P-inefficiency from the last section. Suppose the density function of the distribution of Δz is g. Then the density function of $s \equiv \Delta z^2$ is $g(\sqrt{s} / \sqrt{s})$, which means that the distribution density of the square of a variable goes to infinity at the value 0 unless $g(0) = 0$. It is not appropriate to assume the density at 0 is zero because we have assumed a symmetric distribution around the mean.[4]

On the other hand, for all types of families of distribution assumed for technical inefficiency the density does not go to infinity at the most efficient point. This provides us with a distinction between G-inefficiency and P-inefficiency. In practice, the difference will appear in the observed value of skewness and kurtosis of the distribution of discrepancies from the production frontier. Those values are independent from the variance (in this case of allocative inefficiency, the value of $f_{zz}/2$). Hereafter we confine our analysis to the case that the symmetric disturbance of allocative inefficiency is normally distributed.

Where do these differences in the shapes of distribution between allocative and X-inefficiency come from? An asymptotic distribution of X-inefficiency is a product of the balance of the two forces which equilibrate the asymptotic distribution of the level of inefficiency. One of the forces is a tendency to depart from frontier efficiency, the other is the pressure to return to the frontiers. In the neighbourhood of the most efficient point, the latter force is not assumed to go to infinity, nor is the first force assumed to be zero. The level of efficiency drifts incessantly. It is hard to imagine that the pressure increases rapidly as efficiency increases, or that the tendency to depart from the frontier is very limited near the frontier. Therefore the distribution density is bounded everywhere.

On the contrary, allocative inefficiency is a stationary concept. In the neighbourhood of the most efficient point $(\Delta z \to 0)$, the ratio of the departure from frontier $(\Delta z)^2$ to the degree of allocative inefficiency Δz is infinitesimal, so that the distribution density goes to infinity.

When the half-normal distribution is assumed for technical inefficiency, the values of skewness and kurtosis are $\sqrt{2}(\pi - 4)(\pi - 2)^{-3/2}$ (about -0.9953, denoted as s_h) and $(3\pi^2 - 4\pi - 12)(\pi - 2)^{-2}$ (about 3.869, k_h) respectively. On the other hand, these statistics for the distribution of the square of the normal distribution with zero mean are $2\sqrt{2}$ and 15 respectively (s_a and k_a). Note that these values are independent from the variance. However, observed skewness and kurtosis are averaged with those of symmetric distribution (especially the normal distribution with skewness 0 and kurtosis 3), and these averages are weighted by the relative values

Table 15.1 *Distribution of estimates of skewness*

Range	Skewness
-5.5 to -5.0	1
-5.0 to -4.5	6
-4.5 to -4.0	0
-4.0 to -3.5	3
-3.5 to -3.0	6
-3.0 to -2.5	4
-2.5 to -2.0	19
-2.0 to -1.5	19
-1.5 to -1.0	50
-1.0 to -0.5	66
-0.5 to -0.0	83
0.0 to 0.5	52
0.5 to 1.0	24
1.0 to 1.5	4

of the variances. Therefore when half-normally distributed inefficiency is assumed, the skewness of composed error term should lie in interval $[s_h, 0]$. If skewness is greater than 0, the situation is refered to as 'type I error', and if less than s_h 'type II error' according to Aigner *et al.* (1977).

The next table (drawn from Torii, 1992, tables 2–8) summarises the distribution of observed skewness in an empirical study of the manufacturing industries in Japan. Fewer than half of the investigated industries have skewness in the range $[s_h,0]$. The relatively high variance of the estimators of the third moments is not enough to explain most type II errors.[5] About a quarter of negative skewness (92 industries) which caused the type II errors can be explained as P-inefficiency. It looks as if observed technical inefficiency does include allocative inefficiency.

These type I and II errors stem from the inability to calculate σ_u and σ_v from moment estimates. The relation between (σ_u, σ_v) and (m_2, m_3) is:

$$m_2 = \sigma_v^2 + \frac{x-2}{x}\sigma_u^2,$$

$$m_3 = \sqrt{\frac{2}{x}}\frac{x-4}{x}\sigma_u^3.$$

From these relations we get:

$$m_2 = \sigma_v^2 + K_h m_3^{2/3},$$

here

$$K_h \equiv \frac{x-2}{x}(\sqrt{\frac{2}{x}}\frac{x-4}{x})^{\frac{2}{3}}$$

is a constant, 1.003. Similarly when we assume that P-inefficiency exists with a distribution density squared of zero mean and the normal distribution in place of half-normally distributed technical inefficiency, we get the same form of equation with the constant changed to K_a which has the value of 0.5.

We have to assume some distribution for σ_v a priori to test whether the constant is K_h or K_a. If the mean of the distribution of σ_v is far larger compared to the standard error of the distribution, OLS estimates are effective. Nevertheless, in practice this simple method is not appropriate. Figure 15.1 shows the distribution of $m_2 - K_{h(a)} m_3^{2/3}$ calculated from the empirical result of Japanese manufacturing industries. The figure suggests that the assumption that the mean of the distribution of σ_v is far greater than the standard error is not appropriate. The part of the distribution with values less than zero implies a type I error. With the P-inefficiency assumption, the ratio of type I errors is less than that with the G-inefficiency assumption. Nevertheless note that this observation is not enough to explain whether most of observed technical inefficiency is due to allocative inefficiency or specification error in models, as the variance of the estimator of the third moments is quite large. Moreover a relatively large proportion of type I errors does not deny the existence of G-inefficiency, however it is suggested by the existence of P-inefficiency. The most natural assumption is the co-existence of G-inefficiency and P-inefficiency. The elements of P-inefficiency easily overcome and hide the property of G-inefficiency. As the absolute value of the skewness of the distribution generated by P-inefficiency, s_a, is greater than that by G-inefficiency, s_h, someone who sees a value of skewness which is in the range $[s_a, 0]$ cannot tell whether there is no G-inefficiency. Skewness with such values may be an outcome of a mixture of P-inefficiency and a normally distributed symmetric error term, or of P-inefficiency and G-inefficiency.

In examining the relation between moments without any knowledge the distribution of σ_v, higher moments offer some information. We assume the distribution of Δz is $N(0, \sigma_z)$. First we consider when $f_z = 0$. If there is only P-inefficiency, we will observe a composed deviation from frontier, $u^* + v^*$, here

$$v * \tilde{N}(0, \sigma_v), \frac{U^*}{a} \tilde{X}^2(1), \text{ here } a \equiv \frac{f_{zz}}{2} \sigma_z^2.$$

$m_2 - K_a(m_3)^{(2/3)}$

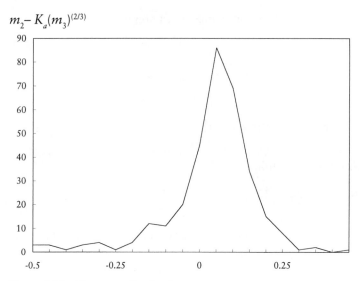

Figure 15.1a *Skewness distribution*

$m_2 - K_b(m_3)^{(2/3)}$

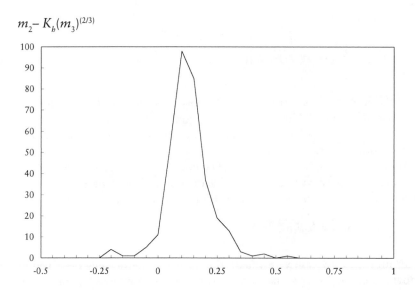

Figure 15.1b *Skewness distribution*

The first four moments of this composition are:

$$m_1 = a\sigma_z^2,$$

$$m_2 = \sigma_v^2 + 2a^2\sigma_z^4,$$

$$m_3 = 8a^3\sigma_z^6,$$

$$m_4 = 60a^4\sigma_z^8 + 12a^2\sigma_v^2\sigma_z^4 + 3\sigma_v^4.$$

From the last three equations, we get:

$$m_4 = 3m_2^2 + 3\left|m_3\right|^{4/3}.$$

In the same manner, if we assume that G-inefficiency is only half-normally distributed we get:

$$m_4 = 3m_2^2 + K_m\left|m_3\right|^{4/3}.$$

Here

$$K_m \equiv 8\frac{\pi-3}{\pi^2}\left[\sqrt{\frac{\pi}{2}}\frac{\pi}{\pi-4}\right]^{4/3}$$

which is about 0.8747, from the equations appearing in the appendix of Olson *et al.* (1980). Note that neither equation includes the σ_i s. Therefore the relation can be examined without any knowledge about the distribution of σ_i s.

When f_z is not 0, the composition becomes hard to analyse. Figure 15.2 shows a result of a Monte-Carlo experiment into the estimate of the coefficient (β_1) of the regression analysis for $a = -1$ and various values of f_z:

$$m_4 - 3m_2^2 = \beta_0\beta_1 m_3^{4/3}.$$

From this, how can we evaluate the technical inefficiency observed in Japanese studies? The estimated regression equation on those Japanese samples is:

$$m_4 - 3m_2^2 = 0.0237 + 3.42 \ m_3^{4/3} \quad \overline{R}^2 = 0.866$$
$$(0.077) \qquad N = 310$$

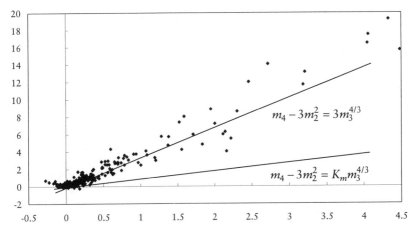

Figure 15.2 *Monte-Carlo experiment*

Comparing the results in figure 15.2, we see that f_z should be relatively small compared to the later departure from the frontier, $-a(\Delta z)^2$, which implies that the implicit price of the constraint expressed by term z is also very small.

We have argued that the relative nature of optimality is not a problem when the implicit price of that constraint is zero. The factor is more than mere optimal conduct, at the same time the data shows the departure from the production frontier. Therefore there is no doubt that the inefficiency detected has the property of X-inefficiency. If we observed some positive price implicit or explicit, the missed factor could be the result of a control mechanism to maximise something. In such cases an important factor omitted from the set of the inputs of the production function caused the observed P-inefficiency.

Recall that the COLS estimator of average technical efficiency is calculated only from the estimate of the third moment. The average departure by P-inefficiency, the average shift caused by the inefficiency, can also be derived from the third moment,

$$E(m_1) = \frac{[E(m_3)]^{1/3}}{2}$$

Therefore the COLS estimator has a meaning as an index of the departure from the frontier caused by P-inefficiency. We know that COLS estimates of inefficiency have systematic relations with the competitive structure of markets.[6] As the level of P-inefficiency has the same property, P-inefficiency can be understood as having the property of X-inefficiency.

Notes

2 PRODUCTIVITY GROWTH IN THE 1980s

1 This research was financed by Economic and Social Research Council grant no: R000233658 for which we are most grateful. The basic data analysis has been undertaken by Dave Watts, Lance Green and colleagues at the Central Statistical Office, Newport and we also acknowledge helpful assistance with our research from Ingo Albrecht, Andy Blake, Hassan Feisal, Paul Gregg, and Nico Vaughan at NIESR. The presentation has been improved by comments from Sig Prais and the participants at the Fulbright Colloquium.

2 Net output per head in UK manufacturing industry (NOPH) increased by 35.1 per cent between 1960 and 1970, 17.6 per cent between 1970 and 1980 compared with 57.1 per cent between 1980 and 1990, all expressed in 1985 prices (Annual Census of Production (ACOP), Summary Reports). We quote NOPH rather than the better known 'value added' as this variable is more readily available in the ACOP results. The difference in definition between the two terms is small. Net output is calculated by deducting from gross output the cost of purchases (adjusted for fluctuations of stocks of materials, and so on during the year) and the cost of industrial services received and, where applicable, duties, and so on. Value added (gross value added at factor cost) is calculated by deducting from net output the cost of non-industrial services, for example rent of buildings, hire of plant, machinery and vehicles, advertising, rates, bank charges, and so on. As an indication of the importance of the difference between these two definitions, value added per head increased by 53 per cent between 1980 and 1990. All variables used are defined in the Appendix.

3 Nickell *et al.* (1992) find that higher levels of debt are associated with increases in levels and growth rates of productivity.

4 Plants employing 1000 or more workers.

5 However, Professor Prais at NIESR has told us that visits to engineering firms made by himself and his team have suggested that the tail of low productivity has been 'chopped off', resulting in a sharper tapering of the distribution rather than

amputation. It could be that our method of analysis is not well adapted to discern this, although we do consider the change in the shape of the productivity distribution.

6 The first comparison of these results is shown in Caves (1992) and a comprehensive description of the UK analysis for a single year (1977) in Mayes *et al.* (1994).

7 In our earlier work (Mayes *et al.*, 1994) we explored the consequences of using both measures. Here we have perpetuated the resulting choice.

8 This generates only a 133-industry breakdown of manufacturing compared with our own 182 and many of these have overlapping boundaries.

9 This would be consistent with some aspects of the process of substitution as the number of shifts worked might be reduced.

10 S. Smith-Gavine (De Montfort University) and A. Bennett (University of Aston Business School) have been producing the PUL index for over twenty years. It is circulated by them in the form of a regular Bulletin.

11 The difference between the two measures in the case of the USA is much smaller, 58 per cent per employee hour compared with 54 per cent per employee, and since the overall gap between the two countries is so large this difference has no important impact on the conclusions one might draw.

12 Prais describes the estimates as 'unrealistic' and GDP estimates are certainly complicated by the need to deal with productivity in the services industries, a problem which makes the arguments over estimates in manufacturing seem rather trivial.

13 Taking exact matches may not be a fair comparison because tastes and other differences among economies may mean that the products which are common in one economy are unusual in the other and hence not surprisingly produced with different levels of efficiency. Comparing typical plants does not avoid the problem but offers a helpful alternative viewpoint.

14 In the metal products and machinery industries production statistics data suggested an advantage for the Netherlands over the UK of 30 per cent, while Mason and van Ark's (1993) plant comparison suggests 36 per cent.

15 This is covered in its clearest form in the CSO *Business Monitor, Report on the Census of Production*, Summary volumes for the years 1980 to 1990.

16 Standard Industrial Classification (SIC(68) as opposed to SIC(80) for our data). Data will be available for 1991 on the same basis soon but 1992 and subsequent years will be on SIC(92) which is again not comparable at our level of disaggregation. Our earlier research on 1977 is also on SIC(68) so comparability is limited. Cost constraints precluded trying to trace through those industries whose definition was largely unchanged over a longer period of years.

17 We have made a proposal to create a database along US/Canadian lines.

18 Using single deflation by output prices to express it in constant prices. Ideally double deflation would have been used but the input prices are not available at this level of detail. Stoneman (1992) shows that productivity calculations at a much more aggregate level can be so seriously altered by the use of double rather than single deflation that the validity of the data is called into question.

19 With the exception of some very limited non-response and suspect data.

20 As from the next Annual Census the smallest companies (fewer than twenty employees) will also be sampled. It has become clear that many of the most important changes in the economy are occurring in this category which contained 114,115 businesses in 1990, some 80 per cent of the total in manufacturing by number although only 10 per cent of employees. This omission therefore applies to our own analysis.

21 It is clear from the aggregated data shown in Appendix table 2A.3 that there are serious problems in comparing the data drawn from the original business with the published version, grossed up from ACOP, as discrepancies between the measures can be as large as a quarter.

22 The sectoral classification in SIC(80) is shown in the Appendix.

23 That is, not motor cars.

24 Results using value added weights show a consistently larger discrepancy.

25 Three other industries with productivity levels closer to the mean have also shown below average rates of productivity growth (food, drink and tobacco; paper, paper products, printing and publishing; non-metallic minerals).

26 The characteristics of this dataset are explained at the beginning of the next section of this chapter.

27 Neither the Chemical Industries Association nor British Pest Control were able to offer an explanation in terms of specific restructuring within the industry over that period.

28 The proportions will change when value added weights are used.

3   ENTRY, EXIT, OWNERSHIP AND THE GROWTH OF PRODUCTIVITY

1 Shown here by the coefficient of variation to allow for the fact that higher means permit higher variances.

2 We have not at this stage explored the distribution of changes in the coefficient of variation in each industry, which would show whether there was merely a whole series of fairly small changes in each industry or whether in fact the distributions had changed markedly and industries showing large reductions in variance were merely being offset by others showing large increases.

3 This is caused by an outlier in the data. In shipbuilding and repair, SIC 3610, average productivity fell by roughly a half in 1988.

4 Clearly this area can be explored in greater depth when resources permit.

5 Bailey used SIC(68).

6 The dataset she was dealing with relates to the original genesis of the present research. The work was originally begun in the mid-1970s at the National Development Office as part of the Industrial Strategy developed for the government. Among the tasks which were set was the identification of areas where productivity performance was weak, both in static and dynamic terms. The concern was whether these weaknesses lay in particular industries in particular size classes of firms – SMEs being an expected target. The estimation of the 1977 frontier production functions (Mayes *et al.*, 1994; Caves, 1992) was a second step

in this process stemming from a collaboration with Richard Caves at Harvard. While the 1974–9 government did not last long enough for the strategy to be implemented, NEDO has not lasted long enough to see the full fruits of the work, having been closed at the end of 1992.

7   As Bailey (1992) shows, this had rather limited success.

8   Earlier versions of this chapter expressed some doubts about the robustness of the data on entrants and exits because of their small number but the CSO has reiterated that they feel that the data are reliable.

9   The change in the structure of the firms which make up industry through entry, exit, acquisition, mergers, and so on.

10 Our data distinguish three forms of 'entry/exit'.
    1 – a new business is 'formed'/an old one is 'closed'. Here entry and exit refer to entry and exit into the sampling frame, that is, being a business with over twenty employees. Firms which remain small do not feature in the dataset and a business deemed 'closed' may in fact re-emerge later on if it regains adequate size.
    2 – an existing business is sold/purchased.
    3 – an existing business changes its principal product and hence shifts from one category into another.
    Category 2 is treated as a continuing business and is matched with itself under its previous ownership in computing the impact on productivity. Category 3 is added to Category 1 and treated as a genuine exit/entry. This can be very misleading as a firm which produces 40 per cent product 1 and 60 per cent product 2 will be classified under product 2. Yet even if it increases output of product 2 by 40 per cent, while doubling output of product 1, it will be treated as an exit as product 1 now becomes the principal product. (Fortunately there are limits to the range of products over which these combinations are plausible within a single business and strikingly different operations by single firms even though they take place under one roof are likely to be categorised as two businesses. For example, the transport division may be treated as a different business.)

11 Using the DTI data on liquidations, Bowden *et al.* (1992) shows that there was a marked increase in both voluntary and compulsory liquidations. Robson (1992) on the other hand argues on the basis of VAT registrations that 1980–90 saw a reduction in business formations and an increase in closures.

4   SHIFTS IN THE PRODUCTION FRONTIER AND THE DISTRIBUTION OF EFFICIENCY

1   I_t is thus an isoquant.

2   In a sense the corresponding problem is the behaviour of total factor productivity as this requires a similar approach to the weighting of the change with respect to changes in the inputs of both capital and labour (Mayes *et al.*, 1994).

3   Our actual specification had to be amended further, imposing the restrictions $a_1 + a_2 = \frac{1}{2}a_4$, which in effect uses a CES approach.

4   It is arguable that this bunching of performance close to the frontier is not a good representation of reality and that the frontier is likely to represent rather

unusually good performance and that the bulk of observations will lie inside it, with their frequency peaking at some intermediate level of efficiency.

5 These specification and estimation issues are discussed in detail in Mayes *et al.* (1993) to which the reader is referred.

6 One of the main reasons for concentrating on labour productivity in the earlier sections of this chapter was our unhappiness with the measures of capital for businesses that exist. Although figures for investment and disposals for the main categories of equipment, buildings and vehicles have been recorded annually for all businesses with over one hundred employees, no attempt has been made to capitalise this information as it is not held in the form of a longitudinal database. Although the PIM method for estimating the capital stock is used at the sectoral level (Mayes and Young, 1994), it is done on the basis of aggregate investment, not the aggregation of estimates of individual businesses capital stock. Even so there are worries that the estimated capital stock is perhaps overestimated by as much as a third. (We are currently engaged in improving these estimates in a contract for the CSO.) Our capital data are therefore capitalised on the basis of each individual year's investment, which will introduce an important element of noise into the study. (See Mayes *et al.*, 1994, for a detailed description of the method.)

7 λ is the ratio of the variation of the inefficiency distribution to that of the symmetric stochastic residual.

8 This also fits with the findings in the previous chapter over the changes in the shape of the industry productivity distributions.

9 Expectations are obtained from the National Institute Domestic Model using forecast values from November of the previous year.

10 The variable reported in the empirical analysis is labelled *GEOG* 2 as it excludes some implausibly valued outliers, whose explanation we are still seeking.

11 This is an independent phenomenon from the relation between the number of businesses in the industry and inefficiency also noted in table 4.4 (the cross-correlation is small and the inverse of the matrix of simple correlation coefficients indicates little multicollinearity among these variables).

12 The annual dummies are measured relative to 1990.

13 In this instance these are plants within British Steel as well as separate companies.

5 PRODUCTIVITY, QUALITY AND THE PRODUCTION PROCESS. A COMMENT ON CHAPTERS 2–4

1 A monumental work relating to the United States for the period 1947–83.

2 It should be noted at this point that although Gordon's work points to an upward bias in the unadjusted durables price index, earlier work on automobiles in the United Kingdom suggested that the major impact of quality adjustment was to reveal a greater cyclical variability in the price index, Cowling and Cubbin (1972). It was speculated that greater quality improvement in periods of recession

could be expected on the basis of oligopolistic rivalry. This raises the interesting question that if the tendency over the past forty years or so has been towards a slower rate of growth, then Gordon's results may be identifying a trend towards quality improvement which actually reflects an oligopolistic reaction to changing macroeconomic conditions.

3 The seminal contribution in the neoclassical literature is that of Shapiro and Stiglitz (1984). Now a lengthy discussion of the implications of unemployment as a worker disciplining device has been incorporated into a leading graduate text (Blanchard and Fischer, 1989, pp. 455–61). Layard *et al.* (1991) features a chapter on efficiency wages.

4 A positive response of worker effort to increases in aggregate unemployment not counteracted by a negative response to wage cutting by the firm in these circumstances can be justified in such models in a number of ways. Green and Weisskopf (1990) suggest that institutional rigidities prevent real wages from responding to unemployment in the short run, so that all the burden of adjustment falls on worker effort. Rebitzer (1993, p. 1399) relies on the near rationality of wage nonadjustment under monopolistic competition in the product market to justify such an effort rather than wage response to unemployment. Chouliarakis (1992) shows that if an industry is collusively oligopolistic a rise in unemployment must see either the optimal pricing or labour discipline rules displaced. In these circumstances wages may remain fixed and the burden of adjustment again fall on effort. Lastly, Rebitzer (1993, p. 1399) reminds us that even under full real wage adjustment by the firms a rise in unemployment can bring not only a fall in real wages but also a rise in effort, depending on the exact specification of the effort function.

5 This sort of innovation had taken place earlier in some industries, as we have already noted, but it became more general towards the end of the 1980s.

6 PRODUCTIVITY, MACHINERY AND SKILLS IN ENGINEERING: AN ANGLO-DUTCH COMPARISON

1 This chapter provides an extended account of a comparative study which was first reported in summary form in Mason *et al.* (1992). We are grateful to Sig Prais (NIESR) for generous advice and comments throughout the study; responsibility for errors is ours alone. We also acknowledge financial support for the project which was kindly provided by the Economic and Social Research Council; the Council is not responsible in any way for the views expressed in the chapter.

We are grateful to the many engineering companies and machinery suppliers who have given generous amounts of time to assist us with this research. In addition we would like to thank the following trade and educational experts in each country for their help and advice:

In the Netherlands: J. van Hoof (SISWO, University of Amsterdam); B. Hövels (ITS, Nijmegen); S. Kelder, J. Fledderus, H. Spronkers (LBO De Nieuwe

Vaart, Zaandam); G. Kraan, A. van der Wielen, S. Broeksma (Scholengemeenschap De Hamrik, Groningen); H. Mulder (Middelbare Vakschool Wageningen); R.J. Schuitema (Metaalunie, De Bilt); A. Timmers (Damland College, Sector Techniek, Zaandam); P. Verhoeven (Stichting Opleidingen Metaal, Woerden).

In Britain: M. Brennan, P. Hiscock (City College, St Albans); B. Glanfield (British Pump Manufacturers Association); A. Henderson (British Valve and Actuator Manufacturers Association); D. Saynor (Spring Research and Manufacturers Association); T. Wilson-Hooper, N. Burgess (Bromley College of Technology).

2 Full details of the selected product areas cannot be given for reasons of confidentiality. However, the individual products chosen for our comparisons of physical productivity levels were typically at the 'small' end of the range of products made by the plants in question. For example, centrifugal pumps with a discharge diameter of 100–200 mm; valves of flange diameter 100 mm; and compression springs made from steel wire of gauge 1.5–2.5 mm.

3 DE, *Employment Gazette* and CBS, *Sociale Maandstatistiek*, various issues.

4 Output and employment estimates derived from CSO, *Report on the Census of Production* and *Monthly Digest of Statistics*, various issues (gross value-added deflated by producer price indices).

5 Estimates derived from CBS, *Produktiestatistieken* and *Sociale Maandstatistiek*, various issues.

6 CSO, *Monthly Digest of Statistics* and CBS, *Statistiek voor de Buitenlandse Handel*, various issues. In the case of metal goods, exports in 1989 accounted for 13 per cent of British sales and 28 per cent of Dutch sales.

7 Estimates of Anglo-Dutch productivity differentials in 1990 for engineering and for manufacturing as a whole are based on extrapolations (using indices of production and employment in each country) of 1984 'benchmark' estimates in van Ark (1990a, b).

8 If a simple comparison of average set-up times for matched operations is made (taking no account of the average number of components to be machined in each case), then the average Dutch advantage in setting-up operations declines from an estimated 60 per cent to 44 per cent; the effect on the weighted average productivity differential for all 23 matched operations, as shown in table 6.4, is a small reduction from 36 per cent in the Dutch favour to 32 per cent. In the main text the more complex measure is preferred since, clearly, the larger are component batch sizes for any given machine set-up, the smaller will be the associated average labour input per unit of production. In both countries great importance was attached by pump and valve producers to the design skills required to postpone 'customisation' of individual products to as late a stage as possible in the production process so that the main components could be effectively standardised and put through early stages of machining in at least medium-sized batches (see main text for further discussion of this point).

9 In both national industries the shares of final output which are processed on CNC equipment tend to be much higher than suggested by these figures on CNC

penetration. In both pump and valve manufacturing, for example, key components (such as pump casings or valve bodies) are now frequently all put through CNC machines. Our sample findings on CNC penetration may be compared with survey information on the diffusion of microelectronics-based production equipment in the two countries which shows just under half of Dutch mechanical engineering firms operating 'at least one CNC machine' in 1988 compared to some 63 per cent of British mechanical engineering establishments doing so in 1987 (unweighted percentages in each case); Sources: Northcott and Walling (1988, table 57); Bilderbeek (1990, p. 216). In our study, based on just three narrowly defined sectors of mechanical engineering and metal goods, all the Dutch plants visited and all but two of the twelve British plants had 'at least one' CNC machine in operation. These apparently above average rates of CNC penetration in both our national samples reflect the high-precision and increasingly 'customised' nature of the product areas in question.

10 For further details of recent Dutch tax credits on fixed-asset investments under the 'WIR' scheme – now greatly reduced in scope – see *Financial Times*, European Investment Locations Survey, 4 April 1991, p. IV. Dutch managers made clear to us that these incentives mainly affected the timing rather than the volume of new investment.

11 For example, in pump and valve manufacturing the machining of relatively small batches of complex components invariably requires a machine to operator ratio of 1:1 but this ratio is frequently increased to 2:1 in both countries whenever batch sizes and more straightforward component specifications allow. In spring manufacturing batch sizes vary greatly but are sometimes large enough for operators in each country to be responsible for three or four machines at a time.

12 This is confirmed by another study of British manufacturers of fluid handling equipment (including pumps and valves) which found, in respect of CNC machine tools, that 'it is now common for cost to be minimised by multi-machine manning' (Hamblin, 1989, p. 22).

13 As a result of recent reforms to the Dutch apprenticeship system, there has been a sharp rise in the number of trainees enrolled in the primary phase of the system since the mid-1980s but this growth has taken place from a low base and apprenticeships continue to absorb only a small proportion (about 10 per cent) of each age cohort. For further details see van Dijk *et al.* (1988) and Mason and van Ark (1993, Appendix A). KMBO ('short intermediate') courses have developed over the past ten years as an alternative means of acquiring vocational qualifications for school-leavers who have been unable (or have not sought) to find employment and who lack the qualifications to enter intermediate vocational (MBO) schools. Although college-based, these courses include extensive workshop practice (in technical subject areas) as well as providing students with the opportunity of work placements.

14 It will be understood that the definition of 'craft-qualified' in each industry involves some simplification of a more complex reality: in the British case, for instance, older 'time-served' employees are included alongside younger craft workers who have completed a standards-based training and further education

programme; on the Dutch side, the great majority of employees designated as craft-skilled have acquired LTS qualifications and subsequently followed employer-specific programmes of on-the-job training which inevitably differ in respect of length and breadth of content; only a small proportion have completed a formal apprenticeship. Nonetheless, our comparisons of exam papers in each country leave us in no doubt as to the broad equivalence between the two sets of workers identified as craft-qualified in each national sample.

15 These estimates of average initial on-the-job training times refer to the periods during which new recruits are regarded as being 'in training', that is, in receipt of regular instruction and detailed supervision. No attempt has been made to compare the allocation of training times in each country between 'instruction periods' (when there is little or no output) and periods of 'learning by experience' when some productive contribution is made.

16 Daly et al., 1985, p. 57.

17 The average ratio of direct workers to supervisors was fairly similar in both national samples: 14.5:1 in Britain, 16:1 in the Netherlands.

18 For a recent study which emphasises the increasing technical and managerial demands being placed on supervisors, see IPRA (1993). The 'effective partnership' between many technicians and Meister-trained supervisors in German manufacturing is examined in detail in Steedman et al., 1991, pp. 62–3. The parallel between MTS-qualified supervisors and German Meister should not be drawn too far as MTS courses are primarily geared towards technical training and rarely cover the more 'people-oriented aspects of Meister courses' (for example, training in instructional techniques) or topics in 'business organisation' (for example, production planning and costing). In both the Netherlands and Britain the main way of developing these kinds of supervisory competence is through short courses of off-the-job training which generally lack technical content.

19 Roughly half the CNC users in each national sample allocated the programming function to office-based technicians but skilled shopfloor workers were in most cases permitted to make modifications to programs. In both countries sole reliance on shopfloor programmers tended to occur in smaller plants with roughly one hundred or fewer employees.

20 The relatively large proportion of craft-qualified technical support staff in the British sample reflects the continued employment (mainly in larger plants) of specialist apprentice-trained inspectors. In the Dutch plants the inspection function is generally carried out either by production workers themselves or by broadly defined 'technical departments'.

21 For a discussion of the relative distribution of technician training costs in Britain compared to France and Germany, see Steedman et al., 1991, pp. 69–70.

22 It is important to note that the relatively high attainments (by international standards) in Dutch vocational schools apply to general subjects such as mathematics as well as to vocational subjects (Mason et al., 1992).

23 For further details of current and prospective educational reforms in the Netherlands, see van den Dool (1989).

7 KNOWLEDGE, INCREASING RETURNS AND THE PRODUCTION FUNCTION

1 This research was supported by ESRC grant R000234954. We are grateful to Christine Greenhalgh, Steve Nickell and Steve Redding for helpful comments on an earlier draft, but the usual disclaimer applies.
2 The R&D data are for the years 1958, 1968, 1972, 1978 and 1981.
3 Setting $\rho = 1$ assumes that there is no depreciation of knowledge capital (see later for discussion of this issue). Setting $\phi = 1$ assumes constant returns to R&D.
4 Data for 1961, 1964, and 1966–9 are from CSO *Studies in Official Statistics* No. 21, and the datum for 1972 is from CSO *Studies in Official Statistics* No. 27. Data for 1973–85 are from the OECD Structural Analysis Database (STAN) and data for 1986–91 are from CSO Press Release *Business Enterprise Research and Development: 1991*.
5 CSO *Studies in Official Statistics* Nos. 21 and 27, and CSO (1993).
6 The index of average earnings of administrative, clerical and technical employees in manufacturing is taken from *Historical Record of Census of Production 1907 to 1970*, various *Employment Gazettes* and various editions of the *Census of Production* from 1970 to 1990.
7 The producer output price implicit deflator for manufacturing is taken from *Economic Trends Annual Supplement*.
8 Implicit GDP deflator (expenditure measure at market prices).

8 ANGLO-GERMAN PRODUCTIVITY PERFORMANCE SINCE 1973

1 This chapter is concerned only with the productivity record of the Federal Republic of Germany as it existed before unification.
2 These differences do need to be treated with caution since the types of workers included in the upper level category may not be comparable in the two countries. Thus the UK data include persons who are members of professional institutions such as accountants and engineers whose qualifications come from certified institutes rather than from a university degree. The certified qualifications are comparable to those obtained from universities and so should be included in the upper qualification category. However it is not clear whether comparably qualified personnel are included in the German data. In Britain members of professional institutions accounted for about a third of those qualified at upper level at the end of the 1970s but this had fallen to about a quarter by 1989.
3 Note that we could achieve a similar coefficient value for total manufacturing if we assumed some depreciation rate and cumulated expenditure over a greater number of years. However it is not clear what depreciation rate should be used. For example Schott (1976) used a depreciation rate of under 10 per cent whereas Cameron and Muellbauer (chapter 7) argue that the stock of knowledge does not depreciate in the sense that physical capital does and hence they assume no depreciation. The latter is not satisfactory for growth accounting exercises since

the share of R&D as a percentage of total non-human capital would increase indefinitely. The use of any depreciation rate requires more historical data on R&D by industry than is available to us, hence our use of the sudden death assumption. However we acknowledge that this assumption is somewhat arbitrary.

9 PRODUCTIVITY AT THE PLANT AND INDUSTRY LEVELS IN AUSTRALIA

1 The views expressed in this chapter are those of the author alone, and are not those of the Bureau of Industry Economics.
2 BIE (1992d) surveys recent developments in theories of economic growth and assesses possible implications for industry policy.
3 However, Dowrick and Nguyen (1989) found that adjustment for cyclical fluctuations, for technological catch-up and for rates of population growth accounted for most of the gap between Australian and average OECD rates of growth.
4 Some empirical analysis suggests that the results from the Accord include a substantial reduction in industrial disputes (Beggs and Chapman, 1987), combined with lower real wages and higher employment and profit shares than those which would have occurred in its absence (Lewis and Kirby, 1987, 1988; Chapman, 1990; Watts and Mitchell, 1990; Flatau et al. 1991). Other studies have reached different conclusions. For example, Simes and Horn (1988) concluded that the Accord had very little effect on wages growth, whereas Pissarides (1991) found that the Accord had no effect on wages over and above the effects of changes in underlying economic conditions. According to Pissarides, the recovery in employment after 1983–4 was brought about by the same factors that caused it to fall before, working in reverse. In particular, investment collapsed, bringing wages down with it, and this was the biggest single contributor to the employment recovery.
5 A flat pay rise of $A16 per week was available to all workers. Further pay rises of up to 4 per cent depended on work restructuring and efficiency. In particular, measures could be implemented to improve work and management practices, change work patterns, reduce demarcation barriers, and advance multi-skilling, training and re-training, and broad-banding (National Labour Consultative Council, 1988).
6 Subsequent developments in the framework for enterprise bargaining are discussed in the section beginning on page 215.
7 The current account deficit in Australia became of particular concern to the Australian government in the mid- and late-1980s. In the latter period, the current account deficit increased from $A2.5 billion in the June quarter of 1988 to over $A6.6 billion in the September quarter of 1989. In response, monetary policy was tightened. The commercial 90-day bill rate rose from under 11 per cent at the start of 1988 to over 18 per cent in October 1989. The result was a decline in the rate of GDP growth and, from mid-1990, falls in the levels of imports, inflation, and

job vacancies, and a substantial increase in the rate of unemployment. With subsequent improvements in the current account and inflation, interest rates were allowed to fall to around their pre-1988 levels by April 1991. However, the recovery in demand and decline in unemployment have been very gradual.

8 This statement is not intended to suggest that the wage rates observed in the Australian plants were consistent with those of a 'competitive' labour market.

9 The effect is equivalent to the impact of inflation (p) on the real after-tax return derived from interest paid on deposits in financial institutions. The retained earnings discount rate in real terms is $r - p = (r + p)(1 - m) - p = r(1 - m) - pm$ which declines with the rate of inflation for positive, marginal rates of personal tax.

10 Promotion on the basis of seniority rather than a manager's perception of merit can support union bargaining power by curbing competition between employees for promotion (Macdonald, 1989). However, promotion on the basis of seniority could lessen the overall incentive to perform, as individuals' efforts would not be a factor in selection for promotion, and this approach could lead to the advancement of senior employees who were less qualified and able than their more junior colleagues (Medoff and Abraham, 1980, 1981; Abraham and Medoff, 1985; Mills, 1985). Such provisions can also perpetuate inequalities of opportunity associated with gender, ethnic origin and socio-economic background. Such factors were evident at the Sydney plant at the time of the BIE inspection team's visit during 1990.

11 National Rail Corporation was established to centralise the control of all interstate freight marketing and operations. It commenced operations on 1 February 1993, and expects to be fully operational by 1996.

12 The NRTC was established in January 1992 under commonwealth legislation as an independent body funded by commonwealth, state and territory governments to develop an acceptable framework of national rules, regulations and charges for the road transport industry.

13 However, Captain Richard Setchell, the head of the stevedoring firm, Conaust, comments (Korporaal, 1993): 'But attitudes in the people that are left [in the union] have got worse. They are endeavouring to turn the clock back.'

14 See Harris (1992), other papers in Caves and Barton (1990), and Caves (1992).

15 DEA models were run by the BIE on an Apple Macintosh computer, using Microsoft Excel 4.0 and the Solver Add-in option (an iterative solution method). Each DMU was run as a separate problem.

16 The Australian Capital Territory does not produce its own electricity.

17 Ross Bunyon, the Chief Executive of Pacific Power, the New South Wales utility, warned that the (AFR, 1994) 'slavish implementation of the theories and ideologies of economic rationalists would put at extreme risk the gains made by our industry in meeting customer needs, protecting the environment for future generations and operating in Asia'.

18 In April 1992, the advent of a new carrier 'Tele2' to compete with the Swedish publicly owned telecom (Televerket) across a full range of services was announced. The ombudsman regulates telecommunications in Sweden under

normal consumer protection law.

19 Commenting on Telecom's operating costs, its Chief Executive assesses that (Lewis, 1993): 'We're about 30 per cent off the mark but it used to be 70, 80, 90 per cent off the mark, so we're making great progress on that and I'm very pleased with the progress'.

20 These issues are addressed in more detail by Harris (1992).

21 In the period since Wooden's analysis, policy outcomes include falls in the current account deficit and inflation, but there was also a substantial increase in the rate of unemployment.

22 Management at the Sydney plant had been willing to make concessions in an attempt to gain industrial peace, and to prevent disruptions in one business unit on the site spreading to others. In this case, the rents over which the parties 'bargained' arose from the company's high market share in many products, lack of competition from water heater imports (due mainly to significant transport costs, and to a lesser extent to product performance regulations that operate to a degree as a non-tariff barrier to trade) and the deterrence to entry provided by large fixed costs.

23 Lockouts have been used only rarely in Australia, owing to doubts about the employer's liability to pay the workforce. Although the legislation will relieve the employer of this obligation, the lockout will not be protected action unless written notice has been given to the union 'and to each employee who will be affected by the action', even those employees who are away sick, on leave and so on (Ludeke, 1993).

10 NONPARAMETRIC APPROACHES TO THE ASSESSMENT OF THE RELATIVE EFFICIENCY OF BANK BRANCHES

1 This is part of a paper that was presented at the Workshop 'Eficiencia en Banca' held at Instituto Valenciano De Investigaciones Economicas (IVIE), Valencia, Spain, December 9–10, 1993. Acknowledgements are due to Philippe Vanden Eeckaut and Pierre Berquin for their help. This text presents results from research conducted at an early stage under support from CIM (Collège Inter-universitaire d'études doctorales dans les sciences du Management), and FRFC (Fonds de la Recherche Fondamentale Collective; convention no. 2.4505.91 with the first author) and pursued later on under the programme *Pôles d'Attraction Inter-universitaires* (PAI) initiated by the Belgian State, Prime Minister's office, Science Policy Programming. The scientific responsibility is assumed by its authors.

2 To our knowledge, FDH frontiers were first used in a significant empirical application by Deprins *et al.*, 1984.

3 The present chapter contains most of the empirical contents of Tulkens and Vanden Eeckaut, 1991.

4 An alternative technique is the one proposed by Berg *et al.*, 1993.

5 Regions 8 and 10 were not used, as the paucity of observations for those regions makes their frontier too unreliable.

6 When averages are not statistically significantly different from one, they are set to one.

11 PRODUCTIVITY GROWTH, PLANT TURNOVER AND RESTRUCTURING IN THE CANADIAN MANUFACTURING SECTOR

1 For other studies that examine the effect of turnover on productivity, see Hazledine (1985), Baily *et al* (1992), Griliches and Regev (1992).
2 These are derived from Statistics Canada (1992).
3 Baldwin and Gorecki (1991).
4 See Baldwin and Gorecki (1990, 1991) for a breakdown of new plants between continuing plants and greenfield entrants.
5 See Baldwin (1995) for a description of the data. For the purpose of this study, all plants in manufacturing were used except those which were classified as head offices. Market share is calculated using manufacturing output; employment is the sum of all salaried and production workers.
6 In Canada, there are 235 industries in the longitudinal files that are consistently defined over the period of study.
7 Since the averages were calculated across all plants, the lower average productivity of entrants will be the result partially of entrants being less productive than plants in the same industry and partially because entrants are more heavily concentrated in industries with lower productivity on average. An alternative method is used in figure 11.7, where entrants' productivity is calculated relative to continuers' productivity in each industry, and then means are taken across industries.
8 Baldwin and Caves (1991).
9 These are means of relative productivity statistics calculated at the industry level. The relative productivity statistics at the industry level are calculated as employment-weighted labour productivity averages.
10 Greenfield entrants are new plants that are created by firms that are new to an industry.
11 Average productivity of each group was calculated using employment weights.
12 For a more detailed discussion, see Baldwin and Caves (1991) and Baldwin and Rafiquzzaman (1994)

12 DOWNSIZING AND PRODUCTIVITY GROWTH: MYTH OR REALITY?

1 The views expressed herein are solely the authors' and do not necessarily reflect those of the Board of Governors of the Federal Reserve System or its staff. We wish to thank the staff and visiting researchers at the Center for Economic Studies, US Bureau of the Census, for providing a stimulating research environment. We would also like to thank participants of the NBER Summer 1993 workshop for valuable comments and suggestions.

2 Manufacturing employment as we describe it here is based upon the Censuses and Surveys of Manufacturing Establishments. Household surveys show that manufacturing employment has been pretty much flat over the last twenty years, barring cyclical downturns. The difference in the conclusions arises because R&D and head office employees based on so-called 'auxiliary establishments' are not included in the establishment data.

3 Hart (1975) presents a variety of alternative summary statistics that could be used to characterise the skewed nature of the size distribution. In the terminology of Hart, the coworker mean is the ratio of the second moment to the first moment about zero of the employment size distribution of plants.

4 Davis *et al.* (1994) describe the methodology for using the coverage code information in the plant level data to clean up residual matching problems in the LRD. In this work we match solely on the basis of Census permanent plant number (ppn).

5 In an earlier version of this chapter, we used 1977 as a base year. This yields a higher growth rate of output and productivity since doing so overstates the contribution to real output of industries with declining relative prices, especially for computers.

6 We report some of the key results using both methods to verify this claim.

7 The figures reported in the table are the average   growth over ten years (cumulative growth divided by ten) rather than the annualised growth rate. We use this average growth measure in all of our tables so that our decompositions add up properly. The implied annual growth rate for productivity is 2.85 percent.

8 Interestingly, the contribution of net entry falls to 20 per cent if industry 357 (computing equipment) is excluded from the calculation.

9 Note that for the entire sample, including those with negative value added, employment declined by 0.42 per year.

10 Shown in table 12A.1 in the Appendix are the summary statistics for the manufacturing sector excluding industry 357, computer equipment. This industry has shown extraordinary productivity growth captured by the rapidly falling deflator for computer equipment. With this industry removed from the total, productivity increase drops to 2.99 per cent a year for the whole sector and to 2.89 per cent for the continuers. Comparing these results with those for total manufacturing shows that 357 by itself has obviously accounted for a non-trivial share of the sector's productivity increase. Note that the relative contribution of industry 357 is affected by the choice of the base year. The relative contribution increases if 1977 is chosen as the base year and decreases if 1987 is chosen as the base year.

11 To ensure that these terms add up properly, the percentage change between 1977 and 1987 is divided by ten to get the average growth. Unless otherwise stated, growth rates are not calculated at an average annual rate.

12 Note that the inclusion of the average productivity term, Π_{t-1} is possible because $\sum_i \Delta\varphi_{t,i} = 0$.

13 In the Appendix table 12A.2 we show the same calculation, but with the computer equipment industry removed from the sample. The main impact is on

the quadrant 1 plants. This group now contributes 1.88 percent rather than 2.18 percent to overall productivity growth.

14 Given the striking similarity in results in tables 12.2 and 12.3, results in subsequent sections are reported only for the value added measure. As with tables 12.2 and 12.3, the subsequent results are very similar using either measure.

15 Excluding computers (SIC 357), the remainder of industry 35 also falls squarely into this group.

16 The equivalent table excluding industry 357 shows that this surprising result on New England is not driven by the computer equipment industry. That is, even excluding computer equipment, New England is still disproportionately in quadrant 1.

17 The use of average size to allocate plants into size classes is motivated by the findings in Davis et al. (1994). They show that regression to the mean fallacy problems arise in using a point in time measure of size to allocate plants into size classes given the large transitory changes in employment that are present in the plant level data.

18 Davis et al. (1993) document the reasons why the claim that small businesses are the dominant sources of job growth is inaccurate.

19 There may be a host of factors underlying these results which deserve further investigation. For example, small plants may be making unique products whose prices are not well captured by the 4-digit deflator. See also the discussion of wages below.

20 Baily et al. (1992) also explore the relation between wages and productivity (TFP). Their findings are consistent with these results. The McKinsey (1993) study of manufacturing productivity shows case study evidence of process and product design innovations in manufacturing (often but not always initiated in Japan) that reduced the need for unskilled workers per unit of output produced. Recent work by Hellerstein and Neumark (1993) and Hellerstein et al. (1994) finds a close association between plant differences in productivity, wages, and the skill mix of the workers at individual plants.

21 We do not consider the role of plant real wage growth in this context given the obvious endogenity problems. We are treating the other observables as capturing exogenous characteristics or at least initial/predetermined conditions. Concerns about endogeneity are nevertheless relevant for the size class measure given that it represents the average size in 1977 and 1987. As discussed in note 16, the use of the average size rather than initial size is motivated by the results of Davis et al. (1994). For this purpose, a preferable method might be the average size in 1972 and 1977 since this would mitigate the transitory component problem. However, a large fraction of plants present in 1977 are not present in 1972 and thus this would reduce our sample in a systematic way – that is, small plants are more likely to fail than large plants.

14 PRODUCTIVITY OF NORWEGIAN ESTABLISHMENTS: A MALMQUIST INDEX APPROACH

1 The material in the chapter draws on a dissertation for the cand oecon degree at Department of Economics, University of Oslo, 'Produktivitetsutvikling i tolv norske industrisektorer analysert ved DEA-metoden' by Marie W. Arneberg, for which the author was the thesis adviser.

2 In this chapter we will use the input-based measure. The definition of the output-based measure, based on scaling the output vector, follows straightforwardly from applying the output-increasing Farrell efficiency measure, see Førsund (1990).

3 Chaining means that $M_i(1,3) = M_i(1,2)M_i(2,3)$. Inserting from (1) on the right hand side yields $(E_i2 /E_i1)(E_i3 /E_i2) = E_i3/E_i1 = M_i(1,3)$.

4 Some preliminary experiments with stochastic frontiers did not yield frontiers significantly different from average functions.

5 If output-increasing efficiency is adapted the frontier technology can be relaxed to constant and decreasing returns by introducing the restriction that the sum of weights shall be less or equal to one, as done in Färe et al. (1989).

15 X-INEFFICIENCY IN MEASURED TECHNICAL INEFFICIENCY

1 The author is greatly indebted to Professor David G. Mayes, NIESR, and other participants of the conference on Sources of Productivity Growth.

2 It also does in the author's case (Torii, 1992a, b).

3 Frantz (1988) cites Førsund et al. (1980) in support of the X-inefficiency theory.

4 When the assumed allocative inefficiency is not symmetric and the mean of Δz is far from zero relative to the standard error of Δz, $g(\sqrt{s}/\sqrt{s})$ does not diverge to infinity. In those cases most of the deviations caused by the allocative inefficiency are observed as a shift of the frontier and the symmetric error term.

5 See results of Monte-Carlo experiences shown in the same study.

6 See the results in Caves et al. (1992).

References

Abraham K.G. and Medoff, J.L. (1985), 'Length of service and promotions in union and non-union work groups', *Industrial and Labor Relations Review*, 38, p. 87.

Aghion, P. and Howitt, P. (1992), 'A model of growth through creative destruction', *Econometrica*, pp. 323–51.

Aigner D.J., Lovell C.A.K. and Schmidt, P. (1977), 'Formulation and estimation of stochastic frontier production function models', *Journal of Econometrics*, 6, pp. 21–37.

Aly, H. and Grabowski, R. (1989), 'Measuring the rate and bias of technical innovation in Japanese agriculture: An alternative approach', *European Review of Agricultural Economics*, 16, pp. 65–81.

Asterhaki, D.J. (1984), 'A dynamic translog model of substitution technologies in UK manufacturing industry', Bank of England Discussion Paper, Technological Series, No. 7.

Atkinson, A.B. and Stiglitz, J.E. (1969), 'A new view of technological change', *Economic Journal*, 79, pp. 573–8.

Australian Bureau of Statistics (ABS) (1990), *Australian National Accounts Input–Output Tables 1986–87*, Cat. No. 5209.0, Canberra.

Australian Bureau of Statistics (ABS) (1993a), *Australian National Accounts Capital Stock 1991–92*, Cat. No. 5221.0, Canberra, April.

Australian Bureau of Statistics (ABS) (1993b), *The Labour Force August 1993*, Cat. No. 6203.0, Canberra, September.

Australian Bureau of Statistics (ABS) (various issues), *Australian National Accounts National Income, Expenditure and Product*, Cat. No. 5206.0, Canberra.

Australian Financial Review (AFR) (1993), 'The foreign investment challenge', *Australian Financial Review*, 2 December, Editorial.

Australian Financial Review (AFR) (1994), 'Power monopolies must go', *Australian Financial Review*, 6 January, Editorial.

Australian Gas Association (AGA) (1993), *Gas Industry Statistics 91-92*, Australian Gas Association, Canberra.

Baily, M.N. and Gordon, R. (1989), 'Measurement issues, the productivity slowdown, and the explosion of computer power', CEPR Discussion Paper, No. 305.

Baily, M.N., Hulten, C. and Campbell, D. (1992), 'Productivity dynamics in manufacturing plants', Brookings Papers in Economic Activity: Microeconomics.

Bailey, S. D. (1992), 'The intraindustry dispersion of plant productivity in the British manufacturing sector, 1963–79', in Caves (1992).

Baldwin, J.R. (1992), 'Industrial efficiency and plant turnover in the Canadian manufacturing sector', in Caves, R.E. (ed.), Industrial Efficiency in Six Nations, Cambridge, MA, MIT Press, pp. 273–310.

Baldwin, J.R. (1995), The Dynamics of Industrial Competition: A North American Perspective, Cambridge, Cambridge University Press.

Baldwin, J.R. and Caves, R.E. (1991), 'Foreign multinational enterprises and merger activity in Canada' in Waverman, L. (ed.), Corporate Globalization through Mergers and Acquisitions, Calgary, University of Calgary Press, pp. 89–122.

Baldwin, J.R. and Gorecki, P.K. (1990), Structural Change and the Adjustment Process: Perspectives on Firm Growth and Worker Turnover, Ottawa, Economic Council of Canada.

Baldwin, J.R. and Gorecki, P.K. (1991), 'Firm entry and exit in the Canadian manufacturing sector 1970–82', Canadian Journal of Economics, 24, pp. 300–23.

Baldwin, J.R. and Gorecki, P.K. (1991), 'Productivity growth and the competitive process: the role of firm and plant turnover', in Geroski, P.A. and Schwalbach, J., Entry and Market Contestability: An International Comparison, Oxford, Basil Blackwell, pp. 244–56.

Baldwin, J.R. and Rafiquzzaman, M. (1994), Structural Change in the Canadian Manufacturing Sector: 1970–1990, Research Paper no. 61, Analytical Studies Branch, Statistics Canada.

Banker R.D., Charnes A. and Cooper, W.W. (1984), 'Some models for estimating technical and scale inefficiencies in data envelopment analysis', Management Science, 30, p. 1078.

Banker R.D. and Morey, R.C. (1986), 'The use of categorical variables in data envelopment analysis', Management Science, 32, p. 1613.

Barro, R.J and Sala-i-Martin, X. (1991), 'Convergence across regions and states', Brookings Papers on Economic Activity, No. 1, pp. 107–82.

Bartelsman, E.J. and Dhrymes, P.J. (1992), 'Productivity dynamics: U.S. manufacturing plants, 1972–1986', FEDS Working Paper No. 94–1, Federal Reserve Board, January.

Bates G. (1993), 'Good electricity reform achieved', Australian Financial Review, 31 March, Letter to the editor.

Baumol, W.J. (1986), 'Productivity growth, convergence and welfare: what the long run data show', American Economic Review, 76, December.

Baumol W.J., Batey Blackman, S.A. and Wolff, E.N. (1989), Productivity and American Leadership: The Long View, Cambridge, MA, MIT Press.

Beggs J.J. and Chapman, B.J. (1987), 'Declining strike activity in Australia 1983–85: an international phenomenon?', Economic Record, 63, p. 330.

Bell C. (1993), 'Assessing the performance of the Australian gas and electricity supply industries: an application of data envelopment analysis', paper presented at the twenty-second Conference of Economists, Curtin University, Perth.

Berg, S.A., Førsund, F.R. and Jansen, E.S. (1992), 'Malmquist indices of productivity growth during the deregulation of Norwegian banking, 1980–89', *Scandinavian Journal of Economics*, 94, Supplement, pp. 211–28.

Berg, S.A., Førsund, F.R., Hjalmarsson, L. and Suominen, M. (1993), 'Banking efficiency in the Nordic countries', *Journal of Banking and Finance*, 17, pp. 371–88.

Berndt, E.R. and Fuss, M.A. (1986), 'Productivity measurement with adjustments for variations in capacity utilisation and other forms of temporary equilibrium', *Journal of Econometrics*, 33, pp. 7–27.

Berndt, E.R., Fuss, M.A. and Waverman, L. (1977), 'Dynamic models of the industrial demand for energy', Research report EA–580, Palo Alto CA, Electric Power Research Institute.

Berndt, E.R., Fuss, M.A. and Waverman, L. (1980), 'Dynamic adjustment models of industrial energy demand: empirical analysis for US manufacturing, 1947–1974', Research report EA–1613, Palo Alto CA, Electric Power Research Institute.

Bilderbeek R. (1990), 'The diffusion of programmable automated systems and its work and training implications in the Netherlands', in Warner, W., Wobbe, W. and Brodner. P. (eds), *New Technology and Manufacturing Management*, Wiley.

Blanchard, O. and Fischer, S. (1989), *Lectures on Macroeconomics*, London.

Blandy, R. (1989), 'The industrial relations revolution', *Labour Economics and Productivity*, 1, p. 139.

Bollard, A.E., Harper, D. and Mayes, D.G. (1993), 'Product market flexibility: concepts and indicators', Report to Her Majesty's Treasury.

Bolt, C. (1994), 'Enterprise agreements: maybe not such a bargain', *Australian Financial Review*, 12 January.

Bosworth, D. (1976) 'The rate of obsolescence of technical knowledge – a note', *Journal of Industrial Economics*, 26, 3, pp. 273–9.

Bowden, S., Coutts, A. and Turner, P.M. (1992), 'Compulsory and voluntary liquidations in the UK economy by industrial sector, 1971–1990', University of Leeds School of Business and Economic Studies, Discussion Paper No. 5.

Bowles, S. (1985), 'The production process in a competitive economy: Walrasian, Neo-Hobbesian and Marxian models', *American Economic Review*, 75, 1, pp. 16–36.

Britton, A. (ed.) (1992), 'Industrial investment as a policy objective', NIESR Report Series No. 3.

Broadberry, S. (1993), 'Manufacturing and the convergence hypothesis: what the long run data show', *Journal of Economic History*.

Budd, A. and Hobbis, S. (1989), 'Cointegration, technology and the long-run production function', Centre for Economic Forecasting, Discussion Paper No. 10–89.

Bureau of Industry Economics (1988), 'Technical efficiency in Australian manufacturing industries', Occasional Paper 4, Canberra, Bureau of Industry Economics.

Bureau of Industry Economics (1990), 'International productivity differences in manufacturing – photographic paper, Research Report 34, Canberra, AGPS.

Bureau of Industry Economics (1991), 'International comparisons of plant productivity – domestic water heaters', Research Report 38, Canberra, AGPS.

Bureau of Industry Economics (1992a), 'International performance indicators: electricity', Research Report 40, Canberra, AGPS.

Bureau of Industry Economics (1992b), 'International performance indicators: rail freight', Research Report 41, Canberra, AGPS.

Bureau of Industry Economics (1992c), 'International performance indicators: road freight', Research Report 46, Canberra, AGPS.

Bureau of Industry Economics (1992d), 'Recent developments in the theory of economic growth: policy implications', Occasional Paper 11, Canberra, AGPS.

Bureau of Industry Economics (1993a), 'International performance indicators: rail freight update', Research Report 52, Canberra, AGPS.

Bureau of Industry Economics (1993b), 'International performance indicators: telecommunications', Research Report 48, Canberra, AGPS.

Bureau of Industry Economics (1993c), 'International performance indicators: waterfront', Research Report 47, Canberra, AGPS.

Bureau of Industry Economics (1993d), 'Multinationals and governments: issues and implications for Australia', Research Report 49, Canberra, AGPS.

Bureau of Industry Economics (1994), 'International performance indicators: overview', Research Report 53, Canberra, AGPS.

Cabinet Office (1993), *Annual Review of Government Funded R&D 1993*, London, HMSO.

Caves, D.W., Christensen, L.R. and Diewert, D.E. (1982), 'The economic theory of index numbers and the measurement of input, output and productivity', *Econometrica*, 50, 6, pp. 1393–1414.

Caves R.E. (1992), *Industrial Efficiency in Six Nations*, Cambridge, MA, MIT Press.

Caves R.E. and Barton, D.R. (1990), *Efficiency in U.S. Manufacturing Industries*, Cambridge, MA, MIT Press.

Chand S., Forsyth P. and Vousden, N. (1993), 'Efficiency and adjustment in Australian manufacturing', paper presented at the second Conference of Industry Economics, Sydney University.

Chapman, B. (1990), 'The labour market', in Grenville, S. (ed.), *The Australian Macro-economy in the 1980s*, Sydney, Reserve Bank of Australia.

Charnes, A., Clark, C.T., Cooper, W.W. and Golany, B. (1985), 'A developmental study of data envelopment analysis in measuring the efficiency of maintenance units in the U.S. air forces', in Thompson (ed.), *Normative Analysis for Policy Decisions, Annals of Operations Research*, 2, Basel, J.C. Balzer Science Publishers.

Charnes, A., Cooper, W.W. and Rhodes, E. (1978), 'Measuring the efficiency of decision making units', *European Journal of Operations Research*, 2, 6, November, pp. 429–44.

Chouliarakis, G. (1992), 'Unemployment, conflict and income distribution', unpublished thesis proposal, University of Warwick.

Clark, D. (1992), 'Importance of better productivity', *Australian Financial Review*, 3 June.

Clark, D. (1993), 'Fortress trade walls tumbling down', *Australian Financial Review*, 24 March.

Coe, D. and Helpman, E. (1993), 'International R&D spillovers', CEPR Discussion Paper, No. 840.

Cohen, A. and Ivins, L. (1967), 'The sophistication factor in science expenditure', Department of Education and Science, Science Policy Studies, no. 1.

Corrigan, M. (1993), 'Industrial policy change under fire', *Australian Financial Review*, 10 November.

Court, A.T. (1939), 'Hedonic price indexes with automotive examples' in *The Dynamics of Automobiles Demand*, Detroit, General Motors, pp. 99–117.

Cowling, K. and Cubbin, J. (1972), 'Hedonic price indexes for UK cars', *Economic Journal*, 82, September, pp. 963–78.

Crafts, N. (1988), 'British economic growth before and after 1979: a review of the evidence', Centre for Economic Policy Research, Discussion Paper No. 292.

Crafts, N. (1991), 'Reversing relative economic decline? The 1980s in historical perspective', *Oxford Review of Economic Policy*, 7, 3, pp. 81–98.

Craine, R. (1975), 'Investment, adjustment costs and uncertainty', *International Economic Review*, 16, pp. 648–61.

Cripps, T. F. and Tarling, R. J. (1973), *Growth in Advanced Capitalist Economies, 1950–70*, Cambridge, Cambridge University Press.

CSO (1993), *Business Expenditure on R&D 1993*, London, CSO.

Daly A., Hitchens D. and Wagner K. (1985), 'Productivity, machinery and skills in a sample of British and German manufacturing plants', *National Institute Economic Review*, February.

Darby, J. and Wren-Lewis, S. (1988), 'Trends in manufacturing productivity', National Institute Discussion Paper No. 145.

Darby, J. and Wren-Lewis, S. (1989), 'UK manufacturing productivity in an international perspective', NIESR Discussion Paper No. 152.

Dasgupta, P. and Maskin, E. (1987), 'The simple economics of research portfolios', *Economic Journal*, 97, pp. 581–95.

David, P.A. (1975), *Technical Choice, Innovation and Economic Growth*, Cambridge, Cambridge University Press.

Davies, S. and Caves, R. (1987), *Britain's Productivity Gap*, Cambridge, Cambridge University Press.

Davis M. (1991), 'Plan for private IR system', *Australian Financial Review*, 18 October.

Davis, S.J. and Haltiwanger, J. (1990), 'The distribution of employees by establishment size: patterns of change in the U.S., 1962–1985', draft.

Davis, S.J. and Haltiwanger, J. (1992), 'Gross job creation and destruction, and employment reallocation', *Quarterly Journal of Economics*, 107, 3, pp. 819–63.

Davis, S.J., Haltiwanger, J. and Schuh, S. (1993), 'Small business and job creation: dissecting the myth and reassessing the facts', NBER Working Paper No. 4492.

Davis, S.J., Haltiwanger, J. and Schuh, S. (1994), *Job Creation and Destruction in U.S. Manufacturing.*

DeLong, J. and Summers, L. (1991), 'Equipment investment and economic growth', *Quarterly Journal of Economics*, 106, pp. 445–502.

Denison, E. (1989), *Estimates of Productivity Change by Industry: An Evaluation and an Alternative*, Washington D.C., The Brookings Institution.

Deprins, D., Simar, L. and Tulkens, H. (1984), 'Measuring labour efficiency in post offices', in Marchand, M., Pestieau, P. and Tulkens, H. (eds), *The Performance of Public Entreprises: Concepts and Measurement*, Amsterdam, North-Holland.

De Vries, A.S.W. (1980), 'The Verdoorn law revisited', *European Economic Review*, 14, pp. 271–7.

Doornik, J. and Hendry, D. (1992), *PC GIVE Version 7*, Oxford, Institute of Economics and Statistics.

Dowrick S. (1990), 'Australian labour productivity growth: trends and causes', Bureau of Industry Economics Contributed Paper 5, Canberra, AGPS.

Dowrick S. and Nguyen, D.-T. (1989), 'OECD comparative economic growth 1950–85: catch-up and convergence', *American Economic Review*, 79, p. 1010.

Dowrick S. and Quiggin, J. (1993), 'Australia, Japan and the OECD: GDP rankings and revealed preference', *Australian Economic Review*, 1st Quarter, 21.

Dunne, T., Roberts, M.J. and Samuelson, L. (1989), 'The growth and failure of U.S. manufacturing plants', *Quarterly Journal of Economics*, 104, 4, pp. 671–98.

Dwyer M. (1993), 'High jobless our choice: Evans', *Australian Financial Review*, 29 October.

Earl G. (1993), 'Indonesia slow on tariff reform: Cook', *Australian Financial Review*, 29 October.

Economic Planning and Advisory Council (EPAC) (1993), *Medium-term review: opportunities for growth*, Canberra, AGPS.

Edgerton, D. (1993), 'British research and development after 1945: A re-interpretation', *Science and Technology Policy*, April.

Electricity Supply Association of Australia (ESAA) (1993), *Electricity Australia 1993*, Victoria, Electricity Supply Association of Australia Ltd.

Englander, J. and Mittlestädt, A. (1988), 'Total factor productivity: macroeconomic and structural aspects of the slowdown', *OECD Economic Studies*, 10, pp. 7–56.

Engle, R. (1982), 'Autoregressive conditional heteroscedasticity, with estimates of the variance of United Kingdom inflations', *Econometrica*, 50, pp. 987–1008.

Färe, R., Grabowski, R. and Grosskopf, S. (1985), 'Technical efficiency of Phillippine agriculture', *Applied Economics*, 17, 2, April, pp. 205–14.

Färe, R., Grosskopf, S. and Li, S. (1992), 'Linear programming models for firms and industry performance', *Scandinavian Journal of Economics*, 94, 4, pp. 599–608.

Färe, R., Grosskopf, S., Lindgren, B. and Roos, P. (1989), 'Productivity developments in Swedish hospitals', Discussion paper 89–3, Department of Economics, Southern Illinois University, Carbondale.

Färe, R., Grosskopf, S., Lindgren, B. and Roos, P. (1992), 'Productivity changes in Swedish pharmacies 1980–1989: A non-parametric Malmquist approach', *Journal of Productivity Analysis*, 3, 1/2, pp. 85–101.

Färe R., Grosskopf S. and Lovell, C.A.K. (1985), *The measurement of efficiency of production*, Boston, MA, Kluwer-Nijhoff.

Färe, R., Grosskopf, S., Yaisawarng, S., Li, S. and Wang, Z. (1990), 'Productivity growth in Illinois electric utilities', *Resources and Energy*, 12, pp. 383–98.

Farrell, M.J. (1957), 'The measurement of productive efficiency', *Journal of the Royal Statistical Society*, series A – General, 120, part 3, pp. 253–81.

Farrell M.J. and Fieldhouse, M. (1962), 'Estimating efficient production functions under increasing returns to scale', *Journal of the Royal Statistical Society*, Series (General), 125, p. 252.

Fase, M.M.G. and van den Heuvel, P.J. (1988), 'Productivity and growth: Verdoorn's law revisited', *Economics Letters*, 28, pp. 135–9.

Fischer, S. (1988), Symposium on the slowdown in productivity growth, *Journal of Economic Perspectives*, 2, 4.

Flatau P., Lewis, P.E.T. and Rushton, A. (1991), 'The macroeconomic consequences of long-term unemployment', *Australian Economic Review*, Fourth Quarter, 48.

Førsund, F.R, (1990), 'The Malmquist productivity index', Memorandum from Department of Economics, University of Oslo.

Førsund, F.R. (1993), 'Malmquist indices of productivity growth: an application to Norwegian ferries', in Fried, H.O., Lovell, C.A.K. and Schmidt, S.S. (eds), *The Measurement of Productive Efficiency: Techniques and Applications*, Oxford, Oxford University Press, pp. 352–73.

Førsund, F.R. and Hjalmarsson, L. (1974), 'On the measurement of productive efficiency', *Swedish Journal of Economics*, 76, p. 141.

Førsund, F.R. and Hjalmarsson, L. (1979), 'Generalised Farrell measures of efficiency: an application to milk processing in Swedish dairy plants', *Economic Journal*, 89.

Førsund, F.R. and Hjalmarsson, L. (1987), *Analysis of Industrial Structure: A Putty Clay Approach*, Stockholm, Almqvist & Wicksell International.

Førsund F.R., Lovell C.A.K. and Schmidt, P. (1980), 'A survey of frontier production functions and of their relationship to efficiency measurement', *Journal of Econometrics*, 13, p. 5.

Frantz, R. (1988), *X-inefficiency: Theory, Evidence, and Applications*, Norwell, Kluwer Academic Press.

Freeman R.B. (1986), 'Effects of unions on the economy', in Lipset, S.M. (ed.) *Unions in Transition – Entering the Second Century*, San Francisco, Institute for Contemporary Studies.

Fritsch, R. (1936), 'Annual survey of general economic theory: the problem of index numbers', *Econometrica*, 5, pp. 1–38.

Giokas, D. (1991), 'Bank branch operating efficiency: a comparative application of data envelopment analysis and the loglinear model', *OMEGA, the International Journal of Management Science*, 19, pp. 549–57.

Gomulka, S. (1971), *Inventive Activity, Diffusion and the Stages of Economic Growth*, Aarhus.

Gordon, R.J. (1990), *The Measurement of Durable Goods Prices*, Chicago, NBER, University of Chicago Press.

Grabowski, R., Kraft, S., Mehdian, S. and Pasurka, C. (1988), 'Technological change in Illinois agriculture, 1982–84', *Agricultural Economics*, 2, pp. 303–18.

Grant, R.M. (1985), 'Capacity adjustment and restructuring in the UK cutlery industry 1974–84', NEDO Working Paper No. 21.

Green, F. (1988), 'Neoclassical and Marxian conceptions of production', *Cambridge Journal of Economics*, 12, pp. 299–312.

Green, F. and Weisskopf, T. (1990), 'The worker discipline effect: a disaggregative analysis', *Review of Economics and Statistics*, 72, pp. 241–9.

Griliches, Z. (1980), 'Returns to R&D expenditures in the private sector', in Kendrick, K.W. and Vaccara, B. (eds.) *New Developments in Productivity Measurement*, Chicago, University of Chicago Press.

Griliches, Z. (ed.) (1984), *R&D, Patents and Productivity*, Chicago, University of Chicago Press.

Griliches, Z. (1988), 'Productivity puzzles and R&D: another non-explanation', *Journal of Economic Perspectives*, San Francisco, 2, pp. 9–21.

Griliches, Z. (1990), 'Hedonic price indexes and the measurement of capital and productivity: some historical reflections', in Berndt, E. R. and Triplett, J. E. (eds), *Fifty Years of Economic Measurements*, Chicago, NBER University of Chicago Press.

Griliches, Z. (1991), 'The search for R & D spillovers', NBER Discussion Paper No. 3768, July.

Griliches, Z. and Lichtenberg, F. (1984), 'R&D and productivity growth at the industry level: is there still a relationship?', in Griliches (ed.).

Griliches, Z. and Regev, H. (1992), 'Productivity and firm turnover in Israeli industry: 1979–1988', NBER Working Paper No. 4059.

Griliches, Z. and Ringstad, V. (1971), *Economies of Scale and the Form of the Production Function; an Econometric Study of Norwegian Manufacturing Establishment Data*, Amsterdam, North-Holland.

Grosskopf, S. (1986), 'The role of the reference technology in measuring productive efficiency', *Economic Journal*, 96, pp. 299–513.

Grossman, G. and Helpman, E. (1991), *Innovation and Growth in the Global Economy*, Cambridge, MA, MIT Press.

Hamblin D. (1989), *The Effectiveness of AMT Investment in UK Fluid Handling Equipment Manufacture*, Cranfield Institute of Technology.

Harris C.M. (1992), 'Technical efficiency in Australia: Phase I', in Caves, R.E. (ed.), *Industrial Efficiency in Six Nations*, Cambridge, MA, MIT Press.

Harris. R.I.D. (1985), 'Interrelated demand for factors of production in the U.K. engineering industry, 1968–81', *Economic Journal*, 95, pp. 1049–68.

Harvey, A. (1981), *The Econometric Analysis of Time-Series Data*, Oxford, Philip Allan.

Harvey, A. (1989), *Forecasting, Structural Time Series Models and the Kalman Filter*, Cambridge, Cambridge University Press.

Haskel, J. and Martin, C. (1993), 'Do skill shortages reduce productivity? Theory and evidence from the UK', *Economic Journal*, 103, 417, pp. 386–94.

Haynes W. (1993), 'Will electricity reforms deliver lower prices?', paper presented at a Committee of Economic Development of Australia Conference, 26 October.

Hazledine, T. (1985), 'The anatomy of productivity growth slowdown and recovery in Canadian manufacturing', *International Journal of Industrial Organization*, 3, pp. 307–26.

Hellerstein, J. and Neumark, D. (1993), 'Sex, wages, and productivity: an empirical analysis of Israeli firm-level data', draft.

Hellerstein, J., Neumark, D. and Troske, K. (1994), 'Wages, productivity, and worker characteristics', draft.

Hilmer, F.G. (1993), see Independent Committee of Inquiry into Competition Policy in Australia.

Hogan, W.W. (1984), 'Patterns of energy use', Discussion Paper Series, E84–04, Cambridge, MA, Energy and Environment Policy Center, Harvard University.

Hogan, W.W. (1989), 'A dynamic putty-semi-putty model of aggregate energy demand', *Energy Economics*, January, pp. 53–69.

Hulten, C.R. (1986), 'Productivity change, capacity utilisation, and the sources of efficiency growth', *Journal of Econometrics*, 33, pp. 31–50,

Hulten, C.R. (1992), 'Growth accounting when technical change is embodied in capital', NBER Working Paper No. 3971.

Independent Committee of Inquiry into Competition Policy in Australia (1993), (Chairman: F.G. Hilmer), *National Competition Policy: Report by the Independent Committee of Inquiry into Competition Policy in Australia*, Canberra, AGPS.

Industry Commission (IC) (1990), *Annual Report 1989–90*, Canberra, AGPS.

Industry Commission (IC) (1991), *Annual Report 1990–91*, Canberra, AGPS.

Industry Commission (IC) (1993a), *Annual Report 1992–93*, Canberra, AGPS.

Industry Commission (IC) (1993b), *Port Authority Services and Activities*, Report 31, Canberra, AGPS.

Industrial Relations Commission (IRC) (1989), *February 1989 Review, Reasons for Decision*.

Ingram, P. (1991), 'Changes in working practices in British manufacturing industry in the 1980s: a study of employee concessions made during wage negotiations', *British Journal of Industrial Relations*, 29, 1, pp. 1–13.

International Telecommunications Union (ITU) (1992), *Yearbook of Common Carrier Telecommunication Statistics*, 19th edition, International Telecommunications Union, Geneva.

IPRA (1993), *Manufacturing Supervision*, report to the NEDC Engineering Skills Working Party by Innovation Policy Research Associates Ltd, London.

Jankowski, J. (1993), 'Do we need a price index for industrial R&D?', *Research Policy*, 22, pp. 195–205.

Jarque, C. and Bera, A. (1980), 'Efficient tests for normality, homoscedasticity and serial independence of regression residuals', *Economics Letters*, 6, pp. 255–9.

Jay C. (1993), 'Dispute resolution allows vital funds to be released', *Australian Financial Review*, 1 November.

Johansen, L. (1972), *Production Functions*, Amsterdam, North-Holland.

Johnson, K.H. (1994), 'Productivity and unemployment: review of evidence', draft.

Jorgenson, D. (1990), 'Productivity and economic growth', *Harvard Institute of Economic Research*, Discussion Paper No. 1487.

Jorgenson, D.W., Gollop, F.M. and Fraumeini, B.M. (1987), *Productivity and U.S. Economic Growth*, Cambridge, MA, Harvard University Press.

Kaldor, N. (1966), *Causes of the Slow Rate of Growth of the United Kingdom*, Cambridge, Cambridge University Press.

Kaldor, N. (1975), 'Economic growth and Verdoorn Law – a comment on Mr Rowthorn's article', *Economic Journal*, December, pp. 891–6.

Kokkelnberg, E.C. (1983), 'Interrelated factor demands revisited', *Review of Economics and Statistics*, 65, 2.

Korporaal, G. (1993), 'Industrial warfare: back to the good old days', *Australian Financial Review*, 13 December.

Layard, R., Nickell, S. and Jackman, R. (1991), *Unemployment*, Oxford, Oxford University Press.

Ledic, M. and Silbertson, A. (1986), 'The technological balance of payments in perspective', in Hall, P. (ed.), *Technology, Innovation and Economic Policy*, Oxford, Philip Allan.

Leibenstein, H. (1966), 'Allocative efficiency vs. X-efficiency', *American Economic Review*, 56, pp. 392–415.

Leibenstein, H. (1976), *Beyond Economic Man: A New Foundation for Microeconomics*, Cambridge, MA, Harvard University Press.

Leslie, D. and Wise, J. (1980), 'The productivity of hours in UK manufacturing and production industries', *Economic Journal*, 90, March, pp. 74–84

Lewis, S. (1993), 'The Blount approach', *Australian Financial Review*, 23 December.

Lewis, P.E.T. and Kirby, M.G. (1987), 'The impact of incomes policy on aggregate wage determination in Australia', *Economic Record*, 63, p. 156.

Lewis, P.E.T. and Kirby. M.G. (1988), 'A new approach to modelling the effect of incomes policies', *Economic Letters*, 28, p. 81.

Lovell, C.A.K. (1993), 'Production frontiers and productive efficiency: an introduction and readers' guide', in Fried, H., Lovell, K. and Schmidt, S. (eds), *The Measurement of Productive Efficiency: Techniques and Applications*, Oxford, Oxford University Press.

Lucas, R.E. (1988), 'The mechanics of economic development', *Journal of Monetary Economics*, 22, p. 3–42.

Ludeke, J.T. (1993), 'Industrial reform in action', *Australian Financial Review*, 31 December.

Lynde, C. and Richmond, J. (1993) 'Public capital and long-run costs in UK manufacturing', *Economic Journal*, 103, 419, pp. 880–93.

McCombie, J.S.L. (1982), 'Economic growth, Kaldor's laws and the static-dynamic Verdoorn law paradox', *Applied Economics*, 14, pp. 279–94.

McCombie, J.S.L. (1987), 'Verdoorn's law', in Eatwell, J., Milgate, M. and Newman, P. (eds), *The New Palgrave*, London, Macmillan, pp. 804–6.

Macdonald D. (1989), 'The use of seniority in labour selection and job allocation', *Journal of Industrial Relations*, 31, 46.

MacKinnon, J. (1991), 'Critical values for cointegration tests' in Engle, R. and Granger, C. (eds), *Long-Run Economic Relationships*, Oxford, Oxford University Press.

McKinsey (1993), *Manufacturing Productivity*, report prepared by the McKinsey Global Institute with the assistance of Baily, M., Bator, F., Hall, T. and Solow, R., Washington DC.

Maddison, A. (1991), *Dynamic Forces in Capitalist Development: A Long Run Comparative View*, Oxford, Oxford University Press.

Malcolmson, J.M. (1980), 'The measurement of labor costs in empirical models of production and employment', *Review of Economics and Statistics*, 62, pp. 521–8.

Malmquist, S. (1953), 'The best and the average in productivity studies and in long-term forecasting', *Productivity Measurement Review*, 9, 37–49.

Mankiw, N., Romer, P. and Weil, D. (1992), 'A contribution to the empirics of growth', *Quarterly Journal of Economics*, pp. 407–38.

Mansfield, E. (1980), 'Basic research and productivity increase in manufacturing', *American Economic Review*, 70, pp. 863–73.

Mansfield, E. (1985), 'How rapidly does new industrial technology leak out?', *Journal of Industrial Economics*, December.

Marglin, S. (1974), 'What do bosses do?', *Review of Radical Political Economy*, 6.

Mason, G., Prais, S. and van Ark, B. (1992), 'Vocational education and productivity in the Netherlands and Britain', *National Institute Economic Review*, May.

Mason, G. and van Ark, B. (1993), 'Productivity, machinery and skills in engineering: an Anglo-Dutch comparison', NIESR Discussion Paper (New Series), No. 36.

Mason, G., van Ark, B. and Wagner, K. (1993), 'Productivity, product quality and workforce skills: food processing in four European countries', NIESR Discussion Paper No. 34.

Mason, G. and Wagner, K. (1993), *High Level Skills and International Competitiveness: Postgraduate Engineers and Scientists in Britain and Germany*, Report No. 6, NIESR, London.

Mayes, D. G. (1983), 'A comparison of labour practices and efficiency between plants in the UK and seven foreign countries', National Institute Discussion Paper, March.

Mayes, D. G., Harris, C. and Lansbury, M. (1994), *Inefficiency in Industry*, Hemel Hempstead, Harvester-Wheatsheaf.

Mayes, D. G. and Young, G. (1994), 'Improving the estimates of the UK capital stock', *National Institute Economic Review*, February.

Medoff, J. L. and Abraham, K. G. (1980), 'Experience, performance and earnings', *Quarterly Journal of Economics*, 95, p. 703.

Medoff, J.L. and Abraham, K.G. (1981), 'Are those paid more really more productive? The case of experience', *Journal of Human Resources*, 16, p. 186.

Meeusen, W. and van den Broeck, J. (1977a), 'Technical efficiency and dimension of the firm: some results on the use of frontier production functions', *Empirical Economics*, 2, pp. 109–22.

Meeusen, W. and van den Broeck, J. (1977b), 'Efficiency estimation from Cobb-Douglas production functions with composed error', *International Economic Review*, 18, p. 435.

Metal Trades Industry Association of Australia (MTIA) (1991), *A Risky Business: Deregulation of the Labour Market*, Canberra, Metal Trades Industry Association of Australia.

Metcalf, D. (1989), 'Water notes dry up: the impact of the Donovan reform proposals and Thatcherism at work on labour productivity in British manufacturing industry', *British Journal of Industrial Relations*, 27, 1.

Metcalf, D. (1993), 'Industrial Relations and Economic Performance', Centre for Economic Performance, London School of Economics, Discussion Paper No. 129.

Mills, D.Q. (1985), 'Seniority versus ability in promotion decisions', *Industrial and Labor Relations Review*, 38, p. 421.

MIT Commission on Industrial Productivity and Dertouzos, M. L., Lester, R. K. and Solow, R.M. (1989), *Made in America: Regaining the Productive Edge*, Cambridge, MA, MIT Press.

Morrison, C.J. (1986), 'Productivity measurement with non-static expectations varying capacity utilisation', *Journal of Econometrics*, 33, pp. 51–74, Amsterdam, North-Holland.

Muellbauer, J. (1984), 'Aggregate production functions and productivity measurement: a new look', CEPR Discussion Paper No. 34.

Muellbauer, J. (1986), 'Productivity and competitiveness in British manufacturing', *Oxford Review of Economic Policy*, 2, 3, pp. 1–25.

Muellbauer, J. (1991), 'Productivity and competitiveness', *Oxford Review of Economic Policy*, 7, 3, pp. 99–117.

Nadiri, M. I. and Rosen, S. (1969), 'Interrelated factor demand functions', *American Economic Review*, 59, pp. 457–71.

National Labour Consultative Council (1988), *Wages Policy and Productivity Improvement, Achieving a Better Balance between Macro and Micro Objectives*, Canberra, AGPS.

Nguyen, S. and Kokkelenberg, E. (1992), 'Measuring total factor productivity, technical change and the rate of returns to research and development', *Journal of Productivity Analysis*, 2, 4, pp. 269–82.

Nickell, S, Wadhwani, S. and Wall, M. (1992), 'Productivity growth in UK companies, 1975–1986', *European Economic Review*, 36, 5, pp. 1055–85.

Norris, K. (1989), 'Wages policy and wage determination in 1988', *Journal of Industrial Relations*, 31, p. 111.

Norsworthy, J. and Harper, M.J. (1983), 'Dynamic models of energy substitution in US manufacturing', in Berndt, E.R. and Fields, B.C. (eds.), *Modeling and Measuring Natural Resource Substitution*, Cambridge, MA, MIT Press.

Northcott, J. and Walling, A. (1988), *The Impact of Microelectronics*, Policy Studies Institute, London.

NUS International (1993), *1993 International Telephone Price Survey*, NUS International Pty Ltd.

Olson, J.A., Schmidt, P. and Waldman, D.M. (1980), 'A Monte Carlo study of estimators of stochastic production functions', *Journal of Econometrics*, 13, pp. 67–82.

O'Mahony, M. (1992a), 'Productivity levels in British and German manufacturing industry', *National Institute Economic Review*, 139, February, pp. 46–63.

O'Mahony, M. (1992b), 'Productivity and human capital formation in UK and German manufacturing', NIESR Discussion Paper No. 28, October.

O'Mahony, M. (1993), 'Capital stocks and productivity in industrial nations', *National Institute Economic Review*, 45, August, pp. 108–117.

O'Mahony, M. (1994), 'Anglo German productivity differences: the role of broad capital', NIESR, mimeo.

O'Mahony, M. and Oulton, N. (1990a), 'Industry-level estimates of the capital stock in UK manufacturing, 1948–1986', NIESR Discussion Paper No. 172.

O'Mahony, M. and Oulton, N. (1990b), 'Growth of multi-factor productivity in British industry', [Part 1: Text and tables; Part 2: Appendices], NIESR Discussion Paper No. 182.

O'Mahony, M., Wagner, K. and Paulssen, M. (1994), *Changing Fortunes: An Industry Study of British and German Productivity over Three Decades*, National Institute Report Series, No. 7.

Organisation for Economic Cooperation and Development (OECD) (1985), 'Purchasing power parities and real expenditures, 1985', Department of Economics and Statistics, Paris, OECD.

Organisation for Economic Cooperation and Development (OECD) (1987), *Structural Adjustment and Economic Performance*, Paris, OECD.

Organisation for Economic Cooperation and Development (OECD) (1990), 'Performance indicators for public telecommunications operators', *Information Computer Communications Policy* 22, Paris, OECD.

Organisation for Economic Cooperation and Development (OECD) (1992a), *OECD Economic Surveys: Australia*, Paris, OECD.

Organisation for Economic Cooperation and Development (OECD) (1992b), 'The 1992/93 communications outlook: Part 1: Background statistics', Working Party on Telecommunication and Information Services Policies, DSTI/ICCP/TSP(92)9 Part 1, dist. 3 June, Paris, OECD.

Oulton, N. (1987), 'Plant closures and the productivity miracle in manufacturing', *National Institute Economic Review*, 121, pp. 53–59.

Oulton, N. (1992), 'Investment, increasing returns and the pattern of productivity growth in UK manufacturing, 1954–86', NIESR Discussion Paper No. 5.

Oulton, N. (1994), 'Increasing returns and externalities in UK manufacturing: myth or reality?', paper presented at the Fulbright Colloquium, February, London, NIESR.

Oulton, N. and O'Mahony, M. (1994), *Productivity and Growth: A Study of British Industry, 1954–1986*, Cambridge, Cambridge University Press.

Pakes, A. and Schankerman, M. (1984), 'The rate of obsolescence of patents, research gestation lags, and the private rate of return to research resources', in Griliches, Z. (ed.), pp. 73–88.

Pavitt, K. and Patel, P. (1988), 'The international distribution and determinants of technological activities', *Oxford Reviews of Economic Policy*, 14, 4.

Piesse, J., Thirtle, C. and Turk, J. (1993), 'The productivity of private and social farms: a non-parametric analysis of Slovene dairying enterprises', mimeo, London, Birkbeck College.

Pissarides, C.A. (1991), 'Real wages and unemployment in Australia', *Economica*, 58, 35.

Prais, S. (1981), *Productivity and Industrial Structure*, Cambridge, Cambridge University Press.

Prais, S. (1988), 'Two approaches to the economics of education: a methodological note', *Economics of Education Review*, 7, 2.

Prais, S. (1989), 'Qualified manpower in engineering: Britain and other industrially advanced countries', *National Institute Economic Review*, February.

Prais, S. J. (1993), 'Economic performance and education: the nature of Britain's deficiencies', NIESR Discussion Paper No. 52.

Prais, S.J. *et al.* (1970), 'Productivity, education and training. Vol. II', NIESR working papers.

Prais, S., Jarvis, V. and Wagner, K. (1989), 'Productivity and vocational skills in services in Britain and Germany: hotels', *National Institute Economic Review*, November.

Prais, S. and Wagner, K. (1988), 'Productivity and management: the training of foremen in Britain and Germany', *National Institute Economic Review*, February.

Price, S., Meen, G. and Dhar, S. (1990), 'Employment, capital scrapping and capital utilisation: some results for UK manufacturing', Oxford Economic Forecasting, Discussion Paper No. 1.

Prices Surveillance Authority (PSA) (1993), *Monitoring of Stevedoring Costs and Charges*, Report 1, Melbourne, Prices Surveillance Authority.

Ramaswamy, R. and Rowthorn, R.E. (1991), 'Efficiency wages and wage dispersion', *Economica*, 58, pp. 501–14.

Ramsey, J. (1969), 'Tests for specification errors in classical linear least squares regression analysis', *Journal of the Royal Statistical Society*, Series B, 31, pp. 350–71.

Rebitzer, J.B. (1988), 'Unemployment, labor relations and unit labour costs', *American Economic Review*, 78, 2, pp. 389–94.

Rebitzer, J.B. (1993), 'Radical political economy and the economics of labour markets', *Journal of Economic Literature*, 31, pp. 1394–434.

Robson, M.T. (1992), 'Macroeconomic factors in the birth and death of UK firms: evidence from quarterly VAT registrations', University of Newcastle upon Tyne Discussion Paper No. 9.

Robson, M., Townsend, J. and Pavitt, K. (1988), 'Sectoral patterns of production and use of innovations in the UK, 1945–83', *Research Policy* 17, pp. 1–14.

Romer, P. (1986), 'Increasing returns and long run growth', *Journal of Political Economy*, 94, pp. 1002–37.

Romer, P. (1987), 'Crazy explanations for the productivity slowdown', *NBER Macroeconomics Annual*, 1, pp. 163–201.

Romer, P. (1990a), 'Endogenous technological change', *Journal of Political Economy*, October, S71–S102.

Romer, P. (1990b), 'Capital, labour and productivity', Washington, *Brookings Papers*, Microeconomics.

Rowthorn, R.E. (1975), 'What remains of Kaldor's law?', *Economic Journal*, 85, March, pp. 10–9.

Rowthorn, R.E. (1979), 'A note on Verdoorn's law', *Economic Journal*, 89, March, pp. 131–3.

Salter, W.E.G. (1966), *Productivity and Technical Change*, 2nd edition, Cambridge University Press.

Schankerman, M. (1981), 'The effects of double-counting and expensing on the measured returns to R&D', *Review of Economics and Statistics*, pp. 454–9.

Scherer, F. (1993), 'Lagging productivity growth: measurement, technology and shock effects', *Empirica*, 20, pp. 5–24.

Schor, J.B. (1988), 'Does work intensity respond to macroeconomic variables?: evidence from British manufacturing, 1970–1986', Harvard Institute of Economic Research Discussion Paper No. 1379, April.

Schott, K. (1976), 'Investment in private industrial research and development in Britain', *Journal of Industrial Economics*, 25, 2, pp. 81–99.

Scott, M. (1989), *A New View of Economic Growth*, Oxford, Oxford University Press.

Shapiro, C. and Stiglitz, J.E. (1984), 'Equilibrium unemployment as a worker discipline device', *American Economic Review*, 74, 3, pp. 433–44.

Sherman, H.D. and Gold, F. (1985), 'Branch bank operating efficiency: evaluation with data envelopment analysis', *Journal of Banking and Finance*, 9, pp. 297–315.

Siegel, D. and Griliches, Z. (1991), 'Purchased services, outsourcing, computers, and productivity in manufacturing', NBER Working Paper No. 3678, April.

Simes, R.M. and Horn, P.M. (1988), 'The role of wages in the Australian macroeconomy', paper presented to the 1988 Australian Economics Congress, Australian National University, Canberra, September.

Sloan, J. (1993), 'Bill doesn't fix the central issue', *Australian Financial Review*, 4 November.

Sloan, J. (1994), 'Wages of awards may turn sour', *Australian Financial Review*, 13 January.

Smith, G. (1993), 'IR flavour an acquired taste', *Australian Financial Review*, 1 November.

Solow, R. (1957) 'Technical change and the aggregate production function', *Review of Economics and Statistics*, 34, pp. 312–20.

Soskice, D. (1993), 'Social skills from mass higher education: rethinking the company based initial training paradigm', *Oxford Review of Economic Policy*, 9, 3.

Spooner, K. (1989), 'Australian trade unionism in 1988', *Journal of Industrial Relations*, 31, p. 118.

Statistics Canada (1990), *Canadian Economic Observer*, July.

Statistics Canada (1992), *Aggregate Productivity Measures*, Cat. No. 15–204. Ottawa.

Steedman, H., Mason, G. and Wagner, K. (1991), 'Intermediate skills in the workplace: deployment, standards and supply in Britain, France and Germany', *National Institute Economic Review*, May.

Steedman, H. and Wagner, K. (1987), 'A second look at productivity, machinery and skills in Britain and Germany', *National Institute Economic Review*, November.

Steedman, H. and Wagner, K. (1989), 'Productivity, machinery and skills: clothing manufacturing in Britain and Germany', *National Institute Economic Review*, May.

Sterlacchini, A. (1989), 'R&D, innovations, and total factor productivity growth in British manufacturing', *Applied Economics*, 21, pp. 1549–62.

Stigler, G. (1976), 'The Xistence of X-Efficiency', *American Economic Review*, 66, p. 213.

Stoneman, P. (1990), 'The adoption of new technology: theory and evidence', paper presented at ESRC Conference on New Technology and the Firm, December.

Stoneman, P. (1992), 'Productivity in UK manufacturing: double deflation and a real cost index', Warwick Business School Research Papers, No. 47.

Telstra Corporation (1993), *Annual Report 1993*, Telstra Corporation Ltd, Melbourne.

Terleckyj, N. (1980), 'Direct and indirect effects of industrial research and development on the productivity gowth of industries', in Kendrick, J. and Vaccara, B. (eds), *New Developments in Productivity Measurements Analysis*, Chicago, University of Chicago Press.

Thirwall, A.P. (1980), 'Rowthorn's interpretation of Verdoorn's law', *The Economic Journal*, 90, pp. 386–8.

Torii, A. (1992a), '"Dual structure" and difference of efficiency between Japanese large and small enterprises', in Caves, R.E. (1992).

Torii, A., (1992b), 'Technical efficiency in Japanese industries', in Caves, R.E. (1992).

Torii, A. (1993), 'A memorandum about technical efficiency and business cycles', mimeo, Yokohama University.

Treu, T. (1992), 'Labour flexibility in Europe', *International Labour Review*, 131, 4–5, pp. 497–512.

Triplett, J. (1988), 'Price index research and its influence on data: a historical review', paper presented to Fiftieth Anniversary Conference of the Conference on Research in Income and Wealth, Washington D.C., 12 May.

Tulkens, H. (1986), 'La performance productive d'un service public: Définitions, méthodes de mesure, et application à la Régie des Postes de Belgique', *L'Actualité Economique, Revue d'Analyse Economique, Revue d'Analyse Economique* (Montréal), 62, 2, pp. 306–35, June.

Tulkens, H. (1989), *Efficacité et Management*, Charleroi, Centre Interuniversitaire de Formation Permanente (CIFOP).

Tulkens, H. (1993a), 'On FDH analysis: some methodological issues and applications to retail banking, courts and urban transit', *Journal of Productivity Analysis*, 4, 1/2, pp. 183–210.

Tulkens, H. (1993b), 'Efficiency dominance analysis: a frontier free efficiency evaluation method', paper presented at the Third European Workshop on Efficiency and Productivity Analysis, CORE, Louvain-la-Neuve, October, mimeo.

Tulkens, H. and Vanden Eeckaut, P.H. (1991), 'Nonparametric efficiency measurement for panel data: methodologies and FDH applications to retail banking', paper presented at EURO XI, the 11th European Congress on Operational Research, RWTH Aachen, July 16–19.

Tulkens, H. and Vanden Eeckaut, P.H. (1993), 'Non-parametric efficiency, progress and regress measures for panel data: methodological aspects', *European Journal of Operations Research*, 80, pp. 474–99.

Tybout, J. and Westbrook, M. D. (1994), 'Trade liberalisation and the dimensions of efficiency change in Medican manufacturing industries', Georgetown University U.S.A., working paper.

van Ark, B. (1990a), 'Comparative levels of labour productivity in Dutch and British manufacturing', *National Institute Economic Review*, 131, pp. 71–85.

van Ark, B. (1990b), 'Manufacturing productivity levels in France and the UK', *National Institute Economic Review*, 133, pp. 62–77.

van Ark, B. (1992), 'Comparative productivity in British and American manufacturing', *National Institute Economic Review*, 142, pp. 63–73.

van Ark, B. (1993), 'International comparisons of output and productivity', Groningen Growth and Development Centre, Monograph Series No.1.

van Dijk, C., Akkermans, T. and Hovels, B. (1988), *Social Partners and Vocational Education in the Netherlands*, Berlin, CEDEFOP.

van den Dool, P. (1989), 'The Netherlands: selection for vocational education starts early', *European Journal of Education*, 24, 2.

Vassiloglou, M. and Giokas, D. (1990), 'A study of the relative efficiency of bank branches: an application of data envelopment analysis', *Journal of the Operational Research Society*, 17, pp. 591–7.

Veerdoorn, P.J. (1949), 'Fattori che regolano lo sviluppo della produttività del lavoro', *L'Industria*, 1, pp. 3–10.

Verdoorn, P.J. (1980), 'Verdoorn's law in retrospect: a comment', *The Economic Journal*, 90, pp. 382–5.

Wadhwani, S. and Wall, M. (1988), 'A direct test of the efficiency wage model using UK micro data', Centre for Labour Economics, London School of Economics, June.

Walfridson, B. (1987), 'Dynamic models of factor demand', Doctoral dissertation, Gothenburg University.

Walfridson B. (1989), 'Adjustments for capacity utilization in productivity measurement', Department of Economics, Gothenburg University.

Watts, M.J. and Mitchell, W.F. (1990), 'Australian wage inflation: real wage resistance, hysteresis and incomes policy: 1968(3)–1988(3)', *Manchester School*, 58, p. 142.

Weisskopf, T. (1987), 'The effect of unemployment on labour productivity: an international comparative analysis', *International Review of Applied Economics*, June, 1, 2, pp. 127–51.

Wenban-Smith, G. (1981), 'A study of the movements of productivity in individual industries in the U.K. 1968–79', *National Institute Economic Review*, 97.

White, H. (1980), 'A heteroskedasticity-consistent covariance matrix estimator and a direct test for heteroskedasticity', *Econometrica*, 48, pp. 817–38.

Whiteman, J. L. (1993), 'Case study: bench-marking Australian utilities against best international practice', mimeo, Bureau of Industry Economics, Canberra.

Wooden, M. (1990), 'Corporatism and wage setting: the Accord in hindsight', *Economic Papers*, 9, p. 51.

Yetton, P., Davis, J. and Swan, P. (1992), *Going International: Export Myths and Strategic Realities*, Australian Manufacturing Council, Melbourne.

Yoo, S.-M. (1992), 'Technical efficiency over time in Korea, 1978-88: exploratory analysis', in Caves, R.E. (1992).

THE NATIONAL INSTITUTE OF ECONOMIC AND SOCIAL RESEARCH PUBLICATIONS IN PRINT

published by
THE CAMBRIDGE UNIVERSITY PRESS
(available from booksellers or, in case of difficulty, from the publishers)

ECONOMIC AND SOCIAL STUDIES

OCCASIONAL PAPERS

OTHER PUBLICATIONS BY CAMBRIDGE UNIVERSITY PRESS

THE NATIONAL INSTITUTE OF
ECONOMIC AND SOCIAL RESEARCH

publishes regularly

THE NATIONAL INSTITUTE ECONOMIC REVIEW

A quarterly analysis of the general economic situation in the United Kingdom and overseas with forecasts eighteen months ahead. The last issue each year usually contains an assessment of medium-term prospects. There are also in most issues special articles on subjects of interest to academic and business economists.

Annual subscriptions, £90.00 (UK and EU) and £110.00 (rest of world), also single issues for the current year, £25.00 (UK and EU) and £30.00 (rest of world), are available direct from NIESR, 2 Dean Trench Street, Smith Square, London, SW1P 3HE.

Subscriptions at a special reduced price are available to students and teachers in the United Kingdom on application to the Secretary of the Institute.

Back numbers and reprints of issues which have gone out of stock are distributed by Wm. Dawson and Sons Ltd, Cannon House, Park Farm Road, Folkestone. Microfiche copies for the years 1961–89 are available from EP Microform Ltd, Bradford Road, East Ardsley, Wakefield, Yorks.

Published by
SAGE PUBLICATIONS LTD
(Available from Sage and from booksellers)

ECONOMIC CONVERGENCE AND MONETARY UNION IN EUROPE
Edited by RAY BARRELL. 1992. pp. 288. £35.00 (hardback), £12.95 (paperback) net.

ACHIEVING MONETARY UNION IN EUROPE
By ANDREW BRITTON and DAVID MAYES. 1992. pp. 160. £25.00 (hardback), £9.95 (paperback) net.

MACROECONOMIC POLICY COORDINATION IN EUROPE:
THE ERM AND MONETARY UNION
Edited by RAY BARRELL and JOHN D. WHITLEY. 1993. pp. 294. £37.50 (hardback), £14.95 (paperback) net.